Joan of Arc

Significant Figures in World History

Charles Darwin: A Reference Guide to His Life and Works,
by J. David Archibald, 2019.

Leonardo da Vinci: A Reference Guide to His Life and Works,
by Allison Lee Palmer, 2019.

Robert E. Lee: A Reference Guide to His Life and Works,
by James I. Robertson Jr., 2019.

John F. Kennedy: A Reference Guide to His Life and Works,
by Ian James Bickerton, 2019.

Florence Nightingale: A Reference Guide to Her Life and Works,
by Lynn McDonald, 2019.

Napoléon Bonaparte: A Reference Guide to His Life and Works,
by Joshua Meeks, 2019.

Nelson Mandela: A Reference Guide to His Life and Works,
by Aran S. MacKinnon, 2020.

Michelangelo: A Reference Guide to His Life and Works,
by Lilian H. Zirpolo, 2020.

Winston Churchill: A Reference Guide to His Life and Works,
by Christopher Catherwood, 2020.

Catherine the Great: A Reference Guide to Her Life and Works,
by Alexander Kamenskii, 2020.

Golda Meir: A Reference Guide to Her Life and Works,
by Meron Medzini, 2020.

Karl Marx: A Reference Guide to His Life and Works,
by Frank Elwell, Brian Andrews, and Kenneth S. Hicks, 2020.

Eva Perón: A Reference Guide to Her Life and Works,
by María Belén Rabadán Vega and Mirna Vohnsen, 2021.

Adolf Hitler: A Reference Guide to His Life and Works,
by Steven P. Remy, 2021.

Sigmund Freud: A Reference Guide to His Life and Works,
by Alistair Ross, 2022.

Henry VIII: A Reference Guide to His Life and Works,
by Clayton Drees, 2022.

Harriet Tubman: A Reference Guide to Her Life and Works,
by Kate Clifford Larson, 2022.

Joseph Stalin: A Reference Guide to His Life and Works,
by David R. Marples and Alla Hurska, 2022.

Joan of Arc: A Reference Guide to Her Life and Works,
by Scott Manning, 2023.

Joan of Arc

A Reference Guide to Her Life and Works

Scott Manning

ROWMAN & LITTLEFIELD
Lanham • Boulder • New York • London

Published by Rowman & Littlefield
An imprint of The Rowman & Littlefield Publishing Group, Inc.
4501 Forbes Boulevard, Suite 200, Lanham, Maryland 20706
www.rowman.com

86-90 Paul Street, London EC2A 4NE, United Kingdom

Copyright © 2023 by Scott Manning

All rights reserved. No part of this book may be reproduced in any form or by any electronic or mechanical means, including information storage and retrieval systems, without written permission from the publisher, except by a reviewer who may quote passages in a review.

British Library Cataloguing in Publication Information Available

Library of Congress Cataloging-in-Publication Data

Names: Manning, Scott, 1980- author.
Title: Joan of Arc : a reference guide to her life and works / Scott
  Manning.
Description: Lanham : Rowman & Littlefield, [2023] | Series: Significant
  figures in world history | Includes bibliographical references and
  index. | Summary: "Joan of Arc: A Reference Guide of Her Life and Works
  focuses on her life, her works, and legacy in fifteenth-century France.
  It features a chronology, an introduction offers a brief account of her
  life, a dictionary section lists entries on people, groups, places,
  events, topics, terms, and medieval documents central to Joan's life"—
  Provided by publisher.
Identifiers: LCCN 2022030921 (print) | LCCN 2022030922 (ebook) | ISBN
  9781538139165 (cloth) | ISBN 9781538139172 (epub)
Subjects: LCSH: Joan, of Arc, Saint, 1412–1431—Encyclopedias.
Classification: LCC DC103 .M36 2023 (print) | LCC DC103 (ebook) | DDC
  944.026—dc23/eng/20221006
LC record available at https://lccn.loc.gov/2022030921
LC ebook record available at https://lccn.loc.gov/2022030922

To Dawn, the first Joan in my life

Contents

Acknowledgments	ix
A Note about Anglicizing French Names	xi
Map	xiii
Chronology	xv
Introduction	1
ENTRIES #, A–Z	5
Appendixes	
A Roles and Responsibilities for the Condemnation Trial	229
B Key Battles, Sieges, and Captured Cities	231
C Selected Treaties and Truces during the Time of Joan of Arc	233
D Joan of Arc's Immediate Family	235
E Surviving Letters of Joan of Arc	237
F Popes during the Time of Joan of Arc	239
G Selected Monarchs and Rulers	241
H Constables and Marshals of France	243
Bibliography	245
Index	267
About the Author	281

Acknowledgments

I would like to thank Gail Orgelfinger whose support and encouragement, as well as her years of scholarship on Joan of Arc, continue to be sources of inspiration for me.

I'm grateful to Kevin J. Harty who has provided wise counsel and candid feedback, which managed to talk me out of *and then* into this project. I spent years searching for a mentor, and Kevin came into my life like a wildfire. His passion for medievalism is infectious, and I could not have found a more generous friend.

The International Joan of Arc Society and their yearly panels at the International Congress of Medieval Studies in Kalamazoo, Michigan, have provided an outlet for my research and exposed me to brilliant Johannic scholars. I have been humbled and thankful to partner with Tara B. Smithson in stewarding the organization of the society's panels for the past few years. Tara has been a superb collaborator and friend while we both continue our journeys to understand the world of Joan of Arc. Tara has also provided critical feedback on portions of this book as we collaborated on our different Joan projects.

Thanks to Tapestry Comics for publishing my first piece on Joan of Arc, as the epilogue to the graphic novel *A Flower in a Field of Lions: The Trials of Joan of Arc* (2018).

I am grateful to my father, who demonstrated that the best time to continue your education is now. He acquired his bachelor's and master's degrees after he was fifty, which inspired me to pursue higher education in my thirties. He instilled a love of history and storytelling in me from an early age.

The Free Library of Philadelphia, especially its interlibrary loan department, helped me track down numerous papers and obscure books during my research for this book. It is a superb institution of the city and a wonderful environment in which to write.

While I wrote much of this book while quarantined at home during the COVID-19 pandemic, I am grateful to Pairings Cigar Bar in Media, Pennsylvania, which provided me with a refuge during the hot summers and bitter cold winters while I toiled away on this manuscript.

Finally, this would not have been possible without Dawn Manning, who first took me to a viewing of Luc Besson's *The Messenger: The Story of Joan of Arc* in 1999, after which she spent the rest of the day explaining to me how poorly the movie portrayed Joan. That day started my fascination with Joan. As a writer and editor herself, Dawn has been my coach, cheerleader, teacher, and partner. She graciously read this manuscript in several incarnations and provided invaluable feedback and direction. All mistakes are, of course, my own.

A Note about Anglicizing French Names

The anglicizing of French names is often inconsistent in histories written in English. There is no hard rule that historians have followed, but there are some common approaches. For example, if a person or ruler has a nickname appended to their name, then the whole name is typically translated and anglicized. Thus, *Philippe le Bon* is consistently translated to Philip the Good, never partially as Philip le Bon, and *Jean san Peur* is always John the Fearless, never Jean the Fearless or John san Peur.

However, when there is no appended nickname, the anglicization can vary. John and Jean become interchangeable, as do Henry and Henri. Sometimes there can be two Jeans in a work, and one is always Jean while the other is always John. This is often a situation where an individual has become so well known in the English-speaking world that the anglicized version is more prominent or was at least propagated at a particular time in history. Thus, Joan of Arc or Joan the Maid are much more common than Jeanne d'Arc or Jeanne la Pucelle. There are also works where the writer, translator, or editor have insisted on anglicizing every single name. The guiding principle, however, is that the name for an individual should remain consistent throughout a work.

The use of *de* or *d'* partitive articles in names such as Jean de Metz or Jean d'Estivet have the same meaning, as *d'* is a contraction of *de* when the following word begins with a vowel. The use of either can indicate nobility or simply where the person is from. The anglicized version for either is *of*. Thus, Jean de Metz becomes John of Metz.

This book follows an approach using the most common version of a name in previous English-speaking works to make entries easier to find and cross-reference.

Map

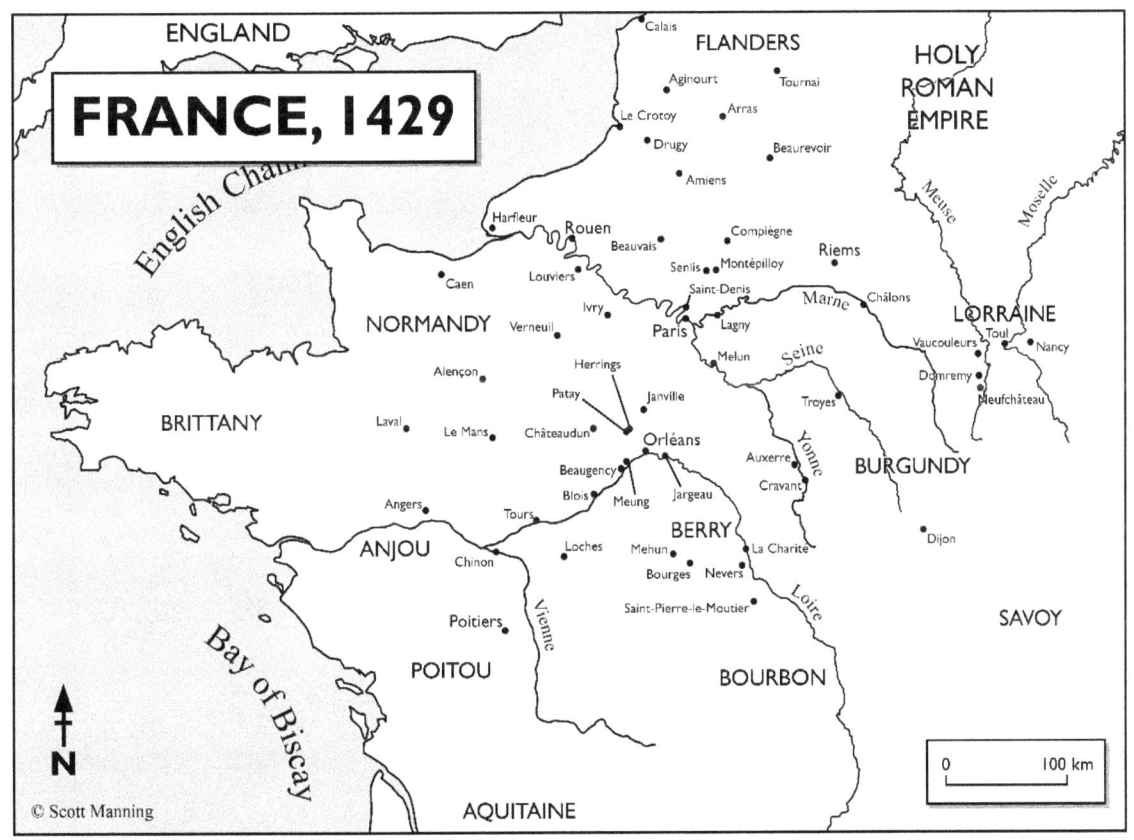

Map of France

Chronology

1403 **22 February:** Future Charles VII born.

1407 **23 November:** Men acting on orders from Duke John the Fearless of Burgundy assassinate Duke Louis of Orléans, marking the traditional start of the French Civil War between the Armagnac and Burgundian factions.

1412 **6 January:** Traditional date of Joan of Arc's birth in Domremy. **18 May:** Armagnacs sign Treaty of Bourges with English, seeking military aid in their war against Burgundy. **11 June:** John the Fearless captures Bourges and uses an order from King Charles VI to break the Treaty of Bourges. **10 August:** English send expedition force to assist Armagnacs. The English expedition force conducts raids, seeking compensation. **14 November:** Treaty of Buzançais commits payments to English to withdraw expedition force.

1413 **23 August:** Armagnac faction takes control of Paris.

1415 **18 August–22 September:** English besiege and capture Harfleur. **25 October:** English defeat the French at Agincourt, capturing numerous nobles, including Duke Charles of Orléans. **18 December:** Dauphin Louis, duke of Guyenne dies. Jean, duke of Touraine becomes the new dauphin.

1417 **5 April:** Dauphin Jean dies. Future Charles VII becomes the new dauphin. **1 August:** Henry V arrives with an expedition force for his conquest of Normandy. **19 September:** English capture Caen.

1418 **16 February:** English capture Falaise. **29 May:** Burgundian faction takes control of Paris. Dauphin Charles flees city. **29 July:** English begin siege of Rouen.

1419 **19 January:** English capture Rouen after a nearly six-month siege, marking the traditional end to Henry V's conquest of Normandy. **10 September:** John the Fearless assassinated while meeting with Dauphin Charles. Philip the Good becomes new duke of Burgundy.

1420 **21 May:** Henry V, Charles VI, and Philip the Good sign the Treaty of Troyes. Charles VI adopts Henry V as his son, making Henry and his descendants the heirs of the French crown. Henry made regent of France. **2 June:** Henry V marries Catherine of Valois, daughter of Charles VI.

1421 **3 January:** Charles VI disinherits son, Dauphin Charles. **23 February:** Coronation of Queen Catherine in Westminster Abbey. **22 March:** Henry V's brother Clarence defeated and killed at the battle of Baugé. **6 December:** Future Henry VI born.

1422 **31 August:** Henry V dies. **21 October:** Charles VI dies. Future King Henry VI is too young to rule France and England. John, duke of Bedford, acts as regent of France after Philip the Good turns down the role. **30 October:** Those loyal to Dauphin Charles declare him King Charles VII of France.

1423 **13 April:** Dukes of Bedford, Burgundy, and Brittany sign the Treaty of Amiens, recognizing Henry VI as the king of France. **13 May:** Duke of Bedford marries Anne of Burgundy, sister of Philip the Good. **3 July:** Dauphin Louis, future Louis XI, born. **31 July:** Anglo-Burgundian forces soundly defeat Franco-Scottish forces at the battle of Cravant. **26 September:** French forces defeat English army at the battle of La Brossinière. **10 October:** Arthur de Richemont, brother of the duke of Brittany, marries Margaret of Burgundy, sister of Philip the Good.

1424 **28 March:** Treaty of Durham signed, which included seven-year Anglo-Scottish truce and the release of Scottish King James I. **17 August:** English forces soundly defeat Franco-Scottish forces at the battle of Verneuil. **24 September:** Philip the Good and Charles VII agree to the truce of Chambéry, ceasing hostilities until 1 May 1425, which was later extended to 25 December 1425.

1428 **13 May:** Earliest possible meeting between Joan of Arc and Robert de Baudricourt in Vaucouleurs. Baudricourt sends Joan away. **22 June:** Burgundian troops invade Lorraine, besieging Vaucouleurs and raiding Domremy. Joan's family flees to Neufchâteau. **July:** Earl of Salisbury sets sail from England to France with expedition force. **17 July:** Charles VII and King James I of Scotland sign treaty, which includes a marriage contract with their children, Dauphin Louis and Margaret Stewart. **September 5:** Earl of Salisbury captures Meung. **September 25:** Salisbury captures Beaugency. **5 October:** Salisbury captures Jargeau. **12 October:** Siege of Orléans begins. **24 October:** English capture the Tourelles bastille. Salisbury mortally wounded by a cannonball. **November 3:** Salisbury dies in Meung. **Mid-November:** Earl of Suffolk takes over command of English forces.

1429 **January–February:** Joan meets with Duke Charles of Lorraine and René of Ajou. Robert de Baudricourt finally agrees to send Joan to meet Charles VII. **12 February:** English defeat Franco-Scottish forces en route to resupply Orléans at the battle of the Herrings. **March 6:** Joan finally meets Charles VII at Chinon. **11–22 March:** Joan interrogated at Poitiers concerning her mission. **22 March:** Joan dictates letter to the English, demanding they leave France. **24 March:** Joan returns to Chinon. **5 April:** Joan travels to Tours where her armor and standard are made. **17 April:** Duke of Bedford nixes a proposal for Orléans to surrender directly to Philip the Good. Philip withdraws Burgundy troops from the siege. **21 April:** Joan joins army en route to Orléans. **29 April:** Joan of Arc arrives at Orléans with reinforcements and supplies. **4 May:** French assault and capture the Saint Loup boulevard. **5 May:** French occupy the Saint Jean le Blanc boulevard, which had been abandoned by the English. **6 May:** French assault and capture the Augustins boulevard. **7 May:** French assault and capture the Tourelles bastille. **8 May:** English abandon siege of Orléans. **14 May:** Theologian Jean Gerson writes the first version of his pamphlet in support of Joan of Arc, which is distributed widely. **11–12 June:** French capture Jargeau by assault, massacring most of the English defenders. **15 June:** French capture the bridge at Meung. **15–18 June:** French army bombards Beaugency before negotiating the town's surrender. **18 June:** French army defeats the English army at the battle of Patay. Janville closes its gates to the retreating English. **29 June:** Charles VII begins the march to Reims. **30 June–2 July:** Auxerre surrenders to the French army after negotiations. **5–9 July:** French besiege and force surrender of Troyes. **17 July:** Charles VII crowned at Reims. **31 July:** Christine de Pizan writes *The Tale of Joan of Arc*. **15 August:** French and English standoff at Montépilloy without engaging their full forces. Battle ends in a stalemate. **28 August:** Charles VII and Philip the Good agree to a four-month truce set to begin on 28 September. **8 September: French attack Saint-Honoré Gate at Paris. Joan wounded in the thigh. **9 September:** Charles calls off the siege of Paris. **4 November:** French capture Saint-Pierre-le-Moutier. **6 November:** Henry VI crowned king of England. **24? November–23? December:** Siege of La Charité.

1430 **19 January:** Orléans hosts a banquet in honor of Joan, who is in attendance. **29 March:** Battle of Lagny. **22 May:** Siege of Compiègne begins. **23 May:** Joan captured outside of Compiègne by Burgundian forces. **11 June:** Burgundian forces are defeated at Anthon. **July:** Joan transferred to Beaurevoir. **October:** Plausible date of Joan's failed escape attempt from the tower of Beaurevoir. She is severely injured in the process. **25/26 October:** Siege of Compiègne lifted. **21 November:** Burgundians ransom Joan to the English. **23 December:** Joan arrives in Rouen.

1431 **3 January:** Joan handed over to the Church for an inquisition. **9 January:** Preliminary process for inquisition begins. **21 February–March 3:** Public sessions held during trial. **10–17 March:** Joan interrogated with a smaller audience in her prison cell. **27–28 March:** Seventy articles of accusation reviewed with Joan. She comments on each point. **2–5 April:** Seventy articles whittled down to twelve articles. **12 April:** Twelve articles notarized for distribution to the University of Paris. **2 May:** Jean de Hulot Châtillon admonishes Joan of Arc. **19 May:** Opinion from the University of Paris on the twelve articles arrives in Rouen, reviewed by judges and assessors. **23 May:** Twelve articles, opinion of University of Paris, and warning presented to Joan. Trial concluded. **24 May:** Joan's abjuration. She agrees to wear women's clothing and spend life in prison. **28 May:** Joan resumes wearing men's clothing. **30 May:** Joan condemned as a relapsed heretic and is executed in Rouen. **16 December:** Henry VI crowned king of France in Paris.

1432 **5 March:** Charles VII and Arthur de Richemont reconcile. **August:** Anglo-Burgundian force fails to capture Lagny. **14 November:** Anne of Burgundy dies.

1433 **22 April:** Duke of Bedford marries Jacquetta of Luxembourg.

1435 **5 August:** The Congress of Arras officially begins. **14 September:** Duke of Bedford dies. **21 September:** Charles VII and Philip the Good sign the Treaty of Arras, undoing the Treaty of Troyes and recognizing Charles as the heir to the French crown, effectively ending the French Civil War.

1436 **13 April:** Arthur de Richemont enters Paris in the name of Charles VII. **25 June:** Louis XI and Margaret Stewart of Scotland wed.

1437 **12 November:** Charles VII officially reenters Paris.

1440 **February–July:** Praguerie rebellion. **26 October:** Gilles de Rais executed after trial. **9 November:** Duke of Orléans freed after twenty-five years of captivity in England.

1442 **18 December:** Pierre Cauchon dies.

1444 **20 May:** English and French agree to truce at Tours.

1445 **January–May:** Charles issues military reforms, establishing a state army and banishing private armies.

1449 **31 July:** Charles VII rekindles war against the English. Reconquest of Lancastrian Normandy begins. **10 December:** Charles VII officially reenters Rouen where the records of Joan of Arc's condemnation trial are kept.

1450 **15 February:** Charles VII initiates an investigation into the condemnation trial of Joan of Arc.

1453 **17 July:** French defeat English at Castillon, marking the traditional end to the Hundred Years War.

1455 **11 June:** Pope Calixtus III orders a new trial with Joan's surviving family acting as plaintiffs. **7 November:** Proceedings for the Nullification of Condemnation begin.

1456 **28 January–11 February:** Thirty-four witnesses interviewed in Lorraine. **22 February–16 March:** Forty-one witnesses interviewed in Orléans. **2 April–11 May:** Twenty witnesses interviewed in Paris. **12–14 May:** Nineteen witnesses interviewed in Rouen. **7 July:** Nullification trial concludes, and the 1431 condemnation trial of Joan of Arc is rendered null and void.

1461 **22 July:** Charles VII dies and his son is coronated as Louis XI, king of France.

1462 **27 June:** Louis of Orléans born, son of duke of Orléans.

1465 **5 January:** Duke of Orléans dies.

1467 **15 June:** Philip the Good dies. Charles the Bold becomes the new duke of Burgundy.

1477 **5 January:** Charles the Bold dies.

1483 **30 August:** Louis XI dies and his son coronated as Charles VIII.

1498 **7 April:** Charles VIII dies. Louis of Orléans coronated as Louis XII, king of France.

Introduction

Alongside Henry V and the battles of Poitiers, Crecy, and Agincourt, Joan of Arc (c. 1412–1431) and the siege of Orléans are the most recognizable names from the Hundred Years War (1337–1453). The number of "Joan" biographies in English are too voluminous to list in the bibliography of this work. Yet there is no reference guide in English to the people, places, events, documents, and terms surrounding the brief but incredibly well-documented life of Joan. At only nineteen years old, this teenage soldier is celebrated as the most-documented medieval figure, who participated in the most-documented medieval siege, and defended herself in the most-documented trial of the Middle Ages.[1] For both new and seasoned scholars, such a breadth of information is overwhelming, and today's leading Johannic scholars in the English-speaking world—Kelly DeVries, Deborah Fraioli, Kevin J. Harty, Gail Orgelfinger, and Bonnie Wheeler, to name a few—spend entire books tackling niche aspects of Joan's world and reception. While biographers such as Helen Castor and Julia Taylor have done remarkable jobs in producing fresh and engaging biographies for the twenty-first century,[2] what has been lacking in the field is an A-to-Z reference guide to Joan and her world accessible in English. It is the sort of book I wish I had access to twenty years ago.[3]

Anyone new to the world of Joan of Arc is immediately confronted with a host of unfamiliar names, titles, and customs. For English speakers, the names of one person vary from Joan to Jeanne to Jehanne to Johanne, often with little explanation on the differences. For those unfamiliar with France, place names such as Lorraine, Chinon, Poitiers, and Jargeau add another level of complexity. Then there are the endless titles—dauphin, duke, bishop—some still in use today, but certainly foreign, and with a particular medieval nuance not readily apparent for today's readers.

The characters in Joan's life become easy to confuse as well. First, there's Charles. In 1429 France, the current and previous two kings of France, the king's cousin, the count of Clermont, and the dukes of Lorraine and Orléans were all named Charles. There are more Jeans: the dukes of Alençon, Berry, Brittany, and Bourbon; the marshal of Boussac; the bastard of Orléans; the count of Luxembourg; Joan's brother, Joan's confessor, and at least five of Joan's other companions in arms were all named Jean. During her trial, the inquisitor, examiner, promoter, and executor were also named Jean. In many English histories, some, but not all, of the Jeans have been anglicized to John, causing yet more confusion. Then there are names wholly unfamiliar to English speakers. Two of the three notaries at Joan's trial were named Guillaume, and some historians differentiate between them by using one of their nicknames, Boisguillaume. Similarly, the captain of Compiègne where Joan was captured and the man who captured Joan were both named Guillaume.

The roles and titles are even more foreign or at least misunderstood, as Joan interacted with captains, barons, dukes, kings, knights, squires, and pages in the secular world, as well as cardinals, bishops, priests, friars, priors, and inquisitors in the Church. Many of these men were educated at universities, boasting degrees in theology, canon law, civil law, and medicine. Then there are the ceremonies such as coronations, councils, and of course, inquisitions.

There are also the names for groups of people, some of which modern historians swap for variety. Depending on the battle or siege, a reader may encounter Armagnacs, Orleanists, royalists, loyalists, or dauphinists, all fighting on the same side. In some instances, one descriptor may be precise, but in another, several of these descriptors could be accurate. Meanings may overlap somewhat, but they're by no means as loosely interchangeable as readers will find in some works concerning Joan of Arc.

The hot topics of the day become confusing as well. The interpretations of Joan's cross-dressing, militancy, monarchist fervor, virginity, evocation of "Jesus Mary," and encounters with saints have evolved over the centuries. Thus, depending on the period and location of a written work, the explanations can vary wildly from sparse details to epics of mythic proportions. Was Joan's evocation of the divine genuine, or did she understand what it took for a woman to gain access to the world of authority regulated by men?

Readers tend to focus solely on Joan of Arc while missing out on the complicated world that created and destroyed her, the same world she dramatically impacted. It is difficult for the uninitiated to heed the direction of Daniel Hobbins, who tells us, "Joan of Arc was not a contradiction of her world but its product, and she is comprehensible only within the terms of reference of that culture."[4]

And the world of Joan of Arc is deceptively simple. With six hundred years of hindsight, it is easy to wrap up the life of a nineteen-year-old soldier into several paragraphs. Any basic history on Joan is going to mention the sieges of Orléans and Compiègne. The next layer will include the battle of Patay, the cities along the Loire River, and Paris. But these are just over half the known battles and sieges in which Joan participated. Then there are at least an additional thirty-two known towns that opened their gates to Joan's armies without firing a shot.[5] Of the fourteen battles and sieges featuring Joan, eight of these are typically described as victories.[6] Yet, even though Joan was captured outside the gates of Compiègne, the siege was ultimately lifted, bringing Joan's total victories to nine, if we are maintaining such a ledger in the sense of a traditional military history.

The numbers soon become overwhelming. At a single siege, there were at least ninety-five known captains on the English side, let alone those among the French, Burgundians, and Scottish present.[7] There were roughly 131 men who participated in the inquisition to prosecute Joan. They initially presented seventy articles against her, which were whittled down to twelve. During the proceedings that ultimately nullified the verdict of her condemnation, at least 115 people testified, some at length and multiple times. These numbers are by no means complete, and it quickly becomes possible to present an A-to-Z list of entries numbering near a thousand.[8]

Before she became a saint or an icon of feminist, trans, spiritual, and nationalist movements, Joan was a teenager, a soldier, and a staunch monarchist. More than anyone else, she supported the divine right of Charles VII to the throne of France, even while many of her compatriots lacked this consistency before or after her brief career. Claiming to be sent by God, Joan declared that she alone could relieve the siege of Orléans with the king's backing. Although Charles and his allies had been calling him king since 1422, Joan argued that all French kings must be properly crowned in Reims, deep within enemy territory. She successfully pressed the king to march his army there for the ceremony. As long as Joan was successful militarily, she maintained an air of divinity. With the failure outside the gates of Paris, her credibility diminished. She kept fighting, sometimes where directed, but eventually where she believed she could make a difference, until the moment she was captured by Burgundians, ransomed to the English, tried in Rouen, and executed by secular authorities following a supposed relapse

INTRODUCTION

as a heretic for wearing men's clothing and speaking directly with saints.

This book aims to provide a quick reference for the most common people, places, events, documents, and topics mentioned in the story of Joan of Arc from her birth through the nullification proceedings (1450–1456) that annulled the relapse verdict in 1431, more than twenty-five years after her execution. For those that are entirely new to the world of Joan of Arc, I recommend starting with the entries below. These are the most reoccurring references, and reading them in this order will provide the reader with a rough outline of Joan and her world. From there, you can follow the associated entries throughout the book and peel back the numerous layers of people, events, topics, and documents.

> Hundred Years War
> French Civil War
> Treaty of Troyes
> Charles VI
> Isabeau of Bavaria
> Charles VII
> Philip the Good
> Duke of Bedford
> Anglo-Burgundian Truce
> France
> Mission
> Voices
> La Pucelle
> Poitiers
> Letters
> Artillery
> Battle
> Siege
> Siege of Orléans
> Loire Campaign
> Coronation of Charles VII
> Siege of Paris
> Siege of Compiègne
> University of Paris
> Pierre Cauchon
> Condemnation Trial
> Nullification Proceedings

While this book contains multiple entries for military terms and equipment, it is not all-inclusive. Rather, the scope has been limited to the components that appear often in Joan of Arc's story. Thus, there are detailed entries for **ladder** and **artillery**, as these feature prominently in several sieges and testimonies from Joan and her peers, but the mantelet is only briefly described in the entry for **siege**. Although the mantelet was common in medieval sieges, it was never mentioned explicitly in the medieval narratives of Joan.

Because Joan has become a lightning rod for women's rights and, more recently, women's right to serve in the military, critics are quick to heap upon her all the credit for success or blame for failure in her campaigns, while at other times promoting her as a mere figurehead. I have focused strongly on which military minds were present at which campaign. Some histories about Joan might describe her as leading *her* armies and *her* commanders, meaning they reported to her, while others will focus on the commanders' actions and describe Joan's involvement as that of a cheerleader. In reality, Joan's involvement was much more complex and varied. Her ability to influence and lead troops ebbed and flowed based on the situation, the military commanders present, and the authority she obtained. In the battle entries, care has been taken to emphasize what sort of role Joan and the nobles present played.

When you get past the popular myth and lore that has built up around Joan of Arc prevalent in pulp magazines and the internet, many historians will claim she did not turn the tide of the Hundred Years War. If you read past 1431, then you'll learn her companions in arms hardly shared her vision of monarchist purity through Charles VII, let alone the French. Others were simply bad people by any measure, before and after they met Joan. Some of her closest companions in arms were scoundrels or eventually found themselves in rebellion against the monarchy she sought to bolster. For example, the duke of Alençon and the bastard of Orléans both took part in rebellions against Charles VII, the former of which was arrested multiple times, convicted of treason, and ultimately died in prison. Then there is Gilles de Rais, a serial rapist and murderer who killed at least a hundred, and possibly hundreds, of children between the ages of six and eighteen, the age of Joan when she was captured in 1430. It seems grossly incongruous to reconcile the actions committed by these individuals after they had served alongside *the* Joan of Arc.

This book covers not only the important people, places, and events in Joan's world, but also the objects, roles, odd terminology, sources, and themes that impacted her world or that come up often in subsequent histories about her. It is easy to get caught up in the inner workings, such as what to call the men present at Joan's trial, and different works on Joan can conflict on these details. Were they judges? Were they assessors? If there were both judges *and* assessors present, then which men judged and which men assessed? The answers are remarkably not forthcoming in many books on Joan, and it has led to a girth of material that, while it may not be wholly incorrect or incomplete, is not precise. Why, for example, should a military historian waste ink explaining the difference between a judge and an assessor at Joan's trial, especially when the focus of a military historian is what Joan had to say about her campaigns? This book aims to bridge these gaps for those who dive deep into the world of Joan of Arc.

Joan of Arc: A Reference to Her Life and Works focuses purposefully on Joan's world up to the nullification proceedings, and ventures into historiography only where it demonstrates the evolving perspectives of specific documents, people, and events over time. The bibliography at the end focuses on works in English, but also includes some of the necessary French and Latin works. It is my hope that this book will serve as a useful quick reference guide to Joan and her world for the newly curious reader and expert alike.

NOTES

1. Historians often make at least one of these statements. For Joan as the most-documented medieval person, see Larissa Juliet Taylor, *The Virgin Warrior: The Life and Death of Joan of Arc* (New Haven: Yale University Press, 2010), xix–xx. For Orléans as the most-documented military engagement, see Kelly DeVries, *Joan of Arc: A Military Leader* (Phoenix Mill: Sutton Publishing, 1999), 57. He takes it further, stating the "battles of Crecy, Poitiers, Agincourt, Formigny, and Castillon together cannot boast the number of pages devoted to the siege of Orleans." For the most-documented trial, see Daniel Hobbins, editor and translator, *The Trial of Joan of Arc* (Cambridge: Harvard University Press, 2005), 1.

2. Helen Castor, *Joan of Arc: A History* (New York: HarperCollins, 2015); Taylor, *The Virgin Warrior*.

3. The definitive French work today is Philippe Contamine, Olivier Bouzy, and Xavier Hélary, *Jeanne d'Arc: Histoire et dictionnaire* (Paris: Robert Laffont, 2012).

4. Hobbins, *Trial of Joan of Arc*, 28.

5. DeVries rattles off thirty-two individual cities that surrendered to Joan throughout his book. Several times he cuts his list short by saying "and more." DeVries, *Joan of Arc*, 114, 116, 122–23, 126–27, 132–33, 136, 138–39.

6. Orléans, Jargeau, Meung-sur-Loire, Beaugency, Patay, Troyes, Saint-Pierre-le-Moutier, and Lagny.

7. L. Jarry, *Le compte l'armée Anglaise au siège d'Orléans* (Orléans: H. Herluison, 1892), 205–26.

8. See, for example, Pascal-Raphël Ambrogi and Dominque Le Tourneau, *Dictionnaire et encyclopedique de Jeanne d'Arc* (Paris: Desclée De Brouwer, 2017).

Entries, A–Z

12 ARTICLES. *See* TWELVE ARTICLES

70 ARTICLES. *See* TWELVE ARTICLES

1428 EXPEDITION. *See* SALISBURY'S 1428 EXPEDITION.

ABBOT. An abbot was the male superior of a religious community, typically locally elected for life, but sometimes appointed or transferred by bishops or secular authority. The most common community was a monastery, but they could also include canons or groups of clerics. The abbot's leadership role was firm, and he was responsible for disciples and their behavior under his care. Depending on the prestige, age, and wealth of the location, abbots could exert more power and influence over the local community, both religious and secular.

There were numerous abbots present at Joan of Arc's **trial**, observing and giving opinions. Their authority came not only from their rank of abbot, but also in the various degrees they boasted in **canon law**, theology, and **civil law** (*See* EDUCATION). In France during this period, there were women in the equivalent abbess role, ruling over a community of nuns, but none were present at Joan's trial. *See also* DUREMORT, GILLES DE; PRIOR.

ABJURATION OF JOAN OF ARC (24 MAY 1431). At the end of Joan of Arc's **condemnation trial**, the judges and assessors (*See* ROLES) read the surmised **twelve articles** of accusation against her along with the opinion on each article from the **University of Paris** (23 May 1431). Afterward, they urged Joan to submit to the **Church Militant**, which she refused. She further stood by her previous statements made throughout the trial. The judges then concluded the trial and determined to read their final verdict the next day (24 May).

This scene was held in public in the Saint-Ouen Abbey cemetery, complete with a scaffold ready for execution. **Guillaume Érard** then preached a sermon to Joan, the full contents of which do not survive. The **transcripts** of the trial tell us that he led by quoting from John 15:4, "No branch can bear fruit by itself; it must remain in the vine" (NIV), the vine being the Church and Joan the fruitless branch. Then **Pierre Cauchon** began to read the verdict, but Joan interjected and said she would submit to the judges and abandon men's **clothing**. Next was presented an abjuration document, which **Jean Massieu** read aloud before Joan signed it. The judges then presented a different verdict, sentencing Joan to life in prison and wearing women's clothing for the rest of her days. Joan was then escorted away. The judges and some assessors met with her later that afternoon to ensure she wore women's clothing. Joan also had her **hair** shaved at her request, which was previously in a pageboy style, an act meant to signify repentance.

During the **nullification proceedings**, witnesses said the English were furious with the results, but Cauchon was adamant that he was interested in saving her soul, not killing her. There was also contention over what document Joan actually heard and signed during the spectacle. Jean Massieu, the reader of the document, claimed that what survived in the Latin transcripts of the trial was not the same document he read. Others such as Guillaume de La Chambre (*See* PHYSICIANS) attested that what was read was much shorter than what survives in the Latin transcripts of the trial. In the surviving French minutes from the trial, a shorter version of the abjuration document appears, aligning with the six to eight lines in length described by witnesses. In both versions, Joan admits and agrees to stop sinning, as well as submit to the Church. In both versions, she admits to falsifying her **visions, voices, and revelations**. However, the Latin version provides more details about her sins including leading others astray, wearing men's clothing, and seeking war. She also admits to being a **blasphemer, idolator,** and **schismatic**. The Latin version also has more procedural information about the legitimacy of the inquisition, the judges, and their authority from Rome and the **pope**.

Contentions over the abjuration and the signed document have raged since the nullification proceedings. Some argue that Joan was misled into signing the document and/or she signed a different document than what was read to her. Guillaume de La Chambre further confused the situation by claiming Joan was promised freedom if she simply signed the document. While no one else made this claim, witnesses did attest to Joan believing she was promised her freedom, or at least relocation to an ecclesiastical prison. Part of the argument made during the nullification was that if Joan did not genuinely abjure, then she could not **relapse**, as she was found guilty of doing on 30 May 1431.

AGE OF JOAN OF ARC. The only contemporary source that provides an exact day for the birth of Joan of Arc is a letter written by **Perceval de Boulainvilliers**, in which he claimed Joan was born on 6 January 1412, or the day of the Epiphany. Because this is the only source that provides an exact date, some historians dismiss it outright, but most supply the date with an asterisk, emphasizing that it is suspect.

Deriving at least a birth year for Joan from other surviving contemporary chroniclers and testimonies, typically from the **nullification proceedings**, provide us years between 1407 and 1413. For example, Joan's childhood friend, Hauviette, put her birthdate at 1407 or 1408; Burgundian chroniclers **Jean Chartier** and **Monstrelet** went with 1409; **Gilles le Bouvier, Martin Ladvenu,** and **Jean Le Fèvre** went with 1410; **Perceval de Cagny** and Pierre Miget gave us 1411; the author of the *Journal d'un Bourgeois de Paris*, **Isambard de La Pierre, Nicolas Taquel,** and Pope Pius II give us 1412; and finally, **Jean d'Aulon, Thomas Marie,** and **Christine de Pizan** give us 1413. Deriving these dates is often done by taking the age they associated with Joan during an event for which we know the date. That the years vary so wildly should not surprise us, especially given some of them received their information secondhand or were remembering events from more than twenty-five years prior. It is very easy to get in one's head that someone is sixteen years old and continue to cite that age regardless of how much time has passed.

During her **condemnation trial**, Joan's age seems to have been of little consequence when compared with her gender, claims, or deeds. In the first public session (21 February 1431), Joan was asked her age, and she indicated that she was around nineteen years old, but there is no indication that the assessors followed up for a precise date. If Joan was indeed born on 6 January, she would have been forty-six days past her nineteenth birthday at this point in the trial. Joan would have been seventeen when she first encountered **Charles VII** in **Chinon**, relieved the siege of **Orléans**, served in the **Loire Campaign**, participated in the **coronation of Charles VII**, failed to capture **Paris**, and was **injured** at least three times. She was eighteen when she was captured outside of **Compiègne**, attempted to **escape**, and was eventually **ransomed** to the English. By the first public session of her condemnation trial, she had been in captivity for 274 days, during which it is likely she turned nineteen at some point, if not on 6 January.

AGINCOURT, BATTLE OF. *See* HUNDRED YEARS WAR.

ALBRET, CHARLES II D' (?–1471). Charles II d'Albret was a well-connected noble in the French court. His father was constable of France, as well as a commander and casualty at Agincourt; his cousin was **Charles VII**; his half-brother was **Georges de La Trémoille**. Albret was involved in political and martial maneuvering throughout the 1420s to increase the power of Charles VII, and he was with the king when he seized **Chinon** in 1428. He is mentioned explicitly being present at the battles of **Patay** and **Jargeau**, and the **march to Reims** where he held a prominent position at the **coronation** of Charles. At **Montépilloy**, Albret commanded the troops where Joan of Arc, **La Hire**, and the **bastard of Orléans** were stationed. He was also the commander in the presence of Joan at the sieges of **Saint-Pierre-le-Moutier** and **La Charité**. Before the siege of the latter, he and Joan both sent letters to **Riom** requesting gunpowder, saltpeter, sulphur, arrows, and crossbows. After the failed siege of La Charité, Albret became Lieutenant General in **Berry** and continued fighting in campaigns for Charles until the latter's passing in 1461. During the reign of King **Louis XI**, Albret, like many other French nobles, took part in the **League of the Public Weal** and other aristocratic rebellions. *See also* ARTILLERY.

ALENÇON, JOHN II, DUKE OF (C. 1409–1476). John II, the duke of Alençon, was a companion in arms of Joan of Arc, participating in the **Loire Campaign**, the **march to Reims**, and the siege of **Paris**. His candid testimony during the **nullification proceedings**, as well as the chronicle of his servant, **Perceval de Cagny**, provide an exhaustive and positive perspective on the duke and his interactions with Joan.

John II became duke of Alençon upon the death of his father at Agincourt in 1415 (*See* HUNDRED YEARS WAR). However, in 1420, **Henry V** conquered the duchy of Alençon during his campaigns in France and gave it to his brother, the **duke of Bedford**. Alençon and his mother fled to the court of the dauphin (*See* CHARLES VII). In 1423, Alençon married Jeanne, daughter of the **duke of Orléans**. On 17 August 1424, Alençon was captured at the battle of **Verneuil** and was eventually released on **ransom** on 3 October 1427. He was then brought before the duke of Burgundy (*See* PHILIP THE GOOD), who tried to persuade Alençon to switch sides in the **French Civil War**, but Alençon maintained his loyalty to Charles VII. This earned him praise upon his return to the king's court.

According to his testimony, Alençon first met Joan of Arc in **Chinon** where she claimed God would restore the kingdom of France to Charles VII. Alençon revealed the monarchist attitude of Joan who immediately took to him because of his royal ancestry, as the duke was a descendant of French King Philip III (1245–1285). Alençon was impressed with Joan's jousting skills, and he gave her a **horse**. Alençon participated in the preparations for Joan's relief of the **siege of Orléans**, but he did not participate in the relief itself due to his ransom not being fulfilled yet. However, Alençon and Joan led Charles VII's army during the **Loire Campaign**, the **march to Reims**, and the failed siege of **Paris**. At the **coronation of Charles VII**, Alençon took part in the ceremony by arming the king, after which the king then knighted him in turn.

After Paris, Alençon led an army to Lancastrian **Normandy**, but not before he unsuccessfully sought Joan's aid. The royal council ultimately sent Joan elsewhere to capture **Saint-Pierre-le-Moutier**. Alençon and Joan never served together in combat again.

After the **execution** of Joan (30 May 1431), Alençon's career was turbulent. He was arrested in 1439 for taking part in a noble-led rebellion against Charles VII, and he was not released until 1449. He took part in the reconquest of Normandy and then participated in the nullification proceedings, after which he was arrested again, this time for trying to marry his daughter to the duke of York in England. He was convicted of treason in 1458 and remained imprisoned until the death of Charles in 1461. **Louis XI**, the new king of France and godson of Alençon, released the duke. However, after a fallout with Louis, Alençon was arrested and condemned to death in 1474. He was never executed and instead died in prison in 1476.

Alençon provided colorful commentary and anecdotes on Joan of Arc. He spoke of her antagonism toward **camp followers** in the army, including the oft-told story of her breaking a **sword** on the back of one of the women at **Saint-Denis**, after the siege of Paris. He attested to Joan's crusade against profanity, and he admitted watching his words in front of her. Alençon also slept near Joan while on campaign and saw her breasts while she dressed on several occasions, but he emphasized he felt no carnal desire for her. Alençon attested to Joan's martial skill, telling of her ability to sight and direct gunpowder **artillery**. At **Jargeau**, she told him to move from his position. He did and was amazed when it was struck by an enemy cannon, killing another soldier in the same spot.

Historians often read Alençon's accounts of Joan in battle through a tactical or strategic lens, but he displayed a mix of martial and divine awe. He was emphatic about her ability to direct artillery, but the capture of some of the English fortifications outside of Orléans, which he did not witness in person, he described as miraculous.

ALESPÉE, JEAN (1357–1434). Jean Alespée (or Alépéé) was one of the assessors at Joan of Arc's **condemnation trial**. He boasted a licentiate in **civil law** and a bachelor of **canon law**, but the trial transcripts only ever mention the former, likely because there were so few civil law degrees and an abundance of canon law doctors (*See* EDUCATION). He served as canon of multiple cathedrals including **Rouen** where he also served as treasurer, and later led the construction effort of the library. He had close ties to the English, and **Henry V** nominated him as canon of multiple cathedrals, expanding Alespée's influence and wealth. When Rouen surrendered to the English in 1419 after a lengthy siege, Alespée represented Henry during the negotiations.

During Joan of Arc's condemnation trial, Alespée sat in on at least ten sessions, gave an opinion on the **twelve articles**, took part in Joan's sentences as a **heretic**, and then later as a **relapse**, and he attended Joan's **execution**. Concerning the twelve articles, Alespée deferred to the other scholars' opinions. He died well before the **nullification proceedings**, and no commentary of his survives. He would seem quite unremarkable in Joan of Arc's story; however, at the proceedings, **Jean Riquier** claimed Alespée wept openly and declared he wished his soul to go with Joan's soul, a statement often repeated by historians.

ALLEMAGNE. *See* HOLY ROMAN EMPIRE.

ALNWICK, WILLIAM (C. 1390–1449). In the final days of Joan of Arc, William Alnwick was the **bishop** of Norwich, a member of **Henry VI**'s royal council, and keeper of the king's privy seal. Prior to then, he was close with **Henry V** during the king's final days, accompanying him during his last trip to England, being present at his death in France, and traveling with the body back to England. He joined the council to rule on behalf of the young Henry VI and became keeper of the privy seal, holding both positions for a decade.

William Alnwick appears to have been present at Joan of Arc's **condemnation** trial only during the spectacle that led to Joan's **abjuration** (24 May 1431), and he was likely a witness of her **execution** (30 May). Although no commentary from Alnwick survives, he supported scare tactics and executions of heretics. For more than three years leading up to the moment, Alnwick's court at Norwich had tried upwards of one hundred suspected Lollards, followers of John Wycliffe, allowing them to recant of their accused **heresy**. Alnwick handed three of the accused over to secular authorities for execution after they reneged on their recantations. However, whether it was owing to the end of the Wycliffe heresy scare or perhaps seeing a nineteen-year-old Joan burned alive, there were no further executions as a result of Alnwick.

Given his closeness to Henry VI, it is very likely Alnwick kept the young king informed on the trial. After Joan's execution, Alnwick's name appears along with the privy seal on Henry VI's letter concerning Joan of Arc and her trial. Alnwick would remain active in the church and in politics, becoming Henry VI's confessor in 1433. He was part of the English envoy at the Congress of **Arras** (1435), which resulted in the fresh alliance between Burgundy and France. He served as bishop of Lincoln from 1436 until his death.

AMIENS, TREATY OF (1423). The Treaty of Amiens was an agreement between the dukes of **Bedford, Brittany,** and Burgundy (*See* PHILIP THE GOOD). After the deaths of Henry V (31 August 1422) and Charles VI (21 October), Bedford became **regent** of France. The duke of Burgundy had already signed the **Treaty of Troyes** (1420), which disinherited the dauphin (*See* CHARLES VII) as the heir of the French throne and instead identified the future firstborn son of Henry V and **Catherine of Valois** as the next king of France. However, in 1422, Charles VII was still laying claim to the throne, and with **Henry VI** at such a young age, Bedford, as regent, sought to strengthen his alliance with Brittany and Burgundy.

Negotiations for the treaty began in February 1423 with all three dukes arriving in Amiens to negotiate the terms, officially signing on 13 April. The terms were somewhat loose with little explicit military commitment, but the treaty did recognize Henry VI as the king of France and England.

In addition, Bedford also negotiated a marriage with **Anne of Burgundy**, the younger sister of Philip the Good in December 1422. Bedford and Anne wed on 13 May, and she would go on to play a pivotal role in maintaining the alliance with Burgundy until her death in 1432. In addition, Jean V's brother, **Arthur de Richemont**, would marry Margaret of Burgundy, another sister of Philip the Good, on 10 October.

Both dukes of Brittany and Burgundy undermined the treaty as they saw fit. Brittany more often remained neutral during the war between France and England, sometimes wavering support between the two as one side gained strength over the other. Burgundy at times made overtures toward peace or possibly recognizing Charles VII as king of France, but these were often delaying tactics before resuming hostilities (*See* FRANCO-BURGUNDIAN TRUCE). Although typically overshadowed by the Treaty of Troyes in narratives of Joan of Arc, the Treaty of Amiens reinforced Troyes while also demonstrating how adherence to such documents could be halfhearted, depending on the circumstances.

ANGLO-ARMAGNAC ALLIANCE. *See* BOURGES, TREATY OF.

ANGLO-BURGUNDIAN ALLIANCE (1420–1435). Although England and Burgundy experienced some fleeting alliances and moments of neutrality (*See* FRENCH CIVIL WAR) before 1420, the root of their fifteen-year alliance was the assassination of John the Fearless, duke of Burgundy on 10 September 1419. With the dauphin (*See* CHARLES VII) implicated in the plot, **Philip the Good**, the son of John and the new duke of Burgundy, was open to an alliance with England.

On 21 May 1420, **Henry V, Charles VI,** and Philip signed the **Treaty of Troyes**, which officially disinherited the dauphin as heir to the French throne, made Henry **regent** of France, and further determined that the firstborn son of Henry and **Catherine of Valois**, daughter of French King Charles VI, would be the heir to the French throne. With the death of Henry V on 31 August 1422 and Charles VI on 21 October, the **duke of Bedford** became the regent of France while the seven-month-old **Henry VI** was too young to rule.

Bedford sought to solidify the alliance with Burgundy, negotiating the **Treaty of Amiens** (13 April 1423) in which the dukes of Burgundy and Brittany officially recognized Henry VI as the king of France and England. In addition, the dukes became bound through marriage contracts with Philip's sisters. First, Bedford married **Anne of Burgundy** on 13 May, and **Arthur de Richemont**, brother of the **duke of Brittany**, married Margaret of Burgundy on 10 October.

Militarily, the high watermark of Anglo-Burgundian efforts came at the battle of **Cravant** (31 July 1423), where they soundly defeated the army of Charles VII and his Scottish allies. At the battle of **Verneuil** (17 August 1424), Bedford again soundly defeated the army of Charles, but not without first sending away Burgundian troops who did not participate in the victory. Although the medieval record is not explicit on the reasons or repercussions of this exclusion, historians have concluded that it resulted in a slight on the part of Bedford that sent a message of mistrust to Philip. On 28 September 1424, Philip agreed to a truce with Charles VII at **Chambéry**, which was scheduled to last until 1 May 1425 but was later extended to 25 December. In the text of the truce, Charles is referred to as the "king of France." Although there were violations of this truce, the English and Burgundians effectively waged their own wars against Charles while the Anglo-Burgundian Alliance became little more than a non-aggression pact.

During the **siege of Orléans**, a force of Burgundians joined the English army in December 1428. However, after Philip the Good was unable to convince Bedford to let the city surrender directly to him on 17 April 1429, he withdrew his troops. Thus, the remaining siege, the **Loire Campaign**, and the battle of **Patay** were fought entirely between Charles's forces and the English.

In the summer of 1429, Bedford moved to rekindle the war between Burgundy and Charles VII. On June 14, Bedford changed his will to leave his holdings throughout France to his wife, Anne of Burgundy, and their future children. With no offspring in their marriage yet, the next in line in the will was Philip the Good. In addition, to continue the war against Charles, Bedford promised compensation to Philip.

Still, representatives of Philip and Charles negotiated the **Franco-Burgundian Truce**, which officially began on 28 September. Both sides found ways around the truce and still attacked each other's holdings. The Burgundians brought a large army against **Compiègne**, besieging the town on 22 May 1430. On 23 May, the Burgundians captured Joan of Arc outside the town's gates. The siege was ultimately unsuccessful, and the Burgundians abandoned it on 25 October over payment disputes between Bedford and Philip, the former of which was as late as two months' payments.

During disputes between Bedford and Philip, Anne of Burgundy was instrumental in quelling arguments. Thus, the moments of disparity were often fleeting and there were only temporary truces between Philip and Charles. Anne's death in 1432, followed by Bedford's decision to marry Jacquetta of Luxembourg on 22 April 1433, put strains on the alliance.

In addition, in June that same year, a shake-up in Charles's court expelled **Georges de La Trémoille**, a vocal enemy of Philip, and reintroduced some of Philip's allies including his brother-in-law, Arthur de Richemont. Thus, the familial bonds for an alliance with England and against Charles had eroded entirely.

By 1435, Burgundy and France were in discussions for a lasting peace, and England ultimately abandoned the negotiations. Bedford died on 14 September and the **Treaty of Arras** was signed on 21 September. As part of the treaty, Charles agreed to punish those involved with the assassination of John the Fearless, the two settled territorial disputes, and Philip recognized Charles as king of France.

During Joan of Arc's prominence, the Anglo-Burgundian Alliance represented one of the biggest obstacles to her **mission**. She was unsuccessful in convincing Philip to attend the **coronation of Charles VII**, let alone join in her cause of expelling the English from France. In addition, after her capture, the Burgundians **ransomed** her to the English, which led to her **condemnation trial** and **execution**. Although the Anglo-Burgundian Alliance never again achieved the same level of military coordination as at the victory at Cravant, Joan was unable to break the bonds of the alliance during her lifetime.

ANGLO-SCOTTISH TRUCE. See DURHAM, TREATY OF.

ANJOU, MARIE OF. See MARIE OF ANJOU.

ANNE OF BURGUNDY, DUCHESS OF BEDFORD (1404–1432). Anne of Burgundy was the fifth daughter of John the Fearless and sister of **Philip the Good**, born on 30 September 1404. As early as 1414, John offered her hand in marriage to **Henry V** to create an alliance with the English during the **French Civil War**, but nothing came of it. After the death of John, Philip signed the **Treaty of Troyes** (1420), initiating the **Anglo-Burgundian Alliance** (1420–1435). With the death of Henry in 1422, his brother, **duke of Bedford**, sought ways to solidify the alliance with Burgundy against **Charles VII**. The result was a marriage contract between Bedford and Anne on 12 December 1422. They were officially wed on 13 May 1423. At the time, Anne was eighteen and Bedford was thirty-three.

Although struck for political reasons, their marriage was by all surviving accounts a happy one. Several contemporaries, including the *Bourgeois de Paris*, described Anne and Bedford as often inseparable, and **Monstrelet** described Bedford's joy with Anne.

Anne became instrumental in maintaining the sometimes-rocky relationship between Bedford and Philip with explicit interventions in 1424 and 1425. On 14 June 1429, Bedford moved to rekindle the war between Burgundy and Charles VII by changing his will to leave his holdings throughout France to Anne and their future children. However, with no offspring in their marriage, the next in line in the will was Philip.

During the **nullification proceedings**, it was revealed that Anne prevented guards from **sexually assaulting** Joan of Arc in 1430, and she had clothes made for the prisoner. In addition, Anne was involved in the examination that determined that Joan was still a **virgin**. The results of the examination were never included in the **condemnation trial**.

In 1432, Anne contracted a fever while helping victims of an epidemic in Paris, dying on 14 November. Monstrelet described Bedford's sadness upon her death and further calculated the political implications. Historians often identify Anne's death as the last bond in the Anglo-Burgundian Alliance, which would officially end in 1435 after the death of Bedford and with the **Treaty of Arras**.

ANTHON, BATTLE OF (11 JUNE 1430). The battle of Anthon was a major victory for the forces of **Charles VII**. Louis de Châlon, prince of Orange, purchased the duchy of Dauphiné and led a force of four thousand troops from Burgundy and Savoy to stake his claim. **Raoul de Gaucourt**, governor of Dauphiné and a previous companion in arms of Joan of Arc, led a force of some sixteen hundred French troops and Lombard and Castilian mercenaries to meet Châlon. Attacking a marching column that emerged from the forest with cavalry while simultaneously using infantry to attack the sides of the column still in the forest, Gaucourt inflicted about fifteen hundred casualties. Châlon escaped across the Rhône River, but four hundred of his troops drowned in the process. The battle put an end to Châlon's claim to Dauphiné and secured France in the southeast.

Although a major battle of the **Hundred Years War**, it has remained relatively obscure as it is overshadowed by the capture of Joan of Arc, nineteen days prior (23 May). Some historians have begun evoking this battle to demonstrate that even with Joan's capture, the war continued in favor of Charles VII.

APPELLATE TRIAL. *See* NULLIFICATION PROCEEDINGS.

APOSTATE. An apostate is someone deemed to have completely abandoned their faith, which could occur through simple neglect, obstinance, or conversion. Among the **twelve articles** leveled against Joan of Arc during her **condemnation trial**, she was explicitly labeled an apostate for cutting her hair and refusing to wear women's **clothing**. For claiming that she would not disobey her **voices** regardless if the Church asked her to do so, she was labeled both a **schismatic** and an apostate.

During her **execution**, they placed a cap on her head that read "relapsed heretic, apostate, idolater." *See also* HERETIC; IDOLATER; INQUISITION.

ARC, CATHERINE D'. There is still debate on whether Joan of Arc's sister, Catherine, was older or younger than Joan. It has been theorized that she died before Joan began her **mission**, as Catherine is not listed in the **ennobling** of Joan's family (*See* COAT OF ARMS). However, it was discovered that Catherine had married Colin, son of Jean Colin of Greux, which could also explain her exclusion. At the **nullification proceedings**, Colin is described only as a childhood friend of Joan, and he made no mention to his connection with the family, indicating that she had passed away some time prior. However, Colin tells us that Joan and Catherine dutifully carried candles to the local chapel every Saturday afternoon so often that he and other boys teased them for their piety.

ARC, ISABELLE D', ROMMÉE (1380?–1458).

Isabelle Rommée was born possibly in 1380 in Vouthon, about six kilometers northwest of **Domremy**. Isabelle's father was Jean de Vouthon. She had two brothers, Henri and Jean, as well as one sister, Aveline. Jeanne, the daughter of the latter, married **Durand Laxart**, who escorted Joan to **Vaucouleurs** to meet with **Robert de Baudricourt** in 1428. There are theories about the origin of Isabelle's name, including it being a nickname after a pilgrimage to Rome, but there is no evidence of this. The name was likely regional.

Isabelle later married **Jacques d'Arc**, and in 1428 they had five surviving children: **Jacquemin, Pierre, Jean, Catherine**, and Joan of Arc. Due to the mortality rate of infants, it is possible Isabelle had more children and Joan may not have been the last. Joan tells the assessors at her **condemnation trial** that she learned prayers from her mother.

After the passing of her husband, Isabelle moved to **Orléans** in 1440 where she was celebrated as the mother of Joan of Arc and was provided a pension by the city. Records as late as 1453 reveal that she was receiving a yearly payment that was modest, but sufficient for an elderly widow to live alone in the city. Her son, Pierre, moved to Orléans in 1442, but there is no evidence that she lived with him.

During the **nullification proceedings**, Isabelle traveled to Norte-Dame-de-Paris on 7 November 1455 to formally present her request to nullify the verdict of Joan of Arc. She traveled there again in 1456 where she was questioned, and she was present for the nullification verdict on 7 June. She was back in Orléans on 20 July when the verdict was formally announced to the city.

Isabelle died in 1458. If she was buried in Orléans, there is no evidence in records, and none were found during the excavations in the 1980s.

ARC, JACQUEMIN D' (C. 1392–C. 1450).

Jacquemin was the eldest brother of Joan of Arc, possibly twenty years older than his little sister. Although he was married in 1419, the name of his wife is uncertain. For a time, he lived in Vouthon where his mother, **Isabelle d'Arc**, had land. Unlike his brothers, **Jean** and **Jacques**, he did not join Joan's army and he instead returned to **Domremy** in 1429, perhaps to fill the gap left by his brothers. Jacquemin likely died sometime before 1452, as he was not interviewed for the **nullification proceedings**.

Jacquemin had at least one daughter, Jeanne. Jeanne had two children, Claude and Thévenin, nine grandchildren, and eleven great-grandchildren. His descendants supposedly survive today, but the legitimacy of their ancestry is disputed.

ARC, JACQUES D' (?–C. 1439).

Jacques d'Arc was the father of Joan of Arc. Estimates for his birth year range from 1360 to 1380. His death year is often cited as 1431, having died from grief because of his daughter's **execution**. Other historians place his death in 1439, as his wife, **Isabelle**, settled in **Orléans** the following year.

Based on documentation and testimony, we can confirm that Jacques was a farmer in **Domremy**, owning land and animals, but there is no certainty what animals he owned. Throughout the 1420s, he was a leader in Domremy, and he represented the town in several claims and disputes in Toul, and to **Robert de Baudricourt** in **Vaucouleurs**, as late as 1428. Joan shared in her **condemnation trial** how her father had dreams of her leaving with soldiers, which at the time meant she did so as a **camp follower**, a role associated with sex work. Jacques then made his sons promise to drown Joan or he would do it himself if that ever came to pass. Others seem to have known this concern, as they testified during the **nullification proceedings** that Joan was under close watch when the family visited **Neufchâteau** due to the presence of soldiers. The assessors at her condemnation trial grilled her on leaving Domremy without her parent's permission. Joan admitted that she left without their knowledge, as she believed they would try to stop her.

Jacques seems to have come around concerning Joan's military career, as he was present for the **coronation of Charles VII**, having his expenses paid for by **Reims**. After the coronation, there is no other surviving documentary evidence of Jacques. If he was alive, he would have benefited from the **ennoblement** of the Arc family in December 1429.

ARC, JEAN D', DU LYS (?–C. 1476). Jean was the youngest of Joan of Arc's brothers, and his known actions regarding Joan were mostly entwined with his brother **Pierre**. The two traveled with Joan initially to **Neufchâteau** in 1428. However, they did not follow her to **Chinon** in February 1429. Instead, the brothers appear only to join her in March or April 1429, after her examination in **Poitiers**. The brothers were present at the **siege of Orléans** when Joan entered the city, at the **coronation of Charles VII**, and at **Compiègne**. However, unlike Pierre, Jean managed to avoid capture. After his **ennoblement** in 1429, he began styling himself Jean du Lys, as do his descendants.

In 1436, Pierre and Jean backed imposter **Claude des Armoises** as the real Joan of Arc, claiming she escaped her **execution**. The ruse continued until 1440 when it was seemingly put to rest in **Paris**, but not before Claude and Joan's brothers benefited from lodging and gifts from various cities including **Orléans**.

During the **nullification proceedings**, Jean was commissioned to bring witnesses, but he did not provide his own testimony. In 1461, there is record of Jean petitioning the newly crowned King **Louis XI** for an office, listing among his credentials that he was brother of Joan of Arc and served **Charles VII** in his wars.

Jean is on record receiving a yearly pension as early as 1454 and as late as 1472. By 1476, Jean was dead.

ARC, PIERRE D', DU LYS (?–C. 1478). Pierre was one of Joan of Arc's brothers, and his known actions regarding Joan were mostly entwined with his brother **Jean**. The two traveled with Joan initially to **Neufchâteau** in 1428. However, they did not follow her to **Chinon** in February 1429. Instead, the brothers appeared only to join her in March or April 1429, after her examination in **Poitiers**. The brothers were present at the siege of **Orléans** when Joan entered the city, at the **coronation of Charles VII**, and at **Compiègne**. However, unlike Jean, Pierre was captured alongside Joan, and he had to pay a hefty **ransom** for his release. After his **ennoblement** in 1429, he began styling himself Pierre du Lys, as did most of his descendants.

In 1436, Pierre and Jean backed **Claude des Armoises** as the real Joan of Arc, claiming she escaped **execution**. The ruse continued until 1440 when it is seemingly put to rest in **Paris**, but not before Claude and Joan's brothers benefited from lodging and gifts from various cities including **Orléans**.

Pierre was later knighted by **Charles, duke of Orléans**. Pierre retired to the city where he was given the farm of Baigneaux. For the remainder of his life, there are records of pensions and donations given to him by **Charles VII** and the city of Orléans as late as 1463. He also served as provost of **Vaucouleurs** and captain of Chartres. Pierre's son, who styled himself Jean de la Pucelle, inherited his father's pension, and there are records of him receiving payments as late as 1476 and 1478.

ARCHBISHOP. Meaning "chief bishop," an archbishop was typically a local of the region he oversaw and was often appointed by the **pope**. By the fifteenth century, archbishops did not hold the same power they did in the early Middle Ages, but their ceremonial roles were still important. For example, although **Catherine of Valois** married **Henry V**, he ensured that she was officially coronated as queen of England and France by the archbishop of Canterbury in Westminster Abbey. The role also came with considerable wealth, as can still be seen today in the archbishop's palace in **Reims**.

Joan of Arc encountered **Regnault of Chartres**, the archbishop of **Reims**, during the **coronation of Charles VII**. Similarly, **Jean Juvénal des Ursins**, a later archbishop of Reims, would oversee the proceedings and final verdict during the **nullification proceedings**. *See also* BISHOP.

ARMAGNAC, JEAN IV, THE COUNT OF (1396–1450). Jean IV, the count of Armagnac, inherited the title from his father, Bernard, after the latter's assassination in 1418. In the early years of the **French Civil War**, Bernard had leant his title to the name of one of the warring factions: **Armagnacs**. Although some of those opposing **Charles VII** during the time of Joan of Arc continued to use the term "Armagnac," it is not an apt description of those supporting Charles's claim to the throne.

Since 1418, the new count of Armagnac had found himself wavering between support of **Henry V** and Charles VII. In 1429, Armagnac was excommunicated as a **schismatic** and **apostate** for his continued support of Clement VIII as **pope**, but by 30 March 1430 he repented and was pardoned by Pope Martin V. Armagnac was not present at the **coronation of Charles VII**, and his remaining years involved conspiracies, attempts to wed his daughter to **Henry VI**, and eventual imprisonment. A contemporary, **Georges Chastellain**, described him as only obeying the French king if he felt like it.

With such a tumultuous history and personality, Armagnac's contribution to Joan of Arc's story comes from a single letter he sent that was received on 22 August 1429 in **Compiègne**. In this letter, the count asked Joan for her opinion on the true pope, listing three possible choices. Joan's response is short and non-committal (*See* LETTER TO JEAN IV). During her **condemnation trial** on 1 March 1431, the assessors presented both Armagnac's letter and Joan's response, grilling her on whether she knew the true pope. Both letters were again presented in articles 26 to 30 of the **seventy articles** originally brought against Joan.

ARMAGNAC, TERMES D'. *See* TERMES, THIBAUT DE.

ARMAGNACS. During the **French Civil War**, the Armagnacs represented one of the two warring parties, the other being the **Burgundians**. Those labeled as or willingly identified as the so-called Armagnacs changed throughout the war. In 1410, Duke **Charles of Orléans** married Bonne, the daughter of Count Bernard VII of Armagnac. Armagnac was thus brought into Orléans's raging dispute with Duke John the Fearless of Burgundy, for the assassination of Charles's father, Louis I (1407). In 1411, Orléans and Armagnac formed the League of Gien along with the duke of Brittany and the counts of Alençon and Clermont against Burgundy. The strong influence of the count of Armagnac led to those in dispute with Burgundy taking on the name Armagnacs. Through ebbs and flows in the civil war, and a rekindled war with England, the leaders of the original Armagnac faction were decimated: Alençon was killed at Agincourt while Orléans and Clermont were captured; Armagnac was assassinated in 1418; and John the Fearless was assassinated in 1419, leading to the **Treaty of Troyes** the next year. The dauphin (*See* CHARLES VII) was implicated in John's assassination, and the new duke of Burgundy (*See* PHILIP THE GOOD) worked directly with the English. The treaty disinherited the dauphin as heir to the French throne and established the dual monarchy between French King **Charles VI** and English King **Henry V**, with the latter's descendants becoming the heirs to the French throne.

With the original leaders of the civil war dead or imprisoned and the entirely new cause in favor of the dauphin being taken up, this new party did not refer to itself as Armagnacs. They were sometimes known as **dauphinists**. However, the English and French who favored the dual monarchy, and thus the **Anglo-Burgundian Alliance**, referred to those supporting the dauphin's cause for the throne as "Armagnacs." Although the new count of Armagnac, Jean IV, did not garner the same influence as his slain father, nor was he consistently in the camp of Charles VII, English and French continued to evoke the term. For example, **Jean Pasquerel** tells us that the English referred to Joan of Arc as the "Armagnacs' whore." The author of the *Journal d'un Bourgeois de Paris* referred to the supporters of Charles VII, before and after his coronation at Reims, as Armagnacs, and he did not stop using the term until Charles reentered **Paris** in 1436. Thus, after 1420, the term evolved into a derogatory moniker to differentiate the French who did not support the Treaty of Troyes.

Today, historians often use the term to differentiate between the two sides of the three-decade-long French Civil War, the Burgundians and Armagnacs, with the latter acting as shorthand for whichever collection of French is opposing the Burgundians and their allies at the time. *See also* LOYALISTS, ORLÉANAIS, ROYALISTS.

ARMOISES, CLAUDE DES. Between 1436 and 1440, a woman named Claude appeared in France, claiming to be Joan of Arc, having escaped her **execution**. Married to Robert des Armoises, she wore armor and rode a horse. She apparently duped citizens of multiple cities including **Orléans**. Her story would hardly be worth mentioning if it was not for the implication of Joan's brothers, **Pierre d'Arc** and **Jean d'Arc**, as well as **Gilles de Rais**, who all purportedly gave Claude credence.

Records survive of Orléans exchanging letters with Claude. She visited the city in the summer of 1439 where gifts and banquets were held in her honor, or at least to the honor of who she claimed to be. On the night of one such banquet, Claude did not show up, and she disappeared from the city. Elsewhere, one inquisitor apparently watched Claude tear up a napkin and smash a glass before reassembling both. Another account claims that upon meeting **Charles VII**, Claude fell to her knees, admitting her scam.

While in **Paris** in 1440, the author of *Journal d'un Bourgeois de Paris* tells us how Claude had deceived many people into believing that Joan survived. However, upon interrogation by the **University of Paris** and Parlement, Claude admitted her ruse and left, never to be heard from again.

Although there are records of other women claiming to be Joan, Claude des Armoise was the most successful and has received the most attention by far. The evidence is scant and conflicting, and her marriage certificate has not survived. Other accounts are not recorded until the early sixteenth century, well after the events, leaving open questions. When and where was her ruse exposed? To what extent were Joan's brothers involved? Were they duped or in on it? Still, there are histories as recently as the twentieth century theorizing that Joan did indeed survive and has living descendants. Most historians chalk this up to the stuff of conspiracy theorists who have gone as far as to claim that she was a bastard of Duke Louis I of Orléans, even though he was assassinated in 1407 (*See* FRENCH CIVIL WAR) well before Joan's probable birth year in 1412 (*See* AGE).

The supposed survival of Joan of Arc is easy to dismiss as the English were keen on seeing Joan executed, going so far as to demand her custody in the event the **condemnation trial** found her innocent. **Jean Massieu**, who escorted Joan to and from her cell throughout the trial, later testified to watching her executed at Rouen. Eyewitnesses such as **Jean Riquier** testified to seeing the executioner dig through the charred pyre so that people could see Joan's burned body.

Most historians agree that there was a desire by people to see Joan escape her fate. Believing that she was sent by God, as she claimed, her execution forced them to contemplate that she was either abandoned or lying. Thus, people saw what they wanted to see in a woman roughly the same age and, presumably, the same build as Joan had been, five to ten years after they last saw her.

ARRAS, FRANQUET D'. *See* LAGNY, BATTLE OF.

ARRAS, TREATY OF (1435). The Treaty of Arras officially marked the end of the **French Civil War** (1407–1435), as well as the **Anglo-Burgundian Alliance** that was formed as part of the **Treaty of Troyes** (1420).

Since 1432, there were serious discussions of a peace conference in France with the selection of papal delegates to mediate. Duke **Philip the Good** of Burgundy did not overtly commit to such a conference until his advisors found a legal loophole out of the Treaty of Troyes, which was used as the basis for **Henry VI**'s claim to the French throne. Philip's advisors argued that since **Henry V** never inherited the crown himself, his son could not then inherit it. Instead, Troyes had made Henry V **regent** of France, while **Charles VI** remained king. The untimely deaths of Henry V (31 August 1422) followed by Charles VI (21 October) had not left a clear succession of the crown to the infant Henry VI. With this new argument, Philip openly supported a peace conference in early 1435. He began preparations in May to host the conference in Arras, and the Congress of Arras opened on 5 August with thousands of representatives from England, Burgundy, **Charles VII**, and the Church.

The negotiations were contentious. The English believed Philip was betraying them for abandoning Henry VI's claim to the French throne. They were prepared to offer some territorial concessions to Charles VII and possibly hand over the imprisoned **duke of Orléans**, but they wanted to keep their conquered territory in **Normandy** and Henry's claim to the French throne while Charles VII could be king of the territory he currently possessed and pay homage to Henry. Conversely, delegates of Charles argued that Henry must relinquish his claim to the French throne. The English eventually left the conference in the first week of September, and the delegates of Charles and Philip continued discussions in earnest.

On 21 September, the conference concluded with the Peace of Arras. Burgundy agreed to recognize Charles as the king of France but was not required to pay homage. In return, Charles made territorial concessions to Philip including some towns that the English claimed. Charles also identified and agreed to punish individuals involved with the plot to kill Philip's father, John the Fearless (*See* FRENCH CIVIL WAR), erect a monument to John, and send a delegate to Philip to officially apologize on bended knee.

The Congress of Arras fell short of a general peace in France, but it did mend the relationship with Burgundy. Although its implementation was not seamless and Burgundy would at times be accused of not fully committing to the war against the English, the treaty was an official legal document supported by the Church that recognized Charles VII as the king of France.

Historians often view the Treaty of Arras as a turning point in the **Hundred Years War**, something Joan of Arc aimed and failed to achieve as part of her **mission** during her lifetime. However, debate still rages on the extent her actions played into ultimately bringing about the peace, five years after her **execution**. *See also* FRANCO-BURGUNDIAN TRUCE.

ARTILLERY. The complexion of warfare during the time of Joan of Arc conflicts at times with the popular "medievalism" found in today's film and television. While there were armored knights on horseback, archers, and crossbowmen, the predominant form of artillery was gunpowder weaponry.

Gunpowder was invented in China sometime between the sixth and ninth centuries, but it did not make its way to Western Europe until the second half of the thirteenth century. The transmission came from a combination of Muslims in Byzantine lands, invading Mongols, Spain, and/or Russia, or possibly from all. The first guns appeared in Europe in the early fourteenth century and slowly evolved in their effectiveness. **Henry V** used them in his campaigns in France (*See* HUNDRED YEARS WAR) and by 1428, they were a staple in fortified towns and among besieging armies.

Surviving chronicles and records attest to the sheer amount of gunpowder weapons present in the wars of Joan of Arc. For example, at least 135 gunpowder weapons were provisioned for **Salisbury's 1428 expedition** (D. Spencer 2015, 183). Looking at Joan's first and last engagements, one historian has concluded that the siege of **Orléans** "involved more gunpowder weapons" than any other engagement up to that time (DeVries 1996, 8), and then at the siege of **Compiègne**, "there was perhaps no power with a stronger or more numerous gunpowder weaponry arsenal than the Burgundians" (DeVries 2007, 193). Thus, Joan of Arc's military career was bookended by two record-breaking gunpowder engagements, and gunpowder was described explicitly at each of the campaigns in between them.

The question now becomes to what extent did Joan of Arc understand and successfully employ gunpowder artillery? Based on chronicles and eyewitness accounts, Joan possessed an uncanny skill in deploying the weapons as she did at **Troyes**, which led to the town's capitulation. The **bastard of Orléans** described this moment and other actions by Joan of Arc with a sense of awe, emphasizing that he "believed that Joan was sent by God, and that her deeds of arms came from divine inspiration rather than human talent" (Taylor 2006, 277). One of the most oft-cited stories of Joan and artillery comes from the **duke of Alençon** who tells us that at **Jargeau**, Joan told him to move from his position, otherwise "that engine [presumably a cannon] will kill you" (Taylor 2006, 307). After following her instruction, another soldier was killed by the cannon in the duke's previous position. While he was amazed by this event, the duke took a different view of Joan's skill in warfare, which he believed was on par with commanders possessing twenty or thirty years' experience, and "above all with regard to the preparation of artillery . . . she excelled" (Taylor 2006, 310).

Regardless, Joan of Arc understood the use and logistics of gunpowder artillery. After the successful capture of **Saint-Pierre-le-Moutier**, she and **Charles d'Albret** wrote nearby towns, requesting supplies. In her surviving **letter to the people of Riom (9 November 1429)**, Joan explained that they had exhausted their supplies and they needed "gunpowder, saltpetre, sulphur." Saltpeter, sulphur, and charcoal were the three ingredients necessary for making gunpowder, and Joan emphasized that she did not want to see the anticipated siege of **La Charité** "prolonged for lack of gunpowder and other military supplies" (Taylor 2006, 130–31).

Due to the imprecision of chroniclers who may refer to all gunpowder as simply artillery, cannons, or engines and the lack of complete inventory records, it is impossible to construct the types or numbers of such weapons at each of Joan of Arc's engagements. In surviving detailed inventories, the vocabulary was still evolving and thus inconsistent at the time, making it hard to distinguish between types and sizes with confidence. *Cannon*, the French word for gun, began as the catch-all term for any sort of gunpowder weapon in the fourteenth century, but by 1429, there had been some classification of types of cannons in the forms of *bombards*, *veuglaires*, and *culverines*.

Bombards, sometimes called "large gun" in English inventories, were by far the largest of cannons but had no standard size, ranging widely between 1.0 to 5.2 meters in length and weighing as much as twenty tons (DeVries and Smith 2012, 149). Individual bombards were often named, and the *Journal du siège d'Orléans* tells of one named Bergerie or Bergere from Orléans that was responsible for taking down a tower at Jargeau after three shots.

If there was an attempt to further classify cannons during the time of Joan of Arc, the records most commonly mention *veuglaires* and *culverines*. *Veuglaires*, known as "fowlers" in English inventories, were shorter cannons with a large bore. Both **Monstrelet** and **Jean de Wavrin** mention *veuglaires* present at Compiègne. *Culverines* were portable rifle predecessors that still required two people to transport them and also required support from a fork in the ground. *Culverines* were by far the most common distinct form of artillery aside from bombards, and chroniclers attest to their presence at Orléans, Jargeau, **Paris**, and Compiègne. But again, these records are incomplete and often imprecise, and it was likely that all sorts of these guns appeared in the military engagements of Joan of Arc while being referred to simply as "artillery," "cannons," or "cannons and bombards." Depending on the chronicler, they could describe a large gun as a bombard and all other gunpowder weapons simply as cannons. Of course, their definition of large could vary wildly.

During this time, guns were made from bronze but increasingly became made of forged, cast, or wrought iron due to the cost. The projectiles were made from stone for the larger guns and lead for the smaller guns. Calibers were not consistently standardized until the eighteenth century, and some projectiles were cut or melted on demand for individual pieces. Transportation relied on standard sized carts for smaller guns pulled by a team of horses and then large, reinforced carts for the bombards. Deploying these large guns required the use of cranes to place them on wooden frames.

The **earl of Salisbury** was mortally wounded by a cannon shot at Orléans. Although the earl was in the wrong place and was not specifically targeted, some gunners demonstrated accurate skill, especially with *culverines*. One such gunner was **Jean de Montéclair**, who was described by multiple sources as targeting and killing individuals at different engagements, sometimes on command. From **Lorraine**, historians have theorized that Montéclair had an influence on Joan's understanding of gunpowder. The resources and expertise necessary for forging, transporting, deploying, and employing gunpowder weapons brought new demands to medieval armies, and **Christine de Pizan** presented lengthy details on their logistics in her military treatise.

Finally, among the non-gunpowder artillery was the trebuchet, a counterweighted arm used to throw large stones with great precision. These weapons were large, difficult to transport, and labor intensive to construct onsite, as they were never transported whole. Although they are listed in inventories in the fifteenth century, these would have been easy targets for guns, and historians have concluded that by the time of Joan of Arc, trebuchets were possibly used only defensively, but more likely they remained unused in armories once gunpowder weapons took over the military arsenal.

The effectiveness of gunpowder weapons continued to evolve after Joan of Arc. The complexity and cost grew such that only the king could afford to build and maintain an armory. During the reconquest of Lancastrian **Normandy**, the French used gunpowder weapons exclusively and succeeded against the English.

ASSESSOR. See ROLES AND RESPONSIBILITIES.

ASTESAN, ANTOINE (1412–1461?). Antoine Astesan was a poet, writer, and teacher of Latin in Asti, a county under possession of the then-imprisoned **duke of Orléans**. Although Astesan never met Joan of Arc, his association with her comes from one of his Latin poems entitled *Sur Jeanne*, written in 1435. Loosely based on a 21 June 1429 letter from **Perceval de Boulainvilliers**, Astesan creatively told the story of Joan from her birth to the lifting of the **siege of Orléans**. He compared Joan to ancient queens and warriors, including Amazons, emphasizing that the French believed that Joan had saved the country. No details of Joan's demise are included in the poem. Instead, he declares that God had decided the French must complete their efforts on their own.

In 1435, Astesan sent his work to the duke of Orléans, as a sort of newsletter. Upon the release of the duke in 1440, he made Astesan his secretary, and the poet wrote further works on **Paris** and the exploits of the duke and **Charles VII**.

AULD ALLIANCE. See FRANCO-SCOTTISH ALLIANCE.

AULON, JEAN D' (1390–1458). Jean d'Aulon was close with Joan of Arc during her military campaigns, and he later provided one of the most intimate portraits of her during the **nullification proceedings**. He first met her during the **Poitiers** examination, after which he was charged by **Charles VII** to guard and escort her, as Aulon described it. At the time, Aulon was a **squire**, which has led historians to misrepresent him as a servant or page of sorts (*See* COUTES, LOUIS DE). In reality, Aulon was a well-equipped, experienced cavalryman, and he would lead and train many of the troops that campaigned with Joan. He was often right beside Joan in battle. For example, he used Joan's own **standard** to rally troops at **Orléans**, he cautioned her right before the successful assault of **Saint-Pierre-le-Moutier**, and he was captured alongside her outside **Compiègne**.

Aulon was freed shortly after his capture, and he continued to serve Charles VII, receiving the honor of holding the bridle of the king's horse during his grand entry into **Paris** in 1437. Aulon would go on to serve in various roles including captain of Corbeil (1441), governor of Castelnaudary (1445), and **seneschal** of Beaucaire (1455). It was at the battle of Harcourt (1449) where he was officially knighted.

Aulon initially sent a written testimony to the nullification proceedings. However, **Jean Juvénal des Ursins** asked Aulon to share his story in person. Aulon's testimony is unique, as it is the only one recorded in French, as opposed to Latin, and it was spoken plainly, as opposed to answering a set of questions. The result is a raw narrative and portrait of Joan from a man who was with her daily from Poitiers to Compiègne (March 1429–May 1430), and who slept in the same room with her and her pages. He goes into extreme detail about the siege of Orléans but also talks about Saint-Pierre-le-Moutier. Joan is depicted as always eager to get into the thick of the fighting to rally the troops, often leaving Aulon behind.

Aulon spoke with adoration of Joan, whose success he believed was divine and miraculous. Thus, outside of battle, he supported this notion by emphasizing her devout and pure lifestyle, as she attended Mass almost daily, confessed often, and never swore. Aulon tells us how he saw Joan's breasts on several occasions, as well as her bare legs while tending to her wounds (See INJURIES), but he never had any sexual desire toward her, a claim made also by **Jean de Metz** and **Bertrand de Poulengy**. He also tells of how after the Poitiers examination, Joan was examined to confirm her **virginity**. Going further, Aulon claimed that in his gossiping with women who had attended to Joan, they never knew her to menstruate. He believed this circumstantial evidence added to Joan's divinity.

AUXERRE. *See* REIMS, MARCH TO.

AUXERRE, TREATY OF. *See* BOURGES, TREATY OF.

B

BACHELOR OF THEOLOGY. *See* EDUCATION.

BAILIFF. The role of the bailiff in medieval France had evolved from a low-level tax collector to an enforcer of the royal government's justice, policing, and financing within a designated province or district. The role paid well, sometimes very well, depending on the size and wealth of the province. To avoid impropriety, those selected were typically not from the province, they were not supposed to hold property within their bailliages, and they were transferred regularly. However, these rules were not always followed. By the fifteenth century, bailiffs in France still had considerable power, but the title was sometimes more honorific in nature.

The role in France differed from that of the more commonly known role of bailiffs in England, especially in terms of power and the non-local nature, and thus, English-speaking historians sometimes prefer the French word *bailli* to distinguish the two. *See also* SENESCHAL.

BAILLI. *See* BAILIFF.

BANNER. *See* STANDARD.

BARETTA, BARTOLOMEO. Baretta Bartolomeo, also known as Barthélemy Barette, was an Italian **squire** and mercenary who participated in campaigns for **Charles VII** in the 1420s. He entered **Orléans** on 25 October 1428, taking part in the defense and relief of the city (*See* ORLÉANS, SIEGE OF). Baretta was with Joan at the **battle of Lagny** (29 March 1430) and the **siege of Compiègne** but evaded her fate of captivity on 23 May. There survive records from Compiègne contracting Baretta and some of his nearly one hundred men to help with the defense of the city against the Burgundians.

BARON. In fifteenth-century France the baron title was used for any nobleman who lacked a higher title such as **count** or **duke**. The most famous baron that Joan of Arc encountered was **Gilles de Rais**, who stylized himself as Baron de Rais.

BASEL, COUNCIL OF. *See* COUNCILS.

BASIN, THOMAS (1412–1490). Born the same year as Joan of Arc, Thomas Basin grew up in a noble family from **Normandy**. During his childhood, his father sided with the duke of Burgundy (*See* PHILIP THE GOOD) but managed to avoid the war by moving at least seven times before settling in 1429 in Caudebec, in Lancastrian Normandy. In 1424, Basin enrolled at the **University of Paris**, and he would receive his master of arts around the early age of eighteen. There, he likely heard the reports of Joan of Arc's successes in 1429, and he may have been present during her attack on **Paris**. However, it is unknown what his thoughts were at the time. Basin continued his academic career at the University of Louvain in Burgundian Netherlands (1430–1433) and then the University of Pavia in Italy, studying **civil law** (1433–1434).

Basin's career as a clergyman is a lengthy and active one, as he traveled to London, Pisa, Ferrara, Florence, and Hungary in various roles to participate in church matters. He eventually settled as professor of **canon law** at the University of Caen in 1441 in Lancastrian Normandy. The next year, Basin became rector, the same role initially held by the **duke of Bedford**, founder of the school in 1432. In 1447, Basin became **bishop** of Lisieux in Normandy. It was in this same role that during the French reconquest of Normandy in 1449, he negotiated a surrender of the city to French forces commanded by Count Jean of Dunois, formally known as the **bastard of Orléans**. To the relief of both the inhabitants and the conquerors, the process resulted in the bloodless transition of the city, unlike the recent sacking of nearby Pont-Audemer. The experience at Lisieux then became the model used for the rest of Normandy, which was brought entirely under **Charles VII** by August 1450. Basin claimed that he was among the commanders during this campaign, recommending which towns to negotiate with first and later representing the king in these negotiations. Regardless of how integral his role was in the campaign, he certainly met and spent considerable time in the company of Dunois, one of Joan of Arc's fiercest supporters.

Basin's tangential encounters with Joan culminated in 1453 when he was among the experts consulted for the **nullification proceedings**. This gave him access to all the documentation, questions, testimony, and opinions of her **condemnation trial**. Basin wrote a thoroughly documented opinion that argued there were no grounds for the conviction and the verdict should be nullified, which was the conclusion of the proceedings in 1456.

Basin continued to serve Charles until the king passed in 1461, but he ultimately fell out of favor with the new king, **Louis XI**, especially for his role in the **League of the Public Weal** and other aristocratic rebellions. Basin eventually left France permanently in 1468, and Louis used Basin's imprisoned brother to force the bishop to resign from Lisieux in 1474. In response, Pope Sixtus IV granted Basin the title of **archbishop** of Caesarea. By 1477, he settled in Utrecht, his final residence until he passed in 1490.

During these final decades, Basin was active in public debate and writing, including the production of his massive Latin history, *The History of Charles VII and Louis XI*, a work that was meant to defend his own actions while critiquing the reforms of the two kings. Concerning Joan of Arc, Basin was explicit that she struck fear in the English, something he possibly witnessed firsthand. He also believed the attack on Paris was doomed to fail. Concerning her trial, he repeated many of the points from his opinion in the nullification proceedings, including what he deemed baseless accusations and trap questions from the judges. He believed the unclean environment and bad food weakened Joan during the process, theorizing that this treatment led to her renouncing her **visions**, followed by an almost immediate recantation. Although the work was well-known in France, authorship was often misattributed to others, as Basin wrote in the third person. He remained an obscure figure until the mid-nineteenth century when he was confirmed as the original author of the work. *See also* BOURGEOIS DE PARIS, JOURNAL D'UN; CHASTELLAIN, GEORGES.

BASSET, JEAN (1381–1454). Jean Basset held a master's in arts and a licentiate in **canon law** (*See* EDUCATION). He acquired several **benefices** and served in numerous positions in **Rouen** since the beginning of English occupation in 1420. In 1429, he became the *official* for the diocese, a position that was appointed by the bishop to represent him in ecclesiastical cases. As such, when there was a dispute over whether **Pierre Cauchon**, a refugee from Beauvais, was the appropriate bishop to lead the **inquisition** of Joan of Arc, the other option would have been the bishop of Rouen who would have likely sent his official, Jean Basset, to conduct the trial (*See* ROLES).

Instead, Basset was an assessor, attending sessions on 21, 22, and 27 February and 1 March 1431. He was present for the reading of the **seventy articles** of accusation against Joan (27–28 March), and his opinion was solicited for the **twelve articles** before they were sent to the University of Paris for review. Historians often note the reserved tone of Basset, which was mimicked by others. He admitted that Joan's **voices, visions, and revelations** were possibly from God, but he assumed they were not, deferring to theologians. He believed she was wrong to wear men's **clothing** and should submit to the **Church Militant**.

Basset was briefly imprisoned in May 1431, but there is no confirmation this had anything to do with Joan of Arc's **condemnation trial**, as some historians have theorized since the twentieth century.

After Joan's trial, Basset continued his ecclesiastical career, even after **Charles VII** reclaimed Rouen.

BASTARD. In fifteenth-century France, the term bastard was a title to denote someone born out of wedlock, but it did not carry the insulting connotation it has today. Joan of Arc often referred to Jean the **bastard of Orléans** simply as "bastard," as one would refer to a captain or sergeant. The title was not always permanent, as **canon law** allowed for a change in title if the person's parents later married. The title could also be superseded by a new one. For example, well after Joan's execution, the bastard of Orléans was granted the title count of Dunois in 1439, which in turn became his more commonly used title. Still, some that knew him during Joan's time still referred to him as the bastard during the **nullification proceedings**.

BASTARD OF ORLÉANS. See ORLÉANS, BASTARD OF.

BASTILLE. See SIEGE.

BATTLE. Traditionally, battles, defined as armies fighting outside of a fortification, have received the lion's share of attention from medieval chronicles and post-medieval histories. Historians of the latter twentieth and early twenty-first centuries have correctly emphasized that **sieges** played a more important role in conquest, especially during the **Hundred Years War**. Thus, while Agincourt (1415), **Patay** (1429), and Castillon (1453) receive most of the attention, the capture of **Rouen** by the English (1420), the successful defense of **Orléans** by the French (1429), and the recapture of Rouen by the French (1449) were more important to the outcome of the war.

This hindsight view should not negate the importance that those of the medieval world placed on battles, nor should it diminish their occurrence. One historian has calculated at least 186 battles among peoples in Europe between 1295 and 1525, "giving an average of .08 per annum" (Curry 2002, 365). Battles gave nobles and those who aspired to be nobles the opportunity to prove themselves. To medieval people, the outcomes of battles were determined by God, as the divine way of deciding who was right or wrong, and they commemorated the battles through chronicles, poetry, and art. These works meticulously documented the victors, captured, slain, and cowards.

During the time of Joan of Arc, the way battles were conducted was evolving with the introduction of gunpowder (See ARTILLERY), but they still featured cavalry, armored troops, archers, and crossbowmen. The size and length of these battles could vary dramatically. **Montépilloy** is considered a battle even though it did not involve a full encounter between the armies, while Patay lasted a day. Fighting was often preceded by lengthy maneuvers, lasting days as was the case of Agincourt. Deployment alone could take up half a day. Before the fighting, messengers often gave terms, delayed, and debated locations.

The English developed tactics to address their weakness in numbers and placed a heavy emphasis on their archers who employed longbows. This meant establishing a defensive position with stakes in the ground. The French, who relied heavily on armored cavalry, struggled when charging these positions, as they did at Agincourt, **Cravant** (1423), **Verneuil** (1424), and the **Herrings** (1429). Although arrows typically could not pierce the heavy plate armor worn by cavalry, it could wreck havoc on the horses, and the archers could move behind their stakes while foot soldiers could help attack cavalry caught up in these defenses. Patay was the antithesis of these scenarios, as the French were able to attack the English before they could establish their positions.

Although no one ever saw Joan fight in battle, numerous eyewitnesses testified that she was at the frontlines, rallying troops. At Patay, Joan was successful in convincing the French leaders to attack the English, but she arrived after much of the fighting was complete. She was at the frontlines during the battle of **Lagny** (29 March 1431). She also led charges outside of **Compéigne** up until she was captured (23 May). These examples aside, the majority of Joan's military engagements were sieges, involving fortifications.

BAUDRICOURT, ROBERT DE (C. 1400–1454).

Robert de Baudricourt was the captain of **Vaucouleurs**, a fortified city loyal to **Charles VII** in the **Lorraine** duchy. He had held the position since at least 1419, the same year he defeated **Burgundian** forces at Maxey-sur-Meuse, near the Meuse River opposite of Joan of Arc's hometown, **Domremy**. Baudricourt held a tenuous position at Vaucouleurs, being one of the few fortified towns still loyal to Charles in a region surrounded by Burgundians. Still, he remained defiant, and throughout the 1420s he raided Burgundian territory, ransoming captives on several occasions.

Based on Joan's testimony at her **condemnation trial** and corroboration from witnesses during the **nullification proceedings**, we know that Joan met with Baudricourt in Vaucouleurs on at least three occasions, but the timeline is somewhat disputed. According to **Bertrand de Poulengy**, their first meeting took place on 13 May 1428. Escorted by her uncle **Durand Laxart**, Joan claimed she immediately recognized Baudricourt, having never seen him before. Baudricourt ultimately turned her away after she failed to convince him to take her to see Charles VII so that she could lead his armies in fighting the English. Laxart tells us that Baudricourt instructed him to give Joan a good beating before taking her back to her father (See ARC, JACQUES D'). Historians dispute the dating of this first meeting because Joan testified that she approached Baudricourt by claiming that she would lift the siege of **Orléans**, which did not begin until October that year.

On 22 June 1428, Burgundians invaded Lorraine, besieging Vaucouleurs and raiding Domremy, which forced Joan and her family to take refuge in **Neufchâteau**. Baudricourt agreed to an armistice with Burgundian forces in July. Although the terms remain unknown, he was left in possession of Vaucouleurs. It is also likely he agreed not to leave the city or at least to avoid any more raids. The terms might have also prevented future incursions by Burgundians into towns such as Domremy.

Joan's second encounter with Baudricourt probably occurred in December 1428 or January 1429. During the nullification proceedings, Marguerite la Touroulde testified this meeting came about because **Charles II, duke of Lorraine**, requested to meet Joan. Other historians have theorized Baudricourt agreed to see Joan again out of guilt for the summer raid on Domremy. Either way, Durand Laxart escorted Joan to Vaucouleurs and then to Nancy or Toul in order to meet with the duke. Some historians have theorized that Baudricourt's close friend, **René of Anjou**, organized Joan's journey and exchanged letters with the captain throughout January 1429 about Joan.

Upon Joan's return to Vaucouleurs on 13 February 1429, and thus her third encounter with Baudricourt, the captain brought in a priest to attempt an exorcism on her. It was at this point, according to **Catherine Le Royer** at the nullification proceedings, that Joan evoked the prophecy of the maid from Lorraine to Baudricourt (See PROPHECIES FORETELLING JOAN OF ARC). In addition, Joan vaguely predicted the loss of Franco-Scottish forces at the battle of the **Herrings**, an event taking place the same day, but much too far away for news to reach Vaucouleurs. Historians vary on the timeline after this prediction. Some have Joan leaving Vaucouleurs within a day (14 February) while others have her waiting nearly two weeks (26 February) to allow time for the news of Herrings to arrive to Baudricourt, and thus convince him of Joan's legitimacy. Regardless, Baudricourt was convinced enough to send Joan to **Chinon** with **Jean de Metz** and Bernard de Poulengy as escorts, as well as a personal letter introducing Joan to Charles VII. According to **Simon Charles**, the letter was critical for her to gain an audience with the king. When Joan left Vaucouleurs, she had male **clothing**, a **horse**, and a **sword**, all of which Baudricourt either gave to her directly or provided reimbursement to other townsfolk who contributed them to her.

Once Joan left for Chinon, Baudricourt's activities remain obscure. While he likely attended the **coronation of Charles VII**, there is no evidence of it. He fought at the battle of Bulgnéville (2 July 1431) and earned a reputation as the "Fugitive of Bulgnéville" for fleeing, but modern historians have shown sympathy to the captain in what was a poorly led battle. In 1437, he became **bailiff** of Chaumont en BasSigny, a position he held until his death in 1454. His son, Jean, went on to become **marshal of France** and served as governor of Burgundy from 1481 to 1499.

Baudricourt passed shortly before he could testify at the nullification proceedings, so his story comes predominantly through the recorded testimony of Joan and others.

BAUGÉ, BATTLE OF (22 MARCH 1421). The battle of Baugé was a Franco-Scottish victory over English forces that featured several commanders who would later play roles in Joan of Arc's campaigns.

In February 1421, **Henry V** returned to England with **Catherine of Valois**, his new wife, after spending the previous three and a half years campaigning in France to great success. Having won her hand in marriage as part of the **Treaty of Troyes**, Henry needed to make an appearance in his homeland and see that Catherine was officially coronated as queen in Westminster Abbey (23 February). The previous month, Henry elevated his eldest brother and heir presumptive, Duke Thomas of Clarence, to commander of his army in **Normandy** (18 January).

In March, Clarence began campaigning with a force of some five thousand to six thousand troops in the Anjou duchy, north of the **Loire River** in western France. In the same region were forces of the dauphin (*See* CHARLES VII), consisting of French troops and newly imported Scottish troops, led by Earl John Stewart of Buchan and **Gilbert Motier de La Fayette**. The **bastard of Orléans** and **La Hire** were also among their ranks. When Clarence caught wind of the **dauphinist** army's position near Baugé, he left with roughly fifteen hundred to two thousand cavalry and ordered the **earl of Salisbury** to follow quickly with the rest of the army. Fighting dismounted in order to cross a river, Clarence was ultimately overwhelmed by the much higher numbers and killed along with upwards of one thousand of his troops. Another five hundred or so were captured, including Clarence's stepson, Duke John Beaufort of Somerset. Salisbury managed to escape with the rest of the English army, and the Dauphinists did not pursue.

The immediate effects were dramatic. This was the first major defeat for the English since Henry began his conquest of France (1415), and it was the first time an English heir presumptive had been killed in battle. According to **Clément de Fauquembergue** and the **Bourgeois de Paris**, news arrived in Paris on 4 April, and by 11 April, orders were issued to arrest anyone who spoke out against the **Treaty of Troyes**. Similarly, letters went to **Reims** and other major cities in the name of **Charles VI**, asking them to stay diligent and faithful. The mystique of English invincibility on the battlefield was tarnished.

Conversely, the victory bolstered the dauphin's cause, and it solidified the fledgling **Franco-Scottish alliance**. Scots would be present at nearly all major battles and sieges of Charles VII up until **Herrings** (1429). Although any gains the dauphin made in terms of recapturing cities after Baugé were mostly wiped out during Henry's return campaign later in 1421, the victory effectively transformed Anjou into a battlefield for the next decade. There was also the notion that English success was tied only to the presence of Henry himself, but that fell to the wayside with English victories at **Carvant** (1423) and **Verneuil** (1424). Baugé was an important battle recorded by all major chroniclers including **Monstrelet** and **Thomas Basin**, and it demonstrated how quickly fortune could turn in warfare, especially in France.

BEAUCHAMP, RICHARD. See WARWICK, RICHARD BEAUCHAMP, EARL OF.

BEAUFORT, HENRY (C. 1375–1447). Henry Beaufort was a rich and influential English bishop and cardinal who served under four English kings. He personally funded and reinforced multiple expeditions in France. He secured Joan of Arc as a prisoner, partially funded her **condemnation trial** (1431), and was present for her **abjuration** (24 May) and **execution** (30 May).

Born around 1375 as one of several illegitimate sons of John of Gaunt, duke of Lancaster, Beaufort pursued his education at the University of Oxford. He was legitimized in 1397 by King Richard II, and he became bishop of Lincoln in 1398, the first of many of his **benefices**. He joined the royal council of King Henry IV in 1402, and he conducted the wedding of the king. He then served as chancellor from 1403 to 1405. From 1410 to 1412, he supported the efforts of his nephew, Prince Henry (See HENRY V), to meddle in the **French Civil War** on the side of John the Fearless, duke of Burgundy. With the coronation of Henry V in 1413, Beaufort once again served as chancellor until 1417, focusing on securing support and funding for the war in France. Beaufort also provided the first of many loans secured for the war. Beaufort rejected the final offer of peace from France in 1415, and he announced the news of the victory of Agincourt in London later that year (See HUNDRED YEARS WAR). In 1416, he became the official prelate of the Order of the Garter, the most exclusive order in England, where he conducted ceremonies for joining knights.

In 1417, Beaufort resigned as chancellor and traveled to Rome to take part in the Council of Constance (See COUNCILS), as well as put an end to the **Great Schism**. He had a mandate from Henry V to secure a new **pope** favorable to England's interests in France. With the election of Martin V as pope who appointed Beaufort as cardinal, Beaufort lost favor with Henry who believed he had colluded to enrich himself. After returning from a pilgrimage in Jerusalem (1418), he was forced to deny his cardinalship if he was to keep his benefices in England. Although he managed to regain some favor from Henry when the king needed more money, Beaufort never achieved the same status he previously celebrated under the king.

With the death of Henry V in 1422, Beaufort joined the council of the late king's infant son (See HENRY VI). In 1424, he became chancellor again, secured funding, and loaned his own money for the **duke of Bedford**'s campaign in France that led to the victory at **Vernuil**. As uncle of Bedford and granduncle of Henry VI, Beaufort had secured his position in England for the foreseeable future. In 1426, he was able to accept his cardinalship while keeping his benefices, including the lucrative Winchester. That same year, he ended his third stint as chancellor and the next year, the pope appointed him leader of the church's crusade against the Hussites in Bohemia.

After seeing the military situation in Bohemia firsthand, Beaufort sought to raise a crusader army from England and Burgundy. He secured verbal support from the dukes of Bedford and Burgundy (See PHILIP THE GOOD) before heading to England in 1428 to recruit more crusaders. However, he met resistance as the focus had now turned toward the fledgling siege of **Orléans** and the recent death of the **earl of Salisbury**, commander of the siege (3 November). By the time Beaufort arrived in France en route to Bohemia in July 1429, Bedford pushed Beaufort to relinquish his crusader force to fight against the army of **Charles VII**. The crusaders joined Bedford in time for the standoff at **Montépilloy** (15 August). As a result, Beaufort lost favor with the pope, but retained the support of Bedford.

After a brief stint back in England, Beaufort returned to France with Henry VI on 30 April 1430 for his coronation as king of France. After Joan of Arc was captured outside **Compiègne** (23 May), Beaufort paid part of the ransom to secure her from **John of Luxembourg**. He was present in **Rouen** in May 1431 and instructed **Pierre Cauchon** to accept Joan's abjuration (24 May). He was also present for Joan's execution (30 May), where **Isambart de La Pierre** tells us Beaufort was one of many people who wept at the spectacle. Afterward, Beaufort ordered Joan's ashes thrown into the Seine River.

On 16 December 1431, Beaufort conducted the coronation ceremony of Henry VI as king of France. Over the next few years, he continued to secure reinforcements, funding, and loans for Bedford's attempts to undo the French successes in 1429. However, by 1435, the papacy wanted to see an end to the Anglo-Franco wars. During the negotiations for what became the **Treaty of Arras**, Beaufort represented England, and he failed to convince Philip the Good to maintain the **Anglo-Burgundian Alliance**.

Throughout the 1420s and 1430s, Beaufort was often at odds with his nephew, the duke of Gloucester, who continually upset relations with Burgundy and confronted Beaufort's and Bedford's influence in England. With the death of Bedford in 1435, Beaufort lost much of his influence. In 1439, he made his last diplomatic mission, which failed to secure a twenty-year truce with France. The following year, Beaufort began withdrawing from politics, and he died on 11 April 1447.

In contemporary texts, Beaufort is often referred to as the cardinal of England or the bishop of Winchester. He remains a prominent figure in Joan of Arc's story for his support of Bedford through funding and reinforcements, as well as his efforts to secure Joan for an **inquisition**, the acceptance of her abjuration, and the discarding of her ashes.

BEAUGENCY, BATTLE OF (15–18 JUNE 1429). Beaugency is located on the Loire River halfway between **Orléans** and **Blois**, featuring a strategic bridge across the river. Within its walls were a castle and towering keep, known as the Tour de César (Tower of Caesar). Defending French retreated to the keep during **Salisbury's 1428 Campaign**. The **earl of Salisbury** negotiated the town's surrender on 25 September.

After the relief of the siege of Orléans (8 May 1429), **John Talbot** stationed himself and his troops at Beaugency. During the **Loire Campaign** led by the **duke of Alençon** with Joan of Arc, the French captured **Jargeau** (12 June) and then the bridge at **Meung** (15 June) before arriving outside Beaugency the next day (16 June). Talbot withdrew the night before, leaving his second in command, Richard Guétin, with a garrison of roughly five hundred troops. On 17 June, **Arthur de Richemont** arrived with reinforcements for the French (*See* LOIRE CAMPAIGN). After a small skirmish between the English and French forces, Guétin withdrew to the keep. Its massive height prevented an assault similar to the one that had been successful at Jargeau, so instead Alençon bombarded the keep with cannons for several hours until Guétin asked to negotiate (*See* ARTILLERY). It was agreed that the English could leave with their arms and horses if they agreed not to fight for ten days. The next morning, the English left Beaugency and headed for Meung. They then headed north to meet up with other English forces that were defeated at **Patay** (18 June).

Beaugency still features some of the original structures from the time of Joan of Arc including churches, an abbey, the original castle, and the Tour de César, as well as ruins of some ramparts and the original bridge.

BEAUPÈRE, JEAN (C. 1377–1463). Jean Beaupère was a professor from the **University of Paris** and an assessor at Joan of Arc's **condemnation trial**. Born around 1377, he received his master of arts from Paris in 1397 and went on to receive his doctorate in theology (*See* EDUCATION). In 1420, he became **canon** of Notre-Dame de Paris, one of many **benefices** he would hold throughout his life. Like most of his fellow professors and students at the University of Paris, he supported the **Treaty of Troyes**, and he flourished in the 1420s. By 6 September 1430, his benefices had grown to include canons of Sens, Beauvais, and Rouen, as well as parish priest of Saint-Jean-en-Gréve in Paris.

Beaupère was among the assessors questioning Joan of Arc in her prison cell on 22, 24, and 27 February 1431. When **Pierre Cauchon** sought an official opinion from the University of Paris, Jean Beaupère was sent with **twelve articles**, and he then returned with the university's assessment of Joan, which he proclaimed he agreed with on 22 May.

On 5 March 1450, Beaupère was among the first of the assessors questioned regarding the trial for what would eventually become the **nullification proceedings**. His perspective is unique because he did not shy away from Joan's **visions** and he provided a matter-of-fact perspective that revealed no shame or guilt in her demise. Instead, he believed her visions were not divine but imagined. He claimed he visited her the day before her **abjuration** (24 May), pleading with her to submit to the Church. Afterward, Beaupère said he and **Nicolas Midi** heard that Joan regretted discarding men's **clothing** and was considering donning them again, an act forbidden according to her abjuration. He and Midi hoped to meet with her in her cell to encourage her not to **relapse**, but they could not find the guard with the key. They were also threatened by English soldiers, so they fled. Beaupère missed Joan's **execution** (30 May), leaving for the Council of Basel (*See* COUNCILS) a few days prior (28 May). Beaupère was not summoned for further testimony in 1456, likely due to the contents of his 1450 testimony, his remoteness, and his age.

In 1450, Beaupère was at an impasse in his career. He had been canon of Rouen up until **Charles VII** retook the city the previous year. He successfully petitioned to remain canon, arguing that he was not present for the conquest of Rouen, and he was instead in a neutral city. Beaupère died in 1463.

BEAUREVIOR, TOWER OF. *See* ESCAPE.

BEDFORD, JOHN OF LANCASTER, DUKE OF (1389–1435). John of Lancaster was the brother of **Henry V**, uncle of **Henry VI**, duke of Bedford, **regent** of France, and the principal antagonist to Joan of Arc and her professed **mission**. Among those opposing Joan, Bedford was perhaps the most experienced in military and political arenas, having served in wars from a young age in Wales, Scotland, and France, on land and sea, as well as embroiling himself in politics in England, France, and the Low Countries. He set the stage for Joan's **condemnation trial** and is often credited with its orchestration.

John of Lancaster was the third son of English King Henry IV, born on 2 June 1389. From an early age, he benefited from riches and accumulated lands, titles, servants, and wealth, while also receiving the best possible education, which included both French and Latin. In 1399, he was knighted. In 1414, he became the duke of Bedford, a title that was made hereditary in 1433 and that which contemporaries and historians most often associate with him. By the time of his death in 1435, he owned, or at least collected revenues from, multiple titles and lands in England and northern France.

Between 1415 and 1420, Bedford was either in England defending the realm while Henry V was campaigning or joining his brother in France. In 1416, he commanded the fleet responsible for breaking the French-Genoese blockade at Seine, and he then participated in the siege of Harfleur in **Normandy**. In May 1420, he brought reinforcements to France and was present for the **Treaty of Troyes**, which established the **Anglo-Burgundian Alliance** and determined the firstborn son of Henry and **Catherine of Valois** to be the heir to the French throne. On 1 December, Bedford was part of Henry's official entry into **Paris**.

In 1421, Bedford returned to England for the coronation of Catherine as queen of England. While in England, Bedford's older brother, duke of Clarence, died at the battle of **Baugé**, fighting the dauphin's army on 22 March. With the death of Clarence, Bedford became heir to the throne of England until the birth of Henry VI on 6 December. From June 1421 to May 1422, Bedford remained in England while Henry V returned to France to continue his campaigns against the **dauphin** (*See* CHARLES VII).

The untimely death of Henry V on 31 August 1422 followed by the death of Charles VI on October 21 created a crisis for the fledgling dual monarchy instituted by the Treaty of Troyes, and Bedford was instrumental in sustaining it. Although Henry V wanted the duke of Burgundy (*See* PHILIP THE GOOD) to serve as regent of France while Henry VI was too young to rule, Bedford took up the role when Philip turned it down. On 19 November, the infant Henry VI was proclaimed king of France and England.

Bedford immediately sought to solidify the alliance with Burgundy, beginning negotiations for a marriage with **Anne of Burgundy**, one of Philip's sisters, in October 1422. A marriage contract was signed on 12 December, and on 13 May 1423, the two were married. In addition, on 17 April, the dukes of Bedford, Burgundy, and Brittany signed the **Treaty of Amiens**, an agreement to support Henry VI as king of France and to further unite against Charles VII. **Arthur de Richemont**, brother to the **duke of Brittany**, married Margaret of Burgundy, another sister of Philip. The treaty and unions provided a united front against Charles, a remarkable feat in less than a year after the deaths of the kings of both England and France.

The Anglo-Burgundian Alliance was not without its issues. Bedford commanded the English force that defeated Charles's army at **Verneuil** (1424), but not before first sending away the Burgundian troops, which caused a rift in the alliance with Philip the Good. Similarly, while the Burgundians participated in the siege of **Orléans** (1428–1429), Philip abandoned the siege when Bedford refused an offer from the city to surrender explicitly to Philip who would then decide its fate. In moments like these, Anne of Burgundy was instrumental in soothing the disputes between Bedford and Philip, so they would at least discuss their differences if not find a solution. For example, on 14 June 1429, Bedford rewrote his will, leaving all his possessions to Anne and their descendants, of which there were none. The will ensured that the next in line was Philip. This, coupled with new land grants and agreements to pay for Burgundy's war effort, ensured that the alliance would continue in some form, all while Philip bought time through ploys (*See* FRANCO-BURGUNDIAN TRUCE). Burgundian troops would be present at the battle of **Montépilloy** and the siege of **Paris**, and they would conduct the siege of **Compiègne** where they captured Joan of Arc on 23 May 1430. In addition, the Burgundians **ransomed** Joan to the English in November. While by no means a perfectly harmonious alliance, Bedford was able to keep the Burgundians pitted against Charles VII.

Joan of Arc and Bedford both wrote letters mentioning and threatening each other. Joan's **letter to the English (22 March 1429)** commanded Bedford to lift the siege of Orléans, return all occupied cities including Paris to the kingdom of France, withdraw all English troops from France, and recognize Charles VII as the king. Although Bedford never addressed Joan directly, he mentioned her in his letter to Charles VII (7 August 1429), attacking Joan for wearing men's **clothing** and mentioning her in the same sentence as **Friar Richard**, a well-known **heretic**. After the **execution** of Joan, Bedford was also likely the author of multiple letters in the name of Henry VI (8 and 28 June 1431), which described the results of the trial and again condemned Joan for her male **clothes**. He also described her as a witch who allowed herself to be worshipped. Bedford's letters were well-distributed and are preserved in multiple chronicles, including **Monstrelet** and **Jean de Wavrin**.

Bedford's involvement in Joan of Arc's condemnation trial is somewhat debated among historians. To describe him as its architect would be accurate, as he sought the transfer of Joan to English custody. She was brought to **Rouen**, his main home in France, and he ensured that the **inquisition** would fall under the jurisdiction of Bishop **Pierre Cauchon**. There is, however, no further documentary evidence of his involvement, as he left Rouen for Paris on 13 January 1431, not returning for the remainder of the trial or Joan's **execution**.

Afterward, Bedford was able to make inroads against some of the advances made by Charles VII and his armies. Politically he sought to mitigate the **coronation of Charles VII** by bringing the young Henry VI to France and holding a coronation ceremony on 16 December 1430 in Paris. However, with the death of Anne of Burgundy on 14 November 1432, his decision to marry Jacquetta of Luxembourg on 20 April 1433, and his failing health, the Anglo-Burgundian Alliance wavered and eventually crumbled. His last meeting with Philip the Good was in May 1433, and beginning in June, he spent much of the next year defending himself in England over the deteriorating situation in France. In a memorandum from June 1434, Bedford outlined his case and pleaded for more funds and resources. He further described how he did not agree with the strategy to besiege Orléans in 1428, but he still did his best to support it. He again mentioned Joan, reassociated her with Friar Richard, and accused her of enchantment and sorcery, but he also credited her with inspiring the French loyalty to Charles VII and striking fear into the English and Burgundians.

When he returned to France in July 1434, his health was failing. In 1435, Philip the Good had found a loophole in the Treaty of Troyes and he began earnest discussions to host a conference for a general peace in France. Although Bedford did not attend, English representatives argued their case to papal mediators at the Congress of Arras before abandoning negotiations. Bedford died in Rouen on 14 September 1436, childless. The **Treaty of Arras** was signed on 21 September, officially ending the Anglo-Burgundian Alliance.

BENEDICITE. *See* ESTIVET, JEAN D'.

BENEFICE. A benefice typically refers to an ecclesiastical office such as **bishop**, **canon**, or priest, which included a permanent source of income for the holder. These benefices came in the form of a gift, often from nobility, a royal court, or a town that dedicated a revenue-producing piece of land or taxes to the office. In fifteenth-century France, there was a wide range of benefices, and the papacy had consolidated the appointments of the most important and highest-income offices such as bishops and archbishops. There was often friction between the Church and local rulers over who held the office and how they used the money. Even if an appointment was purely political in nature, the Church often had minimum educational requirements for would-be office holders.

Students and professors at schools such as the **University of Paris** would hope to secure benefices for income to continue their studies. Other enterprisers would secure numerous benefices, and in some instances, rarely visited the churches, chapels, and monasteries where they held their titles. The number of benefices, as well as who bestowed them, are useful gauges in understanding the influences on clergymen.

BENEDICTINE ORDER. *See* FRIAR.

BERMONT CHAPEL. *See* DOMREMY.

BERNARD VII, COUNT OF ARMAGNAC. *See* ARMAGNACS; FRENCH CIVIL WAR.

BERRI, HERALD OF. *See* BOUVIER, GILLES LE.

BERRY. Made a duchy in 1360, Berry is in central France and makes up roughly the region on the southwestern side of the Loire River that peaks northwest and then traces south. Its capital is **Bourges**, the city where **Charles VII**—first as **dauphin**, then as disputed king—made the seat of his royal government. Those challenging Charles's claim to the French throne often referred to him as the king of Bourges, as an insult.

The duchy was subject to frequent raids from **Perrinet Gressart** in the second half of the 1420s from his base in **La Charité**. In October through December, Charles sent an army led by **Charles d'Albret** and Joan of Arc to target the towns occupied by Gressart.

BERWOIT, JOHN. *See* ROLES AND RESPONSIBILITIES.

BÉTHUNE, JEANNE DE. *See* LUXEMBOURG, JOHN OF.

BIRTH YEAR. *See* AGE.

BISHOP. A bishop was a church officer, typically the head of a diocese, a territorial division, or province, over which he had spiritual authority over laypeople and other clergy. A bishop was typically local, but some could achieve the position through a transfer. Bishops were involved in local politics and royal courts, going so far as to broker treaties, garner appointments, and write laws, or at least advise in all these matters. Similarly, leaders of countries may push for their preferred clergyman to the role of a bishop. The role came with **benefices** and prestige, enhanced by the location.

During the time of Joan of Arc, bishops such as **Thomas Basin** were involved in negotiating the surrender of cities. A bishop's local jurisdiction was often enforced, but it still required secular authorities to cooperate. This was the case with **Pierre Cauchon**, bishop of Beauvais, as Joan was captured in his province. The **University of Paris** pushed for him to oversee an **inquisition** focused on her. However, it took months of prodding from Cauchon and the university to convince **Henry VI** and **John of Luxembourg** to hand her over. This was only achieved under the condition that if the church did not find her guilty, they agreed to give her back. *See also* ARCHBISHOP.

BLASPHEMY. Blasphemy has evolved over the centuries in its meaning, initially starting as a verbal sin against God or His character to include words or actions that go against the Church, **saints**, or even people. It was an act that was taken seriously, as an unrepentant blasphemer could bring divine judgment upon themselves and those around them.

During her **condemnation trial**, Joan of Arc was accused of denying God and His saints on two occasions: first, after learning that the captain of Soissons had surrendered the town to the English; then again after her attempted **escape** that left her injured. Joan denied making any such statements and further said that she must have been misunderstood.

Although these two instances made it into the initial **seventy articles** of accusation brought against Joan, they were scrubbed from the **twelve articles**. Blasphemy, however, appeared in the conclusions from the **University of Paris** based on the twelve articles, highlighting her wearing men's **clothing**, including "Jesus Mary" in her **letters** and on her **standard**, disobeying her parents, and in her claims to converse with saints **Catherine** and **Margaret**. In her **abjuration**, "blaspheming God and his saints" was listed among her sins and in the final judgment after her **relapse**, Joan was described as a "blasphemer against God and his saints" (Hobbins 2005, 192, 202).

During the **nullification proceedings**, the topic of blasphemy was thoroughly examined. Several eyewitnesses testified how Joan aggressively confronted those who swore using the name of God, including **La Hire** and the **duke of Alençon**. *See also* GODDAM.

BLOIS. Blois was a fortified town on the Loire River, roughly thirty-five kilometers southwest of **Beaugency**, and a major staging area for Joan of Arc and the efforts to reinforce, resupply, and relieve the siege of **Orléans**. The town was under the domain of the imprisoned Charles, **duke of Orléans**, after his father, Louis, had purchased it in 1391. Although it was under threat in the 1420s, it remained firmly in the camp of **Charles VII**. Joan of Arc arrived from Tours around 24 April 1429 on her way to Orléans, staying in Blois until possibly 27 April. During this time, she delivered her **letter to the English (22 March 1429)**. She also first met the **bastard of Orléans** and **La Hire** who traveled from the siege to meet her there. Joan arrived at Orléans on 29 April, after which the bastard of Orléans and others traveled back to Blois, gathering more troops and supplies, and returning to Orléans on 4 May. Although other towns along the Loire such as Beaugency had fallen during **Salisbury's 1428 expedition**, Blois remained untouched while Orléans continued to resist.

BOISGUILLAUME. *See* COLLES, GUILLAUME.

BOMBARD. *See* ARTILLERY.

BOSQUIER, PIERRE. Everything known about Pierre Bosquier is found in his recantation and sentence for speaking out against the **condemnation trial** and judges of Joan of Arc during her **execution** (30 May 1431). He was a Dominican **friar** who did not attend any of the sessions. According to his recantation, once Joan was handed over to secular authorities for her execution, Bosquier was vocal that the judges' actions were evil. The judges—**Pierre Cauchon** and **Jean Le Maistre**—brought the case before **Jean Graverent**, the Grand Inquisitor of France. They believed criticizing the judges and the trial was tantamount to supporting Joan, who had just been condemned as a relapsed **heretic**. On 8 August 1431, they officially accepted Bosquier's recantation and punished him with imprisonment and a diet of only bread and water until the following Easter (1 April 1432).

BOUILLÉ, GUILLAUME (?–1476). Doctor of theology, professor at the **University of Paris**, dean of the cathedral in Noyon, and counselor to **Charles VII**, Guilluame Bouillé was instrumental in the **nullification proceedings** (1450–1456), which examined and ultimately overturned the verdict of Joan of Arc's **condemnation trial** (1431). Although initiated on behalf of the king, most historians argue that it was Bouillé who instigated the process in 1450, as he argued that a soldier condemned as a heretic in the king's army was a stain on the throne.

Bouillé officially began his inquiry with a letter from the king on 15 February 1450. On 4–5 March, he interviewed seven witnesses in **Rouen** who had attended the original trial. Based on this testimony, Bouillé concluded that the **twelve articles** drafted against Joan were misleading and altered her original statements. Thus, those who gave their opinions on the articles, namely the University of Paris, were also misled. Conversely, he saw in Joan someone who sought glory for France, not herself. Even her predictions had come true. As for her male **clothing**, he saw them as necessary while in the company of soldiers. Based on all of this, he believed the original verdict did not hold up. Since Bouillé's original inquiry was secular, not ecclesiastical, and held under the auspices of the king, it could not overturn the verdict of an **inquisition**.

When Cardinal **Guillaume d'Estouteville** began his own inquiry in 1452, Bouillé was part of the process and continued his participation until the nullification of Joan's condemnation trial in 1456.

BOULAINVILLIERS, PERCEVAL DE. Perceval de Boulainvilliers was an active and well-connected French noble in the court of **Charles VII** in 1429. Among the titles and offices held by this **knight**, he was **bailiff** of **Bourges** (1422–1426 and 1429–1434), **seneschal** to the duke of Berry, and counsellor and **chamberlain** to Charles VII. It was likely in the seneschal role where he was responsible for recruiting Scottish and Lombard auxiliary troops for the war. He had a natural connection for the latter, as he had married the daughter of the governor of Asti in Italy.

Boulainvilliers seemingly had a front row seat to the arrival of Joan of Arc, or at least access to eyewitnesses and reports of her exploits from **Orléans** and the **Loire Campaign**, when he wrote his 21 June 1429 letter to the duke of Milan in Italy. Composed in Latin, the letter celebrates the arrival of Joan with fanciful tales from her childhood: the roosters crowed when she was born, she seemingly flew across the ground while racing her childhood friends, and she never lost a sheep while the beasts were tamed by her presence. Historians believe that Boulainvilliers heard some of these stories from the investigative reports in **Domremy**, sent by the **Poitiers** examination. Boulainvilliers also marvels at how Joan was so skilled in riding **horses** and able to support full plate armor for days at a time. Concerning the victories at Orléans and the Loire Campaign, he follows the pattern of the celebratory letter of Charles VII (19 June), describing the same highlights (capture of **John Talbot**), misinformation (capture of **John Fastolf**), and figures, indicating he had access to Charles's letter.

There are two details that make Boulainvilliers's letter important. First, he is the only contemporary source that provides an exact birthdate for Joan, specifically the "day of the Epiphany" or 6 January (*See* AGE). The holiday or date are never mentioned in the **condemnation trial**, the **nullification proceedings**, or any other source, leading most historians to cite the date with a qualifier that it is likely suspect.

Second, Boulainvilliers is the earliest surviving source that makes mention of Joan's **voices**. He recounts that while Joan was playing with some friends, an unknown young man approached Joan to tell her that her mother wanted her home. Upon returning home,

Joan's mother denied sending for her, so Joan went back to her friends. While heading back to her friends, a shining cloud came down from the sky and told Joan of her **mission** to help Charles VII.

Boulainvilliers's letter was well received. **Antoine Astesan**, a poet born near Asti in Italy, rewrote the letter in 1435, poetizing it into verse and explicitly making classical references to the likes of the queens of the Amazons and Virgil. Astesan also took the story past what was known in 21 June 1429, skipping Joan's **execution** by explaining that she was sent by God and now God wanted the French to complete the work on their own. Astesan dedicated his poem to the **duke of Orléans**, who was also the ruler of Asti and, at the time, a captive in England. Upon Charles's ransom in 1440, he would eventually meet Astesan and appoint him secretary to translate his poetry.

Thus, Boulainvilliers's letter survives today in its original form and its poetized form, both in Latin.

BOULEVARD. See SIEGE.

BOURBON, DUKE OF. See CLERMONT, CHARLES I, COUNT OF.

BOURGEOIS DE PARIS, JOURNAL D'UN. The misleadingly titled *Journal d'un Bourgeois de Paris* is a diary maintained between 1405 and 1449, likely by a cleric of the **University of Paris**, who provided candid updates on events in **Paris** and the surrounding region. The author refers to the wars in France with disdain, lamenting how strangers kill each other. During Joan of Arc's military career, the author clearly supports the **Burgundians**, then the rulers in Paris, and typically the **English**, but the author does not withhold criticism for inaction, incompetence, and greed among any party. The diary is rich with commentary on the death of the **earl of Salisbury**, the battle of the **Herrings**, the lifting of the siege of **Orléans**, the death of **William Glasdale**, the siege of Paris, and the **capture, condemnation trial**, and **execution** of Joan. The anonymous author provides exhaustive detail of the trial content, demonstrating access to the records.

Like the writings of **Clément de Fauquembergue**, another Parisian, the *Bourgeois de Paris* diary is reactionary, and it confirms some of the accounts of Fauquembergue, as Parisians would have heard them in the day. However, the *Bourgeois de Paris* provides more updates and much more color, including the logistical effect of supporting the siege of Orléans with flour and corn, and going so far as to track the inflation of food products. The diary also captures the roller coaster of morale among Parisians as Joan of Arc approached the city, attacked, and ultimately fled. The diary's regular updates demonstrate how war was a constant source of angst for Parisians, as they received news and rumors of raids, battles, and sieges. Although the author was not present, the description of Joan's execution is particularly gruesome, as it describes how the executioners let the fire go out so that the spectators could see a naked and charred body before restarting the fire.

Portions of the *Bourgeois de Paris* first saw print in 1653, and the journal saw a full publication in 1729.

BOURGES. When the **dauphin** (See CHARLES VII) fled **Paris** during the Burgundian takeover in 1418 (See FRENCH CIVIL WAR), he reestablished a government in cities south of the Loire River. Bourges, the capital of the duchy of **Berry**, was left to Charles upon the death of his great-uncle, Duke Jean of Berry (1340–1416). The duke had used the city for his court and administration, and Charles followed suit, making it the royal, financial, and administrative capital of his kingdom. Accordingly, Charles received the moniker "king of Bourges" to deride his claim to the French thrown.

During the prominence of Joan of Arc, Bourges sent supplies to aid against the siege of **Orléans**. After the failed assault on **Paris** (8 September 1429), both Charles and Joan traveled to Bourges. The queen of France (See MARIE OF ANJOU) was staying there. Joan lodged there for at least three weeks, recovering from a wound she sustained at Paris (See INJURIES). Threatened by the raids of the warlord **Perrinet Gressart** from **La Charité**,

Joan and **Charles d'Albret** were tasked with capturing Gressart's strongholds. During their campaign, Joan wrote her **letter to the people of Riom (9 November 1429)** requesting supplies. Although only the letter to Riom survives, she very likely wrote other cities. Bourges was recorded as answering the call, and the city levied a tax for a year to pay for the expense.

After Charles reclaimed Paris in 1436, Bourges remained an important city. He tended to stay south of the Loire in cities such as Bourges, likely wary of the experience he had fleeing Paris in 1418. In 1438, Bourges hosted the ecclesiastical assembly that established the contentious **Pragmatic Sanction**. King **Louis XI**, who was born nearby, later established a university in the town (1463).

BOURGES, TREATY OF (18 MAY 1412). In the continual ebb and flow of the **French Civil War**, the Treaty of Bourges was a pivotal moment when one faction sought to gain an advantage by eliciting England's involvement. Although England had already sided with **Burgundy** in 1411 through marriage, military aid, and agreements for territory swaps and joint conquests, the **Armagnacs** sought their own alliance with England, promising more territories for military aid against Burgundy.

The treaty was signed on 18 May 1412 in Bourges, and King Henry IV sent an army led by his son, the duke of Clarence, who arrived on 10 August. However, before the direct involvement of England, Duke John the Fearless of Burgundy was able to break the Anglo-Armagnac Alliance through diplomacy and force, capturing Bourges and using an order from King **Charles VI** to convince all opposing dukes to renounce their agreements with England through the Treaty of Auxerre. The duke of Clarence and his English army sought compensation for their expedition, leading raids in France and eventually stopping in Buzançais where the Armagnacs agreed to pay off the duke. The Treaty of Buzançais (14 November 1412) committed extensive financial payments to England, which took over thirty years to complete.

The long-term effect of the short-lived Treaty of Bourges was to expose the opportunity of exploiting the shaky relationship between the dukes of France. The prince of Wales, future King **Henry V**, took notice. *See also* HUNDRED YEARS WAR.

BOUSSAC, MARSHAL DE. *See* BROSSE, JEAN DE.

BOUVIER, GILLES LE (1386–C. 1455). Gilles le Bouvier was a herald (*See* COAT OF ARMS) and witness to some of Joan of Arc's campaigns and battles. His rise in influence is documented in his writings where we learn that he became king-of-arms for **Berry** in 1420. This role had him traveling to at least Turkey, Armenia, Bohemia, Rome, Brussels, Metz, and Guyenne. In 1450, he wrote the lavishly illustrated *Armorial de France, Angleterre, Ecosse, Italie et autres puissances*, which provides details on roughly eighteen hundred coat-of-arms designs for France, England, Scotland, and other countries. The next year, he was promoted to king-of-arms for all of France.

Among his other works is *Chronique de Charles VII*, covering 1402 to 1455, and amendments were added later to cover through 1461. Commissioned by King **Charles VII**, the work provides a flattering view of the king while forgoing negative details. Still, Bouvier had access to plenty of official documents, eyewitnesses, and experience from which to write. The chronicle's details on Joan are scant, but he was present for some of the campaigns including the **march to Reims** and the **coronation of Charles VII**. The chronicle provides narratives for **Orlèans**, **Beaugency**, **Patay**, **Troyes**, **Montépilloy**, **Paris**, and **Compiègne**, but it is silent on Joan's **execution**. The chronicle was popular with at least twenty surviving manuscripts. However, it was often misattributed to **Alain Chartier** or **Jean Chartier** until its print publication in 1661.

BOWER, WALTER (1385–1449). Walter Bower was a Scottish abbot who studied at the University of St. Augustine. He was involved in politics, helping secure the **ransom** of King James I in 1423 to 1424 (*See* DURHAM, TREATY OF), and joining the embassy to France to negotiate the marriage of the **dauphin** (*See* LOUIS

XI) and Margaret, daughter of James I (*See* FRANCO-SCOTTISH ALLIANCE).

In the 1440s, Bower wrote the *Sotichronicon*, a Latin history of Scotland up to the assassination of James I (1437). Concerning Joan of Arc, he tells of the relief of **Orléans**, the **Loire Campaign**, the **march to Reims**, the **coronation of Charles VII**, the attack on **Paris** and her wounding there (*See* INJURIES), her capture at **Compiègne**, and her **execution** at **Rouen**. However, Bower is most often quoted by historians for his evocation of the wizard Merlin from Arthurian legend as a **prophecy** foretelling the arrival of Joan of Arc.

BRÉHAL, JEAN (?–C. 1478). Dominican **friar**, **prior** of numerous convents, doctor of theology at the **University of Paris** (*See* EDUCATION), and grand inquisitor of France, Jean Bréhal was the most active participant in the **nullification proceedings** (1450–1456), which focused on the original **condemnation trial** of Joan of Arc (1431).

Joining the proceedings in spring 1452 at the request of Cardinal **Guillaume d'Estouteville** who had recently taken up the cause, Bréhal took over management, aggregated documentation, conducted interviews, and sought opinions from theologians and scholars. With funding from **Charles VII**, Bréhal sought opinions using a document that surmised the main accusations against Joan, her responses, and his commentary. This document has become known as the *Summarium* since the twentieth century. Several fifteenth-century copies survive today, including one with his signature throughout. The document focuses on Joan's **voices**, her bold predictions, the so-called **fairy tree** in **Domremy**, her use of men's **clothing** and participation in war, and her willingness to submit to the **Church Militant** and the **inquisition** brought against her. Finding in Joan's favor, Bréhal pushed for papal support of the proceedings.

In spring 1455, he gained support with a request for an inquiry from Joan of Arc's surviving family including her brothers and mother (*See* ARC, ISABELLE D'). When newly elected Pope Callixtus III gave his blessing for the process (11 June 1455), Bréhal continued his work, interviewing over one hundred witnesses throughout France in 1456. Along with the recorded interviews, Bréhal produced what has become known as his *Recollectio*, an exhaustive document containing roughly nine hundred quotes, examining and disputing every single accusation brought against Joan during the condemnation trial including the **seventy articles** of accusations and the **twelve articles** brought against her. The document further denounced the judges, especially **Pierre Cauchon**, for their lack of partiality and procedural violations. Based on Bréhal's work, the proceedings concluded on 7 July 1456, rendering the original trial null and void.

Bréhal traveled to Rome the next year to present the results to the pope. He remained active as the grand inquisitor of France until 1474. There is record of him still alive as late as 1478, but his exact date of death is unknown. *See also* GRAVERENT, JEAN.

BRETONS. *See* BRITTANY.

BRITTANY. A northwestern peninsula of France, the duchy of Brittany played a pivotal role at times during the **Hundred Years War**, but during the time of Joan of Arc, the region remained relatively independent and neutralized. This independence began during the **French Civil War** (1407–1435), in which **Duke Jean V of Brittany** initially participated, but ultimately sought to strengthen his own nationality and rule. During **Henry V**'s conquest of **Normandy** (1417–1419), he was able to negotiate Brittany's neutrality. Throughout the 1420s, the duke of Brittany wavered between the warring factions. First, he recognized **Henry VI** as the king of France by signing the **Treaty of Amiens** (1423), then he recognized **Charles VII** as king with the Treaty of Saumur (1425), and finally returned to Henry VI with a reaffirmation of the Treaty of Amiens on 8 September 1427. Although the duke of Brittany sent a delegation to the **coronation of Charles VII** in 1429, Brittany signed yet another treaty with the English, assuring Brittany would stay out of the war with France.

Several figures in Joan of Arc's life came from Brittany, most prominently the **duke** of Alençon. Arthur de Richemont was the brother of the duke of Brittany, and Richemont would become the duke of Brittany himself in 1457 until his death the next year. **Gilles de Rais** was also from Brittany, serving alongside Joan during most of her 1429 campaigns and remaining loyal to Charles VII. Finally, the brothers **Guy XIV de Laval** and **André de Laval** from Brittany met Joan after the siege of **Orléans** and joined her on the **Loire Campaign** and the **march to Reims**.

BRITTANY, JEAN V, DUKE OF (1389–1442). Jean V, duke of Brittany, was the brother-in-law of **Charles VII**, having married the latter's older sister, Joan (1391–1433), in 1396. He was also brother of **Arthur de Richemont**, an ally and companion in arms of Joan of Arc. As duke, he maintained a policy of putting the interests of Brittany first, which, as the northwestern region of France, had grown in power and autonomy since the 1350s. **Charles VI** requested his presence at what became the battle of Agincourt in 1415, but he did not arrive in time to contribute (*See* HUNDRED YEARS WAR).

In 1420, the duke of Brittany was taken prisoner and was released with the intervention of **Gilles de Rais**, but Charles VII was implicated in the plot. Brittany signed the **Treaty of Amiens** (1423), recognizing **Henry VI**, not Charles VII, as the king of France. Although he briefly aligned with Charles VII in 1425, he once again sided with the English in 1427.

However, the duke's brother, Arthur de Richemont, joined the French in their victory over the English at **Patay** (1429). Afterward, the duke sent a delegation to the **coronation of Charles VII**. In her **letter to Reims (28 March 1430)**, Joan of Arc informed the citizens that the duke of Brittany was sending troops, but this never materialized. Yet the duke did not appear to move toward the English side again. He was not present to pay homage to Henry VI during his coronation in Paris (1430). It is well recorded that the Bretons were anglophobes, thus bringing them closer to the camp of Charles VII as the war continued in his favor. In addition, Joan of Arc remained popular in Brittany among the people, but there are no recorded perspectives from the duke on her.

BROSSE, JEAN DE (1375–1433). Jean de Brosse was a well-connected noble, seasoned military commander, and a companion in arms to Joan of Arc throughout her campaigns and battles in 1429.

Brosse's military career is uneven throughout much of the 1420s, but mostly successful. His cousin, **Louis de Culant**, brought him into the French court in 1422. Brosse rose through the ranks of the army, first as captain of forty troops in 1423 and then one hundred troops in 1424. In 1426, Brosse and his men formed the personal guard of **Charles VII**, which he served as captain until the following year. During this time, Brosse became **marshal of France**. However, from mid-1427 through mid-1428, Brosse participated in an open rebellion against Charles, in support of the recently banished **Arthur de Richemont**. Brosse captured **Bourges** in May 1428, but was then surrounded and forced to capitulate, after which Charles forgave Brosse for his transgressions.

This appears to be the only spell of rebellion, and from then on Brosse was loyal to Charles. Brosse fought at the battle of the **Herrings**. At the siege of **Orléans**, he and Joan of Arc arrived with reinforcements and supplies on 29 April 1429, and he returned on 4 May with more supplies. He then participated in the capture of the Augustines boulevard and the Tourelles bastille outside Orléans. Brosse was active in the **Loire Campaign**, the **march to Reims**, the siege of **Paris**, and the siege of **La Charité**. He was explicitly credited with breaking the lines of the English at **Patay**. For his service, Brosse was honored as one of the four guardians of the holy oil used in the **coronation of Charles VII**.

After the capture of Joan of Arc, Brosse's military career continued. On 25 October 1430, Brosse was part of the army that forced the Burgundians to lift the siege of **Compiègne** where Joan had been captured earlier that year (23 May). Brosse forced the **duke of Bedford** to lift the siege of Lagny in 1432.

Brosse died in 1433, highly respected, but drastically in debt. His name is often stylized as the *Marshal de Boussac* in medieval and modern histories, pairing his title with one of his lands.

BURGUNDY. During the time of Joan of Arc, Burgundy was a powerful duchy, making up the northeastern area of France, bordering and encroaching into other areas of France, the Low Countries, and the **Holy Roman Empire**. The duchy's size and autonomy shifted throughout the preceding centuries and especially during the fifteenth century.

In 1363, French King John II (1319–1364) granted Burgundy to his son, Philip the Bold (1342–1404). After Philip's brother, Charles V (1338–1380), became king in 1364, Philip began expanding the duchy through marriage, diplomacy, and conquest. **Charles VI** (1368–1422) became king upon the death of Charles V in 1380. When Charles VI began showing signs of mental illness in 1392, Philip took advantage, expanding his influence in the royal government to further his interests until his own death in 1404. His son, John the Fearless (1371–1419), became the new duke of Burgundy, and disputes between the king's brothers, uncles, and cousins led to the **French Civil War** (1407–1435). John himself was expelled from the government in 1413, and he did not take part in defending the kingdom during **Henry V**'s 1415 campaign or the conquest of **Normandy** in 1417 to 1419 (*See* HUNDRED YEARS WAR).

John the Fearless explored the opportunity to end the civil war in 1419, but was assassinated, and the **dauphin** (See CHARLES VII) was implicated in the plot. John's son, Philip the Good (1396–1467), became the new duke of Burgundy and signed the **Treaty of Troyes** (1420), allying with the English. The **Anglo-Burgundian Alliance** ebbed and flowed in military and diplomatic coordination, but Philip always sought opportunities to expand Burgundy's power. In 1435, Philip negotiated with King Charles VII (1403–1461) to end the civil war and thus the Burgundian alliance with England (See ARRAS, TREATY OF). Still, Burgundy remained sidelined during the remainder of the Hundred Years War. The high watermark of Burgundy's expansion came in 1440 with the conquest of Luxembourg, at which point Philip had successfully doubled the size of the duchy since he became duke in 1419.

Although the Treaty of Arras recognized Charles VII as the king of France, Philip tried and failed to gain recognition as king of Burgundy from the Holy Roman Empire in 1447. Upon Philip's death in 1467, his son, Charles the Bold (1433–1477), became duke and ruled until his own death in battle. With no male heirs, Burgundy began to wane in power and influence, and much of the original duchy was slowly absorbed back into France.

From the perspective of Joan of Arc's monarchist zeal, Charles VII was the divine rightful king of France. She saw Philip the Good and Burgundy as part of Charles's domain, as Philip was descended from King John II, the same House of **Valois** as Charles. Her efforts to reconcile Charles and Philip during her lifetime were stymied by preceding decades of the dukes of Burgundy expanding their influence, territory, and autonomy. Joan's family had experience with Burgundian soldiers who raided **Lorraine** in 1428, and her journey to meet with the king in **Chinon** (1429) sent her through Burgundian-controlled territory. It was Burgundians who captured her during her effort to relieve the siege of **Compiègne** (23 May 1430). They held her captive until they **ransomed** her to the English on 21 November, who then transferred her to **Pierre Cauchon** for her **condemnation trial**.

BUZANÇAIS, TREATY OF. See BOURGES, TREATY OF.

CABOCHIAN REVOLT. *See* FRENCH CIVIL WAR.

CAGNY, PERCEVAL DE. Robert "Perceval" de Cagny served under the counts and dukes of Alençon for three generations including **Duke John II of Alençon**, one of Joan of Arc's commanders and strongest supporters. Between 1436 and 1438, he wrote a lengthy chronicle (forty-four thousand words in Middle French), which includes the career of Joan of Arc. Serving under Alençon, Cagny personally met Joan and was eyewitness to some of her battles, sieges, and other key events including the **march to Reims**. Although the chronicle covers most of Joan's career, Cagny was relying on other chronicles and eyewitnesses for his narrative of events after Reims. The chronicle maintains a very favorable view of Joan and Alençon while providing details on logistics, planning, and disputes. Cagny portrays Joan taking a leadership role in the campaigns, as when she pushed Alençon to attack at **Jargeau** and when she sent threatening messages to cities before she arrived in person. From Cagny came the enduring narrative that Joan's successes were miraculous and only thwarted due to **Charles VII** and his jealous advisors, including **Georges de La Trémoille**. Although written shortly after the life of Joan, Cagny's chronicle did not see prominence until the nineteenth century. *See also* CORONATION; LOIRE CAMPAIGN.

CALIXTUS III. *See* POPE.

CALOT, LAURENT. Laurent Calot was a French notary for **Charles VI**, and later, **Henry VI** under the regency of the **duke of Bedford**. He was forced to flee **Paris** in 1413 before returning in 1418 to begin his service for the kings (*See* FRENCH CIVIL WAR). In 1423, Bedford commissioned a poem from Calot propagating the legitimacy of the **Treaty of Troyes** and Henry VI as the king of France, and therefore diminishing **Charles VII**. Surviving manuscripts of the poem include a genealogy tracing Henry's ancestry all the way back to **Louis IX**. The poem was translated into English in 1426 by John Lydgate at the expense of the **earl of Warwick**, and a copy was presented by **John Talbot** to Margaret of Anjou in 1445 upon her marriage to Henry VI.

During the **nullification proceedings**, **Haimond de Macy** recalled Calot being present for the **abjuration** of Joan of Arc. He described the notary pulling a document from his sleeve and demanding Joan sign it. Macy said she mockingly made a circle, after which Calot grabbed her hand and forced a more definitive mark, which Macy could not recall. There is conflicting testimony over *who* physically presented the document to Joan, but Macy's point was that Joan's hand was forced.

After Joan's **condemnation trial** (1431), Calot was the notary for Henry VI's 12 June letter offering protection to the judges and assessors of the trial (*See* ROLES). When Charles VII reclaimed Paris in 1436, Calot fled the city once again. He was recorded in Rouen as late as 1437 but is lost to history after this.

CALTROP. A caltrop is an ancient, defensive weapon that featured spikes (typically four) in a star shape, bent in such a way that when thrown, it would always land with one spike pointed directly up. They varied in size and sometimes featured a weighted ball in the center. **Vegitius** tells us the Romans successfully used them against chariots. In medieval warfare, they were used in battles, sieges, outside camps, and on roads, aimed at hindering cavalry. **Christine de Pizan** recommended that a city preparing for a siege should have them in great quantity. In one of the Burgundian inventories from 1406, there were twenty thousand caltrops in the arsenal.

The *Journal du siège d'Orléans* tells us that the women of the city planted caltrops outside the walls in 1428. The *Chronique de la Pucelle* also tells us that Joan was slightly wounded on 6 May 1429 by stepping on a caltrop while dismounting her **horse** at **Orléans** (*See* INJURIES).

CAMP FOLLOWERS. *Camp follower* is a broad term that can refer to any non-combatant following an army on campaign such as politicians, clergy, or those supplying logistical needs such as cooking or laundry. In the context of Joan of Arc, it most often refers to women with a strong emphasis on sex work, paid or not, and it is common to see historians refer to them as "prostitutes." Medieval armies could have hundreds, sometimes thousands, of such camp followers depending on the size of the army and duration of the campaign. Joan's interactions with camp followers was a strong focal point of her contemporaries, and continues to elicit interest today.

During the **nullification proceedings**, multiple eyewitnesses attested that in addition to pushing the troops to confess, hear Mass, and take communion regularly, Joan pushed them to lead pious lives. According to multiple witnesses, this also meant banishing camp followers from the army unless the

Joan of Arc chases camp followers. *Miniature from Les Vigiles de Charles VII, BnF, fr. 5054, f. 60v. Public domain.*

soldiers were prepared to marry them. Both **Louis de Coutes** and the **duke of Alençon** described Joan as chasing out camp followers with a **sword**, and the latter claimed she broke her sword in the process, although he did not specify how. The stories of when and how Joan broke her sword vary. Alençon placed it at **Saint-Denis**, so most likely at the end of August or beginning of September 1429. However, **Jean Chartier** placed it at the beginning of the **march to Reims** (29 June–16 July). Chartier's account was more salacious, as Joan supposedly broke the sword on the back of a sex worker. Eberhard Windeck, a German chronicler, went so far as to claim Joan killed a sex worker.

Neither Chartier nor Windeck wrote from an eyewitness perspective, and they demonstrate how the stories evolved as chroniclers got further away from events. No one else corroborates Windeck's claim that Joan killed a woman. Chartier attached more meaning to the supposed breaking of Joan's sword, as he believed that her success began to wane as a result of the event. Thus, after the **coronation of Charles VII**, Joan met her first major defeat outside the gates of **Paris** (8 September 1429). Still, Joan chasing camp followers remains a popular image in histories. One of the most common images is found in the colorful miniatures of a copy of *Les Vigiles de Charles VII* from 1484 to 1485. It depicts Joan on horseback with a sword, chasing women.

Although no record survives of Joan speaking directly about her attitude toward camp followers, it is easy to glean her perspective. During her **condemnation trial** we learn that her father (*See* ARC, JACQUES D') was determined to drown her in order to prevent her from becoming a camp follower. He obviously envisioned any woman on campaign being associated with sex work and not as the rallying figure Joan became. In addition, Joan emphasized her own **virginity** through multiple examinations and by adopting the moniker *la Pucelle* ("the Virgin"). Thus, she saw a need to cleanse the armies of women serving in the previously accepted roles, which she chose not to perform.

CANNONIER, JEAN LE, MASTER COULEU-VRINIER. *See* MONTÉCLAIR, JEAN DE.

CANON. Canon has several meanings depending on the context. When used as the title of a person, canon simply means they are a member of the clergy staff at a church or cathedral. For example, **Jean d'Estivet** was often described as a canon of the churches of Bayeux and Beauvais, and **Nicolas Loiseleur** was the canon of Rouen Cathedral.

Canon may also simply refer to the New Testament books of the Bible that the Church considered genuine. Additional books the Church has deemed exemplifying excellence are sometimes referred to as canon as well. *See also* CANON LAW.

CANON LAW. Canon law refers to a set of evolving ecclesiastical laws established and governed by the Catholic Church, dating as far back as the third century. Unlike **civil law**, which could vary from region to region or even town to town, canon law was intended to be universal, governing everything in the church community from marriage to appointing clergy.

By the fifteenth century, canon law had evolved into a career path that empowered academics in the discipline to find work anywhere the Catholic Church had sway, including royal courts, **inquisitions**, and especially **councils**. The discipline had found its grounding in several efforts to solidify the bodies of work that included early writings of fathers of the church, papal decrees, council decrees, and decisions from ecclesiastical courts. For example, the publishing of the *Liber extra* in 1234 boasted nearly two thousand papal decrees. Before 1430, other volumes followed including *Liber Sextus decretalium* in 1298 and *Constitutiones clementinae* in 1317. These volumes, commentary on them, and the precedents established by the decisions based on canon law represented the bulk of the material studied by aspiring canonists at institutions such as the **University of Paris**.

Of the thirty-five known canonists present at Joan of Arc's **condemnation trial**, at least six provided opinions on the **twelve articles** formally brought against Joan. Almost all of them deferred to the decision of the theologians, except for Denis Gastinel who believed if Joan did not abjure, then she should be handed over to secular authorities.

CANONIST. *See* CANON LAW; EDUCATION.

CANNON. French word for gun. *See* ARTILLERY.

CAPTIVITY OF JOAN OF ARC. Upon her capture outside **Compiègne** (23 March 1430), Joan of Arc spent the rest of her days in captivity. Initially under the custodianship of **John of Luxembourg**, Joan was treated as a prized prisoner similar to nobles held for possible **ransom**. Throughout her captivity, she was visited up until the day of her **execution** (30 May 1431) from a wide array of people including nobles, clergy, **physicians**, those involved in her **condemnation trial**, and curious onlookers.

In July 1430, she was transferred to the tower in Beaurevoir, deep within Burgundian territory. On an unknown date, possibly in October, Joan attempted to **escape** from the tower, but fell in the process, suffering a serious **injury** that nearly killed her. From then, she was kept under stricter conditions.

Upon her ransom to the English on 21 November, she was transferred to **Rouen** on 23 December, the site of her condemnation trial. The **earl of Warwick** was the captain of the city, and he locked her in a tower of the Château du Bouvreuil. The details of her cell come from testimony recorded during the **nullification proceedings**. They tell us she was guarded by three Englishmen—John Grey, William Talbot, and John Berwoit—who were assisted by other soldiers. Although little is known about these men, the names Grey and Talbot suggest connections with English nobility. These men took turns watching her and slept in her cell. The window of the cell was fitted with an iron gate. A wooden beam was fitted next to Joan's bed where she was chained at night. During her trial, Joan was escorted from her cell by **Jean Massieu**. She was also questioned in her cell during the so-called prison sessions.

Upon the confirmation of Joan's **virginity**, **Anne of Burgundy** insisted that Joan be protected from the guards. Anne then had Joan fitted for female **clothing**, which she refused to wear. During the fitting, Joan was **sexually assaulted**. In addition, there are multiple instances of sexual assault or attempted rape including by **Haimond de Macy**, and later by some of the guards. The earl of Warwick supposedly intervened with the latter, forbidding the accused from guarding her anymore. After her **abjuration**, several eyewitnesses tell us that Joan claimed the guards yet again tried to rape her. *See also* RANSOM OF JOAN OF ARC; ROLES.

CAPTURE. *See* COMPIÈGNE, SIEGE OF.

CARDINAL OF ENGLAND. *See* BEAUFORT, HENRY.

CATHERINE, SAINT. Saint Catherine dates to the fourth century. She was purportedly a virgin persecuted for her Christianity. After confounding a group of philosophers, she was starved, then tortured, and finally beheaded. The cult of Saint Catherine began in the ninth century with the story that her body was transported by angels to Mount Sinai. Joan and her family would have heard the story of Saint Catherine, as she was the patron saint of Maxey-sur-Meuse near **Domremy**, and Joan's sister was named Catherine (*See* ARC, CATHERINE D').

Joan found a connection with the saint early on, and she claimed a **sword** from Fierbois that was hidden in a sanctuary dedicated to Catherine. Joan would later reveal that it was the saint who told her of the sword's location. On 10 May 1429, Pancrazio Giustiniani, an Italian merchant, wrote to his father in Venice, comparing Joan to Saint Catherine, in part because of her performance at the **Poitiers** examination, confounding the theologians there.

During her **condemnation trial** (1431), when Joan was continually questioned on her **voices**, she eventually clarified they came in the form of saints **Michael**, Catherine, and **Margaret**. Margaret always appeared alongside

Catherine, but sometimes Catherine came to Joan alone to comfort her. During the **nullification proceedings**, **Jean Massieu** claimed that she commended herself to God and saints Micheal and Catherine before her **execution**. *See also* CHARLEMAGNE, SAINT; GABRIEL, SAINT; LOUIS, SAINT; SAINTS.

CATHERINE DE LA ROCHELLE. A follower of **Friar Richard**, Catherine de La Rochelle tried and failed to impress Joan of Arc with her own strategic plans and brand of prophecy. Very little is known about Catherine except that she was married with children and came from La Rochelle. In the autumn of 1429, Catherine tried to dissuade Joan from her planned attack on **La Charité**, blaming the cold. She also believed it was worth approaching **Philip the Good** to make peace.

Joan explained in her condemnation trial that she heeded none of this counsel, blowing her off and telling her to go back to her husband. Joan believed that peace with Burgundy was only possible "at the point of a lance" (Hobbins 2005, 83). At the trial, she was also questioned about the so-called white lady dressed in gold cloth that Catherine claimed to have seen in visions. Joan said she never saw the white lady and she spent two nights in bed with Catherine in an attempt to see it to no avail. She wrote to **Charles VII**, dismissing Catherine in a letter that has not survived. The incident caused consternation between Joan, Catherine, and Friar Richard.

Catherine struck back during her own trial in **Paris** the following summer (1430) where she testified that Joan, freshly captured at **Compiègne**, should be well-guarded or the devil would help her escape. Catherine disappears from the sources after this last jab, but among the initial **seventy articles** brought against Joan, Article 56 included Catherine's warning about the devil helping Joan. The intent was to associate Joan's **voices** with the devil.

After Joan's execution, Inquisitor **Jean Graverent** preached a sermon in Paris where he described Joan and Catherine as both being under the direction of Friar Richard, as an attempt to further discredit them all.

CATHERINE OF VALOIS (1401–1437). Catherine was the daughter of French King **Charles VI** and older sister of the **dauphin** (*See* CHARLES VII). As part of the **Treaty of Troyes** (1420), Catherine wed English King **Henry V** on 2 June, and her coronation as queen of England was held on 23 February 1421. Such marriages had the aim of creating ties between peoples, but the treaty further stated that their firstborn son would become heir to the French throne, disinheriting her brother. With the deaths of Henry V on 31 August 1422 and then **Charles VI** on 21 October, her infant son, future King **Henry VI**, was too young to rule. As such, the **duke of Bedford** ruled as **regent** of France.

Although Catherine was obviously pitted against her brother through marriage and treaty, there is no surviving record of her agency in regard to the war against him. Her fate remained in England, and after the death of Henry V, she eventually married Owen Tudor at an unknown date. From them came the Tudor Dynasty, including Henry VIII.

CAUCHON, PIERRE (1371–1442). Pierre Cauchon spent his life embroiled in the politics of the Church, **Paris**, the **French Civil War**, the **Anglo-Burgundian Alliance**, and the royal courts of England and Burgundy. Today he is best remembered as the bishop who organized the **inquisition** into the accused heresy of Joan of Arc, more commonly known as her **condemnation trial**, serving as one of the two judges (*See* ROLES).

Born near **Reims**, Cauchon attended the **University of Paris**, completing his master of arts (1391), serving as the dean of the college (1397) and then rector twice (1397 and 1405), and also completing his licentiate of **canon law** (1398). He was working on a theology degree when he turned his focus to the papal politics of the **Great Schism** in 1406, taking up a case against Pope Benedict XIII in the Parlement of Paris. In March the next year, he led a delegation to Italy, asking both Benedict XIII and Gregory XII to renounce their competing claims to the papacy. After returning to Paris, the French Civil War began in earnest with the assassination of Duke Louis I of Orléans (1407). Cauchon was subjected to the targeted reprisals by the **Armagnac** party, forcing him to flee the city; he never completed his doctorate.

While in exile, Cauchon acquired several **benefices**, including chaplaincy of Saint Étienne (1408), **canon** at Reims followed by bishop's deputy (1409), and canon at Beauvais (1410). During this time, he also began to counsel John the Fearless, duke of Burgundy. The Burgundians regained Paris in 1411, and the next year Cauchon acted as one of the reformers prosecuting the Armagnacs for their excesses during their reign. In 1413, Cauchon and other academics at the University of Paris contributed to the Cabochian revolt, but when their instituted reforms went too far, they lost favor among the Parisians. Upon entry of Count Bernard VII of Armagnac into Paris (27 September), Cauchon was banished from the city once again. From 1415 to 1418, Cauchon was part of the Burgundian embassy at the **Council** of Constance. While there, he witnessed the trial of John Huss who was condemned as a **heretic**, and he successfully lobbied for the election of Martin V as the new **pope**.

Upon Cauchon's return to France in 1418, French Queen **Isabeau of Bavaria** appointed him to represent Burgundy in hopes of a reconciliation with the Armagnacs. In July that year, he returned to Paris alongside John the Fearless. He also began serving as master of requests for English King **Henry V**. In addition, the bishop of Paris appointed him to try Armagnac clerics imprisoned for treason. In September 1419, all hopes of reconciliation dissipated with the assassination of John the Fearless. The incident led directly to the **Treaty of Troyes** (1420), which, among many things, disinherited the **dauphin** (See CHARLES VII) from the throne of France. The University of Paris sent Cauchon to aid with the formation of the treaty upon his request.

Cauchon continued to build up his benefices during this time, but most significantly, Martin V selected him as the next bishop of Beauvais in August 1420. Although **Philip the Good**, the new duke of Burgundy, attended Cauchon's consecration in Beauvais on 12 January 1421, the new appointment distanced the bishop geographically and politically from the duke while bringing him closer to the English.

In 1422, he began counseling **Henry VI** and became the executor of will for **Charles VI**. Over the next few years, Cauchon helped negotiate the surrender of cities to the English, a similar role **Thomas Basin** played later in the war during Charles VII's reconquest of **Normandy**. This participation in war became regular during the 1420s for Cauchon, and in 1428, he actively solicited funds from cities to aid **John of Luxembourg** in his siege of Beaumont. The war came to Cauchon's doorstep in July 1429 when he was forced to flee Reims when the city decided to open its gates to the approaching royalist army. Cauchon was then absent for the **coronation of Charles VII** even though there was a role traditionally played by the bishop of Beauvais. The next month, Cauchon was forced to flee Beauvais. The battle of **Montépilloy** (15 August) took place a mere 48 kilometers from Beauvais, and nearby cities were rebelling against Anglo-Burgundian control with the success of Charles VII and his recent coronation. Cauchon took refuge in **Rouen**, roughly 150 kilometers to the west of Beauvais. Although the bishop seat in Rouen was vacant and Henry VI lobbied on the bishop's behalf, Cauchon was never transferred there. The English compensated him for lost or inaccessible benefices, paying him for special diplomatic tasks.

When Joan of Arc was finally captured outside of **Compiègne** (23 May 1430), Cauchon was the highest-ranking bishop in the region—Beauvais was fifty-three kilometers to the west. The University of Paris charged him with raising the funds to pay Joan's **ransom** and secure her for an inquisition. On 14 July, he met personally with Philip the Good to provide payment and a letter from the university, demanding Joan be handed over, but to no avail. While Cauchon and others sent numerous letters to Henry VI and Philip the Good, none were able to secure Joan for trial. The University of Paris sent a letter to Cauchon on 21 November, emphasizing their displeasure in his inability to secure Joan for inquisition.

The bishop finally got ahold of Joan in late December. After Joan's **execution** (30 May 1431), Cauchon oversaw the translation and distribution of the condemnation trial **transcripts** possibly until 30 November. From there, Cauchon continued his active career, but with little connection to Joan.

Cauchon participated in the coronation of Henry VI as king of France in Paris (16 December). After becoming the bishop of Lisieux (1432), he continued to represent Henry in numerous efforts, such as at the Council of Basel (1434–1435), the negotiations over the **Treaty of Arras** (1435), the formation of the University of Caen (1436), and the negotiations over the release of the **duke of Orléans** (1438–1440).

Cauchon still faced difficulties and disappointments. He was excommunicated in 1434 for not paying his dues to the Church after becoming bishop of Lisieux, but he was able to reverse the ruling by paying up. When the archbishop of Rouen died in 1436, Cauchon was not given the position even though it was his refuge for several years. Also in 1436, opinion in Paris turned against the war as well as the English, with the signing of the Treaty of Arras. Still, Cauchon had sworn a loyalty oath to Henry VI (15 March), and the author of the *Journal d'un Bourgeois de Paris* called him out explicitly for his continued support of the war. When Charles VII reclaimed Paris (13 April), Cauchon fled once again to avoid capture. Finally, on 18 December 1442, the bishop died while shaving, probably of heart failure.

Although Cauchon had racked up multiple benefices over his career, his enrichment only appeared moderate. He left most of his possessions to the construction of a chapel in Lisieux where he was buried. For years, it was a common story that Cauchon's body was thrown into a sewer shortly after the **nullification proceedings**, but these were Victorian sentiments propagated through the twentieth century. In 1783, his tombstone was destroyed to clear space for burying the bishop of Condorcent, but his coffin was not damaged. In April 1931, his grave was excavated, revealing a 1.68-meter skeleton, a ring, and scepter. His body was reburied in the chapel and remains there to this day, unmarked. His ring and scepter were exhibited in a local museum but were lost during the D-Day landings in June 1944.

If Cauchon expressed any regrets or remorse for his part in the trial and execution of Joan of Arc, nothing has survived. He left no surviving works or treatises, which historians believe underscores his lack of expertise in heresy trials, among other topics. Although he had tried Armagnacs for excesses and treason, it is very likely Joan was his first trial of an accused heretic. He also never acquired a doctorate, another deficiency that historians believe contributed to his desire to invite as many experts to attend Joan's condemnation trial, as well as his penchant for highlighting the degrees of all the assessors present (*See* EDUCATION).

During the nullification proceedings, Cauchon became the villain and scapegoat for the demise of Joan, where there were accusations that he modified or hid some of Joan's responses and suppressed those who tried to help Joan. He was regarded as English during the proceedings, and based on the last few decades of his career, he certainly represented the interests of Henry VI fervently. The great-grandnephews of Cauchon provided their testimony in writing, emphasizing that they were but children during the time of the trial, which has led historians to conclude that his own family disavowed him.

Yet it is because of Cauchon that we know so much about Joan and have the closest thing to direct quotes from her. His efforts to legitimize the trial by documenting everything in French and creating copies in Latin for distribution have ensured that the details of Joan's inquisition survive today.

CHABANNES, ANTOINE DE (1408–1488). Younger brother of **Jacques de Chabannes**, Antoine was first recorded in military action in the 1420s, captured by the English at **Verneuil** (1424). After his release, he served under **La Hire** and then the **count of Clermont**. He was again captured at **Orléans** in 1428, but he was released in time to be recorded at **Jargeau** (11–12 June 1429) and **Patay** (18 June). During the **march to Reims**, he was made **bailiff** of **Troyes**. The following year, he was part of the relief of **Compiègne** (25 October 1430). He continued to serve **Charles VII** until the **Praguerie** rebellion (1440), and he was not reconciled with the king until 1449. When **Louis XI** became king in 1461, the new king imprisoned Chabannes briefly. Although he took part in the **League of the Public Weal** (1465), he was reconciled with the king and became grand master of the Hotel of France. Chabannes retired from military service in 1477 and died in 1488.

Although he was a companion in arms of Joan of Arc, Chabannes did not participate in the **nullification proceedings**.

CHABANNES, JACQUES DE (1400?–1453). Older brother of **Antoine de Chabannes**, Jacques commanded at least 140 men at the **siege of Orléans**. He participated in the battles of the **Herrings** (12 February 1429) and **Patay** (18 June), and the **march to Reims** (29 June–16 July). He was present at **Compiègne** during the capture of Joan of Arc (23 May 1430) and later during the relief of the city (25 October). Chabannes continued to serve **Charles VII** throughout the 1430s, but he was implicated in his brother's participation in the **Praguerie** rebellion (1440). Coming back into the king's graces in 1447, he participated in the reconquest of **Normandy** (1449–1450). In 1451, he was made grand master of the Hotel de France. He was present for the victory at Castillon (13 July 1453), the traditional end of the **Hundred Years War**, after which he sent the crescent of the slain **John Talbot** to the king. Jacques died later that year from the plague, contracted while campaigning (25 October).

CHAMBERLAIN. The chamberlains of the kings and dukes of England, France, and Burgundy were often knights, who served as councilors and oversaw their households. There were often levels of chamberlains with different responsibilities, the grand chamberlain playing the highest role, which included carrying the privy seal for signing documents. Chamberlains during the period of Joan of Arc included **Georges de La Trémoille**, who served as grand chamberlain for John the Fearless (*See* FRENCH CIVIL WAR) and later Charles VII, and **Thomas Rempston** served as chamberlain for the **duke of Bedford**. Some of Joan's companions in arms such as **Florent d'Illiers** and **Jean d'Aulon** would later serve as chamberlains for Charles.

CHAMBÉRY, TRUCE OF (24 SEPTEMBER 1424). The truce of Chambéry was a negotiated period ceasing hostilities between Burgundy and the regions loyal to **Charles VII**. Signed on 24 September 1424 and initially lasting until 1 May 1425, the truce was later extended until 25 December. As this came on the heels of the English victory at **Verneuil** (17 August 1424), before which the **duke of Bedford** sent Burgundian troops away, historians have seen this as a fallout of what was perceived as a slight. In addition to the agreed upon period of truce, there was an exchange of towns including **La Charité** that went to Charles VII (*See* GRESSART, PERRINET). Historians have zeroed in on how the verbiage of the truce referred to Charles as the "king of France," but this was not an official recognition of Charles as king.

Regardless of the reasons for signing it, the truce enabled **Philip the Good** to focus on solidifying his territories to the east while his western and southern borders remained protected through the **Anglo-Burgundian Alliance** and the truce of Chambéry. Both sides found ways around Chambéry, and they would accuse each other of violating the truce for years.

During the prominence of Joan of Arc, she would witness similar periods of open warfare, truces, and fake truces in the form of the **Franco-Burgundian Truce**, which stymied her own war efforts in Burgundian-controlled territory.

CHAPITAULT, SIMON. Simon Chapitault held a master of arts and a licentiate in **canon law** from the **University of Paris** when he was selected as promoter by the three judges of the **nullification proceedings**: **Jean Juvénal des Ursins, Guillaume Chartier,** and **Richard Olivier de Longueil**. Like **Jean d'Estivet**, the promoter of the **condemnation trial** against Joan of Arc, Chapitault was responsible for building a case by presenting and questioning witnesses, documents, and whatever else he deemed necessary. Receiving his appointment on 15 December 1455, Chapitault built a list of articles to question witnesses in **Domremy**, **Orléans**, **Paris**, and **Rouen** between 28 January and 14 May 1456. In determining his approach and questions, he very likely had input from the judges, from the previously recorded interviews in the process in 1450 and 1452, and from those who had been working in the proceedings such as **Jean Bréhal** and **Guillaume Prévosteau**. Chapitault built his case against the judges, the process, the **abjuration**, the **relapse**, and the verdict and **execution**, which he argued were biased and fraudulent. Chapitault was successful in convincing the judges, who nullified the original trial record and sentences on 7 July 1456. *See also* EDUCATION; ROLES AND RESPONSIBILITIES.

CHARITÉ. *See* LA CHARITÉ, SIEGE OF.

CHARLEMAGNE, SAINT. Charlemagne (748–814) was king of the Franks and emperor. He was canonized in 1165 by an antipope, though the Catholic Church never officially recognized him as a saint. Still, over the centuries, numerous writings, historical and poetic, proliferated throughout medieval Europe on Charlemagne, and in fifteenth-century France, his status as a **saint** persisted. Although Joan of Arc was never recorded as evoking Saint Charlemagne, Jean Dunois (*See* ORLÉANS, BASTARD OF) claimed she prayed to him along with **Saint Louis**. The same exchange is found in the *Chronique de la Pucelle*. *See also* CATHERINE, SAINT; GABRIEL, SAINT; MARGARET, SAINT; MICHAEL, SAINT; VOICES, VISIONS, AND REVELATIONS.

CHARLES, SIMON (C. 1396–C. 1462). Simon Charles was a longtime administrator for **Charles VII**. Before then, he pursued a master of arts and licentiates in **canon** and **civil law** from the **University of Paris** (*See* EDUCATION). However, at some point, he abandoned pursuit of a career in the church, and by the time Joan of Arc rose to prominence, he was a knight and the master of requests for **Charles VII**. In 1431, he became a master in the *chambre des comptes* (chamber of accounts) in **Bourges**, managing the royal finances. In 1437, he became president of the institution, then relocated to Paris where he held that position until 1462.

Simon Charles provided detailed testimony in 1456 during the **nullification proceedings**, offering perspective as a member of the court of the king. Here, we learn that upon the arrival of Joan in **Chinon** (March 1429), the king hesitated to meet with her until he learned that she carried a letter from **Robert de Baudricourt**, revealing that Joan's commitment to gain sponsorship from the captain was worth the effort. Simon Charles was present for the **march to Reims** (29 June–16 July). Like other eyewitnesses, he described how Joan took command of the royal army outside of **Troyes**, prepared for an assault the night before, and how by the morning, the town capitulated (9 July). He also revealed the king's concern over Reims, which Charles VII believed he lacked sufficient **artillery** to capture. However, Joan personally encouraged him to press on, and the town opened its gates upon his arrival (16 July).

Simon Charles also spoke of Joan's military acumen, which was the only craft at which he found her to be exceptionally skilled. He described her regularly admonishing soldiers she thought were misbehaving. Further, he tells us that her **mission** consisted only of lifting the siege of **Orléans** and the coronation of **Charles VII**.

CHARLES II, DUKE OF LORRAINE. *See* LORRAINE, CHARLES II, DUKE OF

CHARLES VI, KING OF FRANCE (1368–1422). Born 3 December 1368, Charles VI became king of France upon the death of Charles V in 1380. He is traditionally referred to as "Charles the Mad" because of his bouts with mental illness, today thought to have been paranoid schizophrenia, which began manifesting in 1392. This illness rendered him incapable of ruling at times, leaving his brothers, cousins, uncles, and nephews to rule in his stead. All of these dukes jockeyed for influence and power, eventually leading to the **French Civil War** (1407–1435). The war continued partially because of Charles's inconsistency in addressing grievances between the warring factions. English King **Henry V** invaded France in 1415, leading to the English victory at Agincourt, and the death or capture of many French nobles, including **Duke Charles of Orléans** who was the nephew of Charles VI (*See* HUNDRED YEARS WAR).

Although Charles VI had two older sons, both had died by 1417. Thus, the new **dauphin** (*See* CHARLES VII) became heir to the throne. In 1419, the dauphin was implicated in the assassination of Duke John the Fearless of Burgundy. The event led to the **Treaty of Troyes** (1420); the disinheriting of the dauphin; the marriage of Henry V and Charles VI's daughter, **Catherine of Valois**; and the future son of Henry and Catherine being named as heir to the French throne. However, the deaths of Henry on 22 August 1422 followed by Charles VI on 21 October left Henry's infant son (*See* HENRY VI) too young to rule, and thus, the **duke of Bedford** acted as **regent** of France. The civil war, English invasion, and Charles's illness paved the way for the turbulent decade that preceded the arrival of Joan of Arc who was determined to bring all of France under the rule of Charles VII. *See also* ISABEAU OF BAVARIA; MISSION.

CHARLES VII, KING OF FRANCE (1403–1461). The story of Joan of Arc is integrally entwined with Charles VII, as her **mission** exuded a monarchist zeal for seeing him rule all of France as the divinely appointed king. Contemporaries and historians have painted Charles as inept, only able to gain determination because of Joan of Arc, and as ignoring her **execution** without intervention, only seeking her posthumous rehabilitation when it was convenient for him. In the latter part of the twentieth century, historians have toiled for a more balanced view.

Born on 22 February 1403, Charles was the fifth son of **Charles VI** and **Isabeau of Bavaria**. During his childhood, France witnessed the start of the **French Civil War** (1407–1435) and the rekindling of the **Hundred Years War**. Charles did not become the heir to the throne of France until the deaths of his older brothers, the last being Duke Jean of Touraine (5 April 1417), after which he became the new **dauphin**, the heir apparent. When Duke John the Fearless of Burgundy captured **Paris** on 29 May 1418, the dauphin fled. On 10 September 1419, the sixteen-year-old dauphin was present during the assassination of John, and he was implicated in the plot. Charles VI was furious with his son. The new duke of Burgundy (*See* PHILIP THE GOOD) and Charles VI signed the **Treaty of Troyes** (21 May 1420) with the English. Charles VI adopted **Henry V** as his new heir who also ruled as **regent** of France. Henry married **Catherine of Valois**, the dauphin's sister. Furthermore, Charles VI disinherited his son entirely on 3 January 1421.

The disinherited dauphin was not without supporters, however, and after a victory over the English at the battle of **Baugé** in 1421, Henry V returned to the continent to solidify his conquests. The sudden deaths of Henry (31 August 1422) and Charles VI (21 October) left the infant son of Henry and Catherine too young to rule (*See* HENRY VI). Henry V's brother, the **duke of Bedford**, became the new regent of France and quickly sought to shore up the **Anglo-Burgundian Alliance** through more treaties and marriages between the families of the dukes of Brittany and Burgundy in 1423 (*See* AMEINS, TREATY OF). Conversely, the dauphin's supporters recognized him as King Charles VII on 30 October 1422. He then married **Marie of Anjou** on 18 December, and the couple would have fourteen children, the first of which became the new dauphin (*See* LOUIS XI).

Throughout the 1420s, the war with England and Burgundy ebbed and flowed. Anglo-Burgundian forces decisively won the battle of **Cravant** (31 July 1423), Charles's forces won the battle of La Brossinière (26 September), and the English won the battle of **Verneuil** (17 August 1424) over Charles and his Scottish allies (*See* FRANCO-SCOTTISH ALLIANCE). After a rift between the dukes of Bedford and Burgundy, Charles was able to negotiate the **truce of Chambéry** with Burgundy (24 September 1424).

Yet, **Salisbury's 1428 expedition** had led to the capture of numerous cities by the English who then besieged **Orléans** on 12 October, the last stronghold loyal to Charles VII north of the **Loire River**. After the disastrous battle of the **Herrings** (12 February 1429), the plight of the French defenders worsened. They went so far as to negotiate directly with Philip the Good to surrender, but after the duke of Bedford spurned this notion, Burgundian troops withdrew from the siege.

It was in this climate that Joan of Arc came to prominence and arrived at the court of Charles VII in **Chinon**, probably on 23 February 1429. He had just turned twenty-six years old. Charles did not meet with Joan until 25 February, allowing others to question her first. There are numerous tales of their meeting, but Joan managed to convince Charles of her mission that included lifting the siege of Orléans. Still cautious, he sent her to **Poitiers** for examination by theologians for eleven days, after which she then returned to Chinon with the caveat that she could prove herself if she indeed lifted the siege.

Charles sent Joan of Arc with a convoy of supplies and reinforcements, arriving at Orléans on 29 April, and after several days of fighting, the siege was lifted on 8 May. A surviving letter from Charles on 10 May describing the success tells the recipients that Joan "has always been present at the accomplishment of all of these deeds" (Taylor 2006, 86). Although some advised Charles to take the success into Lancastrian **Normandy**, Joan, who insisted on calling him "dauphin," pushed for the army march to **Reims** where kings of France had been traditionally coronated. The **bastard of Orléans** described how Joan forcefully convinced Charles "to take the deserved crown" (Taylor 2006, 282).

First came the **Loire Campaign**, which recaptured the cities along the river occupied by English forces since the previous year. Then came the overwhelming victory over the English at the battle of **Patay** (18 June). Charles's army continued to grow with the news of Joan and the successful battles and sieges, and he accompanied the army on its **march to Reims** (29 June–16 July). It is unknown how much Charles and Joan interacted on the march, but there is one recorded encounter during the debate on how to handle a defiant **Troyes**, at which she convinced him to allow her to besiege the city instead of bypassing it as others advised. At the **coronation** (17 July), Joan stood next to the king and his men. Although his coronation was symbolic, it was a powerful symbol that solidified his claim to the throne.

Those closest to Charles were split on the next steps. Joan and the **duke of Alençon** pushed for capturing Burgundian-controlled Paris, but **Regnault of Chartres** and **Georges de La Trémoille** pushed for negotiating peace with Burgundy. Negotiations started while Joan was allowed to besiege Paris, failing on 8 September. The next day, Charles called off the siege and withdrew the army, disbanding it in hopes of not upsetting a newly agreed upon truce with Burgundy (*See* FRANCO-BURGUNDIAN TRUCE). Joan failed to dissuade him at **Saint-Denis** on 10 September.

Although Charles disbanded the royal army deployed at Paris, this was not the end of his military ambitions. The duke of Alençon prepared for an invasion of Lancastrian Normandy and sought Joan's assistance, but Charles's advisers prevented it. By October, Joan was eager to fight, and she was sent to fight south of the Loire through the rest of 1429 (*See* SAINT-PIERRE-LE-MOUTIER, SIEGE OF). By December, Charles began the process for **ennobling** Joan and her family, an uncommon honor for a woman in fifteenth-century France. In the first three months of 1430, Joan was stationary. Eager for action, she left at the end of March, fighting several battles and sieges with an unsanctioned army, finally being captured outside **Compiègne** (23 May). Joan was in custody of the Burgundians until they **ransomed** her to the English on 21 November. After being transferred to **Rouen**, Joan was subjected to an **inquisition** where she eventually signed an **abjuration**, but then **relapsed** several days later, leading to her **execution** on 30 May 1431 (*See* CONDEMNATION TRIAL).

During this period, there are no recorded opinions of Charles or debate within his court on Joan, let alone an attempt to **ransom** or rescue her. Conversely, Joan never stopped speaking favorably of the king in letters and in her testimony at the condemnation trial. During her unsanctioned military initiatives in March to May 1430, she conducted her actions in the name of the king and in her **letter to Reims (28 March 1430)**, she encouraged the city to remain loyal to Charles.

Historians often theorize that Charles had no more use for a rebellious Joan. By 1431, the twenty-eight-year-old king seems to have weighed the benefits and practicality of rescuing an unorthodox soldier who was part of his military successes over the course of a three-month period but was captured after disobeying orders.

The next mention of Joan and Charles comes when he inquired about her condemnation trial on 15 February 1450. Although many historians have lambasted his silence up to this point, recent historians have pointed out how the acquisition of Paris (1436) and capture of Rouen (1449) were necessary to begin any such inquiry. The **University of Paris** was instrumental in conducting the trial and the documents were held in Rouen, where she was tried and executed. A lack of access to these documents had been a problem until 1449. There were several false starts into the inquiries in 1450 and 1452, and it was not until the **pope** supported the effort in 1455 that the **nullification proceedings** began in earnest, leading to a nullification of the original verdict on 7 July 1456.

After Joan's execution, the remainder of Charles's reign was filled with illnesses, conquests, rebellions, truces, treaties, and military and ecclesiastical reforms, ultimately leading to an end of the French Civil War (*See* ARRAS, TREATY OF), a stronger, mostly unified France, and the end of the Hundred Years War. In 1450 to 1456, Charles was still focused on expelling the English from the continent and dealing with a Burgundian-backed rebellion from the dauphin (*See* LOUIS XI). In early 1461, Charles and Philip the Good were at war again, but with the death of Charles on 22 July, Louis XI became the new king of France.

There is much made of Joan's unquenchable loyalty to Charles, which he did not reciprocate at her lowest point. However, her loyalty did not include obeying orders to stay out of war in 1430, and it is plausible that had Joan not been captured by the Burgundians, she would have faced accusations of treason in Charles's court. If her claims that Charles was the king of France by divine right were true, was Joan not also subject to his decisions? Joan's claims of a divine mission gained strength with her victories and then diminished with her defeat at Paris.

Joan was a war hawk in the purest sense, seeking combat and being wary of diplomatic truces, as she stated in her **letter to Reims (5 August 1429)**. Charles's complete victory over the English took twenty-two years to achieve after Joan's execution, and it was accomplished through a combination of truces, treaties, and conquests. Had Charles somehow recovered Joan, it is difficult to see how she would have fit into the equation of the rest of the wars with England and Burgundy.

CHARTIER, ALAIN (C. 1385–1430). Older brother of **Guillaume Chartier**, Alain Chartier from Bayeux was a poet, political writer, administrator, and ambassador first for **Yolande d'Aragon** and then **Charles VII**. He acquired his master of arts from the **University of Paris** (*See* EDUCATION). Chartier began serving Charles when the latter became the **dauphin** in 1417, and the two fled Paris in 1418 when the Burgundians took control of the city (*See* FRENCH CIVIL WAR). In 1426, Chartier became an ordained priest. Throughout the 1420s, he served as ambassador for the king, traveling to Italy, the **Holy Roman Empire**, and Scotland (*See* FRANCO-SCOTTISH ALLIANCE). Chartier's writings were popular, the most renowned of which was *Quadrilogue invectif* (1422). This worked borrowed from **Vegetius**, and it was translated into several languages, including English. **John Talbot** gave a copy to Margaret of Anjou, daughter of **Réne of Anjou**, upon her marriage to **Henry VI** (1444).

In the story of Joan of Arc, Chartier wrote a letter to a foreign diplomat, possibly serving the duke of Milan. Written in Latin from Bourges in July or August 1429, the letter survives today in four manuscripts. Chartier is enthusiastic, recounting Joan's **voices**, her **mission**, her journey to **Chinon**, meeting the king, the **Poitiers** examination, the relief of Orléans, and the **coronation of Charles VII**. He conveys how her **voices** began when she was only twelve, and they were explicit that she should meet with the captain of **Vaucouleurs** (*See* BAUDRICOURT, ROBERT DE) and to wear men's **clothing**. He writes that her divine **mission** included relieving Orléans, the coronation at Reims, the capture of **Paris**, and the reclamation of the entire kingdom for Charles. Chartier is emphatic about Joan's military acumen, as she orders troops, organizes camps, and leads in battle.

The letter demonstrates the euphoria in the court of Charles VII for Joan of Arc between the coronation (17 July 1429) and the failed assault on Paris (8 September), as Chartier compares her to Hector, Alexander the Great, Hannibal, and Caesar. He describes Joan's achievements as divine, miraculous, and impossible, and that she was sent from heaven. Although the letter is lengthy, he emphasized that he was being brief and could have written an entire book on her exploits. Nothing survives that indicates how Chartier felt about Joan after Paris, and he died in March 1430. *See also* PIZAN, CHRISTINE DE.

CHARTIER, GUILLAUME (?–1472). Born in Bayeux, Guillaume was the younger brother of **Alain Chartier**. He acquired doctorates in both **canon law** and **civil law** (*See* EDUCATION), and in 1432, he became professor of canon law at the newly established University of Poitiers. In 1435, he took part in the negotiations for the **Treaty of Arras** as a representative of **Charles VII**. In 1437, he became **canon** of Notre-Dame in **Paris**, and in 1447, he was elected **bishop**.

It was as bishop of Paris that the **pope** selected Chartier in 1455 to serve as a judge during the **nullification proceedings** of Joan of Arc's **condemnation trial**. Chartier was actively engaged, especially in gathering witness testimonies in Paris. After the verdict, Chartier kept a copy of the proceedings, which was later archived in the library of Notre-Dame de Paris. Today, the manuscript resides in Bibliothèque nationale de France. *See also* LONGUEIL, RICHARD OLIVIER DE; URSINS, JEAN JUVÉNAL DES.

CHARTIER, JEAN (?–1464). In November 1437, **Charles VII** tasked Benedictine monk Jean Chartier as "Chronicler of France," a role that would produce a widely read royal chronicle in latter-fifteenth-century France. The new role elevated his station from administrator of the Abbey of **Saint-Denis** outside **Paris**. Chartier held sympathies for Charles, but also lived during the events of Joan of Arc and possibly met her during her attack on Paris, giving his chronicles added value. Between 1437 and 1445, Chartier produced a Latin chronicle that covered the rise and reign of Charles until 1445. Afterward, he translated and greatly expanded the work into Middle French, covering well past the reign of Charles (1461) and venturing into the early reign of **Louis XI**. Both versions of the chronicle provide favorable and extant details on Joan of Arc. Among the events covered by Chartier are Joan's meeting and fabled identification of Charles VII in disguise; her arrival, resupply, and relief of **Orléans**; the sieges and battles of **Beaugency**, **Patay**, **Troyes**, Paris, and **Compiègne**; the **march to Reims** and **coronation of Charles VII**; and the **trial** and **execution** of Joan. Chartier was highly critical of the latter, aggressively condemning the English and judges involved in Joan's **condemnation trial**. With access to a whole host of other documents and chronicles, Chartier provides remarkable details on the transition of cities between English, French, and Burgundian loyalties, as well as the logistics of forming and paying armies.

Jean Chartier is sometimes mistaken as the brother of **Alain Chartier** and **Guillaume Chartier**.

CHARTRES, PEACE OF. *See* FRENCH CIVIL WAR.

CHARTRES, REGNAULT OF, ARCHBISHOP OF REIMS (C. 1380–1444). Regnault of Chartres was the archbishop of Reims and the longest serving advisor of **Charles VII**. During his lifetime, the archbishop participated in or led nearly every major diplomatic negotiation on behalf of the king, including the **Franco-Scottish Alliance**, the **Treaty of Chambéry** (1424), the **Franco-Burgundian Truce** (1429–1430), and the **Treaty of Arras** (1435).

Born around 1380, Chartres became the archbishop of **Reims** in 1414 and would serve in the role until his death. Both his older brother and father served **Charles VI**, the former dying in 1415 at Agincourt (*See* HUNDRED YEARS WAR) and the latter dying during the Burgundian capture of **Paris** in 1418 (*See* FRENCH CIVIL WAR). That same year, the archbishop began serving Charles VII who was, at that time, the **dauphin**. He briefly served as the king's chancellor in 1425 and then again from 1428 until his death.

The interactions between the archbishop and Joan of Arc were brief. He formed the council of theologians that questioned Joan during the **Poitiers** examination (March 1429), but it is not clear if he participated in the process beyond that. During the siege of **Troyes** (5–9 July), he recommended the army abandon the **march to Reims** entirely, but a stubborn Joan successfully pushed for preparing an attack on the city until it capitulated. Upon entering Reims (16 July), it was the first time the archbishop had been there since 1418. At the **coronation of Charles VII** (17 July 1429), he led the ceremony and crowned the king. While Joan was pushing to capture **Paris** in August, the archbishop led a delegation along with **Georges de La Trémoille** and **Raoul de Gaucourt** to negotiate a truce with the duke of Burgundy (*See* PHILIP THE GOOD). The truce, coupled with the failure to capture Paris on the first day of the assault (8 September), led Charles to call off the siege entirely and then disband the royal army. The archbishop was among the group of the king's advisors that prevented Joan from joining the **duke of Alençon** for his campaign in **Normandy** (October 1429).

Upon Joan's capture at **Compiègne** (23 May 1430), the archbishop wrote a letter to the people of Reims, lambasting Joan for her pride and for following her own will instead of the will of God. This was possibly in response to Joan's **letter to the people of Reims** (16 March 1430), encouraging them to resist any attempt by Burgundians to capture the city and proclaiming she would be there soon to help them. Although the Franco-Burgundian Truce had elapsed, the archbishop likely maintained hopes of a reconciliation between Charles VII and Philip the Good.

Before his death on 4 April 1444, the archbishop acquired numerous **benefices** including bishop of **Orléans** and archbishop of Embrun and Agde. The next archbishop of Riems was Jacques Juvénal des Ursins (1444–1449) followed by **Jean Juvénal des Ursins** (1449–1473), the latter of which oversaw the **nullification proceedings**.

CHASTELLAIN, GEORGES (C. 1405–1474). Georges Chastellain graduated from Leuven University in 1432 in **Burgundian** Netherlands and thus never met Joan of Arc or witnessed the events surrounding her. However, Chastellain had access to eyewitness accounts and documents such as **Monstrelet**. His military experience included service under **Philip the Good** in campaigns against the **French** (1433–1434) and then against the **English** (1435–1436), after the **Treaty of Arras**.

In 1455, Chastellain became the official chronicler of the Burgundian court, and he produced a lengthy history on the period 1419 to 1475 in Middle French. It was never distributed and likely passed to his son who continued to edit it. Today, only fragments survive, but particularly useful in the story of Joan of Arc are the surviving pages that cover 1430 to 1431. Chastellain provides a post–**French Civil War**, Burgundian perspective aimed at encouraging the French peace. Although his sources were hostile toward Joan of Arc, he tempered them, portraying her as a strong military commander. This comes out in his details on Joan's battle against Burgundians at **Lagny**. The chronicle also covers **Compiègne**, as well as Joan's **execution**. *See also* BASIN, THOMAS.

CHÂTILLON, JEAN HULOT DE. Jean Hulot de Châtillon held a doctorate in theology (*See* EDUCATION), taught at the **University**

of Paris, and was the archdeacon and **canon** of Évreux during the **condemnation trial** of Joan of Arc (1431), where he was an assiduous assessor (*See* ROLES). Beginning with the first public sessions, he is found in attendance throughout the rest of the trial except for the prison sessions, where it is assumed he did not attend due to the limited capacity of Joan's cell.

Châtillon's most prominent role in the trial came on 2 May where he offered the first admonishment of Joan at the direction of **Pierre Cauchon**. This sermon, which is recorded in detail in the trial **transcripts**, emphasizes the main points of contention in the process thus far. The admonishments included Joan's unwillingness to submit to the **Church Militant**, her insistence on wearing male **clothing** and keeping her **hair** short and round, her claims to interact with saints **Catherine** and **Margaret**, and her claims that she received instructions from these saints for her words and actions. When pressed, Joan responded, "I fully believe in the Church on earth; but as I've said before for my words and actions, I wait upon and trust the Lord God" (Hobbins 2005, 176).

Châtillon is recorded attending the rest of the trial, including the threat of **torture** (9 May), the reading of the opinions from the University of Paris (19 May), the second admonishment delivered by **Pierre Maurice** (23 May), Joan's **abjuration** (24 May), the vote to abandon Joan to secular authorities after her **relapse** (29 May), and her **execution** (30 May). After the trial, Châtillon would go on to serve as archdeacon of Vexin (1437–1442).

Based on the trial record, Châtillon's perspective on Joan seems clear, but testimonies from the **nullification proceedings** (1450–1456) cloud his character. **Jean Massieu** claimed that Châtillon challenged questions presented to Joan, believed the trial was wrong, and stopped attending at one point, all of which conflict with the trial record. **Guillaume Manchon** claimed that Châtillon argued that Joan was not required to answer some of the questions, causing an uproar between him and Cauchon. **Thomas Courcelles** claimed that Châtillon advised Joan before her abjuration. Although these testimonies are by no means consistent, they do paint a more complex picture of Châtillon as one who believed Joan was wrong but who also questioned the partiality of the trial.

CHAUSSE-TRAPE. *See* CALTROP.

CHINON. Situated south of the Loire River in what was the Touraine duchy, Chinon features one of the largest castles in Western Europe. It is the site where Joan of Arc first met **Charles VII** in late February 1429. Although popular history depicts it as the king's "headquarters," the meeting there was not inevitable. The city had only returned to the king's control in 1428. He arrived in October, hosting what has become known as the estates general, a meeting of leaders throughout his loyal regions where he gained approval to levy taxes to fund the fight with the English. Charles, who was an itinerant king, often stayed at **Bourges**, **Poitiers**, and **Mehun**. His presence in Chinon was a recent development and by no means permanent.

As the king's stay coincided with the **siege of Orléans** (12 October 1428–8 May 1429), the various defending captains took turns visiting Chinon to provide updates. For example, the **bastard of Orléans** was there in October, **La Hire** in November, and **Poton de Xaintrailles** in December. At the time of Joan's arrival, **Raoul de Gaucourt** was the captain present.

The exact dates of Joan's first visit to Chinon are unknown, and historians often reconstruct them by working backward from her stay in Poitiers (11–22 March 1429). When Joan arrived, possibly on 23 February, the king did not meet with her at first, relying on others to question and examine her. Eyewitnesses tell us she told them of her **mission**. When the king finally met with Joan, possibly as late as 6 March, the fabled stories of her identifying the disguised king begin (*See* CHARLES, SIMON; CHARTIER, JEAN). This is also possibly when the event of the **sign** occurred, as attested by Joan during her **condemnation trial**. Although the details of what Joan said to Charles remain scant with plenty of conjecture, Charles determined to have Joan further questioned and examined in **Poitiers**, leaving with her on 10 March.

Joan was present at Chinon shortly after returning from Poitiers, and several more times, between 22 May and 2 June. It was there that Charles agreed to support what became known as the **Loire Campaign**. Although Charles would return to Chinon again, he spent most of his time elsewhere. Much of the surviving structures of the Chinon castle are later additions, but two walls of the king's hall still stand where Joan and Charles probably met.

CHRONIQUE DE JEAN CHARTIER. *See* CHARTIER, JEAN.

CHRONIQUE DE LA PUCELLE (C. 1467). From 1661 and until the mid-nineteenth century, the *Chronique de la Pucelle* was considered the earliest and most important of the chronicles on Joan of Arc. It was later discovered to be predominantly a compilation of the *Journal du siège d'Orléans*, Jean Chartier, and testimony from the **nullification proceedings**. Composed in Middle French, the anonymous work starts seven years before the arrival of Joan and ends just after the siege of **Paris**. Although disregarded today, the work was highly influential on the lore that sprung up regarding Joan.

CHRONIQUE DE L'ÉTABLISSEMENT DE LA FÊTE DU 8 MAI (C. 1456). Written with the purpose of encouraging citizens to participate in the yearly commemoration of the lifting of the siege of **Orléans** on May 8, the *Chronique de l'établissement de la fête du 8 mai* was written by an eyewitness of the siege who also relied on the experiences of others in the city. Due to its religious tone, some have theorized it was compiled by someone with a religious degree (*See* EDUCATION). Covering July 1428 before the siege began through **Patay** in June 1429, many events in the *Chronique* are treated miraculously where Joan of Arc is involved. Conversely, events such as the killing of the **earl of Salisbury** with a cannonball are treated as an accident. Only two manuscripts survive today. Its existence remained obscure until one of the manuscripts was discovered in 1847 in the Vatican along with a copy of the *Journal du siège d'Orléans*, as well as two letters of indulgence, dated 1452 and 1453, encouraging the citizens of Orléans to participate in the yearly commemoration. *See also* KIRKMICHAEL, JOHN OF.

CHRONIQUE DITE DES CORDELIERS. Most likely completed in 1432, the so-called *Chronique dite des Cordeliers*, named for the monastery where the sole copy was discovered, was a **Burgundian** chronicle written in French vernacular, covering events from the Biblical creation to 1431. The author was most likely a Parisian, which may explain the access to other Burgundian chronicles (e.g., **Monstrelet**) and documents. Particularly useful to the story of Joan of Arc is the **Franco-Burgundian Truce**, including negotiation details and a copy of the truce. Although written from a Burgundian perspective, it is sympathetic toward Joan and provides extant details on her **escape**. The chronicle reveals that, instead of simply throwing herself from the tower as some suggested during her **condemnation trial**, she had attempted to climb down from the window using a makeshift support, which broke and caused her to fall.

CHRONIQUES DE CHARLES VII. *See* BOUVIER, GILLES LE.

CHURCH MILITANT. The term "Church Militant" is no longer in use by the Catholic Church, and it has been repurposed today by right-wing extremists for a so-called culture war. In 1431, however, it had a completely different, non-militaristic meaning to the judges and assessors at Joan of Arc's **condemnation trial**. For them, a key theological belief divided the Catholic Church into the Church Triumphant and the Church Militant. As several assessors explained to Joan, the Church Triumphant (in heaven) included God, **saints**, angels, and saved souls, whereas the Church Militant (on earth) included the **pope**, bishops, clergy, and all good Christians, as the representatives of God. They went so far as to claim that when the Church Militant assembled, they could not err in their judgment.

When Joan claimed to interact and receive directions from saints and angels without the intercession of clergy or bishops, Joan was bypassing the Church Militant and claiming to interact directly with the Church Triumphant. These finer points of theology were explained to Joan during her inquisition and when pushed to submit to the authority of the Church Militant, she was often elusive in her responses. Initially, she refused to respond (15 and 17 March). Then when Article 61 of the initial **seventy articles** brought against her (27–28 March) accused her of refusing to submit to the Church Militant, she was given an opportunity to respond, but she delayed, telling them to ask her again on Saturday (31 March). When her assessors followed up, she said she would submit to the Church Militant if they did not ask her to retract her words and deeds, which included her **voices**. She also clarified that her voices did not command her to disobey the Church, but she would always put God first.

The questioning turned to pleading, cajoling, and finally, admonishing from the assessors. **Nicolas Midi** explained the differences again, quoted scripture, and begged her to submit (18 April). Yet Joan persisted, emphasizing she was a good Christian, baptized, and loved God. They also offered to let her take communion, which they had forbidden for her until she stopped wearing men's **clothing**, but she persisted. After the admonishments from **Jean de Châtillon** (2 May), other assessors pleaded with her to submit to the Church Militant, but she again answered as before.

When some of the assessors were asked to contemplate **torture** for Joan, **Isambard de La Pierre** believed it would be inexpedient. Instead, she should be warned a last time about submitting to the Church Militant. **Jean Le Maistre** did not comment on whether to torture her but believed she should again be asked to submit.

Among the condensed **twelve articles** formally brought against Joan and distributed to the **University of Paris**, Articles 1 and 12 both mentioned her delay and refusal to submit to the Church Militant. It was regarding this last article that the university labeled her an **apostate** and **schismatic**. When the articles and the university's conclusions were presented to her (23 May), she again said she would answer no differently. However, on 24 May, Joan agreed to submit (*See* ABJURATION).

Numerous historians have theorized that both Joan and her assessors were talking past each other regarding the Church Militant. No matter how many times they explained it, Joan appears to have understood them not to mean the Church as a whole, but instead the inquisition court handling her trial. There is support for this view in several of Joan's appeals to the **pope** and her statement that she would share some of her secrets directly with him. However, these requests were cast aside, and the judges and assessors reemphasized their point about the Church Militant being the representation of the pope and thus the Church Triumphant.

CHURCH TRIUMPHANT. *See* CHURCH MILITANT.

CIBOULE, ROBERT (C. 1403–1458). Robert Ciboule held a doctorate in theology from the **University of Paris** where he would later serve as chancellor (1451). He represented **Charles VII** diplomatically with the **pope**, the **Council of Basel**, and the **Holy Roman Empire**.

In January 1453, Ciboule was one of the scholars who responded to a request for an opinion to the findings of the fledgling **nullification proceedings** that were examining Joan of Arc's **condemnation trial**. He provided what has become known as his *Consideratio seu opinio* ("Consideration or opinion"), a document numbering more than fifty pages in the most recent edited edition. Ciboule argues that Joan was at worst guilty of a mortal sin and by no means **heresy**. He also concludes that the **twelve articles** presented to the University of Paris were inconsistent with Joan's recorded testimony.

Examining each of the articles, Ciboule forcefully picks each one apart. For example, he argues it was rash to dismiss her **voices, visions, and revelations** with such finality, especially because she had demonstrated the ability to prophecy the victory of **Charles VII**. As for her male **clothing**, like others, he argues that it was out of necessity, but he also evokes Deborah from the Old Testament as an example of a woman who would not shy from cross-dressing in battle. As for Joan's push for war, she was justified to defend the kingdom of France against enemies. Even still, he highlighted that she carried her **standard** in battle, not her **sword**, to avoid killing.

Ciboule by no means saw Joan as infallible. When it came to the question of submitting to the **Church Militant**, he argues that she was a simple, ignorant girl with gifts, but still demonstrating a desire for education. He concedes that while it was wrong to dismiss her voices outright, she likely needed help understanding their instruction.

Given his role as chancellor, there is an obvious desire on Ciboule's part to clear the University of Paris for its culpability in Joan's **execution**. By arguing that the twelve articles were misleading, he puts the blame squarely on the judges and assessors who produced those articles (*See* ROLES). He further argues that it was wrong to deny Joan's appeal to the pope right before her **abjuration**. As such, his opinion was to nullify and void the condemnation trial and its verdict.

CIVIL LAW. Civil law, often referred to as Roman law, was the basis for most legal systems in Europe by the fifteenth century. Derived from the legal systems of the Roman Republic and Empire, as well as Byzantium, Roman law had fallen out of use in Europe until its rediscovery in the twelfth century.

It was unavailable as an academic field at the **University of Paris** but was a specialty of the University of Orléans. Thus, at Joan of Arc's **condemnation trial**, there were only fifteen assessors known to possess any degree in civil law, with five of them also possessing degrees in **canon law**. *See also* EDUCATION.

CLASSIDAS. *See* GLASDALE, WILLIAM.

CLERK. *See* ROLES AND RESPONSIBILITIES.

CLERMONT, CHARLES I, COUNT OF (1404–1456). During the prominence of Joan of Arc, Count Charles I of Clermont was a prominent military commander for **Charles VII**; he was present for several of Joan's campaigns.

Born in 1404, Clermont was the son of Duke John I of Bourbon, who was captured at Agincourt (1415) and held in captivity until his death in 1435, at which point Clermont became the new duke. Before then, Clermont was allied with the **Armagnac** party in 1418, and he was captured when the Burgundians took control of **Paris** (*See* FRENCH CIVIL WAR). At the time, he was engaged to **Catherine of Valois**, future wife of **Henry V**, but the engagement was then broken. As a captive of Duke John the Fearless of Burgundy, Clermont wed John's sister, Agnes of Burgundy. On 10 September 1419, Clermont was with John when the latter was assassinated. The Armagnacs took Clermont captive. In the court of Charles VII, in 1424, Clermont acted as mediator between Charles and the duke of Burgundy (*See* PHILIP THE GOOD) after the battle of **Verneuil** (*See* CHAMBÉRY, TRUCE OF). He continued to serve Charles VII, capturing cities and fighting alongside future companions in arms of Joan of Arc.

Entrusted with leading the king's forces at **Herrings** (12 February 1429), Clermont received much of the blame for the disastrous defeat, refusing to support the overeager Scots. On 18 February, Clermont left the siege of **Orléans** with his troops. As a result, Charles VII entrusted the **duke of Alençon**, not Clermont, with command of his army during the **Loire Campaign**. However, Clermont was with the royal army during the **march to Reims**, and he was present for the **coronation of Charles VII**. After Joan of Arc's failed assault on **Paris** (8 September), Clermont was part of the contingent that arrived to deliver Charles VII's decision to abandon the siege.

During her **condemnation trial** (1431), Joan of Arc evoked Clermont on 10 and 13 March as one of the people who witnessed the **sign** of an angel crowning Charles VII. It is unclear when this sign occurred, but Joan agreed to send a letter to Clermont and others to testify to the validity of the sign on 2 May. The letter, if there was one, along with evidence of its results, have not survived.

After the trial, Clermont experienced a sporadic career. He became duke of Bourbon in 1435 but then participated in rebellions against

Charles VII in 1437 and in 1440 (*See* PRAGUE-RIE). After a failed war against the duke of Savoy, the duke of Bourbon was disgraced. He did not participate in the **nullification proceedings**, and he died on 4 December 1456.

Historians are often split in their assessment of Clermont, who found himself in a precarious situation from a young age. His regions bordered Burgundy, so were often under threat, yet there is no consensus as to whether he was simply ambitious, unstable, or stupid, or a combination of these traits.

CLOTHING. Joan of Arc's male attire was arguably the biggest point of contention for those who supported her and those who condemned her. With nearly six centuries of fashion separating us today, this is one of the most difficult aspects of Joan for the modern mind to comprehend. Deuteronomy 22:5 tells us, "A woman must not wear men's clothing, nor a man wear women's clothing, for the Lord your God detests anyone who does this" (NIV). Although such laws were not strictly taught or enforced in Christianity at the time of Joan of Arc, there were prevailing gender norms in regard to clothes. This was not simply wearing a dress versus a shirt and pants, as soldiers wore surcoats that were the equivalent of dresses, and nobles and clergy wore robes and gowns for formal occasions. However, women typically wore dresses, even while working in the field. Shirts and exposed hose were for men. Both men and women wore head coverings. While there might be deviations or reversals of gender-approved clothing at events such as carnivals, these were relegated to such spaces and moments as exceptional.

When Joan arrived to meet with **Robert de Baudricourt** in **Vaucouleurs**, witnesses tell us she was "dressed in poor female attire, coloured red" (Taylor 2006, 271). It was here that Joan first adorned male attire, supposedly to help conceal her during the journey to **Chinon**, but Joan continued to wear these clothes, even to meet with **Charles VII**. Her male clothes were a topic during the **Poitiers** examination, but the examiners were able to move past it. From there, the woman known as *la Pucelle* was typically recognized by ally and foe alike as the woman wearing men's clothing or armor. The main exception comes from the simple sketch by **Clément de Fauquembergue** that depicts a long-haired girl in a dress, holding a sword and a **standard**. Fauquembergue, however, had not seen Joan, and since the sketch was drawn shortly after the lifting of the siege of **Orléans**, it was likely that tales of Joan's cross-dressing had not reached Paris yet. Conversely, an eyewitness account in the **Laval letter (8 June 1429)** described Joan as "fully armoured except for her head and holding the lance in her hand" (Taylor 2006, 92).

After the capture of Joan of Arc at **Compiègne (23 May 1430)**, she continued to wear male clothing while in captivity. Given the opportunity to wear women's clothing, Joan refused, even when **Anne of Burgundy** had a dress made for her. During her **condemnation trial**, Joan's clothing became a focal point for the assessors who treated the act dogmatically. A letter sent on behalf of **Henry VI**, transferring Joan from the English to **Pierre Cauchon** (3 January 1431), reveals the perspective of her enemies, as it described her as a woman who "abandoned women's clothes and dressed and armed herself like a man, a thing against the divine law and abominable to God, and condemned and forbidden by every law" (Hobbins 2005, 40).

When pressed on who instructed her to wear men's clothing, Joan initially refused to answer, eventually saying she believed it was a "small matter, one of the least," and that she had done it "by the command of God and the angels" (Hobbins 2005, 66). The assessors continued to press Joan on her male attire throughout the trial, and they offered to allow her to attend Mass if only she would wear women's clothing. Joan refused and argued that the clothes kept her safe while on campaign and it further protected her while in a prison guarded by English. Article 13 of the initial **seventy articles** of accusation hones in on the cross-dressing, and it describes her as "wearing short, tight, and immodest men's clothing, undergarments and hose as well as other articles" (Hobbins 2005, 129). Article 5 of the condensed **twelve articles** continues the accusation and describes how she claimed

"God commanded her to wear men's clothes" and she refused to stop (Hobbins 2005, 159). Concerning this article, the **University of Paris** accused Joan of **blasphemy**, further proclaiming "you worship yourself and your clothing" (Hobbins 2005, 185).

Upon her **abjuration** (24 May), Joan agreed to abandon women's clothing, which she did initially. However, by 28 May, Joan was once again wearing women's clothing. The picture that emerges from those testifying during the **nullification proceedings** was that the English guards confiscated Joan's clothing and left her with male clothing. Although she resisted putting them on initially, they refused to let her leave her cell to relieve herself unless she put the male clothes on, which she eventually did. Others such as **Isambart de La Pierre** revealed that there was an attempted rape as well (*See* SEXUAL ASSAULT). None of this made a difference to the judges and assessors who labeled Joan a relapsed **heretic** for continuing to wear men's clothes as well as her claim that she still believed and conversed with her **voices**. Sources are inconsistent on whether she was **executed** in male or female clothing.

For the contemporaries supporting Joan, the male clothes seemed to have shocked at first, but all seemed to find ways to support it. For example, **Jacques Gélu** eventually supported the argument that Joan's choice of clothing was necessary while on campaign and living among soldiers. Reflecting on the Poitiers examination, **Pope** Pius II noted that "the only difficulty was her dress" (Gragg 1988, 195), but they overcame it. Many questioned during the nullification proceedings answered that cross-dressing was not enough to condemn Joan. Thus, as shocking as it was, most people were able to accept Joan's attire as necessary, but those leading her condemnation trial were not.

COAT OF ARMS. During Joan of Arc's time, the coat of arms was the visible image of heraldry, which was the systematic identification of nobles using simple designs on shields, tunics, seals, and **banners**. The origins of the practice are still debated, but the prevalent theory is the nature of warfare in the Middle Ages had evolved such that soldiers covered their bodies and faces in armor, making it difficult to distinguish friend from foe, and the coat of arms aimed at clearly distinguishing someone on the battlefield. Another possible origin was that it was pure vanity. Regardless, the pageantry of displaying a coat of arms was common in **battle** and tournaments by fifteenth-century France.

The varying designs for coats of arms are legion but often were defined by the outline of a shield known as the field. Within the shield would be simplistic shapes, animals, weapons, armor, and short mottoes. The guidelines and rules for designing, modifying, and inheriting a coat of arms varied between countries, but in medieval France, it required an **ennoblement** from the king that could then be passed down to descendants. Heralds were responsible for recording, regulating, and announcing heraldry. Heralds typically reported to a higher-ranking herald known as a king-of-arms, and this role could preside over a city, region, or the kingdom. For example, **Gilles le Bouvier** was initially a herald, then the king-of-arms in Berry, and finally, the king-of-arms for France.

Coat of Arms bestowed to Joan of Arc on June 2, 1429. *Recueil concernant les monnaies, Bibliotheque nationale de France, Ms. Fr. 5524, f. 142.*

During her **condemnation trial**, Joan of Arc demonstrated that she was aware of the practices of heraldry and was learning the various coat of arms designs among her companions in arms. A surviving record indicates that Joan had her own coat of arms bestowed upon her by **Charles VII** by 2 June 1429. Joan claimed she never sported the coat of arms, instead preferring her own design for her standard. She did not ask for it or even want it, and it was instead used by her brothers. However, she was aware of the coat of arms design, describing an azure field outlining a silver sword with a golden hilt pointing up through a golden crown, flanked by two gold fleur-de-lises. During her imprisonment, Joan described the design to a painter who produced an interpretation of it. Among the initial **seventy articles** presented against Joan, Article 58 explicitly lists the coat of arms and the painter's interpretation, citing them as examples of pride and vanity. Today, the coat of arms is common among works about Joan.

COLIN (1405–?). Colin, son of Jean Colin of Greux, was from **Domremy** and a childhood friend of Joan and her sister (*See* ARC, CATHERINE D'). Records indicate that Colin and Catherine were married at some point, but no details exist on when. At the nullification proceedings, Colin testified that he saw Joan, Catherine, and other women dutifully carrying candles to a local chapel almost every Saturday afternoon. He admitted to teasing Joan for her piety. He also testified that Joan performed her chores and duties well, always cheerfully.

COLLES, GUILLAUME (C. 1390–1456). Guillaume Colles, also known as Boisguillaume or Boscguillaume, was a notary of **Rouen** that served in the same role at Joan of Arc's **condemnation trial**. Born to a Norman family, he was a priest of Notre-Dame-de-La-Ronde at least by 1424. In 1430, he served as notary on the **inquisition** trial of Jean Seguent.

Pierre Cauchon appointed Colles along with **Guillaume Manchon** as the notaries for Joan's trial on 9 January 1431. **Nicolas Taquel** joined them as a third notary on 13–14 March when vice-inquisitor **Jean Le Maistre** officially joined the trial (*See* ROLES). Thus, Colles's name is found alongside Manchon's, and later Taquel's, at key points in the trial, as they signed their names, attesting to the legitimacy of the records. For example, these signatures are included when the **twelve articles** were attached to the trial record along with opinions from some of the assessors, as well as on 29 May when the judges summoned Joan after her supposed **relapse**.

During the **nullification proceedings**, Colles attested that he and his fellow notaries wrote down the meaning of Joan's responses to the questions, claiming they were not intimidated into changing anything. Their process involved compiling the questions and answers in the mornings, and then reviewing them together after lunch.

Colles provided other anecdotes, including how the assessors asked Joan multiple times if she was in a state of grace. Colles said they were astonished by her answer, recorded on 24 February 1431 as, "If I'm not, may God put me there; and if I am, may God keep me in it" (Hobbins 2005, 60–61). The reaction of the assessors recounted by Colles is a common story in the histories of Joan.

COMPANION IN ARMS. Companion in arms is not an official title or rank, but historians often use it to refer to the leaders and troops that fought alongside Joan of Arc. The term avoids the implication in referring to them as "Joan of Arc's troops," that she possessed complete leadership or command, although some historians do not shy away from this verbiage. During each of Joan's campaigns, there were often designated commanders of the armies, such as the **duke of Alençon** on the **Loire Campaign** and **Charles d'Albret** at **Saint-Pierre-le-Moutier**. Although Joan was heavily involved in planning, rallying, deploying **artillery**, carrying siege equipment, assaults, and directing troops in the heat of battle, she did not have an official rank. Still, many of the commanders worked with her and some made decisions based on her input. *See also* MEN-AT-ARMS.

COMPIÈGNE, SIEGE OF (22 MAY–25/26 OCTOBER 1430). Compiègne was a highly contested town during the **French Civil War** (1407–1435), but it is best remembered as the site where Joan of Arc was captured (23 May 1430). During the civil war, the town was first captured in February 1414 by Burgundians before being reclaimed in April. In June 1422, Anglo-Burgundian forces captured the town. **Charles VII** reclaimed Compiègne in January 1424 before it was captured again in April. Charles and Joan of Arc entered the town with the royal army on 18 August 1429 after the standoff at **Montépilloy**. While there, Charles appointed **Guillaume de Flavy** as captain, one of the few such appointments he made in the region. Also during her stay, Joan dictated her **letter to Jean IV, count of Armagnac (22 August 1429)** before leaving for **Paris**. Part of the negotiations for the **Franco-Burgundian Truce** was the return of Compiègne to **Philip the Good**. However, Charles left the town to its own devices without any ceremonial handover and the town did not submit to Burgundy.

The volatility of Compiègne's ownership was due to its strategic location, controlling the main roads between **Reims** and **Rouen**, and between Paris and Flanders, with a bridge measuring roughly 138 meters across the Oise River. Along its 2,600-meter-long walls were at least forty-four towers surrounding fifty-six hectares and a large castle (Smith and DeVries 2005, 100–101). In March 1430, the citizens learned that Philip the Good was planning a major assault with a massive **artillery** train, and they began preparations for a siege.

Hearing of Philip's plans and looking for a fight, Joan of Arc arrived in Compiègne on 13 May 1430 along with **Poton de Xaintrailles** and upwards of five hundred troops. Over the next ten days, these troops attempted delaying tactics along the Oise River as the Burgundian army was en route. Joan is recorded as being present at Crépy-en-Valois on 22 May, but historians have theorized that she was likely present for the other small battles during this period, all failing to halt the Burgundians' approach. Unfortunately, the medieval record is sparse on details of the battles and their participants. Joan returned to Compiègne that night (22 May), sneaking past the English and Burgundians outside the town.

On 23 May, Joan led excursions across the bridge into the Burgundian lines. At her **condemnation trial**, Joan told of how she successfully pushed back the Burgundians twice, but upon the third assault, she was cut off from the bridge by English troops. Surrounded, she was captured. **Perceval de Cagny** tells us that upon seeing so many Anglo-Burgundian troops outside the bridge's gate, Guillaume de Flavy ordered it shut. For centuries, popular narratives of Joan of Arc, and some historians, theorized treachery was involved on the part of Flavy, going so far as to claim he was bribed to shut Joan out. However, most historians today dismiss this theory, as there is no record of any bribe among the surviving detailed records of Burgundy, while there are records of bribes made to surrender the city, which Flavy refused to accept.

Burgundian chroniclers credit **Guillaume, bastard of Wandomme**, a soldier serving under **John of Luxembourg**, as the man who captured Joan of Arc, simply by being at the right place at the right time. The details vary, but she was either stripped from her horse or fell when her horse was wounded. Wandomme received payment for his prisoner. Later that night, Philip the Good met with Joan. **Monstrelet**, who claimed to be present for the encounter, said he could not recall what they said to each other. Joan was now a prisoner, and her participation in military campaigns was over (*See* RANSOM).

Meanwhile, with Flavy refusing to surrender, the siege of Compiègne continued. Part of the city's defenses included a bastille with a gate at the end of the bridge crossing the Oise River. The Burgundians built a boulevard facing it named Saint-Ladre. Medieval chronicles record a large array of cannons on both sides with deadly effect to both the besiegers and defenders, including Flavy's brother. By July, the Burgundians had destroyed the bastille, and the bridge was destroyed in the process, likely by the inhabitants. Makeshift bridges were built using boats, but no assault was successful. By 4 August, Philip the Good left the siege to deal with other matters, leaving John of Luxembourg in command. Facing supply and money problems, the besiegers suffered from desertions, but still managed to surround most of the city by mid-October. However, on 25 October, a relief army arrived and helped capture the Saint-Ladre boulevard after multiple assaults. The next day, Luxembourg abandoned the siege, leaving behind most of his artillery.

The aftermath put further strains on the **Anglo-Burgundian Alliance**. Although Monstrelet tells us Philip the Good condemned Luxembourg for abandoning the siege, the duke wrote to **Henry VI**, complaining about the lack of finances provided for Philip's men. They were behind as much as two months' pay, which explains some of the desertions. Conversely, the town began holding yearly celebrations on 25 October similar to those celebrated in **Orléans** on 8 May. In the context of Joan of Arc, Compiègne is often evoked only to note her capture. However, the town continued to resist and ultimately succeeded in lifting the siege.

COMRADE IN ARMS. See COMPANION IN ARMS.

CONDEMNATION TRIAL OF JOAN OF ARC. After Joan of Arc was captured at **Compiègne** by the Burgundians (23 May 1430), the English and the **University of Paris** both strove to secure her as a prisoner. There are surviving letters written from, or on behalf of, the university, **Henry VI**, and **Pierre Cauchon** to the duke of Burgundy (See PHILIP THE GOOD). The process lasted through the end of the year, and Joan was first transferred to the English who then gave her to Cauchon in **Rouen** on the promise that she would be returned to the English if she were found innocent after an **inquisition** (See RANSOM).

There is more surviving documentation for the trial of Joan of Arc than any other trial from the Middle Ages, and historians agree that this was because of the high-profile nature of their prisoner, as well as Cauchon's desire to appear above reproach. This desire explains the length of the trial, about five months depending on how it is examined, as well as the high number of assessors, roughly 131. However, most of these assessors only appeared for a portion of the sessions. Historians typically contrast Joan's trial to that of **Gilles de Rais**, the **marshal of France**, another high-profile defendant, who was certainly higher ranking. His trial lasted a mere two weeks in 1440 and the surviving documentation was less than half that of Joan's trial.

There are competing breakdowns for the condemnation trial, but the common approach is to view it first as a preparatory trial (9 January–24 March 1431), then an ordinary trial (26 March–24 May), and finally a trial for **relapse** (28–30 May). This can be misleading for understanding the experience of Joan herself, who would have seen the whole affair as a trial for her life while she awaited judgment in a prison cell with English guards (See CAPTIVITY).

Breaking it down further, Cauchon and the assessors began the proceedings on 9 January by assigning necessary **roles** such as the promoter and notaries. By 13 January, they had decided to draft a series of articles, or questions, to pose to witnesses about Joan. The articles were finalized and approved on 23 January. The articles, the names of those questioned, and their answers have not survived, but the results were reviewed on 19 February by Cauchon and the assessors. Also on 19–20 February, the question of the role of the inquisitor was settled, as inquisitions required a joint role of two judges that included a local **bishop** and an inquisitor (See LE MAISTRE, JEAN). Although the trial was held in Rouen, Cauchon, who was the bishop of Beauvais, served as the bishop for the inquisition because Joan was captured in his jurisdiction.

The first time Joan was directly questioned was on 21 February, the beginning of the so-called public sessions that lasted until 3 March. Here is where many of the assessors made appearances to observe the trial, if only for a day or two. Joan was questioned in the mornings on 21 and 22 February, after which there was a break on 23 February, most likely to give the notaries time to clean up their notes. After this, Joan was questioned almost every other day (24 and 27 February, and 1 and 3 March). On 4 March, the assessors decided to end the public sessions and moved to questioning Joan in private in the presence of the two judges and a handful of assessors in her prison cell during the so-called prison sessions, which lasted from 10 to 17 March. These sessions were more condensed, focusing on clarifying answers Joan provided during the public sessions. The process moved more quickly, and she was questioned on all but two days during this period (11 and 16 March). Two of these days included morning and afternoon sessions (14 and 17 March). The judges and some assessors gathered on 18 March and determined to review the transcripts thus far (19–21 March). On 22 March, the assessors decided to aggregate the results into a set of articles to bring against Joan, but not before reviewing the transcripts with her. Joan listened and agreed with the record (24 March). On 25 March, Cauchon offered to let Joan hear Mass—a request she had made repeatedly—if she would wear women's **clothing**. She refused.

The so-called ordinary trial began on 26 March, and on 27 and 28 March, the aggregated **seventy articles** were presented to Joan. Originally compiled in Latin by the promoter **Jean d'Estivet**, the articles were translated into French for Joan by **Thomas de Courcelles**, allowing her to respond to each point. She was questioned again in prison on 31 March, and the rest of the trial was a lengthy waiting period with only a few interruptions for Joan. During this time, the assessors collectively agreed to narrow down the seventy articles (2 April). This task was handled by **Nicolas Midi**, who finished his work on 5 April. The result was the **twelve articles** that were reviewed, commentated, and notarized without Joan's review or input, before being sent to the University of Paris for their opinion (12 April).

The progress of the trial was essentially on hold for the next five weeks, but there were other recorded events. On 18 April, Cauchon and a small group of assessors visited Joan in her cell while she was recovering from an illness (*See* PHYSICIANS). They begged Joan to submit to the **Church Militant**, offering her Mass and communion in return, but she refused. On 2 May, another concerted effort was made, this time by **Jean de Châtillon**. He presented six points of error on her part, including refusing to submit to the Church Militant, wearing men's clothing, and claiming divine revelations (*See* VOICES). Joan remained defiant as she faced further questioning and individual pleas from the assessors to submit. On 9 May, Joan was threatened with **torture**, but again to no avail. On 12 May, Cauchon met with a small group of assessors and asked for their opinion on whether they should employ torture rather than just threaten it, but the group voted against it, albeit not unanimously. During this period, individual assessors visited and pleaded with Joan to submit, but the names and dates are not recorded.

It was not until 19 May that the assessment from the University of Paris arrived in Rouen, which determined that based on the twelve articles, Joan was a **schismatic**, an **apostate**, and a liar. If she did not abjure, she should be abandoned to secular authorities. The judges and a small group of assessors determined to bring the twelve articles and the university's opinion to Joan formally and warn her one last time. If she did not abjure, then she would be deemed a **heretic**. On 23 May, Joan heard the twelve articles for the first time along with the university's opinion, read by **Pierre Maurice**. She was not provided the opportunity to respond to each article, as she did with the seventy articles. After the reading, Maurice warned Joan that if she did not submit, her soul and body would be destroyed. Joan refused.

The next day (24 May), Joan was brought to the Saint-Ouen Abbey cemetery where she heard a sermon by **Guillaume Érard**, begging her yet again to submit. Others informally asked her to as well. Joan appealed to the **pope** but was told that he was too far away and that those present represented the Church. She still refused, and the judges began to read a formal verdict. Before the verdict was finished, Joan interjected and agreed to submit. She signed a formal **abjuration**, and she would wear women's clothing, submit to the Church, and spend her days in an ecclesiastical prison.

This ended the so-called ordinary trial that lasted from 26 March to 24 May. During this nearly two-month period, Joan had spent two days hearing and answering the seventy articles, one day answering clarifying questions in her cell, received at least three visits to plead with her to submit, one day resisting the threat of torture, one day hearing the twelve articles, and then one day hearing a sermon and the beginning of the court's sentence. She had been a captive for more than one year (23 May 1430–24 May 1431).

Three days later, rumors circulated that Joan had abandoned women's clothing. When visited by the judges and some assessors (28 May), they found her in men's clothing. When questioned, she stated that she was wrong to forsake her voices and withdrew her abjuration. The next day began the so-called trial for **relapse** when the judges and assessors met and voted unanimously to officially sentence her as a relapsed heretic and hand her over to secular authorities if she did not submit. On 30 May, they brought her out of her cell and read the sentence, after which she was immediately taken to an already prepared stake and executed by being burned alive (*See* EXECUTION).

After the trial, testimony was recorded from some of the assessors on 7 June to describe the events of 30 May, but much of this is disputed and conflicts with testimonies from the **nullification proceedings**. After the trial, Thomas de Courcelles and **Guillaume Manchon** compiled and translated in Latin the trial along with supporting documentation and letters for distribution, three copies of which survive today (*See* TRANSCRIPTS).

Although there were a few English assessors in the trial, most of the assessors were French, as were all those with official roles. The background of many of the participants reveals their loyalties as Burgundian or English, as they lived in English- or Burgundian-controlled cities, swore oaths to the **Treaty of Troyes** (1420), and held **benefices** bestowed from these governments. In addition, records survive demonstrating that the English funded the trial, and paid the participants for their labor. Most of those who survived to participate in the nullification proceedings held the opinion that the trial was a sham meant to discredit **Charles VII**. It becomes easy to form opinions against the architects and participants of the trial based on this evidence. However, over the past quarter century, historians have reexamined the trial and process, noting that its high number of assessors, the public sessions, tedious documentation, lengthy ceremonies around procedure, and drawn-out review process involving the University of Paris all attest to a genuine desire by Cauchon and others to save Joan's soul, if not her freedom. Cauchon believed in his cause and his approach, and he ensured there was a record to support him.

CONSTANCE, COUNCIL OF. *See* COUNCILS.

CORONATION OF CHARLES VII (17 JULY 1429). The coronation of King **Charles VII** at **Reims** traditionally marks the apex of Joan of Arc's influence. By the fifteenth century, the coronation of the king of France had evolved from centuries of pomp and ceremony, claiming tradition as far back as the fifth century. By 1429, it was a symbolic gesture, albeit a powerful one, that resonated with supporters and some detractors of Charles.

The ceremony combined two separate events for the king: his coronation, or crowning, and his consecration, or anointing by the Church. This was not always the practice. Pepin the Short, king of the Franks, kept them as two separate ceremonies in 751. In 816, Louis I the Pious performed the ceremonies together. Later in the ninth century, the archbishop of Reims produced texts that weaved the two ceremonies together into a single event that blurred the lines between secular and ecclesiastical rule. In 1131, Louis VII was anointed with the same holy oil purportedly used for the consecration of Clovis I in 496. The relic became part of the ceremony for future kings, further solidifying the divine nature of the event and its king. The archbishop of Reims was responsible for providing the crown and scepter, and then anointing the king. Also participating in the ceremony were powerful **dukes** and **counts**, representing the unity of France. By the end, the ritual symbolized the king as selected by God. Afterward, there was a Mass followed by a post-coronation banquet, the latter of which was limited to men only.

Reims became the traditional location in 1129 with the coronation of Philip, and future kings followed suit. The city became so central to the ceremony that English King Edward III attempted to capture Reims in 1359 and 1360 to formally crown himself king of France. The Reims Cathedral, finished in 1275, became the location for the ceremony and still stands today.

Some modern historians have downplayed the significance of the coronation of Charles VII, arguing that Charles and his supporters had declared him king since 30 October 1422, nine days after the passing of **Charles VI**. Furthermore, the administration of the royal government changed little after the coronation. However, this ignores the symbolism attributed to the ceremony by the French. Charles himself expressed his desire to campaign to Reims for the ceremony in a letter to the people of **Tournai** in 1423. Joan of Arc insisted on calling Charles "**dauphin**" verbally and in letters until he was crowned in Reims. Similarly, **Clément de Fauquembergue**, writing from Anglo-Burgundian Paris, referred to Charles as the "dauphin" in his writings prior to the coronation, and then "Charles of Valois" afterward. This helps explain why Charles decided that after the victory at **Patay** (18 June 1429), his next military effort would be the **march to Reims** (29 June–16 July), as opposed to conquests in Lancastrian **Normandy**. It was never a foregone conclusion, and Joan was instrumental in convincing the king to make the trek.

On the coronation day (17 July), there were many prestigious nobles and participants from the recent military successes in relieving the siege of **Orléans** and the **Loire Campaign**. The holy oil was presented by four military men: **Jean de Brosse**, **Louis de Culant**, **Gilles de Rais**, and **Jean Malet de Graville**. **Regnault of Chartres**, the archbishop of Reims, applied the oil and crowned the king. **Charles d'Albret** carried the king's sword. The **duke of Alençon** replaced the absent duke of Burgundy (*See* PHILIP THE GOOD) and had the honor of knighting Charles, after which some two hundred more men were knighted. Other titles were bestowed, such as Gilles de Rais becoming **marshal of France**. Prominent nobles in attendance also included **Georges de La Trémoille**, **Charles, count of Clermont**, and **Louis, count of Vendôme**. Absent from the ceremony was **Pierre Cauchon**, who had fled the city before the royal army entered. **Arthur de Richemont** was asked not to attend the ceremony, as he was then in a dispute with La Trémoille.

Joan of Arc is described as standing beside the king, outfitted in her armor and carrying her **standard**. Some modern historians have questioned the scene of someone being on or near the altar in military gear, but chroniclers such as **Jean Chartier** and **Thomas Basin** are clear in their descriptions. Joan was grilled during her **condemnation trial** about why her banner was present at the ceremony, to which she replied that it had earned the honor to be there. After the ceremony, the *Journal du siège d'Orléans* tells us that Joan knelt before the king, kissed his foot, and wept, in front of all the nobles and soldiers who were moved by the scene.

After the coronation, Joan and others wrote letters, describing the ceremony and proclaiming Charles VII as king of France. Historians have lauded Joan with praise for her insistence on the march to Reims, an effort Charles had clearly envisioned for years. If the capture of **Troyes** symbolically attacked the **Treaty of Troyes** (1420), then the coronation at Reims declared it dead. Charles was no longer the disinherited dauphin, but the rightfully crowned king of France.

Not everyone respected the new title, however, and the **duke of Bedford** derided Charles in his public letters as one who fancies himself king. In response, **Henry VI** was crowned king of England on 6 November 1429 and then king of France while in Paris on 16 December 1431, then only ten years old.

CORONATION CAMPAIGN. *See* REIMS, MARCH TO.

COULOVRINE. *See* ARTILLERY.

COUNCILS. Councils in Western Europe were meetings between **bishops**, and sometimes other clergy and laity, to settle debates and establish doctrine within the Catholic Church. Originally called for by the emperor in the early days of the Church, by the fifteenth century they were initiated by the **pope**. Such assemblies are typically referred to as ecumenical or universal, meaning they represented many or all churches. Councils could last days or years.

The most prominent council that occurred during Joan of Arc's lifetime was the Council of Constance, featuring thousands in attendance with forty-five sessions held between 1414 and 1418. Some of the highlights from the council included a general settlement of the **Great Schism** (1378–1417) with the resignation of one pope, the deposing of two others, and finally, the election of Pope Martin V in 1417. The council also established its supremacy over the pope, asking that he schedule them at regular intervals. In addition, the council rejected the doctrines of the late Jon Wycliffe. After a lengthy trial, they condemned John Huss in July 1415, executing him at the stake and exasperating the Hussite problem in Bohemia. The conclusions of this and other councils weighed heavily on Joan of Arc's **condemnation trial**, where assessors sought to avoid further schisms with dueling popes and heresies like they found in Wycliffe and Huss.

At the Council of Basel (1431–1449), at least thirteen of the participants from Joan of Arc's trial, including **Pierre Cauchon** and **Thomas de Courcelles**, spread the news of her **abjuration**, **relapse**, and **execution**. A gathering of so many bishops and other clergy from medieval Europe provided a network of information about Joan's trial and demise.

COUNSELOR. *See* ROLES AND RESPONSIBILITIES.

COUNT. Joan of Arc encountered several counts and would-be counts, but the importance and power of these titles varied dramatically from person to person.

The number of counties in France ebbed and flowed between the tenth and fifteenth centuries, peaking at several hundred and dropping to roughly one hundred. Some counties merged, became duchies, and wildly ranged in size. The notion of counts varied over time as well. The title originated as a royal appointment overseeing well-defined territories while also serving the crown, but at times morphed into a decentralized, hereditary title.

By the fifteenth century, countships were inherited, taken through conquest, or bestowed by King **Charles VII**, as was the case with the **bastard of Orléans** who would later gain the title count of Dunois. Counts could also control multiple counties or in some cases, none. For example, the **count of Armagnac** lost his counties after several rebellions against Charles VII in the 1440s (*See* PRAGUERIE). **John of Luxembourg** held several counties when his forces captured Joan outside **Compiègne**.

The equivalent to a count in England was an earl. Thus, in some English histories, William de La Pole is sometimes referred to as the **earl of Suffolk** or the count of Suffolk.

COURCELLES, THOMAS DE (C. 1400–1469). Born in Amiens around 1400, Thomas de Courcelles received his master of arts from the **University of Paris** in 1426. By 1430, he had become rector of the university. Like his counterparts there, he was a supporter of the **Treaty of Troyes** (1420). In 1431, he was an active assessor at Joan of Arc's **condemnation trial**, participating in at least nineteen of the sessions. On 27 and 28 March, he translated the **seventy articles** brought against Joan from Latin to French, reading them aloud when **Jean d'Estivet** was unavailable. He then delivered the shortened **twelve articles** to the University of Paris for their opinion. On 13 May, he was one of the three assessors who voted in favor of **torture** for Joan. On 19 May, he declared that if she did not submit to the **Church Militant**, then she should be declared a **heretic**. On the morning of 30 May, he visited Joan in her cell with **Pierre Cauchon** to question her on why she resumed wearing male clothing, but he left before Joan was executed later that day. After the trial, Courcelles was tasked along with **Guillaume Manchon** with aggregating and translating into Latin the official **transcripts** of the trial.

After the trial, Courcelles excelled in his career, receiving a special dispensation from the **pope** to teach as a master at the University of Paris in 1433, even though he was not yet thirty-five. In 1435, the university had changed its view of the English and the **Hundred Years War**, and he represented the institution during the negotiations for what became the **Treaty of Arras** (1435). From then on, he was entrusted with negotiations and diplomacy by the university, **Charles VII**, and the pope. In 1461, he gave the funeral sermon for the king. His **benefices** included canons of churches and cathedrals in Amiens, Laon, Thérouanne, and Paris. He was respected by his contemporaries from a young age and after his death in 1469.

Since the nineteenth century, historians have not been so kind to Courcelles, especially considering his 1456 testimony given during the **nullification proceedings**. Here we learn that there are lapses in his memory. He could not recall if the inquisition made any inquiry into Joan's home in **Domremy**, even though he was shown portions of the trial transcript where he was present for a reading of the inquiry. He also claimed he never supported torture and he never declared Joan a heretic, only that if she was one before, then she still was one during the trial. Furthermore, it has been revealed that between translating the trial transcript from French to Latin, the names of those in favor of torture are absent. While recent scholarship has argued this may have been an editorial decision, most historians have concluded that if Courcelles did not regret his part in the trial, then he at least tried to cover up his direct culpability in its most unsavory aspects.

COUTES, LOUIS DE (1414–C. 1483). Louis de Coutes came from a line of serving dukes and kings of France. His father served Duke Louis I of Orléans, and his grandfather served **Charles VI**. In 1429, Coutes was only fourteen or fifteen years old and a page for **Raoul de Caucourt**. Upon the arrival of Joan of Arc that year, he and another person, only known as Raymond, were assigned to her as pages. Coutes was on campaign with Joan from **Orléans** to the siege of **Paris**. After which he no longer saw her, perhaps following the death of Raymond who was killed during the assault on Paris. It is unknown if any other pages served Joan. Afterward, Coutes continued to serve **Charles VII**. He and his siblings received estates from their father in 1447.

By the time of his 1456 testimony during the **nullification proceedings**, Coutes was the captain of Châteauden and **chamberlain** to the **duke of Orléans**. His testimony provides an eyewitness account of Joan's military activities, her daily habits, and her character. For example, he tells us that Joan received her armor while in Tours, and that the **duke of Alençon** provided her with a **horse**. She had a strong desire to be in the thick of the fighting, expressing irritation with the **bastard of Orléans** upon her safe arrival to Orléans, and she was relegated to the rearguard during the battle of **Patay**. Coutes described Joan winning over the confidence of the troops, and her ability to rally them outside the Saint-Loup boulevard (4 May). He also stated that Joan always slept with women in her quarters, and when no women were available on campaign, she slept fully armored, which resulted in bruising (*See* INJURIES). He emphasized Joan's piety and that she prayed often and sometimes wept on her knees. She admonished **blasphemers**, including the **duke of Alençon**. Joan pushed for the troops to confess and often arranged communion. She was distressed at the sight of the dead and wounded, and, when she was able to, she prevented the killing of prisoners. One anecdote from Coutes depicts Joan comforting a dying English soldier and arranging for communion while she held his head. Joan drove women from the camp, including at least one mistress that she chased with a **sword** (*See* CAMP FOLLOWERS). Joan's diet was light, eating no more than twice a day.

CRAVANT, BATTLE OF (31 JULY 1423). The battle of Cravant was the high watermark of the Anglo-Burgundian military coordination against Charles VII. **Louis, Count of Vendôme** and John Stewart, earl of Buchan, commanded the king's forces with upwards of eight thousand French, Scots, and Lombard mercenaries. They besieged the town of Cravant in Burgundy, roughly 145 kilometers southeast of Paris, which by late July 1423 was near capitulation.

In hopes of relieving Cravant was an Anglo-Burgundian force commanded by the **earl of Salisbury**, which consisted of five hundred English men-at-arms, two thousand English archers, and at least another one thousand Burgundian men-at-arms, plus an unknown number of crossbowmen and other troops. On 29 July 1423, the Anglo-Burgundians swore to meet the Franco-Scottish army in battle and relieve Cravant. The next day, they rode toward the town but halted well away from fighting distance, a move which historians attribute to Salisbury shrewdly reforming his troops.

On 31 July, the two armies faced each other on opposing sides of the nearby Yonne River. When the Scots began releasing arrows, the Anglo-Burgundians mitigated their effectiveness with tall shields. The Burgundians responded with cannon fire, which included thirty to forty *veuglaires* (See ARTILLERY), and the English archers released arrows as well. During the exchange, Salisbury forded the river with men-at-arms while another of his commanders took a nearby bridge. The move separated the Scots from the French and Lombard mercenaries, and the latter two fled the battlefield, leaving the Scots outnumbered.

Cravant was relieved. The Franco-Scot army suffered upwards of three thousand killed and another two thousand captured, including both Vendôme and Buchan. The Anglo-Burgundians suffered less than one thousand casualties.

Afterward, Charles VII downplayed the loss, emphasizing that the Scots and other allies took the brunt of the casualties while few of his kingdom's nobles were present. In the long-term, this marked the largest, most successful coordinated effort of the **Anglo-Burgundian Alliance**. Although they would work together again in a few sieges, including briefly at **Orléans**, Charles was not eager to meet these two enemies concurrently in battle after Cravant. Thus, for the next decade, the English and Burgundians largely fought two separate wars against territories in France. *See also* FRANCO-SCOTTISH ALLIANCE; VERNEUIL, BATTLE OF.

CRECY, BATTLE OF. *See* HUNDRED YEARS WAR.

CRÉPY-EN-VALOIS. *See* COMPIÈGNE, SIEGE OF.

CRUISY, JEAN DE. *See* NOTARIES AT THE NULLIFICATION TRIAL.

CULANT, LOUIS DE (C. 1360–1444). Louis de Culant (or Culan) became admiral of France in 1422. That same year he brought his cousin, **Jean de Brosse**, to the court of **Charles VII**, which kicked off Brosse's military career. Culant and Brosse joined the siege of **Orléans** on 25 October 1428 and participated in the battle of the **Herrings** (12 February 1429). Culant was a companion in arms of Joan of Arc at Orléans and during the **Loire Campaign**. The *Journal du siège d'Orléans* tells us that Charles sent Culant ahead to clear the way on the **march to Reims** (29 June–16 July 1429). At the **coronation of Charles VII**, he was one of the four men honored with guarding the holy oil used to anoint the king. After the failed siege of **Paris**, Culant remained as part of the garrison of the captured **Saint-Denis**, deep within Anglo-Burgundian territory. Culant would continue his martial service but was replaced as admiral of France in 1437.

CULVERINE. *See* ARTILLERY.

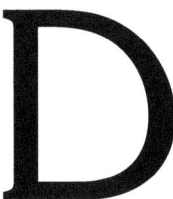

DAUPHIN. The title dauphin, or dauphin of Vienne, was unique to **France**, designating the eldest son of the king as the heir to the throne in the same vein as the Prince of Wales was the heir to the throne of **England**. The origins of the dauphin title began in Dauphiné, a region in southwestern France where Guigue IV (?–1142), **count** of Albon and Vienne, first used the title. Although his exact reasons are disputed, it was perhaps a way to distinguish himself among siblings and descendants all named Guigue. Another theory is that it was a variation of a personal name that was misunderstood to be a title. Regardless, the next baron of Vienne, Guigue V (1125–1162), followed suit and by the 1280s, the count of Albon and Vienne had become the dauphin of Viennois.

Dauphiné was theoretically part of the **Holy Roman Empire**, but by 1337, Humbert II (1312–1355), dauphin of Viennois, had racked up so much debt that he spent the next twelve years shopping around his hereditary rights and eventual kingdom to whoever would provide him financial security. French King Philip VI (1293–1350) initially bought the hereditary rights in 1343 and 1344, but Humbert continued to rule. However, Humbert could not remain within his means and ultimately sold his existing rulership to Philip in 1349 with one of the stipulations being that the title always went to the heir apparent of the French throne. The next year, Philip designated his grandson, future King Charles V (1338–1380) as the dauphin. The title remained in use for the heir apparent of the throne until the French Revolution.

During the time of Joan of Arc, the title became especially important and difficult to follow, as it was bestowed to the four older brothers of **Charles VII** as each died before he finally received it in 1417. With the signing of the **Treaty of Troyes** (1420), **Henry V** and his heirs claimed the French throne upon the death of **Charles VI**. The treaty stripped dauphin Charles of his title, referring to him as the one "who styles himself dauphin in Vienne." With the death of Charles VI (1422), the allies of Charles VII recognized him as king while his enemies derided him as simply the dauphin. Charles passed the dauphin title to his newborn son in 1423 (*See* LOUIS XI). After Charles's **coronation** at Reims, the **duke of Bedford** derided him in a letter as one who refers to himself as king.

Contemporary sources are mixed on how they refer to Charles VII. The *Chronique dite des Cordeliers* only ever calls him king, never dauphin, while **Wavrin** refers to Charles as king upon the death of his father, but his supporters were "Dauphinists." **Clément de Faquembergue** began referring to him as King Charles instead of the dauphin after his coronation. Similarly, Joan of Arc insisted on calling Charles "dauphin" until his coronation. From then on, he was king to her. *See also* THOMASSIN, MATHIEU.

DAUPHINISTS. A generic term sometimes used to denote those loyal to the **dauphin**'s claim to the French throne between the **Treaty of Troyes** (1420) and the **coronation of Charles VII** (1429). Given the range of allies and mercenaries the dauphin incorporated into his military, this could include French, Scots, Lombards, and Spanish. *See also* ARMAGNACS; LOYALISTS; ORLÉANAIS; ROYALISTS.

DE MIRABILIA VICTORIA. *See* SUPER FACTO PUELLAE.

DE PUELLA AURELIANENSI DISSERTATIO. *See* GÉLU, JACQUES.

DE QUADAM PUELLA (1429). Henry of Gorkum was the author of a Latin treatise on Joan of Arc entitled *De quadam puella conversante inter armigeris in habitu virili*, or "On a certain young girl in male clothing, living among soldiers." The work reports on the sudden success of Joan, describing her as prophesying, donning male **clothing**, leading soldiers on horseback with skill, and striking fear in the enemy. Although there is no specific date associated with the text, historians tend to place it in late May or by the summer 1429, after Joan's success at **Orléans** and before the **Loire Campaign**.

The treatise is inconclusive, presenting six arguments supporting Joan of Arc and six arguments against her. The text does not take a position on either side and instead aims to collect them "for those who may see the cause of this present case or a similar one in the future, so that they may be able to reply in some way to those putting forward similar questions" (Taylor 2006, 188).

Like *Super facto puellae*, *De quadam puella* has suffered from confused authorship over the centuries, but to a lesser extent. While it was published in a printed volume of **Jean Gerson**'s works in c. 1483, the same edition contained a total of ten works incorrectly attributed to Gerson. This was corrected in the second edition printed in 1488. Other compilers of Gerson's work continued to reject *De quadam puella* as Gerson's work because it seemed more like that of Henry of Gorkum. It was not until 1894 when a biography of Gerson attributed *De quadam puella* to him, and in 1957 Dorothy Wayman attributed it to Gerson on the point of style. Dozens of historians followed suit or simply proclaimed that we cannot know for certain the author. However, by the twenty-first century, Gerson scholars demonstrated that it was not his work.

DESJARDINS, GUILLAUME. *See* PHYSICIANS IN THE CONDEMNATION TRIAL.

DISSERTATIO. *See* GÉLU, JACQUES.

DITIÉ DE JEHANNE D'ARC. *See* THE TALE OF JOAN OF ARC.

DOCTOR. *See* EDUCATION; PHYSICIANS.

DOMINICAN ORDER. *See* FRIAR.

DOMREMY. Domremy was a town in the duchy of **Lorraine**, and the birthplace and home of Joan of Arc. It resides on the west bank of the Meuse River with **Neaufchâteau** to the south and **Vaucouleurs** to the north. With a population likely between 150 to 250 people, Joan's family owned a farm and Joan's father was a prominent figure in the town (*See* ARC, JACQUES D'). In 1428, the townspeople fled from Burgundian raids and took refuge in Neaufchâteau in the south. During her **condemnation trial** (1431), **Pierre Cauchon** sent investigators to gather information on Joan where they learned of the so-called **fairy tree** that was the sight of local folklore and traditions. However, the recorded information has not survived. During the **nullification proceedings** (1450–1456), local residents were interviewed. They testified that Joan was a shepherd of her father's sheep and frequented the Bermont chapel three kilometers to the north of the town.

Today, it is named Domremy-la-Pucelle to emphasize its connections with Joan. Though it appears as Domrémy on most maps, it should be spelled Domremy. This spelling matches local pronunciation, and the town name in early works (Tavard 2003, 143n1). Although damaged from 1940 bombings during World War II, Domremy still contains the restored home of Joan where two of the original three rooms are preserved; it is a museum open to the public. The Bermont chapel still survives today and has been undergoing restoration since 1992.

DUAL MONARCHY. *See* TROYES, TREATY OF.

DUCHEMIN, JEAN. Jean Duchemin was a lawyer at **Rouen** with a licentiate of **canon law** from the **University of Paris** (*See* EDUCATION). He was present during at least ten sessions of Joan of Arc's **condemnation trial** over the course of three months.

When it came time to render an opinion on the **twelve articles** formally brought against Joan, Duchemin signed a declaration along with **Aubert Morel**, arguing that Joan's revelations were not real and her refusal to wear women's **clothing** was wrong. After spurring the admonishments from the judge and assessors, she deserved excommunication. They hedged their statement that it was *possible* her **voice, visions, and revelations** could be real, but she provided no evidence aside from her own word. Thus, they deferred to the theologians on their validity. Their final recommendation was that if she did not abjure, she deserved prison for life.

Duchemin was present at the public admonishment of Joan on 2 May (*See* CHÂTILLON, JEAN DE). When the University of Paris submitted their opinion on the twelve articles, he agreed with the other assessors that Joan should abjure or be condemned as a **heretic** and handed over to secular authorities. He was present for her **abjuration** (24 May), but he does not appear in the trial records afterward.

DUKE. Derived from the Latin word *dux* for leader, the title duke ebbed and flowed in prominence and power throughout medieval France, going as far back as the late third century AD. By the turn of the fifteenth century, dukes had reemerged as the most powerful rulers in France, second only to the king. Each duke oversaw a territory known as a duchy, which varied greatly in size and power. Over time, duchies expanded, contracted, and absorbed each other, or simply merged back into the administration of the kingdom. There is a tendency for modern cartographers to draw precise lines on maps to indicate absolute borders of territories during this period, but many of these boundaries were fluid and the Kingdom of France was not made entirely of duchies.

When Joan of Arc rose to prominence, the most important duchies were oft-neutral **Brittany**, as well as Lancastrian **Normandy** and their allies in **Burgundy**, collectively covering the northern and northwestern portions of France. The duchies loyal to **Charles VII** included **Anjou, Berry**, Bourbon, **Lorraine**, and Touraine.

Much of the causes and the events of Joan of Arc's military career can be told through the lives (and deaths) of dukes. It was the assassination of Duke Louis of Orléans in 1407 that led to the **French Civil War** and opened the way for English involvement in French political disputes. The capture and captivity of the **duke of Orléans** at Agincourt (1415) led to the creation of part of Joan of Arc's **mission** to see him released. The assassination of Duke John the Fearless of Burgundy (1419) closed all hope of there being a reconciliation between the disputing French, paving the way for the **Anglo-Burgundian Alliance** (1420–1435). It was perhaps at the behest of the **duke of Lorraine** that **Robert de Baudricourt** had a change of heart, when he initially refused to send Joan to meet Charles VII in 1428. When she arrived at **Chinon**, the **duke of Alençon** met her, gave her military training, and led the army during the **Loire Campaign**. At the time, Alençon's duchy was in English possession and claimed by the **duke of Bedford**. Alençon's testimony during the **nullification proceedings** provides numerous anecdotes and insights to Joan on the battlefield. Also joining Joan briefly during the Loire Campaign was **Arthur de Richemont**, but he was excluded from the **coronation of Charles VII** due to political backbiting. Richemont ultimately came back in favor with Charles and worked with the king on military reforms, providing a microcosm of the fluidity of the French court. He became duke of Brittany (1457–1458) upon the death of his brother. Finally, it was subjects of the duke of Burgundy (*See* PHILIP THE GOOD) who held Joan captive after **Compiègne**, ultimately **ransoming** her to the English at the behest of the duke of Bedford and others. She would sit under the **inquisition** organized by **Pierre Cauchon**, a man whose power and influence came from his years of good relations with the dukes of Bedford and Burgundy.

DUNOIS, JEAN, COUNT OF. *See* ORLÉANS, BASTARD OF.

DUPUY, JEAN (C. 1360–1438). Jean Dupuy was a Dominican **friar**, theologian, and **bishop** of Cahors, France, residing in the court of **Pope** Martin V in Rome when he received news of Joan of Arc. Although Dupuy had just completed a short history of the world entitled *Collectarium historiarum* (April 1429), he decided to append it with details on Joan. His enthusiasm is revealed in the first paragraph, telling us "[t]his young girl accomplishes actions which appear more divine than human" (Taylor 2006, 89). In the earliest version of the work, there are blank spaces that were later filled with extracts from *Super facto puellae* by **Jean Gerson**, including a three-point defense of Joan wearing male **clothing**. Dupuy goes on to describe the lifting of the siege of **Orléans**, and Joan's habits of daily confession and weekly communion.

Historians tend to place the writing of the work in late May 1429, as it mentions Orléans explicitly, but not the **coronation of Charles VII** at **Reims**.

DUREMORT, GILLES DE (?–1444). Gilles de Duremort was a Benedictine monk who served as **abbot** of Beaupré (1403), then Beaubec (1413), and finally, the Holy Trinity of Fécamp in **Rouen** (1423). He held a doctorate in theology from the **University of Paris** and was on the faculty from 1423 to 1429 (*See* EDUCATION). In 1428, he became an adviser to **Henry VI**.

Duremort's titles of abbot and doctor earned him top billing among the list of attendees on each day he took part in Joan of Arc's **condemnation trial** (1431). He was an assiduous assessor (*See* ROLES), participating in all the trial preparations, all the public sessions (21 February–3 March), the review of the **seventy articles** (27–28 March), and Joan's **abjuration** (24 May). When it came time to provide his opinion on the **twelve articles**, he deferred to more learned men. When the topic of Joan's supposed **relapse** was discussed (29 May), he initially stated that they should read the text to her to make sure she understood, but he ultimately voted with everyone else to abandon her to secular authorities. It is unclear if he was present for her **execution** the following day.

He later became **bishop** of Coutances (1439) and died in 1444.

Given his regular appearances at the condemnation trial, his name was evoked often among those testifying during the **nullification proceedings** (1450–1456), who were mostly sympathetic to him. For example, **Nicolas de Houppeville** claimed that it was only because of Duremort's interventions that he was spared imprisonment or exile by **Pierre Cauchon**. **Richard de Grouchet** claimed he heard Duremort say that the questions posed to Joan during her trial would have been difficult for even an experienced cleric. Conversely, **Jean Massieu** claimed Duremort acted with prejudicial bias against Joan to please the English. Worse, **Guillaume Manchon** claimed Duremort participated in meetings with Cauchon and others well before any of the recorded proceedings to plan the trial against Joan. Taken together, these statements appear contradictory, but historians have recently theorized that all these assessments could be true, giving us a determined but, at times, conflicted man who ultimately voted with everyone else present to hand Joan over for her execution.

DURHAM, TREATY OF (28 MARCH 1424). James I, who had been a captive of the English since 1406, was the heir to the throne of Scotland upon the death of his father, Robert III, the same year. Robert Stewart, brother of Robert III, served as **regent**. James's time in captivity was luxurious, as he had a salary, maintained an entourage, and attended court. In 1421, **Henry V** knighted James and took him on his 1421 and 1422 campaigns in France.

With the death of Henry, England sought to simmer the tensions with Scotland in the north by marrying James to an English noble and releasing him from captivity to rule. On 2 February 1424, James married Joan Beaufort, daughter of the earl of Somerset and a descendent of English King Edward III.

The Treaty of Durham was sealed on 28 March 1424, which saw the release of King James I for a hefty **ransom** and a cessation of hostilities between England and Scotland for a seven-year period beginning on 1 May. This was especially important on the border with Scotland. During negotiations, there was a clause for all Scottish troops to leave France, but it was not in the final document. Still, at the battle of **Verneuil**, the **duke of Bedford** used the treaty as an excuse to execute all Scottish prisoners under the pretense that they were rebels.

DUVAL, GUILLAUME (C. 1405–?). Guillaume Duval was a Dominican **friar** from **Rouen** who attended one session of Joan of Arc's **condemnation trial**. During the **nullification proceedings**, he testified that he arrived late to the session with **Isambard de La Pierre**, and both of them sat close to Joan. While Joan was questioned, Duval tells us that La Pierre tried to help Joan by touching her and making signs. After the session, Duval and La Pierre went to visit Joan in her cell and were met by the **earl of Warwick**, who admonished and threatened La Pierre for his interference.

EARL. *See* COUNT.

ECCLESIASTICAL LAW. *See* CANON LAW.

EDUCATION OF JOAN OF ARC'S JUDGES AND ASSESSORS. The array of degrees present at Joan of Arc's **condemnation trial** varied wildly and included bachelors and doctors of theology; licentiates and doctors of **canon law**, **civil law**, and **medicine**; and masters of arts. Of the assessors present for some portion of the trial, we know the degrees and fields of roughly one hundred of them, which has required meticulous sleuthing by historians as the trial **transcripts** are not always thorough or consistent. Thus far, historians have identified at least thirty-seven theologians and thirty-five canonists—six of whom also had degrees in civil law. There were an additional nine with degrees only in civil law and five with degrees in medicine. In addition, there were ten university professors—two in medicine and eight in theology. Finally, there were five assessors with masters of arts who had yet to complete further degrees. These numbers exclude the unknown number of professors and students at the **University of Paris** who reviewed the **twelve articles** brought against Joan, but they would have all been trained in theology or canon law.

During the time of Joan of Arc, universities were well established, and male students started by pursuing a bachelor of arts. Students typically enrolled in an arts program around age thirteen or fourteen, focusing on areas such as grammar, logic, astronomy, geometry, arithmetic, and music. Advanced levels could include topics such as natural philosophy, ethics, and metaphysics. To become a bachelor of arts, the student typically needed to complete six years of learning followed by two years of lecturing. Then they qualified for conducting disputations and an examination before a group of masters. As a bachelor of arts, the student could teach under the auspices of a master. The titles varied and typically indicated the student's field, so there were no bachelors of arts at Joan's trial but plenty of bachelors of theology.

To become a master of arts, the student needed to finish specified reading, which typically included books on natural philosophy, astronomy, and ethics by classical authors such as Aristotle and Euclid. During a ceremony, the student would conduct a formal lecture and be accepted by a group of masters. This was rarely completed before the age of twenty-two, and someone like **Thomas Basin** receiving his master of arts before he was eighteen was a notable exception. A master of arts was qualified to teach without another master.

Similarly, a licentiate of canon law, civil law, or medicine was licensed to teach, but the necessary schooling varied depending on the school, and the licentiate could be the equivalent of a bachelor of theology or a master of arts in terms of requirements, time, and effort.

The terminal degree for any field was doctor, and few students achieved it before age thirty-five, given the rigorous amount of education, teaching, and examinations required.

ENGLISH. Among the distinct peoples that Joan recognized in France, there were the French who were loyal to **Charles VII**, the Burgundians who *should* be loyal to Charles, and the English who should leave France immediately. She continually threatened the latter with violence if they did not comply with her demands. She is recorded making these statements during her **condemnation trial**, by eyewitnesses during the **nullification proceedings**, and in several of her surviving **letters**.

There was much made by the assessors during Joan's trial about her attitude toward the English, asking if **Saint Catherine**, **Saint Margaret**, or God hated the English. Joan never gave a definitive answer, claiming she did not know who God loved or hated. However, she was emphatic that the English were to leave France. When asked if Margaret spoke English to her, Joan questioned why she would speak their language when she was not on their side.

That the assessors were concerned about the continued war in France was clear. In response to Article 18 of the original **seventy articles** brought against Joan, she clarified that her desire for war against the English lasted only as long as they remained in France. In Article 53, they attacked Joan's so-called arrogance by taking command in war, to which she replied it was a role she assumed only to defeat the English. When she was asked about the massacre at **Jargeau**, Joan responded that if the English defenders had abandoned their arms and left when instructed, they would have lived.

Historians have examined Joan's attitude toward the English, and although there is clear determination to drive them from the continent, there is a distinct lack of hatred in Joan's words and actions. The most common examples are those of Joan comforting a wounded English soldier and later crying at the sight of slain English, as attested to by **Louis de Coutes** and **Jean Pasquerel**.

Joan also indicated from the beginning that she was willing to make peace with the English once they met her demands. She addressed the **duke of Bedford** directly in her **Letter to the English (22 March 1429)** that she would hope he would eventually join the French on a crusade. These are not the words of someone who *hates* their enemy.

However, Joan certainly feared the English, especially in **captivity**. Her failed **escape** attempt was initiated when she learned that the Burgundians planned to **ransom** her to the English. Her fear was warranted. The English attempted to remain above reproach when it came to her condemnation trial, and it is true that the judges and assessors were almost all French (*See* ROLES). However, the English funded the trial, they gave jurisdiction to **Pierre Cauchon**, they had guards watching Joan, and the **earl of Warwick** was there intervening throughout the trial. Worse, the English handed Joan over for trial with the agreement that they would reclaim her if found innocent.

ENNOBLEMENT OF JOAN OF ARC. On 29 December 1429, **Charles VII** began the process of ennobling Joan of Arc and her family. The meaning of being a noble and the process to achieve this status evolved throughout the Middle Ages and varied by country. The common themes were nobles were wealthy, owned land, and inherited their riches and titles. They often married among each other, creating a difficult barrier for commoners to cross in order to join the noble class. In fifteenth-century France, ennoblement brought Joan and her family into the noble class that could enjoy benefits such as tax exemptions, access to judicial privileges, the ability to arm oneself as a **squire** or apply for knighthood (*See* KNIGHT), and the avoidances of penalties that applied to commoners in certain enterprises. More importantly, nobles recognized each other in peace and on the battlefield, which came into play when negotiating **ransoms**.

The original ennoblement record has not survived, and the earliest copy dates to 1612, maintained by those claiming descent from Joan and her family. From this document, we learn that Charles sought to reward Joan for her efforts by ennobling her, her parents, and her brothers, all mentioned explicitly by name, as well as their male and female lines. They were bestowed with the name "Du Lys," which translates to "of the lily," providing a strong association with the fleur-de-lis. The document listed benefits that explicitly included exclusion from taxes to the crown.

Because we lack the original document, those that survive are sometimes questioned and there are differences between the copies. For example, not all versions state explicitly that the ennoblement could pass through both male *and* female lines, the latter being highly unusual. Those claiming descent from Joan's family sought to certify and protect their claims. A 1614 edict ensured that only those descending from Joan's brothers and their male descendants could claim the title. In addition, the tax exemption expanded and contracted over the years to include all of **Domremy** or to just the male lines of Joan's family.

EPISTOLA DE PUELLA. *See* CHARTIER, ALAIN.

ÉRARD, GUILLAUME (?–1439). Guillaume Érard held a doctorate in theology from the **University of Paris** (*See* EDUCATION) and a **canon** from Langres. He was only present for one interrogation session during Joan of Arc's **condemnation trial** (3 March 1431), but he was active in other aspects including the threat of **torture** against Joan (9 May), the vote on torture (12 May), the presentation of the **twelve articles** against Joan (23 May), and the final sentencing to hand her over to secular authorities (29 May). However, Érard's most significant contribution was made by preaching to Joan right before her **abjuration** (24 May).

The text of the sermon, given in the cemetery of the Saint-Ouen Abbey in **Rouen**, is lost to history. However, portions, or at least tones, of it exist through the **transcripts** of the trial and eyewitness accounts. The trial transcript tells us that Érard led with a passage from John 15:4 that a branch by itself cannot bear fruit. In recounting the accusations against Joan, Érard implored her to submit to the Church and recant. Testimony from the **nullification proceedings** provides more color. **Isambart de La Pierre**, **Martin Ladvenu**, and **Jean Massieu** recalled that Érard labeled Joan a witch, a monster, a **heretic**, and a **schismatic**, and he lambasted **Charles** VII for supporting her. Massieu recalled that Joan interjected to defend the king before being silenced. The contents of the sermon led Ladvenu to conclude that the trial had been wholly an effort to attack Charles.

After the sermon, the trial transcript tells us that Joan offered to submit to God and the **pope**. Her appeal to the pope was denied because of distance, and the judges began to deliver a final sentence on Joan. She interrupted and said she would submit. After this, an official abjuration was read aloud, and Joan signed it. Joan was then sentenced to life in prison.

Érard appears again in the trial transcripts on 29 May, voting to abandon Joan to secular authorities after her **relapse**. However, he does not appear on the day of the **execution** (30 May), which may have just been an oversight. Or, if we add credence to Jean de Lenizeul's testimony during the nullification proceedings, Érard had no desire to participate in Joan's trial. This may account for his appearance at only one of the interrogations, and then only appearing at some of the key moments.

After the trial, Érard continued his career at the University of Paris and added to his **benefices**. In 1433, he represented the university's case against the **duke of Bedford**'s desire to start a university in Caen. In 1435, he broke with many of his university colleagues and represented England's interests alongside **Raoul Rousell** in Arras (*See* ARRAS, TREATY OF). He became a canon and dean of Rouen (1432 and 1438, respectively) and archdeacon of Grand-Caux (1433). Érard died in England in 1439.

ÉRAULT, JEAN. Jean Érault was one of the theologians who questioned Joan of Arc while she was in **Poitiers** (March 1429). Several witnesses mentioned him during the **nullification proceedings** (1450–1456), including **Gobert Thibault**, who identified Érault as the person who transcribed Joan's **letter to the English** (22 March 1429).

ESCAPE. On 14 March 1431, during Joan of Arc's **condemnation trial**, the assessors focused on her disastrous jump from the tower of Beaurevior, where she was then captive of the Burgundians. The exact date of the event is unknown. However, because Joan said she jumped to first help the people of **Compiègne** when she learned there would be a massacre, and second, to escape the English whom she just learned had paid her **ransom**, it was very likely in October 1430, as the siege of Compiègne was not lifted until 25 October. During the questioning, Joan also revealed a moment of dispute with her voices, saying **Saint Catherine** daily told her not to jump, but Joan responded that she would rather die than fall into the hands of the English.

During the questioning, Joan admitted that she was wrong to jump. However, she had confessed, and she claimed Saint Catherine, patron saint of prisoners and escapees, had forgiven her. The assessors asked her explicitly if she was attempting suicide and Joan said no. After reading Article 8 of the **twelve articles** brought against her, the opinion from the **University of Paris** described her as a coward and suggested she was attempting suicide with the jump.

The *Chronique dite des Cordeliers* (1432) provides the detail that Joan's disastrous jump from the tower involved a makeshift support that broke as she climbed down the window.

ESQUIRE. *See* SQUIRE.

ESTIVET, JEAN D' (?–1438). Nicknamed Benedicite, Jean d'Estivet was the assigned promoter, or prosecutor, in Joan of Arc's **condemnation trial** (*See* ROLES).

He had studied at the **University of Paris** and by 16 January 1430, he was **canon** of both Bayeux and Beauvais, the latter of which he also served as promoter. Like **Pierre Cauchon**, the bishop of Beauvais, Estivet fled the region, likely in August 1429, as the battle of **Montépilloy** (15 August) took place a mere forty-eight kilometers away.

Cauchon selected Estivet as the promoter for the inquisition of Joan on 9 January 1431, and he officially took his oath for the office on 13 March. In the records of the trial, Estivet requested copies of the questions and answers Joan had given in public and private sessions, and he produced the **seventy articles** of accusation against Joan. On 27 and 28 March, **Thomas de Courelles** presented the seventy articles to Joan, translating them from Latin to French for her. Over the course of these two days, Joan's response to each accusation was recorded. They also followed up on some of her responses on 31 March. Afterward, **Nicholas Midi** shortened Estivet's original seventy articles down to a more concise set of **twelve articles**.

Estivet and Joan had an antagonistic relationship, even outside the trial proceedings. **Jean Massieu** later claimed that Estivet tried on several occasions to prevent Joan from visiting the chapel she passed on the way to and from her prison cell, going so far as to threaten Massieu and physically block the door of the chapel.

On 18 April, Joan fell sick with fever. Several physicians examined and bled her, after which her fever broke. While recovering, she claimed that Cauchon had poisoned her meal. Several witnesses later testified that Estivet and her exchanged abusive language over the accusation while he purportedly called her a slut and a whore. Guillaume de la Chambre claimed that the fight upset her so much that her fever returned (*See* PHYSICIANS). As a result, the **earl of Warwick** interceded and forbade Estivet from antagonizing Joan further.

During the **nullification proceedings**, multiple participants in the trial derided Estivet for his intentions and behavior, claiming that he not only abused Joan, but also the participants of the trial. They believed he was seeking revenge against **Charles VII** while also trying to please the English.

Estivet died in 1438 near Rouen. The popular belief at the time was he was found dead in a sewer as part of his divine punishment for his participation in the execution of Joan. *See also* CHAPITAULT, SIMON.

ESTOUTEVILLE, GUILLAUME D' (1412–1483). Guillaume d'Estouteville was a prominent cardinal in the Catholic Church and the highest-ranking Church participant in the **nullification proceedings** (1450–1456).

Born around the same time as Joan of Arc in 1412 (*See* AGE), Estouteville was too young to participate in the **Poitiers** examination (March 1429). He came from a powerful Norman family, and his father, Jean, who was the captain of Harfleur in 1415, spent twenty years in captivity after Harfleur's capture by **Henry V** that year (*See* HUNDRED YEARS WAR). His brother, Louis, was captain of Mont-Saint-Michel from 1425 to 1460, a town in Lancastrian **Normandy** that successfully resisted English occupation. Conversely, Guillaume d'Estouteville pursued a career in the Church, acquiring a master of arts and a licentiate in **canon law** in 1435 (*See* EDUCATION). In 1439, he was appointed **bishop** of Angers by Pope Eugene IV (*See* POPE), but **Charles VII** disputed the appointment (*See* PRAGMATIC SANCTION). The pope made Estouteville a cardinal as compensation and Estouteville dropped his claim to bishopric in 1447. Still, by 1450, Estouteville's **benefices** had been numerous, including positions at Saint-Maurice of Angers, Digne, Couserans, Mirepoix, Nîmes, Béziers, and Lodève, and as abbot of Mont-Saint-Michel.

On 13 August 1451, Pope Nicholas V appointed Estouteville to be legate of France and the surrounding regions. The pope sent him to meet with Charles VII to negotiate a peace between France and England, and repeal the **Pragmatic Sanction**. Although Estouteville did not make progress on either of these tasks, he joined the fledgling nullification proceedings, which focused on examining the legitimacy of Joan of Arc's **condemnation trial**. **Rouen** welcomed him to the city on 1 May 1452, and he attended testimonies on 2 to 6 May before appointing **Philippe de La Rose** to serve in his stead alongside **Jean Bréhal**. On 22 May, Estouteville sent Bréhal and **Guillaume Bouillé** to meet with Charles and report on the proceedings thus far. Estouteville later met with the king in July, both agreeing to continue the process. By the fall, Estouteville had returned to Rome and his official participation in the nullification proceedings came to an end. However, in April, he was appointed archbishop of Rouen, succeeding **Raoul Roussel**. Estouteville arrived in Rouen on 28 July 1454 to assume the role.

After the nullification verdict (7 July 1456), Estouteville continued to be a high ranking official in the Church. In 1471, he campaigned to acquire the papacy, but failed. In 1477, he became the *camerlengo* of the Holy Roman Church, a **chamberlain** of sorts that was responsible for declaring the pope dead, securing his property, and executing his will and testament. Estouteville remained *camerlengo*, cardinal, and archbishop of Rouen until his death in 1483.

EUGENE IV. *See* POPE.

ÉVRARD, GUILLAUME. *See* ÉRARD GUILLAUME.

EXAMINER. *See* ROLES AND RESPONSIBILITIES.

EXECUTION OF JOAN OF ARC (30 MAY 1431). The execution of Joan of Arc took place in **Rouen** on 30 May 1431 after the judges and assessors from her **condemnation trial** (*See* ROLES) determined that since her **abjuration** (24 May), she had become a relapsed **heretic**. The events of the day are well-documented from the **transcripts** of her condemnation trial and testimonies recorded during the **nullification proceedings**.

Early in the morning, Joan was visited by **Martin Ladvenu** and **Jean Toutmouillé** who heard her confession and gave her communion. Afterward, Joan was led to a cart and pulled through a large crowd estimated by eyewitnesses to be upwards of eight hundred people. At the old market square in Rouen, a scaffold had been built above a pyre to provide a view for the crowd. As typical with **inquisitions**, a sermon was presented to the defendant and the crowd. **Nicolas Midi** led with a verse from 1 Corinthians 12:26, "Where one part suffers, every part suffers" (NIV). The full contents of the sermon are lost, but Joan purportedly interjected when Midi mentioned **Charles VII**. Then **Pierre Cauchon** delivered the final sentence, releasing Joan to secular authorities. English troops then escorted Joan to the scaffold, tying her to a wooden post. She wore a cap that said "relapsed heretic, **apostate**, idolater." Joan asked for a cross and a makeshift one was presented, which she kissed and held to her chest. Another cross was brought from the nearby church and held up in front of her.

The executioner on retainer in Rouen was Geoffroy Thérage, who had been performing the role in the city at least since 1420. There are records of him beheading, hanging, boiling, and burning people, and then presenting their remains outside the city. He and his assistants were responsible for the pyre and for escorting Joan into the crowd and onto the scaffold. Typically, executioners provided a mercy blow to their would-be victims to knock them unconscious before the execution. However, this was not done for Joan.

As the fire was set, Joan wept and cried out "Jesus" over and over. Most historians believe that she died from smoke inhalation before she was burned. Afterward, Thérage pulled away the burnt pyre to reveal a naked, dead Joan. Witnesses and contemporaries emphasize that the crowd confirmed that Joan was a woman, and she was dead. Another fire was set to burn the remainder of the body. The remaining ashes were gathered and tossed into the Seine River, to prevent the gathering of any relics by Joan's supporters.

EXECUTOR OF MANDATES. See ROLES AND RESPONSIBILITIES.

EXECUTOR OF WRITS. See ROLES AND RESPONSIBILITIES.

FABRI, JEAN. See LE FÈVRE, JEAN.

FAIRY TREE. The so-called fairy tree in **Domremy** was a well-known beech tree in the town, the site of local rituals and folklore in the village. Prior to questioning Joan of Arc during her **condemnation trial**, the assessors gathered information from the town and then used the tree in the questioning of Joan. When questioned on 24 February 1431, Joan freely shared that the tree was situated near a spring that some locals believed had healing power for the sick. Further, some of the locals hung garlands on the tree for the Virgin Mary. In addition, Joan had heard that fairies gathered near the tree. Although Joan admitted to hanging garlands when she was younger, she could not recall if she ever danced near it. Similarly, Joan could not confirm if anyone was ever healed from the spring, and although she heard others claim fairies gathered at the tree, she never saw any. On 1 and 17 March, the assessors revisited the topics of the tree and spring, asking Joan if she heard her **voices** near them or if she hung garlands in the tree for either saints **Catherine** or **Margaret**. Joan did not hang garlands for them nor hear them near the tree, but she did hear them near the spring.

Regardless of her answers, the initial **seventy articles** of accusation brought against Joan presented the tree as evil, harboring spirits known as fairies. Then the articles accused her of visiting the tree, and hanging garlands and dancing around it at night. While Joan was able to respond to these accusations, the first of the surmised **twelve articles** still presented her as hearing the voices of saints by a spring near the evil fairy tree, as a guilt-by-association tactic.

During the **nullification proceedings**, which focused on the validity of the condemnation trial, locals from Domremy emphasized that the tree, the garlands, and the dancing were innocent rituals for young girls, celebrating the Virgin Mary.

The fairy tree garners attention in histories on Joan of Arc for its sensational association with fairies, but it represented one of the numerous attempts by the assessors during Joan's condemnation trial to associate her with evil.

FALSE JOAN OF ARC. See ARMOISES, CLAUDE DES.

FASTOLF, JOHN (1380–1459). John Fastolf was a seasoned and prominent English knight that served in the campaigns of King **Henry V**, as well as those of his brothers, the dukes of Clarence and **Bedford**.

Born in 1380, Fastolf gained initial military experience in Ireland. Although not from nobility, he acquired land and money through marriage (1409). In 1412, he was part of the duke of Clarence's expedition sent to aid the Armagnac faction during the **French Civil War**. In 1415, he joined the expedition with Henry V to France and fought at Agincourt (See HUNDRED YEARS WAR). He continued to serve in Henry's conquests, fighting in battles and sieges, and receiving a knighthood in 1416.

In 1422, he became the steward of the duke of Bedford's household. Two years later, he fought at the battle of **Verneuil**, capturing and **ransoming** the **duke of Alençon**. During the 1420s, Fastolf expanded his land in France along with his wealth, serving in various positions, including governor of Anjou, Le Mans, and Maine, and captain of Verneuil. In 1426, he also became a knight of the Garter, the most exclusive order in England.

During the siege of **Orléans**, Fastolf was responsible for escorting convoys from **Paris** to supply the besiegers. It was at the battle of the **Herrings** (12 February 1429) where he gained considerable notoriety for soundly defeating the Franco-Scottish force that attacked his convoy. However, when the French caught the English unprepared at the battle of **Patay** (18 June), he escaped the rout, earning him considerable infamy. Contemporary reactions to Fastolf's escape were mixed, but mostly negative. Bedford banished Fastolf from the Order of the Garter initially but reinstated him after a formal inquiry into the battle. **John Talbot**, who was captured at Patay, accused Fastolf of cowardice. Fastolf argued his case, but the accusation stuck and haunted him. **Jean de Wavrin**, serving under Fastolf during the battle, provided a lengthy apologist perspective for his commander, arguing that the fog of war, not cowardice, led to the retreat.

While at the Congress of Arras in 1435 (*See* ARRAS, TREATY OF), Fastolf drafted a report that argued the English diplomats should not accept anything that further threatened the **Treaty of Troyes** (1420), which made **Henry VI** the king of France. Furthermore, in anticipation that the Burgundians would betray their commitment to the English, Fastolf argued that Henry should wage a three-year campaign against those whom Fastolf saw as rebels. His very detailed plan called for yearly five-month raids on the countryside (1 June to 1 November), burning and destroying everything. All captives were to be killed with no quarter or **ransom** given. **Sieges** should be avoided because of their cost in men and other resources. He believed that three years' worth of this approach would cause extreme famine and bring the rebels to the negotiating table. Fastolf's document no doubt came from experience, but also from readings into his personal library that included numerous histories and military treatises from authors such as Julius Caesar and **Christine de Pizan**. Nothing came of the approach, but the document provides a window into the mindset of a prominent Englishman who was waging war in France, especially one who had already lost some of his acquired land due to the resurgence of **Charles VII** after the arrival of Joan of Arc.

Upon the death of Bedford in 1435, Fastolf spent considerable time dealing with his master's estates in France, and he retired from campaigning in 1440, returning to England. There, he focused on his local lands and became embroiled in politics. In the last stages of the Hundred Years War (1450–1453), Fastolf was recorded as believing that Normandy belonged to the English by divine right, and it should and could be reclaimed. All of his property in France was lost.

He died childless on 5 November 1459, leaving all his wealth to the fledgling Magdalen College, now part of Oxford University. There is still a Fastolf Society there in his honor. Historians have struggled over the centuries to paint an evenhanded picture of Fastolf. His legacy is often mixed, especially since Shakespeare based Falstaff on him, a character portrayed as a cowardly drunk who serves as comic relief.

FAUQUEMBERGUE, CLÉMENT DE (?–1438). Clément de Fauquembergue was a clerk for the Parlement of Paris during the time of Joan of Arc, a position he held from 1417 to September 1435. His responsibilities included recording all judicial cases before the parlement, and his records are interspersed with brief accounts of current events, typically recorded several days after they occurred due to the speed of news at the time. The result is a matter-of-fact Parisian perspective on key events as they were heard by the city's inhabitants. Regarding Joan, he records the relief of **Orléans**; the battles of **Jargeau**, **Patay**, and **Compiègne**; the **coronation of Charles VII**; and the **condemnation trial** and **execution** of

Joan. He was also an eyewitness to the siege of **Paris**, which he recorded in detail.

Yet Fauquembergue's most significant contribution may be an out-of-character sketch of Joan of Arc, the only surviving contemporary of its kind. Rediscovered and brought to prominence in the nineteenth century, the pen drawing appears in the margin next to his recap of the relief of Orléans. It depicts a long-haired girl in a dress, holding a sword, and a **standard** inscribed with *JHS* for Jesus. Written and drawn several days after the events, he does not mention Joan by name but instead describes the enemy who had in their ranks a "Pucelle" carrying a banner. Although Fauquembergue had never seen Joan, he was obviously impressed by the notion of the maid among the troops holding a standard. Although the complete design of the standard is not depicted, he included part of its contents with *JHS*. The account in the *Bourgeois de Paris*, by another Parisian, describes Joan in **armor** with a banner sporting a single word, "Jesus." It is possible Fauquembergue may not have been able to process the notion of a woman in armor. Thus, the clerk envisioned a woman among troops—long-haired, unarmored, and in a typical dress. *See also* CLOTHING; "JESUS MARY."

FAVÉ, JEAN (C. 1407–?). Jean Favé was a lawyer from **Rouen** and the master of requests for **Charles VII**. Although he was not recorded as participating in Joan of Arc's **condemnation trial** (1431), he testified during the **nullifications proceedings** that he was present for her **abjuration** (24 May) and her **execution** (30 May). Favé provided salacious details that fit with the growing narrative that the trial was a sham funded by the English who aimed to kill Joan and discredit Charles. After Joan's abjuration, which he simply described as a sermon preached to her, Favé tells us that the English were vocal about their disappointment in **Pierre Cauchon** and the assessors (*See* ROLES) for not securing a guilty verdict or her execution. He claimed the English lifted their swords to strike some of the assessors but did not, a detail no one else provided. He also tells us the English openly complained that **Henry VI** had wasted his money with them. During her execution, he tells us she cried out "Jesus" repeatedly (*See* "**JESUS MARY**").

FÉCAMP. *See* DUREMORT, GILLES DE.

FERREBOUC, FRANÇOIS. *See* NOTARIES AT THE NULLIFICATION TRIAL.

FLAVY, GUILLAUME DE (C. 1398–1449). Guillaume de Flavy is one of the most controversial figures in Johannic scholarship, as he was responsible for closing the gate at **Compiègne** the day Joan of Arc was captured outside the city by Burgundians (23 May 1430).

From a noble family in Picardy, Flavy studied at the **University of Paris**, but ultimately chose a life of warfare. Three of his brothers went on to serve under the dukes of Burgundy, while he and two other brothers served under the **dauphin** (*See* CHARLES VII). His half-brother, **Regnault of Chartres**, Archbishop of Reims, often helped him find favor with Charles. In 1417, Flavy unsuccessfully defended **Rouen** against the English. In 1418 and 1419, he unsuccessfully fought in **Paris** against the Burgundians (*See* FRENCH CIVIL WAR). He continued to serve Charles VII throughout the 1420s, capturing Compiègne and fighting in **Normandy**. In August 1427, he defended Beaumont-en-Argonne against **John of Luxembourg**, surrendering the starved city in January 1428. Flavy was present for the **coronation of Charles VII** (17 July 1429). He then took over as captain of Compiègne and negotiated the city's surrender to Charles on 18 August.

In May 1430, still captain of Compiègne, Flavy failed to convince the inhabitants to surrender to **Philip the Good**, who began his siege of the city on 20 May. On 23 May, Flavy is recorded by multiple sources, including **Perceval de Cagny**, as ordering the city's bridge drawn and the gate closed. Outside, Joan of Arc was captured. Afterward, Flavy rebuffed offers to surrender the city before its relief on 25 October.

During the 1430s, Flavy took advantage of the war, fighting and profiting in the surrounding region. When **Arthur de Richemont** entered Compiègne in December 1436, he had Flavy imprisoned. Regnault of Chartres intervened, and Flavy was released, forced to relinquish his captaincy and to promise never again to enter the city under penalty of a hefty fine. However, by 1437, he was again captain, and in 1440, he was again briefly imprisoned. Flavy continued his life of war and was assassinated in 1449, still captain of Compiègne.

The debate over Flavy's culpability in Joan of Arc's capture began during his lifetime. A lawsuit in 1445 described him as shutting the city's gates that fateful day, but it never explicitly stated he did so with the intent of seeing Joan captured. By 1498, chronicles and histories expounded on the story, claiming Flavy took a bribe from Philip the Good for the capture of Joan. Historians have been split on the topic as recently as the twentieth century. His defenders point out that there is no record of a bribe in the detailed archives of Philip the Good, but there are records of him spurning offers to surrender the city *after* Joan's capture. Furthermore, Joan made no mention of the gate being closed during her **condemnation trial**, indicating that she was captured well outside the city. This conflicts with popular re-creations of the capture that depict Joan right outside the gate, and, in some dramatic depictions, banging on it. If there was treason, she made no mention of it.

FONTAINES, RIGUARD DE. Loyal knight of **Charles VII** throughout the 1420s, Riguard de Fontaines was at the siege of **Orléans**, commanding at least thirty men. He was briefly appointed captain of **Compiègne** (22 June 1429) before being replaced by the more popular **Guillaume de Flavy** (15 August). Fontaines was at Compiègne during the capture of Joan of Arc (23 May 1430), and he was there again to help relieve the city (25 October). He continued to serve Charles militarily until at least 1435 with companions in arms such as **La Hire, Poton de Xaintrailles,** and **Jacques de Chabannes.** He was appointed governor and **bailiff** of Valois for the **duke of Orléans**, and again served as captain of Compiègne for Charles in 1457.

FORTIFICATIONS. *See* SIEGE.

FOUR KINGDOMS, QUEEN OF. *See* YOLANDE OF ARAGON.

FRANCE. When historians refer to France or the French people during the time of Joan of Arc, it is necessary to understand the context to which they are referring, as well as the perspective of whatever medieval source they may be citing. Sometimes they will refer to "France" as shorthand to mean those loyal to **Charles VII** as the rightful king. Similarly, some contemporaries of Joan as well as modern historians refer to those loyal to Charles as **"Armagnacs,"** which had become an outdated term, not in use by those to whom it was applied.

It is difficult to see medieval France without a modern, nationalistic view of borders or language. Although France is the only European country where French is the official language, it is at least a co-official language in Belgium and Luxembourg. In addition, colonialism has ensured that French is the official or a common language in countries throughout Africa, the Caribbean, Canada, and South America. This problem is more pronounced in the medieval landscape of the territories that fall within or near France's modern borders. Historians often surmise the situation during Joan of Arc's rise to prominence as being one of simply an **Anglo-Burgundian Alliance** against France, or against Armagnacs. Modern mapmakers may also depict England and **Burgundy** as controlling all the territory north of the **Loire River**, while everything south is all that remains of 1429 France, or at least the regions loyal to Charles VII, but this, too, has issues.

To accurately describe France during the time of Joan of Arc, it is first necessary to understand that the region consisted of duchies (*See* DUKE) and **counties** that varied in size and power, and that, though they were at one point loyal to the king of France, the war with England and the **French Civil War** had made the situation fluid.

Those not loyal to Charles VII included **Brittany**, in the northwest peninsula of France, which had successfully pursued independence from the French crown during the early phases of the French Civil War, and therefore gave this duchy a level of neutrality in the English war on the continent. Much of **Normandy** had fallen under the conquest of **Henry V** in 1419. Burgundy had outright allied with the English as part of the **Treaty of Troyes** (1420), and although that alliance ebbed and flowed in collaboration, they had predominantly remained pitted against Charles with only fleeting periods of truces. Burgundy was by far the largest and most powerful duchy that opposed Charles, with a solidified reign over Flanders and regions within the **Holy Roman Empire**. Finally, Aquitaine, a large southwest duchy, had remained under English rule since 1399, after decades of dispute.

The remaining regions, made up of various duchies, but also individual towns or groups of towns, were loyal to Charles VII. Throughout the 1420s and especially in 1428 to 1431, the regions north of the Loire River and between Brittany, Normandy, Burgundy, and **Paris** were a war zone between the Anglo-Burgundians and those loyal to Charles. Some of these loyal regions were surrounded. This was the situation in **Lorraine** when Joan approached **Robert de Baudricourt**, asking him to send her to France, meaning *through* the territory controlled by Burgundians and *into* the connected territory of Charles.

For Joan of Arc's part, when she spoke of France, she referred to the European continental presence of French speakers, including Burgundy. Hers was a monarchist view, and she believed these towns, regions, and dukes should all be subjects of Charles VII. Today, when historians refer to the French or Armagnacs fighting alongside Joan, they mean the forces loyal to Charles. By the end of the Hundred Years War, most of the French-speaking regions came under the rule of Charles, including Aquitaine, Brittany, and Normandy, whether through conquest or diplomacy. The last English possession was the port city of Calais. *See also* DAUPHINISTS; LOYALISTS; ORLÉANAIS; ROYALISTS.

FRANCISCAN ORDER. *See* FRIAR.

FRANCO-BURGUNDIAN TRUCE (28 SEPTEMBER 1429–16 APRIL 1430). Talks about a truce between **French** and **Burgundian** forces had been in the works since before the **coronation of Charles VII** with **Georges de La Trémoille, Regnault of Chartres**, and **Raoul de Gaucourt** leading the delegation for Charles in the negotiations. On the day of the coronation, **Philip the Good** proposed a fifteen-day truce after which **Paris** would be handed over to Charles, but Philip ultimately reneged on the terms. Negotiations continued until 28 August 1429 when the two sides agreed to a formal three-month truce starting on 28 September and ending on 25 December. This truce initially excluded Paris, allowing Charles to attack and Philip to defend. After the failed siege of Paris (8 September), the city was formally added to the three-month truce on 18 September. Multiple extensions were made, including to 15 March 1430 and finally to Easter (16 April).

The truce has been heavily criticized for multiple reasons. Many have seen the lengthy negotiations by Philip as a means to gain time to bolster his position in Paris, which he never intended to hand over to Charles. During the negotiations with Charles, Philip continued his own negotiations with the English, receiving new counties and a rank second only to the **duke of Bedford**. Historians often credit the truce and the negotiations with ultimately disbanding the royal army and severely undermining Joan of Arc's **mission**.

Joan criticized truces in a **letter to the people of Reims (5 August 1429)**, saying she was not content with them, and she was unsure if she would abide by the fifteen-day truce. At a minimum, she was determined to keep the royal army together if Philip did not follow through with the terms.

The truce was also ineffective at quelling the violence of the **French Civil War**. Although the French and Burgundians were not active against each other officially, **Monstrelet** tells us how troops on both sides found loopholes to attack each other. Burgundians joined with English armies, and the French attacked Burgundian towns claiming they believed they were occupied by English.

FRANCO-SCOTTISH ALLIANCE. The Franco-Scottish Alliance dates back to 1295 and continued through 1560, ebbing and flowing with military, diplomatic, and economic collaboration against England. Before the prominence of Joan of Arc, there were official renewals of the alliance in 1326, 1359, 1371, 1390, and 1407. In 1406, King Robert III of Scotland sent his eleven-year-old son, future King James I, to France for education in the court of King **Charles VI**. However, James was captured by the English in Norfolk and held captive by Henry IV. Robert III died the next year, making James the effective king of Scotland. Robert Stewart, brother of Robert III, served as **regent**. James stayed with the English, joining **Henry V**'s campaigns in France in 1421 and 1422 (*See* HUNDRED YEARS WAR), before his eventual release in 1424 (*See* DURHAM, TREATY OF).

In 1418, the **dauphin** (*See* CHARLES VII) established a personal guard of Scots that became known as the Garde Écossaise, a group that went on to serve future French kings through the nineteenth century. In 1419, the dauphin sought military assistance in his war with England and there are estimates as high as fifteen thousand Scots making the journey to France to fight against the English between 1419 and 1424. Soldiers were paid, and some nobles were given land and titles to participate in the war.

In 1428, Charles VII and James I negotiated another treaty that included another Scottish army and a marriage contract between Charles's son (*See* LOUIS XI) and James's daughter, Margaret, who were four and three years old, respectively. However, the army never made it to France, and the future couple did not meet until 1436 when they were officially wed. **Jean de Metz** later recalled Joan of Arc mentioning the daughter of the king of Scotland in early 1429, which has led historians to conclude that news of the treaty was widely circulated.

The peak of military collaboration with the Scots came at the battle of **Baugé** (1421) where the Franco-Scottish force was victorious over the English. However, at other battles, Scots are reported to have taken the brunt of the casualties, resulting in outright massacres at **Cravant** (1423), **Verneuil** (1424), and **Herrings** (1428). Several prominent Scottish nobles were in these battles including Earl John Stewart of Buchan who led the Franco-Scottish army at Baugé, was captured at Cravant, and then killed at Verneuil. Another John Stewart, of Darnley, also fought at Baugé, was wounded and captured at Cravant, and was then slain at Herrings. Charles VII is recorded coldly dismissing some of these losses, emphasizing that Scots and other foreign allies took the brunt of the casualties, sparing French nobles. Thus, by the time of Joan of Arc, Scots were present, but not numbering in the thousands as they had over the preceding decade. Chroniclers explicitly mention them in the royal army at **Patay**, the **march to Reims**, **Montépilloy**, and the **coronation of Charles VII**. *See also* KIRKMICHAEL, JOHN OF.

FRENCH CIVIL WAR (1407–1435). The French Civil War was a three-decade-long struggle between feuding factions that strove to keep power from each other. The war opened the door for English invasion and occupation in northern France, extinguished the power of the French crown, and provided the impetus for Joan of Arc's **mission**. The details are worth understanding, as it paints the convoluted picture of the political landscape to which Joan entered in 1429.

The kingdom's woes stemmed from the bouts of mental illness experienced by King **Charles VI**, beginning in the 1390s. Modern diagnoses typically settle on paranoid schizophrenia, which came sporadically to the king, leaving him unable to recognize family members, let alone actively rule. But he also had periods of lucidity, resulting in an uneven approach from the king. With no single **regent** assigned to rule during his absence, the power struggle was left to the **dukes** and **counts** who formed alliances and strove to keep power from opposing factions. In the early 1400s, the two major leaders were Duke Louis I of Orléans and Duke Philip the Bold of Burgundy. Louis was brother to King Charles and Philip was uncle to them both.

With the passing of his father, Philip, in 1404, John the Fearless inherited the duchy of Burgundy along with the continuing feud with Orléans. The disputes continued in the form of denying each other funds, lands, and resources, such as when Orléans successfully prevented the royal council from sending reinforcements for Burgundy's siege of the English at Calais in 1405. The traditional start of the French Civil War began with the assassination of Louis I of Orléans, on 23 November 1407. Louis's son, Charles, became the new **duke of Orléans**, and he continued the feud against his cousin, John the Fearless. By 1408, John successfully made the case to Charles VI that the assassination of Louis was justified, as the duke was planning to kill Charles and his family. On 9 March 1409, the Peace of Chartres resulted in Charles VI officially pardoning the duke of Burgundy.

The new duke of Orléans responded by forming the League of Gien on 15 April 1410 with the duke of Brittany and the counts of Alençon, Clermont, and Armagnac. The latter's daughter, Bonne, was wed to the duke of Orléans. Count Bernard VII of Armagnac was so influential that members of the league became known as the **Armagnacs**. On 14 July, they issued the Manifesto of Jargeau, arguing that the pardon of the duke of Burgundy went against divine law and thus the Peace of Chartres was invalid. The Peace of Bicêtre on 2 November seemingly avoided outright war, but this did not last. In the summer of 1411, **Monstrelet** records the contents of public letters released by the Armagnacs and then the Burgundians that amounted to modern-day declarations of war. Both letters served as propaganda to win over the French people to their factions.

Open warfare and the capture of towns were only interrupted by truces and treaties that never lasted, including the Peace of Auxerre in 1412, the Peace of Pontoise in 1413, and the Peace of Arras in 1414. During this time, King Charles VI's son, Duke Louis of Guyenne, attempted to form a third royalist faction. In April 1413, John the Fearless responded by instigating the violent Cabochian Revolt in Paris, which targeted Guyenne's men. The **University of Paris** joined the fray and passed a strict ordinance in which to prosecute Armagnacs and enemies of Burgundy alike. By the summer, the people of Paris grew tired of the excesses. The ordinance was revoked on 5 September, and John the Fearless fled the city. In 1414, John attempted and failed to capture Paris through force.

Both the Armagnacs and Burgundians wooed English King Henry IV into the war and English troops could be found in both armies, but by 1415, Henry V had rekindled English claims to the French throne and invaded France. At Agincourt, the original leadership of the Armagnacs was decimated with the capture of the duke of Orléans, and the death of the counts of Clermont and Alençon. Throughout 1417 to 1419, Henry V conquered **Normandy**. During that time rebellions rose up in Paris in support of Burgundy, but it was not until his siege of Paris (29 May–14 July 1418) that John the Fearless successfully captured the city with the help of rebels from within (*See* VILLIERS, JEAN DE). On 12 July, Count Bernard VII of Armagnac was assassinated, and the **dauphin** (*See* CHARLES VII) fled the city. John entered Paris and was recognized by King Charles VI as the new protector of France.

Although the Armagnacs and the Burgundians tried to reconcile, the assassination of John the Fearless, on 10 September 1419, created a new rift, and the dauphin was implicated in the plot. **Philip the Good**, the new duke of Burgundy, allied with the English at the **Treaty of Troyes** (1420), which also declared Henry's unborn heir the next king of France upon the death of Charles VI. Henry married **Catherine of Valois**, the daughter of Charles VI.

The disinherited dauphin did not recognize the treaty, and his forces defeated the English at **Baugé** in 1421 while Henry was in England for the coronation of Queen Catherine. Henry returned to France and continued his conquests, dying on 31 August 1422. Charles VI died shortly afterward (October 21), and the **duke of Bedford** became the **regent** of France while the nine-month-old **Henry VI** was too young to rule. Meanwhile, supporters of the dauphin declared him King Charles VII of France, and the war continued. Anglo-

Burgundian forces decisively won the battle of **Cravant** (1423), French forces defeated the English at the battle of La Brossinière (1423), and English forces won at the battle of **Verneuil** (1424). After the battle of Cravant, the English and Burgundians fought predominantly separate wars, the English focusing on French-controlled cities to the south of Paris and the Burgundians focusing on territory in the east. After **Salisbury's 1428 expedition**, the English and Burgundians controlled most of the cities north of the **Loire River** and besieged **Orléans**, the last of Charles's strongholds on the river.

With the arrival of Joan of Arc at the siege of Orléans on 29 April 1429, Charles's forces successfully lifted the siege on 8 May, recaptured cities during the **Loire Campaign** in June, and captured additional cities during the **march to Reims**, which then hosted the **coronation of Charles VII** on 17 July. The failure at the siege of **Paris** stymied the momentum of Charles's army (8 September). Another half-hearted truce came during the **Franco-Burgundian Truce** (28 September 1429–16 April 1430), but the French and Burgundians found ways around it during this period. Joan was eventually captured on 23 May 1430 during the siege of **Compiègne**. The civil war continued along with the war against the English, but the French Civil War officially came to an end with the **Treaty of Arras** (1435) with Philip the Good finally recognizing Charles VII as king. *See also* HUNDRED YEARS WAR.

FRIAR. By the fifteenth century, friars were an established norm in France. Texts often describe these religious men as mendicant, because they embraced a life of poverty, typically living only from donations. They are also sometimes described as itinerant because many of them were not tied down to a single abbey, covenant, or monastery, and thus traveled often. Friar means *brother*, and these men may be referred to by one or both terms, sometimes within the same text (e.g., Friar **Richard**, Brother Richard). There were multiple orders of Friars, but the two most mentioned concerning Joan are Dominican and Franciscan. Dominican friars get their name from Saint Dominic and are often referred to as the Order of Friars Preachers or Order of Preachers. Similarly, Franciscans got their name from St. Francis of Assisi and were sometimes referred to as Friars Minor.

Joan of Arc had numerous interactions with friars, starting at an early age. They often traveled through and preached in **Lorraine**. Joan also visited a local friary in Coussey. None of the contents of their sermons survive, but historians suggest they would have contained a mixture of prophecies, political and regional news, and a strong **royalist** sentiment, all of which could have fed or reinforced what Joan claimed to hear from her **voices**.

Dominican friars were present at Joan's **condemnation trial** (1431) and later at the **nullification proceedings** (1450–1456). These men demonstrated sympathy toward Joan, claiming they tried to help her throughout her trial. Friar **Pierre Bosquier** spent time in jail for challenging the validity of the trial, a crime for which he later recanted in writing. *See also* LE MAISTRE, JEAN; PIERRE, ISAMBARD DE LA; PRIOR; TOUTMOUILLÉ, JEAN.

GABRIEL, SAINT. Gabriel is an archangel prominent in texts associated with Judaism, Christianity, and Islam. In fifteenth-century France, Saint Gabriel was most commonly associated with the Annunciation, the angel who delivered the proclamation to Mary about her virgin pregnancy with Jesus Christ (Luke 1:26–38). Gabriel would have been found in art and stained glass throughout France.

During Joan of Arc's **condemnation trial**, she claimed she saw Gabriel along with **Saint Michael** (3 March 1431). When questioned about the angels depicted on her **standard**, the assessors asked if Saint Gabriel was one of them (17 March). However, Joan did not clarify and emphasized the angels were there to glorify God. On 9 May, Joan claimed that Saint Gabriel appeared to her on the Feast of the Invention of the Cross to comfort her (3 May). Like her claims of seeing and interacting with other saints, the assessors believed it was a fabrication. *See also* CATHERINE, SAINT; CHARLEMAGNE, SAINT; LOUIS, SAINT; MARGARET, SAINT; MICHAEL, SAINT; VOICES, VISIONS, AND REVELATIONS.

GARDE ÉCOSSAISE. *See* FRANCO-SCOTTISH ALLIANCE.

GAUCOURT, RAOUL DE (C. 1371–1462). Raoul de Gaucourt was a companion in arms of Joan of Arc with a lengthy military career, serving under John the Fearless, **Charles VI**, and **Charles VII**.

Born around 1371, Raoul de Gaucourt was first recorded campaigning in 1388 alongside Charles VI. In 1396, he joined the crusade of John the Fearless and was captured at the battle of Nicopolis (25 September). When **Henry V** invaded France in 1415, Gaucourt was one of the leaders who surrendered at the siege of Harfleur (*See* HUNDRED YEARS WAR). He remained in captivity for ten years, but he traveled to France on several diplomatic errands for Henry in 1416, returning to England in 1417. Along with the captive **duke of Orléans**, Gaucourt was one of the men that Henry insisted from his deathbed should not be released.

After he was released in 1425, Gaucourt immediately entered the service of Charles VII, and the king put him to work. On 28 March 1426, he became the governor of **Orléans**. In 1427, he served alongside **Arthur de Richemont**, the **bastard of Orléans**, and **La Hire** in the relief of Montargis. In 1428, he became the governor of Dauphiné and served in the role until 1447. When the siege of Orléans began (12 October 1428), Gaucourt was still its governor and was active in its defense. When Joan of Arc arrived at **Chinon** (March 1429), Gaucourt was present as captain of the city. He was also present for Joan's arrival at the siege of Orléans (29 April). **Simon Charles** tells us that on 7 May, Joan admonished Gaucourt, who was leading the troops that stood watch outside the Tourelles bastille, preventing the English from escaping. She wanted an attack, and according to Simon Charles, she convinced the troops to assault the bastille, despite Gaucourt's orders. Regardless of their differences, he was then present on the **Loire Campaign** (10–18 June), **Patay** (18 June), the **march to Reims** (29 June–16 July), and the **coronation of Charles VII** (17 July).

Gaucourt also served the king diplomatically. After the relief of Orléans, a surviving letter from Charles VII celebrating the event and the participation of Joan of Arc was hand-delivered by Gaucourt to the citizens of Narbonne. In August 1429, Gaucourt was with **Regnault of Chartres** and **Georges de La Trémoille** in Arras to begin negotiations with **Philip the Good** for the **Franco-Burgundian Truce**. Gaucourt was still active militarily, and **Perceval de Cagny** listed him as one of the people that physically dragged Joan away after her wounding at **Paris** (8 September).

After Paris, Gaucourt along with Chartres and La Trémoille advised against Joan joining the **duke of Alençon** for his **Normandy** campaign (October 1429). Historians have theorized that Gaucourt joined this group because he saw firsthand what he likely perceived as Joan's recklessness, and he may have been concerned about how the combination of the war-hungry Alençon and Joan may play out while on campaign together again. After all, he witnessed her firsthand at Orléans, **Jargeau**, and Paris, and he understood her propensity to attack, even while wounded and against insurmountable odds.

There are no more documented interactions between Gaucourt and Joan. After her capture (23 May 1430), he continued to serve Charles VII in campaigns and in offices, most notably in the reconquest of Normandy (1449–1450) and as the grandmaster of the king's hotel (1453–1461). During the various noble rebellions against Charles, Gaucourt remained steadfastly in the king's court. He testified briefly at the **nullification proceedings**, telling about Joan's arrival at Chinon. He spoke favorably of her, attesting to her purity and chastity. **Jean Pasquerel** identified Jeanne de Preuilly, Gaucourt's wife at the time, as one of the women who oversaw one of the tests of Joan's **virginity** in March 1429.

Gaucourt's service for Charles VII ended with the king's death in 1461, and the new King **Louis XI** dismissed him from the court. Gaucourt died the next year.

GÉLU, JACQUES (C. 1376–1432). When Joan of Arc arrived in **Chinon** to meet with **Charles VII** (February 1429), the king sought opinions from theologians and experts including Jacques Gélu, the archbishop of Embrun.

Gélu was originally from Luxembourg and attended both the universities of Paris and Orléans, the latter from which he acquired a licentiate in **civil law**. In 1401, he served as counsel to Duke Louis I of Orléans, until the duke's assassination in 1407 (*See* FRENCH CIVIL WAR). In 1410, Gélu became counsel to future Charles VII. He participated in the **council** of Constance (1414–1418) where he was elected archbishop of Tours, and he helped elect Martin V as the new **pope**. He was present in **Paris** during the Burgundian takeover (1418), but he did not flee with Charles initially. Instead, Gélu remained through June, seeing many of his friends and colleagues massacred, eventually escaping on 16 June. From then on, he continued to advise Charles and also serve in diplomatic missions. In 1427, his archbishopric was transferred to Embrun.

It was natural for the king to turn to his seasoned counsel of nearly twenty years for advice on Joan of Arc. The original correspondence of Gélu to the king survived at least until the French Revolution (1789–1799). Today, it survives in seventeenth-century summaries. In four separate letters, Gelu's understanding of Joan evolved as did his opinion. Initially, Gélu only knew Joan was a girl from Lorraine with favorable predictions and prophecies for the king, and he was extremely suspect of Joan. As Gélu received more information, he learned that local theologians and experts in Chinon had found no evil in Joan, which eased his concern somewhat. He also learned of her male **clothing** and her desire to relieve the siege of **Orléans**. While Gélu admitted that God could use women for military victory just as he used men, there was still concern over possible treason and the devil. Treason was a concern, because Joan was from Lorraine, a region surrounded by Burgundy. As for the devil, he urged caution and patience. The longer they kept her waiting, no matter her prophecies or demands to fulfill them, the easier it would become to expose her true intentions. Some historians have theorized this sort of advice is what led directly to the **Poitiers** examination (11–22 March), meant not so much to determine if Joan was genuine through inquiry, but to keep her waiting and expose any evil through time.

Gélu later wrote an undated treatise entitled *De puella aurelianensi dissertatio* ("dissertation on the maid of Orléans"), which historians conclude was written between the victory at Orléans (8 May 1429) and the **coronation of Charles VII** (17 July). This treatise has survived along with a letter addressed directly to the king. By now Gélu's perspective had changed entirely in favor of Joan and her **mission**, which he surmised as defeating and expelling the king's enemies and restoring his kingdom. Gélu argued that male attire was a must if Joan were to live among soldiers and fight like a soldier. Furthermore, God could change and repurpose such laws as He saw fit. Gélu justified God's use of a woman in a traditional man's role in multiple ways, including 1 Corinthians 1:27: "But God chose the foolish things of the world to shame the wise; God chose the weak things of the world to shame the strong" (NIV). The use of Joan and her lowly background, which he emphasized, would further humiliate the English. He also evoked Deborah from the Bible, a female prophet who inspired the Israelites to victory. Although Joan's cause was war, Gélu saw it as justified, arguing that she did so with mercy and with the goal of seeing the king's divine authority upheld and peace restored. Finally, Gélu recommended that the king seek Joan's perspective and follow it, regardless if it seemed contrary to human wisdom (*See* TROYES, SIEGE OF), and to provide her with all the necessary instruments of war to carry out her mission. He again emphasized that time had and would continue to confirm Joan's legitimacy.

After the capture of Joan of Arc at **Compiègne** (23 May 1430), Gélu wrote the king and encouraged him to recover her at all costs, but no record of any attempt survives.

GERMANY. *See* HOLY ROMAN EMPIRE.

GERSON, JEAN (1363–1429). Jean Gerson was a prominent and prolific French theologian, and hundreds of his speeches, sermons, letters, poems, and treatises have survived today, including a widely distributed pamphlet voicing full-throated support of Joan of Arc.

Born in Rethel, thirty-five kilometers northeast of **Reims**, Gerson entered the **University of Paris** in 1377 at the age of fourteen where he would acquire his master's in arts and a doctorate in theology (*See* EDUCATION). He taught at the university for twenty-three years and briefly served as chancellor beginning in 1395. Gerson's life and career were affected by the crises of his day including the **Great Schism** and the **French Civil War**, and he embroiled himself in these issues. He made numerous attempts to reconcile the competing popes beginning in the 1390s before the crisis came to a head at the **council** of Constance (1414–1418) where he and the council members elected Martin V as the new **pope** in 1417.

After the assassination of Duke Louis I of Orléans sparked the French Civil War in 1407, Gerson argued against those who attempted to justify the act on the account of tyrannicide, taking his efforts to the Council of Constance. Duke John the Fearless of Burgundy was implicated in the plot, and he enlisted Gerson's peer, Jean Petit, to justify the act. At Constance, Gerson was able to secure a general condemnation against tyrannicide, but not explicitly against the killing of Orléans. Gerson left Constance on 17 May 1418, but he was unable to return to **Paris**, then controlled by the Burgundians and where many of his previous colleagues had been killed. He eventually settled in Lyons in southern France, under the protection of the **dauphin**, future **Charles VII**. Gerson remained there the rest of his days, continuing to write letters, treatises, and poems.

Among Gerson's numerous works included efforts to examine those claiming to experience divine **voices, visions, and revelations**. He was on record challenging the legitimacy of the revelations from Bridget of Sweden (1303–1373), questioning the reliability of women to act as conduits for God. Thus, when he wrote *Super facto puellae et credulitate sibi prae-*

standa, expressing his full support of Joan of Arc including her male **clothing** and short **hair** (18 May 1429), it was a widely distributed and much discussed piece.

Gerson died on 12 July 1429 while the **march to Reims** was still progressing.

GILLES DE RAIS. See RAIS, GILLES DE LAVAL, BARON OF.

GIRESME, NICOLAS DE (?–1466). Nicolas de Giresme was a knight of the Order of Saint John of Jerusalem, more commonly known today as the Hospitallers. There were few such knights in France at the time, and the mission of Giresme's order was the defense of the island of Rhodes against the Ottoman Turks. Loyal to **Charles VII**, he arrived at the siege of **Orléans** in September 1428 and was wounded on 21 October. The **bastard of Orléans** tells us that Giresme was there when they first met Joan on 29 April 1429. During the attack on the Tourelles (7 May), Giresme remained in the city to lead the defense. However, as Joan and others were making progress on the south side of the Tourelles, the defenders of Orléans toiled to create a passable span across the damaged bridge on the Loire River from the north. According to the *Journal du siège d'Orléans*, Giresme was the first to cross the makeshift bridge and led the attack, further overwhelming the English defenders.

Giresme remained loyal to Charles, and historians theorize he likely participated in the **Loire Campaign** and the **march to Reims**, but there is no record. He later became captain of Melun (1430), captain of Provins (1436), and the grand **prior** of France for his order (c. 1450).

GLASDALE, WILLIAM (?–1429). Based on what survives in muster rolls, we know that William Glasdale rose through the ranks of the English army first as an archer under the **earl of Salisbury** in a 1417 expedition in France to captain of the garrison at Fresnay in 1426. By the siege of **Orléans**, he had considerable campaigning experience, having fought at **Cravant** (1423), **Verneuil** (1424), the expedition to Anjou (1425), the siege of Pontorson (1427), and the recapture of Le Mans (1428), all of which were English-Burgundian victories over French and Scottish forces in France.

It is at Orléans that he is most remembered, as he was placed in command of the captured Tourelles bastille, south of the Loire River. In May 1429, Glasdale confidently and infamously hurled verbal insults at Joan of Arc from the Tourelles, calling her a "whore," "bitch," and "tart," depending on the source and translation. Both the **bastard of Orléans** and **Jean Pasquerel** would testify that she endured verbal abuse from the English defenders. During the French assault on the Tourelles on 7 May, Glasdale and other Englishmen attempted to retreat but drowned when the bridge from the tower collapsed into the **Loire River**. Pasquerel later claimed Joan wept for Glasdale's soul. His body was recovered, identified, cut up, and boiled. The bones were on display in Paris for several days before being sent off to England for burial.

English-speaking historians often refer to Glasdale as "Sir William Glasdale," but he was never officially knighted. Surviving muster roles explicitly list him as an "esquire" (*See* SQUIRE). This trend of erroneously knighting Glasdale dates back to Shakespeare, whose fictional portrayal of Sir William Glansdale in *Henry VI* was based on Glasdale. See also KNIGHT.

GODDAM. The term *goddam*, sometimes spelled *goddon*, *godon*, or *godam*, was a nickname for English soldiers, popular in the fifteenth century among the French. The term was used to denote the supposed English propensity for using profanity. Joan of Arc is recorded as having used the term at least twice, the latter of which incensed **Humphrey Stafford** so much that he had to be stopped from stabbing her. To the modern eye, this appears to go against Joan's admonishments against **profanity**, but the word itself was not recorded as profane until the seventeenth century when it was more closely associated with "goddamn."

GORKUM, HENRY OF (C. 1378–1431). Henry of Gorkum was a Dutch theologian born in Utrecht. He enrolled in the **University of Paris** where he received his master's in arts and began his training in theology. In 1420, he enrolled in the University of Cologne where he received his doctorate in theology and became a professor there. Among his numerous treatises were works on war, the Hussites, and Joan of Arc. The latter, *De quadam puella*, survives today and served to present open-ended questions on Joan, both from a positive and negative viewpoint.

GRAVERENT, JEAN. Jean Graverent, a **friar** with a master's in theology from the **University of Paris** (*See* EDUCATION), was the grand inquisitor of France, a position he had held since 1425. On 16 August 1429, the day after the French and English stalemate at **Montépilloy**, Graverent was among those in Paris who swore a loyalty oath to the **duke of Bedford**, the **regent** of English-occupied France.

As the highest-ranking inquisitor in France in 1431, Bishop **Pierre Cauchon** naturally sought Graverent's involvement in the **condemnation trial** of Joan of Arc, as it was standard for a local bishop and an inquisitor to partner on an **inquisition**. However, he was involved in another trial, and he instead appointed Vice Inquisitor **Jean Le Maistre** as his representative. This seemingly lackluster interest into the most notorious prisoner in France at the time has led some historians to theorize that perhaps Graverent somehow tried to distance himself from what he perceived as a show trial, but this is purely speculative. On 4 July 1431, the author of the *Journal d'un bourgeois de Paris* recorded how an inquisitor of the faith, most likely Graverent, preached a fiery sermon, outlining the case against Joan. He also condemned the heretical **Friar Richard** and his so-called followers such as Joan. Lumping Joan with Richard was an easy guilt-by-association approach to cast more doubt on her while also adding further support for her **execution**.

GREAT SCHISM. The Great Schism, sometimes more specifically called the Western Schism, refers to the period between 1378 and 1417 when there were at least two, and sometimes three, men claiming to be the **pope** of the Catholic Church. For nearly thirty years, these lines of the papacy established their own administrations, appointed their own **bishops**, and garnered support from opposing churches and monarchies. **Canon law** and **theology** scholars were particularly invested in ending the schism or at least propping up their pope of choice. For example, in 1407, the **University of Paris** sent a delegation headed by **Pierre Cauchon** to ask Pope Benedict XIII and Pope Gregory XII to renounce their claim to the papacy. The Schism came to a head at the **council** of Constance (1414–1418) with the resignation of one pope, the deposing of two others, and finally, the election of Pope Martin V in 1417. *See also* SCHISMATIC.

GRESSART, PERRINET (?–1438). Perrinet Gressart was a warlord, likely from Picardy, who fought for and against **Charles VII**, the dukes of Burgundy (*See* PHILIP THE GOOD), and the English. He came from a working-class family, not nobility. His birth year is unknown, but he appears in surviving military records as early as 1416, serving under Burgundy. In 1422, Burgundy captured La Charité on the Loire River, and it is likely that Gressart was among the troops. However, forces of Charles VII recaptured the city later that year. In 1423, Gressart was among the victorious Burgundians at **Cravant**. La Charité was again captured, and this time, Philip the Good appointed Gressart as captain of the city.

La Charité became the central hub of Gressart's operations for the next twelve years, and all his major campaigns and disputes were waged over and from this city. In 1424, the **truce of Chambéry** between Charles and Philip called for the transfer of La Charité to Charles. Gressart refused. In the dispute, Philip stopped paying Gressart. The captain responded by declaring that he did not hold La Charité for the Burgundians, but for the English, playing the dukes of **Bedford** and Burgundy off each other. Gressart's other methods for acquiring wealth became raiding nearby towns in **Berry**, including Nevers, or through **ransoms**, as he did with the capture of **Georges de La Trémoille** (c. 1427).

Still, the French and Burgundians tried negotiating with Gressart, offering him money and three different towns if he agreed to abandon La Charité. He finally agreed on 3 January

1427, but Philip intervened, asking La Charité to be handed to the Burgundians instead of Charles. Then Philip gave the town *back* to Gressart, ensuring the warlord kept La Charité and the newly acquired towns from the negotiation. This may have been Philip's attempt to regain Gressart's loyalty after he had declared it for Bedford, but Gressart continued to declare his loyalty to the English.

After Joan of Arc's failed siege of **Paris** (8 September 1429), she was sent against the strongholds of Perrinet Gressart. It is purely conjecture as to why, but historians often theorize that the advisors of Charles wanted to keep her war-hungry zeal occupied while pointing her at a worthwhile target. And Georges de La Trémoille would not have forgiven his stint as a hostage of Gressart. Regardless, Joan and **Charles d'Albret** besieged **Saint-Pierre-le-Moutier**, south of La Charité, capturing it on 4 November 1429. The victory depleted their resources, and Joan's surviving **letter to the people of Riom (9 November 1429)** requested gunpowder and other supplies. At least **Orléans** and **Bourges** are recorded as answering the call. Still, they failed to capture La Charité after a month-long siege (24? November–23? December), eventually leaving and abandoning all their artillery and supplies.

Gressart continued his raids from La Charité over the years, expanding his territory, and continually reaping rewards from the English and the Burgundians, often at the cost of France. Bedford placed him in command of the forces in Berry where he raided regularly. In 1434, Philip appointed him captain of Nevers.

In 1435, Gressart remained resistant to Philip's overtures of a peace with Charles. He continued to refer to **Henry VI** as the king of France. With the signing of the **Treaty of Arras** (21 September), he remained resistant. It was not until 22 November, when Charles agreed to recognize Gressart's current territorial possessions, that he made peace with France. Gressart was appointed royal captain of La Charité along with other positions including the captain of Nevers, receiving payments from both France and Burgundy. From this point, Gressart essentially retired from active military service, eventually dying in 1438.

Gressart is one of the more unique foes of Joan of Arc. He was a mercenary in every sense of the word, but managed to slice out a portion of territory, which kept him localized like a regional warlord. His loyalties and demands only went so far, and it was possible to buy his obedience. However, he was skilled at staying in power himself while also extracting money from the disputing powers around him. While Joan managed to capture one of his strongholds, La Charité proved too formidable for her and her army.

GREY, JOHN. *See* ROLES AND RESPONSIBILITIES.

GROUCHET, RICHARD DE (C. 1392–?). An assessor at Joan of Arc's **condemnation trial** (1431), Richard Grouchet had acquired a master of arts and a bachelor in theology (*See* EDUCATION). He attended most of the public sessions of the trial (21 February–3 March) and rendered a joint opinion on the **twelve articles** of accusation formally brought against Joan (2 April). Along with two other assessors, Grouchet "insist[ed] as before that a formal answer would require certainty about the origin of the alleged revelations" (Hobbins 2005, 166), arguing they could not definitively determine if Joan's **voices, visions, and revelations** were genuine, good, or evil. Regardless, he eventually agreed that if Joan did not submit to the **Church Militant**, then she should be deemed a **heretic** (19 May), and he later voted to hand her over to secular authorities after her supposed **relapse** (29 May).

In his 1452 testimony during the **nullification proceedings**, Grouchet painted himself and other assessors sympathetically and claimed his opinion on the twelve articles upset **Pierre Cauchon**. He also described how the notaries (*See* ROLES) of the trial were verbally abused but still toiled to record Joan's statements accurately. With Joan, he was impressed with her ability to answer difficult questions at such a young age.

GUARDS OF JOAN OF ARC AT ROUEN. *See* ROLES AND RESPONSIBILITIES.

GUNS. *See* ARTILLERY.

H

HAIR. Joan of Arc made two decisions with her hair that would have shocked people in fifteenth-century France. First, she cut her hair in a pageboy style—that is, shaved around the ears and the nape of the neck with the remaining hair cut in a bowl shape, making a cap of sorts. Second, she did not wear head coverings, or she at least did not wear them often, so that people took note of her unique hairstyle. Women in fifteenth-century France wore head coverings in nearly all situations, and social events had seen the rise of ornate headdresses. Many women went so far as to cut or shave the portions of their head that might extend outside their coverings, ensuring that no strand of hair was exposed in public.

Joan adopted her short hairstyle along with male **clothing** for her journey from **Vaucouleurs** to **Chinon**, to disguise herself as a page while traveling through Burgundian territory. Joan continued to maintain this hairstyle, and historians theorize that, like her clothing, it was for practical reasons. Wearing men's clothing with long hair while among the army could have associated Joan with **camp followers**, whom she drove away. It also may have been too disconcerting to don a headdress while wearing men's clothing or armor. Her unique style emphasized her new persona as *la Pucelle*, which further disassociated her from the class of a mere peasant girl.

Joan's hair was a point of contention during her **condemnation trial** (1431), only overshadowed by her donning men's clothing. This is best illustrated in Article 12 of the initial **seventy articles** of accusation brought against her, which describes how she "cast aside all women's clothing and had her hair cut round [in a bowl shape], like a young man's" (Hobbins 2005, 129). Most of the article focuses on Joan's clothing, which they believed to be indecent, and they quoted scripture to support their stance. The same accusation was coupled with her general appearance in Article 5 of the condensed **twelve articles**, which accused Joan of "leaving nothing about her to indicate the female sex except what nature gave to distinguish her sex" (Hobbins 2005, 159).

Unlike her choice of clothing, the assessors at Joan's trial never questioned her about *why* she cut her hair in this style, but they did admonish her for it. It was always a secondary point mentioned in conjunction with her clothes. For example, on 2 May 1431, when **Jean de Châtillon** evoked her clothing, he described it as "scandalous and against good and decent manners," then adding that she "also has her hair cut round" (Hobbins 2005, 173). He then evoked Apostle Paul that women should cover their heads (1 Cor. 11:5–15). Among the numerous sins listed in Joan's **abjuration** (24 May), she confessed she had her "hair cut round like a man's, against all virtue of the female sex" (Hobbins 2005, 192). After her abjuration, Joan shaved her head, likely to signify she had abandoned her male hairstyle and would grow her hair anew.

Historians typically cite two pieces of evidence to conclude Joan of Arc's hair was possibly black. There is one contemporary description in the Registrar of La Rochelle in western France that describes her with round, black hair. The entry also quotes Joan's **letter to the English (22 March 1429)** in full, but the clerk who made the entry never saw her in person. It is possible he learned of this from someone who had seen her. In 1849, Jules Quicherat claimed to have found a single strand of black hair in the seal on her **letter to the people of Riom (9 November 1429)**. The seal and strand of hair have since been lost.

HENRY V, KING OF ENGLAND (1386–1422).

The man who would become Henry V was born 16 September 1386, the firstborn son of Henry of Derby. In 1389, Henry of Derby deposed his cousin, King Richard II, to become King Henry IV of England. Two days later, the firstborn son of Henry IV was made Prince of Wales, the heir to the English throne. The prince gained military experience from a young age, fighting in Ireland in 1389 where he was knighted, and then in Wales in 1400. In 1412, the warring factions of the **French Civil War** appealed to England to aid their causes. While the prince of Wales differed with the king on which side to choose, the death of Henry IV in 1413 made the prince King Henry V of England.

Henry V immediately sought a policy of demanding lands in **Normandy** and the marriage of **Catherine of Valois**, daughter of French King **Charles VI**. Neither of the French factions were willing to meet his demands, and Henry invaded Normandy on 14 August 1415 (*See* HUNDRED YEARS WAR). After capturing Harfleur, Henry determined to march his army to Calais in order to depart France. The much larger French army harassed his march, eventually forcing a battle at Agincourt on 25 October. The English decimated the French nobility in a surprising and dominating victory.

In October 1416, Henry was finally able to meet with Duke John the Fearless of Burgundy to begin negotiations for an alliance. John continued his campaign against the opposing faction in the French Civil War, capturing Paris in May 1418. Although John was prepared to bring peace in the civil war, he was assassinated in September 1419, leaving his son, **Philip the Good**, the new duke of Burgundy. With the dauphin (*See* CHARLES VII) implicated in the assassination, both Philip and Charles VI were open to negotiations with England. The result was the **Treaty of Troyes (1420)**, which disinherited the dauphin from the French throne, led to the marriage of Henry and Catherine (2 June), and made their firstborn son the future king of France.

Henry and Catherine traveled to England for Catherine's coronation as queen of England (23 February 1421). While Henry was away, his brother, Duke Thomas of Clarence, died fighting at the battle of **Baugé** (22 March), a victory for the dauphin's army. Henry returned to Normandy to restart his campaigns on 10 June. During the siege of Meaux (October 1421–May 1422), his son (*See* HENRY VI) was born (6 December 1421). However, Henry V contracted dysentery during the siege and died on 31 August 1422. With the death of Charles VI on 22 October, the infant Henry VI was too young to rule, and his uncle, the **duke of Bedford**, acted as **regent** of France.

Although Henry V died at the young age of thirty-five and only spent seven years campaigning in France, his efforts established the tumultuous period that followed before the arrival of Joan of Arc. Her **mission** was to expel the English from France and restore the kingdom to Charles VII, undoing the work of Henry V.

HENRY VI, KING OF ENGLAND AND FRANCE (1421–1471).

Henry VI was born on 6 December 1421, a result of the **Treaty of Troyes (1420)**, which led to the marriage of his parents, **Henry V** and **Catherine of Valois**. The untimely death of his father on 31 August 1422 followed by the death of his grandfather, **Charles VI**, on 21 October, left the infant the titular king of both England and France. **Henry Beaufort**, bishop of Winchester and granduncle of Henry VI, led the royal council in England on behalf of the infant king. The **duke of Bedford**, his uncle, ruled as **regent** of France. Meanwhile, his disinherited half-brother, **Charles VII**, was declared king of France. Thus, the events in the **Hundred Years War** and the **French Civil War** played out in the 1420s while Henry VI was not yet actively ruling.

With the lifting of the siege of **Orléans** (8 May 1429) and other French military successes leading to the **coronation of Charles VII** in Reims (17 July), the duke of Bedford pushed for Henry's coronation as king of France on the continent. A coronation ceremony was held for Henry as king of England in the Westminster Abbey on 6 November 1429. Henry was brought to France on 23 April 1430 but traveled to **Rouen** instead of **Paris** on 29 July due to security concerns. He was present in Rouen during Joan of Arc's **condemnation trial** and **execution** (30 May 1431), but he was likely spared the scene of the latter. There is no recorded interaction between the two of them.

On 16 December 1431, Henry, just ten years old, was coronated in Paris as king of France. He left France in January 1432, and he never saw it again.

Numerous letters were sent on behalf of Henry by Beaufort and Bedford regarding Joan of Arc's transfer to the English and announcing her demise. Joan addressed Henry directly in her **letter to the English (22 March 1429)**. During her condemnation trial (14 March 1431), Joan shared that **Saint Catherine** told her that while in captivity by **John of Luxembourg** she would see the king of England and would be handed over to the English, to which she told the saint she would rather die.

Henry did not truly take power until 1437, well after the **Anglo-Burgundian Alliance** had crumbled (1435). He tried to protect his remaining holdings in France in 1445 by wedding Margaret of Anjou, daughter of **René of Anjou** and niece of **Marie of Anjou**. However, the war with France was rekindled in 1449 and by 1453, all English possessions in France, save for Calais, were lost. That same year, Henry began exhibiting the same mental illness that plagued his grandfather, Charles VI. Henry faced civil war in England and was deposed in 1461. He returned to the throne briefly in October 1470 before being deposed again in April 1471, dying in the Tower of London the following month.

HERALDRY. See COAT OF ARMS.

HERETIC. A heretic was a person ostensibly holding a view contrary to fundamental beliefs of the Catholic Church and who had rebuffed correction from church authority. The term originally described those who lost heated theological debates at the earliest **councils**, dating back to the Roman Empire. These heretics would lose their finances, property, and their churches. Throughout the Middle Ages, the response to heretical views varied depending on the region and period. Some heretics continued to exist unmolested, and some successfully challenged the status quo, and yet others suffered mob violence.

Similarly, the church varied in its responses and up until the thirteenth century, the responsibility fell primarily on local **bishops** to deal with heretics. This changed in 1208 when Pope Innocent III initiated what would become known as the Albigensian Crusade, a two-decade prosecution of Cathars, a religious group in southern France. Afterward, the Church established the **inquisition** as a permanent institution. In fifteenth-century France, a reformed version of the inquisition was in place to empower local bishops and papal-appointed inquisitors to work together in order to ferret out heresy and other serious, public charges.

During Joan of Arc's **condemnation trial** (1431), which was an inquisition tribunal, the judges and assessors tiptoed around the term heresy and whether to label Joan a heretic, as opposed to just an **apostate**, **idolator**, or **schismatic**, the latter two of which could easily lead to heresy. When the assessors presented their initial **seventy articles** of accusation against Joan on 27 and 28 March, they introduced them by proclaiming that Joan was "a heretic, or at least greatly suspect of heresy" (Hobbins 2005, 124). Articles 3 and 66 describe how some of her actions and words were heretical or encouraged heresy. Joan was recorded as denying these charges and proclaiming she supported the Church.

When the judges and assessors condensed the rough draft of accusations into **twelve articles** (5 April), all mentions of heresy were gone. However, the judges and assessors, as well as the **University of Paris**, still rendered their opinions on whether Joan was an apostate, idolater, schismatic, and/or a heretic, and to what degree. Some believed there was a suspicion of heresy and the possibility she might lapse into heresy. Most used the term sparingly and then typically only to warn Joan throughout the trial that her words were heretical. On May 2, **Jean de Châtillon** told her some of her statements had already earned her the label "heretic" and would result in execution by fire, but she remained defiant.

Upon her **relapse**, the judges and assessors lost all inhibition against the term, labeling her a relapsed heretic. In reading her final sentence, the judges spoke of the deadly poison of heresy. They were willing to accept her **abjuration** against the charges of being an apostate, idolater, and schismatic, but now, because of her obstinance, she had turned to heresy.

At the **nullification proceedings** (1450–1456), the judges determined that Joan was never truly a schismatic, as demonstrated by her multiple appeals to the **pope**. While she may have sinned or at least erred, she did not sin against the faith. Thus, she never fell into the heresy of holding obstinate counterviews to the Church's basic beliefs. And if there was no heresy, her abjuration was meaningless. Similarly, if she never lapsed, then she could never relapse.

HERRINGS, BATTLE OF THE (12 FEBRUARY 1429). The battle of the Herrings was fought near the town of Rouvray, twenty-two kilometers northwest of **Orléans**, between an English convoy and Franco-Scottish forces on 12 February 1429. The battle was a major English victory, demoralizing **Charles VII** and the inhabitants of Orléans. It also marked the last major offensive by the French to relieve the siege of **Orléans** before the arrival of Joan of Arc at the city on 29 April.

During the siege of Orléans, both the English and French were able to receive reinforcements and supplies seemingly unhindered. After a series of unsuccessful sorties from Orléans by the French, a plan was made to attack a supply convoy from **Paris** before it reached the English. Although sizes vary somewhat in different sources, **Monstrelet** tells us that the convoy was led by **John Fastolf** and made up of five hundred wagons, sixteen hundred soldiers, and another one thousand non-combatants. While near the town of Rouvray, Fastolf received word from scouts that an attack was imminent. He arranged his convoy on an open field, building an enclosure with his wagons with two openings that were guarded by archers.

The French were led by the **count of Clermont**, who commanded around three thousand to four thousand troops. Among his forces were **La Hire** and the **bastard of Orléans**. The Scots were commanded by John Stewart of Darnley. When the Franco-Scottish forces arrived on the field, the English were already waiting in their defensive formation. Clermont had himself been knighted along with others, and Monstrelet tells us the Franco-Scottish forces waited two hours before attacking.

The Franco-Scottish force opened with an artillery bombardment, which destroyed some of the wagons. As the leaders debated on when and how to attack, it is possible that Stewart decided to attack out of frustration, leading his dismounted Scots across the field. The Scots were decimated by the archers' arrows and retreated. Clermont sent a cavalry charge, which was disoriented and also repelled. The English chased the retreating army, causing more casualties. The bastard of Orléans was wounded in the foot. The casualty numbers vary, but most agree few English were hurt, while the Franco-Scottish forces suffered three hundred to seven hundred dead, mostly Scots including John Stewart.

While Joan of Arc was still trying to convince **Robert de Baudricourt** in **Vaucouleurs** to send her to meet Charles VII, the *Journal du siège d'Orléans* credits Joan with predicting the plight at the Herrings. This is often identified as one of her revelations, but with no confirming eyewitnesses, this was likely a romanticized rumor (*See* VOICES, VISIONS, AND REVELATIONS). Historians also identify the battle as an impetus that made Charles more receptive to listening to Joan's demands that she be used in the war against the English.

Although the medieval sources refer to this as the battle of Rouvray, they also use the nickname the "battle of the Herrings," which was coined by the people of Rouvray who found an ample supply of salted fish left behind by the victors. Modern historians typically follow suit, but some historians insist on calling it Rouvray while also mentioning its nickname. *See also* FRANCO-SCOTTISH ALLIANCE.

HOLY ROMAN EMPIRE. The Holy Roman Empire dates back to the coronation of Emperor Otto I (912–973) by Pope John XII. Controlling what was much of modern Germany and parts of eastern France, the empire claimed lineages back to Emperor Charlemagne (747–814) and the Roman Empire. Although its power was waning in the fifteenth century, the presence of the Holy Roman Empire on the frontiers of **Burgundy** and France, especially on the duchy of **Lorraine**, loomed heavily during the time of Joan of Arc. Multiple registers of the empire's cities from this period record some of the exploits of Joan including her **march to Reims**. There is a positive tone toward Joan in these writings and those that followed, likely due to the expansionist policy of **Philip the Good** that encroached into the empire. A register of Holy Roman Emperor Sigismund (1368–1437) preserved a copy of **Joan's letter to the Hussites (23 March 1430).**

The rebellion of the Hussites in Bohemia led to the creation of a crusader army from England under the direction of **Henry Beaufort** (1429). However, this army was commandeered by the **duke of Bedford** after the **coronation of Charles VII**, and it was present in the Anglo-Burgundian ranks during the standoff at **Montépilloy** (15 August), never making it to Bohemia.

HOLY TRINITY OF FÉCAMP. *See* DUREMORT, GILLES DE.

HORSES. In less than two years, Joan of Arc received numerous horses throughout her campaigns, and some estimates have her covering as much as five thousand kilometers on horseback. Her equestrian experience was more than simple transport. Eyewitnesses and chroniclers describe Joan on horseback and in full armor carrying her **standard**, jousting, fording rivers, charging into battle, retreating, riding wounded, and, finally, being captured. There are contemporary descriptions of her calming horses, mounting, dismounting, turning around, curvetting, speeding up, and slowing down on battlefields, among excited crowds, at night, and while incognito. Even her detractors attested to her skill with horses, and the assessors at her **condemnation trial** (1431) included horseback riding in the list of articles brought against her.

Although some historians theorize that Joan may have encountered and learned to ride horses while on her father's farm, this is unconfirmed. It is just as likely her father (*See* ARC, JACQUES D') employed oxen for plowing. The assessors at Joan's condemnation trial seized on her horseback riding and in Article 8 of the original **seventy articles** brought against her declared that she learned to ride and use weapons at a young age while in **Neufchâteau**, frequenting an inn that often housed soldiers and mercenaries. Joan never answered this accusation directly other than to say she was in the town but a few days. Elsewhere, she claimed she knew nothing of riding when she first encountered her **voices**.

The earliest documented horse given to Joan came from the **duke of Lorraine**. While in **Vaucouleurs**, **Robert de Baudricourt** also paid for a horse for Joan for her eleven-day trek to **Chinon** to meet **Charles VII**. Historians theorize that **Jean de Metz** and **Bertrand de Poulengy** provided on-the-job training during the journey, as both of them were **squires** and experienced equestrians. Early in her story, Joan never seemed to be lacking in horses, and, in addition to the duke of Lorraine and Baudricourt, there are records of the dukes of **Alençon** and **Brittany**, and of course, the king, giving her horses. At her condemnation trial, Joan explained that she only asked the king for good horses and weapons and enough money to pay her entourage. She revealed that the king provided five chargers and an additional seven hacks, a common ensemble for a wealthy **knight** or squire. This would have also included men to care for the horses. As for which horse Joan was riding during her capture at **Compiègne**, Joan said she rode upon a demi-charger, meaning something in between a charger typically used on the battlefield and a smaller hackney typically used for transport.

Joan's skill with horses comes through in multiple accounts. While marching into **Orléans** among a crowd, one of the eager onlookers carrying a torch accidentally lit Joan's pennon on fire that was carried by a bearer behind her (*See* STANDARD). The *Journal du siège d'Orléans* tells us that Joan quickly turned around on horseback and rushed over to the scene to extinguish the fire. When fighting began outside the city without her, Joan is described as commandeering a page's horse to get to the action. The **Laval Letter (8 June 1429)** recounts a story of Joan calming a rambunctious horse by moving it in front of a church. The author saw it as a divine moment, but it was likely Joan was simply moving the horse to a calmer spot, a common equestrian tactic.

Although contemporaries were amazed at Joan's endurance on horseback while in full armor—she rarely dismounted while on campaign—her body paid the price. Upon an examination to confirm her **virginity** at her condemnation trial, the examiners found Joan's buttocks were injured due to riding, most likely exhibiting what modern equestrian athletes refer to as saddle sores. There is also an incident recorded in the *Chronique de la Pucelle* when Joan dismounted her horse and stepped on a **caltrop**, **injuring** her foot.

Such equestrian activity was uncommon for women during this period in France, and several chroniclers such as **Monstrelet** noted this fact. In addition, although Joan's family was by no means poor, they lacked the wealth to maintain the horses and equipment necessary for Joan to have gained these skills. Yet, although she is remembered and often depicted on horseback by both her supporters and detractors, she does not appear to have made any real cavalry charges in battle. She was not at the frontlines of **Patay**, she did not have the opportunity to charge at **Montépilloy**, and the details of **Lagny** do not confirm that she was among the cavalry charges, if there were any. Instead, Joan's exploits in the thick of battle were often performed on foot or on a **ladder**.

Joan's final experience with horses came on the day of her **execution** when she was drawn by horses to the stake.

HOUPPEVILLE, NICOLAS DE (C. 1391–?). Nicolas de Houppeville was a native of **Rouen** with a bachelor's in theology and a master's of arts (*See* EDUCATION) when he was called to be an assessor at Joan of Arc's **condemnation trial** (1431). However, testimonies at the **nullification proceedings** confirm that Houppeville was vocal in his disapproval of the trial and thus did not participate. The stories vary, even in his own testimony, but all agree that he was adamant in his disapproval and suffered for it. In 1452, Houppeville testified that he complained to notary **Guillaume Colles**, who then shared the feedback with **Pierre Cauchon**, who then imprisoned Houppeville. He was only released upon the intervention of **Gilles de Duremort**. In his 1456 testimony, Houppeville portrayed himself as more heroic, stating that he complained directly to Cauchon before being imprisoned. This time, he was threatened with exile, but again, saved with the help of Duremort. Setting aside the differences in Houppeville's accounts, others present at the trial, such as **Guillaume Manchon**, **Jean Massieu**, **Martin Ladvenu**, and **Isembard de La Pierre**, all attested that Houppeville refused to participate in the trial and was in some level of danger for it—imprisonment, exile, or drowning.

He believed it was inappropriate that the judges of Joan of Arc were part of the opposing party, namely those in opposition to **Charles VII**. He also believed that questioning Joan was improper since she had already been questioned thoroughly by other theologians in **Poitiers** (March 1429). Joan evoked Poitiers several times when she did not want to rehash similar questions during her condemnation trial. Did these statements inspire Houppeville to make his principled stand, or at least gripe to Colles? It becomes difficult to assess, as Houppeville's name is not in any of the **tran-**

scripts of the trial, and therefore it is uncertain which sessions he attended before he quit and was imprisoned. As for Joan, Houppeville thought she was simple and ignorant of the law, and ill-equipped to defend herself. However, what little of the trial he witnessed led him to believe she demonstrated conviction. He hinted that she may have had spiritual support, but he did not elaborate.

HUNDRED YEARS WAR (1337–1453). The Hundred Years War is a post-medieval construct for a period of wars between England and France that focused predominantly on the French throne. As early as the late seventeenth century, historians identified 1337 as a starting point for a greater war, as it was the year French King Philip VI confiscated lands of English King Edward III on the European continent. The phrase "Hundred Years War" first appeared in the mid-nineteenth century in French (*La Guerre de cent ans*) in several popular histories, and it was then adopted by several English historians. The dates 1337 and 1453 were eventually settled as the beginning and end points, and by 1879, *Encyclopedia Britannica* included an entry for the war.

In the late twentieth century, historians began challenging these dates, pointing out that England and France fought wars for centuries before and after the traditional dates. The kings of England, and later Great Britain, continued to claim the French throne until 1800 when King George III dropped France from his title. In addition, the notion of the Hundred Years War focuses on England and France while ignoring or at least marginalizing all the other countries and duchies involved, including Scotland, the Holy Roman Empire, Iberia, and the Low Countries.

As for the traditional dating of the Hundred Years War, historians are not agreed on its phases. Some have argued for a simple two-phased approach, often grouping the wars up until **Henry V** as the first phase. Others have argued for three phases, but even these vary—one excluding the periods of relative peace (1337–1360, 1369–1389, and 1415–1453) and another encompassing all the years (1337–1360, 1360–1413, and 1413–1453). There is a four-phased approach of 1337–1360, 1369–1389, 1412–1428, and 1429–1453. It is clear that those living through these periods sometimes recognized there was a war greater than themselves, as found in the works of Froissart and others, but none of them appears to place any importance on the date range 1337 to 1453. These constructs are often academic in nature, and the uninitiated should simply recognize the framework employed by the historian in question.

Using the traditional dating of the Hundred Years War, the dispute began when Philip VI confiscated England's lands. Edward III invaded in 1339; by 1340, he declared himself king of England and France. In 1346, the English decisively defeated the French at the battle of Crécy, and the next year they captured Calais. In 1355, Edward's son and heir, the Black Prince, conducted *chevauchées* throughout southern France, a medieval term equivalent to "scorched earth," which razed crops and farms. This led to the English victory over the French army at Poitiers and the capture of French King John II (1356). **Battles**, **sieges**, and *chevauchées* continued until the Treaty of Calais in 1360. Hostilities began again in 1369, and the French recovered most of the land captured by the English save for Gascony and Calais. Another truce was declared in 1389 and extended again in 1396 for another twenty-eight years.

In 1407, the assassination of Duke Louis I of Orléans divided the French into two parties—**Armagnacs** and Burgundians—and marked the traditional beginning of the **French Civil War**. Both sides courted the English to help them in the war. English King Henry IV initially sent forces to aid the Armagnacs and Burgundians, but by 1415, the newly coronated Henry V had rekindled the English claims to the French throne, and he invaded. That year, he captured Harfleur and decisively defeated the French at Agincourt. Throughout 1417 to 1419, Henry conquered **Normandy**. Although the Armagnacs and the Burgundians tried to reconcile, the assassination of Duke John the Fearless of Burgundy created a new rift. **Philip the Good**, the new duke of Burgundy, allied with the English at the **Treaty of Troyes** (1420), which also declared Henry and his descendants heirs to the throne of France upon French King **Charles VI**'s death. Henry married **Catherine of Valois**, the daughter of Charles VI.

The disinherited **dauphin** (*See* CHARLES VII) did not recognize the treaty, and his forces defeated the English at **Baugé** in 1421, while Henry was in England for the coronation of Queen Catherine. Henry returned to France and continued his conquests, dying in 1422. The **duke of Bedford** became the regent of France while the nine-month-old **Henry VI** was too young to rule. He continued the war against Charles VII. Anglo-Burgundian forces decisively won the battle of **Cravant** (1423), French forces defeated the English at the battle of La Brossinière (1423), and English forces won at **Verneuil** (1424), all battles featuring men that Joan of Arc would later fight alongside or against. After the battle of Cravant, the English and Burgundians fought predominantly separate wars, the English focusing on territory south of Normandy and the Burgundians focusing on territories in the east. After **Salisbury's 1428 expedition**, the English and Burgundians controlled most of the cities north of the **Loire River** and besieged **Orléans**, the last of Charles's strongholds on the river.

This is where most histories of Joan of Arc begin their narratives of the war. On 29 April 1429, the arrival of Joan with reinforcements led to the lifting of the siege, the recapture of cities along the river during the **Loire Campaign** (10–18 June), and the French victory over the English at **Patay** (18 June). Charles VII then marched with his army northeast, capturing cities along the way, to **Reims** where they conducted his **coronation**. After an indecisive encounter at **Montépilloy** (15 August) and a failed attempt at capturing **Paris** (8 September), Charles ended his direct participation in campaigns for that year. However, sieges and battles continued on a smaller scale, and Joan was in armies that successfully besieged **Saint-Pierre-le-Moutier** in the south, but failed to capture **La Charité** before the end of 1429. In the spring of 1430, Joan won the battle of **Lagny** against Burgundians, but she was captured outside **Compiègne** (23 May), which the Burgundians were besieging. The siege of Compiègne was not lifted until 25 October. On 16 December 1431, Henry VI was coronated as king of France in Paris.

The French Civil War officially ended in 1435 with the **Treaty of Arras**. The next year, the French retook Paris. French forces slowly retook cities from the English, completing their conquests of Normandy in 1450 and Gascony in 1451. The French won the last major battle at Castillon in 1453, marking the traditional end of the war.

Joan of Arc is often presented as the turning point in the Hundred Years War, though many historians dispute this notion. Although her brief military career was involved in curbing the Anglo expansion past the Loire River, the Treaty of Arras was not signed until four years after her execution, and the major conquests of Normandy and Gascony occurred several decades later. Other historians split the difference and argue that she at least stemmed the tide of Anglo expansion.

HUSSITES. See LETTER TO THE HUSSITES (23 MARCH 1430).

I

IDOLATER. The accusation of idolatry, the worship of something other than God, was typically wrapped up in the greater charges of being an **apostate**, **schismatic**, or **heretic**. However, it was tossed around at Joan of Arc's **condemnation trial** (1431) often in the same way that someone might deem something as "evil" or "offensive."

After reviewing the **twelve articles** of accusation brought against Joan, the **University of Paris** labeled her an idolater or described her as prone to idolatry. For example, they believed it was idolatrous for her to cut her **hair** short and wear men's **clothing** while also receiving the Eucharist. They believed her refusal to stop wearing men's clothing was tantamount to worshipping herself. Similarly, she was labeled an idolater for how she claimed she reacted to seeing Saints **Michael**, **Catherine**, and **Margaret**, specifically kneeling, removing her cap, embracing them, kissing them and the ground beneath their feet, evoking their names, believing them without seeking council from the Church, and swearing her **virginity** to them. The university further deemed these saints to be demons.

After her **execution**, letters from **Henry VI** and the University of Paris reemphasized the accusation that she was an idolater.

During the **nullification trial** (1450–1456), there was an emphasis on the fact that there was no official **canon law** against seeing or speaking with angels and saints, and since she believed them to be good in nature, she was not idolatrous. *See also* INQUISITION; VOICES.

ILLIERS, FLORENT D' (1400–1475). Son of Pierre d'Illiers, Florent succeeded his father after his death as captain of Châdeaudun in 1424. He married Jeanne de Coutes in 1422, the older sister of **Louis de Coutes**. Illiers arrived at the siege of **Orléans** on 28 April 1429 with reinforcements. He was alongside the **bastard of Orléans** the next day to greet Joan of Arc upon her arrival. He then took part in the relief of the siege, earning renown according to the *Journal du siège d'Orléans*. After the siege, he returned to Châdeaudun, but joined up with the royal army again to take part in the **Loire Campaign** (10–18 June). He continued to serve the king as adviser and **chamberlain**, and militarily under **Thibaud de Terms** and the bastard of Orléans.

ILLITERACY OF JOAN OF ARC. *See* LITERACY OF JOAN OF ARC.

INJURIES OF JOAN OF ARC. Joan of Arc suffered injuries on multiple occasions during her military campaigns and her time in **captivity**. The first recorded injury came on 6 May 1429 at **Orléans** when Joan stepped on a **caltrop**, possibly while dismounting from her horse. The event is briefly mentioned in the *Chronique de la Pucelle* after the day's fighting, and Joan retired for the day due to the injury and fatigue. No other chronicles mention the incident nor do any of Joan's companions, indicating that it was likely superficial and certainly overshadowed by her later injuries.

The next day (7 May), Joan suffered her most famous injury: an arrow or bolt, likely from a crossbow. Modern historians vary on the wound's location only because the eyewitnesses vary, but while **Jean Pasquerel** tells us the arrow was above her breast and the **bastard of Orléans** places it six inches deep between her neck and shoulder, Joan herself explained at her **condemnation trial** (1431) that it was in her neck. Pasquerel and the bastard differ on what happened next, but the former tells us that Joan was afraid and weeping, still lucid enough to refuse magical charms from her companions in arms. Instead, she settled for a traditional dressing of olive oil and pig's grease. After confessing, Joan returned to the battle. The bastard claimed she never left the fighting because of the wound, only breaking much later for a prayer, but when she returned with her **standard**, the English were struck with fear. Joan tells us that it took fifteen days for the wound to heal, but she continued to campaign despite it.

During her condemnation trial, Joan also testified that she knew in advance she would be wounded at Orléans and that she had shared this knowledge with **Charles VII**, but not with her companions in arms. Jean Pasquerel, who was not a soldier, claimed she had told him about her impending wound the day before. Another oft-cited source of this prediction comes in the form of a surviving letter from the Lord of Rotseläer, the head of a Burgundian delegation in France who claimed Joan had predicted her wounding at Orléans. The original letter is undated, but Edmond de Dynter (c. 1370–1449) provides a date of 22 April 1429. A canon of Saint Peter's chapel in Leuven and a secretary to several dukes including **Philip the Good**, Dynter copied the letter in full and provided the date in his lengthy Latin chronicle on Burgundy, dedicated to Philip around 1445. Joan's claim that she knew of her impending wound at Orléans disturbed her assessors, as she claimed the knowledge came from Saints **Catherine** and **Margaret**. In Article 33 of the initial **seventy articles** brought against Joan at her condemnation trial, her assessors attacked her claims to know the future, citing this incident.

Joan's next recorded injury came on the second day of the battle of **Jargeau** (12 June 1429). While scaling a **ladder**, a rock hit her in the head and knocked her to the ground. The **duke of Alençon** tells us she remained lucid and stood up to rally the troops.

If Joan's arrow in the neck at Orléans remains her most famous wound today, then her wounding at **Paris** (8 September 1429) was the most discussed by her contemporaries. During the assault on the city, a crossbow bolt struck Joan in the thigh, which took her out of the battle and seemingly ended the assault for the day. The story of the wound appears in most of the surviving contemporary chronicles that tell of Joan including the *Journal du siège d'Orléans* and *Chronique de la Pucelle*, as well as chronicles by **Jean Chartier**, **Jean de Warvin**, **Perceval de Cagny**, and **Monstrelet**. In addition, **Clément de Fauquembergue** and the author of the *Journal d'un bourgeois de Paris*, both inhabitants of the city during the assault, record the incident. The accounts vary, each providing a more dramatic scene than the next. The *Bourgeois de Paris* relished how the crossbow bolt went straight through Joan's thigh, forcing her to retreat. Monstrelet and Wavrin tell how she was left behind in a moat while the rest of the troops retreated, leaving her there until nightfall. Cagny tells us that a wounded Joan cried out loudly from the moat for the attack to continue while the army retreated. They dragged her from the moat against her will. The significance of Joan's wound at Paris is attested to in the later writings of **Pope** Pius II who reflected that it broke the mystique around Joan, proving she was not invincible. At her trial, Joan claimed her wound at Paris took but five days to heal.

Joan's next recorded injury came during her attempted **escape** from captivity at a tower in Beaurevoir, most likely in October 1430. During her condemnation trial, her assessors pressed her on the incident, asking why she jumped from the tower and whether she blasphemed God when she was injured. She claimed she tried to escape because she learned the English were coming to take her from the Burgundians and that she never blasphemed. Regardless, Article 47 of the initial seventy articles brought against her recounted the incident and her blaspheming as fact.

Also among the initial articles was Article 51 that attacked Joan for claiming that during each of her injuries, she was always comforted by Saints Catherine and Margaret. They accused her of fabricating her encounters with saints. The legend of Saint Catherine includes the story of how angels comforted her after torture sessions, a tale possibly known to Joan.

It is probable that Joan suffered other injuries. Her desire to keep pressing on in the heat of battle or campaigning while healing demonstrates her ability to tolerate pain and discomfort. Wearing her heavy suit of armor and riding on horseback surely presented other opportunities for injuries, and while in captivity of the English, they discovered she suffered from saddle sores (*See* HORSES). **Jean d'Aulon** later claimed he had seen Joan's bare legs while dressing her wounds on several occasions, which could have included her wound at Paris, but also perhaps the general chafing that comes from days on horseback wearing armor.

INQUISITION. Prior to the thirteenth century, it fell on local **bishops** to protect the Church from heresy. That changed with the implementation of the inquisition, a new institution that could appoint an inquisitor to a region, very often a Dominican or Franciscan **friar**, to examine and render judgment on the accused. By the fifteenth century, inquisitors and local bishops were required to work together when employing an inquisition. Traditionally associated with combatting heresy, inquisitions could be also used for serious violations of **canon law** including adultery, apostasy, and idolatry.

An inquisition tribunal began with a public accusation. The judges and their selected assessors would determine if the person was an **apostate**, an **idolator**, a **schismatic**, and/or a **heretic**. In addition, they sought to determine the person's degree of intent, ignorance, and willingness to accept correction. Looked at individually, each label has its own degrees of punishment. In a Venn diagram, every heretic is ultimately a schismatic, but they might also be an idolater. Apostates were in a category by themselves but could also exhibit idolatry.

An inquisition was almost always couched in terms of wanting to save the person's soul. The questioning techniques varied, and inquisition manuals evolved and competed around how to draw the truth out of the accused or how to reveal if someone was lying. **Torture** was sometimes employed, but some saw this as unnecessary for an inquisitor who was good at their job. It was certainly possible to successfully defend oneself. However, if the person confessed, they would suffer the consequences determined by the judges. If they were found guilty and refused correction, the judges would hand them over to secular authorities who would punish them. Confessing and later relapsing back into old ways could result in punishment as well. The most severe penalties employed by secular authorities were confiscation of property or execution, but the inquisition judges were not allowed to encourage the latter.

Joan of Arc's **condemnation trial** (1431) was an inquisition, initiated by **Pierre Cauchon**, the local bishop who had jurisdiction where Joan was captured. He followed inquisition procedure by reaching out to **Jean Graverent**, the grand inquisitor of France, but Graverent was already engaged in another trial and ultimately appointed Vice Inquisitor **Jean Le Maistre** to work with Cauchon.

ISABEAU OF BAVARIA, QUEEN OF FRANCE (C. 1370–1435). Isabeau of Bavaria, the queen of France, wife of **Charles VI**, mother of **Charles VII**, and grandmother of **Henry VI**, is one of the most integral and unfairly maligned leaders in the story of Joan of Arc.

Born around 1370, Isabeau traveled to France on the endorsement of Philip the Bold, duke of Burgundy, to meet with Charles VI. Meeting on 14 July 1385, they wed three days later with no official contract or dowry. They would have twelve children during their marriage; the eleventh born in 1403 was the future Charles VII. The mental illness that began afflicting her husband in 1392 crippled their relationship at times, as it did his ability to rule. He would not recognize her and sometimes became violent. While his brothers and uncles jockeyed for power on the royal council during his absences, Charles empowered Isabeau to lead on his behalf in 1402. She naturally sided with Philip the Bold, the man who introduced her to Charles, until Philip passed in 1404. She then began working closely with Duke Louis I of Orléans. Their rule was criticized by their opponents until his assassination in 1407, which is the traditional start of the **French Civil War** (1407–1435). The civil war took a dramatic turn with the invasion of **Henry V** in 1415, who began wooing Burgundian Duke John the Fearless and other dukes for alliances.

With the death of her oldest son, Duke Jean of Touraine, in 1417, the **Armagnacs** imprisoned Isabeau in Tours until her rescue by John the Fearless. Isabeau viewed the king and new **dauphin**, future Charles VII, as prisoners in Paris to the Armagnac faction. When the Burgundians captured the city in May, the dauphin fled the capital, splitting him physically from the king and queen. In November 1419, John the Fearless was assassinated, and the dauphin was implicated in the plot. Isabeau immediately sought to protect the French throne, reaching out personally to Burgundian cities, denouncing the assassination and pleading for their loyalty. The assassination was a watershed moment, as Charles VI, Isabeau, and the new duke of Burgundy (See PHILIP THE GOOD) negotiated the **Treaty of Troyes** (1420) with Henry V. The treaty denounced the dauphin for his part in the assassination of John the Fearless. The treaty also pledged the marriage of Isabeau's daughter, **Catherine of Valois**, to Henry V, whom Isabeau and Charles VI also adopted. Henry would then act as **regent** of France, only becoming king upon the death of Charles VI. With the death of Henry V followed by Charles VI in 1422, the infant **Henry VI** became the titular king of France. Conversely, supporters of the dauphin declared Charles VII king of France.

Although Isabeau remained in Paris throughout the 1420s, rumors spread of her infidelity, going so far as to claim that Charles VII was illegitimate and was actually the son of Duke Louis I of Orléans. These were meant to discredit Charles. Throughout the centuries, similar theories have claimed that Joan of Arc was a product of their affair. Historians have found no credible evidence that there was an affair between Orléans and Isabeau, and no evidence that Charles VII was the product of any affair.

Similarly, with the rise of Joan of Arc, prophecies were aggregated and reinterpreted to identify Isabeau as the woman who ruined France for her part in the Treaty of Troyes and Joan as the woman to save it (See PROPHECIES FORETELLING JOAN OF ARC). Readers of the Treaty of Troyes have sometimes misread its claim of Charles VII being unworthy of the crown as an attack on his birth, but the treaty actually found him illegitimate owing to his part in the murder of John the Fearless.

Isabeau remained in Paris until her death in 1435, the same year as the **Treaty of Arras** and the end of the French Civil War. She was present for the coronation of Henry VI in 1431 and the *Journal d'un bourgeois de Paris* tells us she saw him and wept.

ISABELLA OF BAVARIA. See ISABEAU OF BAVARIA.

J

JAMES I, KING OF SCOTLAND. *See* FRANCO-SCOTTISH ALLIANCE.

JANVILLE. A fortified town thirty-four kilometers north of **Orléans**, the **earl of Salisbury** captured it in September 1428 before capturing other towns along the Loire River. The town remained in English hands, and it was the destination for retreating English after their losses at **Meung** (15 June 1429) and **Beaugency** (16 June). However, when the French army intercepted and defeated the English at **Patay** (18 June), the inhabitants of Janville refused to open its gates to the retreating English, thus surrendering the town back over to **Charles VII.** *See also* LOIRE CAMPAIGN; SALISBURY'S 1428 EXPEDITION.

JARGEAU, BATTLE OF (11–12 JUNE 1429). This two-day battle, which included an assault on the town's walls and a massacre of the defending **English** troops, was the first town recaptured by **French** forces during the **Loire Campaign** (10–18 June 1429).

After Joan of Arc and French forces lifted the siege of **Orléans** (8 May 1429), the commander of the English, the **earl of Suffolk**, opted to hold onto other towns along the Loire River, including Jargeau where he was present. The town was south of the Loire with a bridge crossing to the north and surrounding suburbs outside its main walls. The **duke of Alençon** was in command of the French forces, and among his ranks were the **bastard of Orléans**, **La Hire**, and Joan of Arc.

As French forces arrived on 11 June, the English rushed out to confront them, causing the French forces to waver. Joan rushed to the frontlines and encouraged the troops, who rallied and chased the English back behind the town's walls. The French cleared the surrounding suburbs where they spent the night, deploying **artillery**. During the night, Suffolk asked for a two-week delay in hostilities to allow his reinforcements to arrive, but Alençon rejected it, demanding that the defenders leave, or they would be massacred.

After an artillery bombardment in the morning that stretched over hours or days depending on the contemporary source, the French assaulted the walls. The assault lasted four hours, and Joan was **injured** when a rock hit her helmet and knocked her off a **ladder**. She remained lucid and stood up to rally the troops over the walls. As the English fled across the Loire, Suffolk was captured.

The contemporary casualty estimates vary but indicate that the French massacred most or all of the English, and possibly some of the town's inhabitants. **Monstrelet** estimated the English were three hundred to four hundred strong, and he tells us the French killed three hundred of them. Alençon estimated that eleven hundred were massacred, but he is unclear which of these were occupying English or inhabitants. Conversely, the English troop strengths are found in *Journal du siège d'Orléans* (six hundred to seven hundred) and **Perceval de Cagny** (seven hundred or eight hundred), but they do not provide estimates for those killed.

At Joan's **trial**, the judges pressed Joan on why she did not accept Suffolk's request for a cessation in hostilities. The record of the trial tells us, "For her part, she says she told the people from Jargeau that if they wished, they could leave in their doublets and tunics and escape with their lives; otherwise they would be taken by storm" (Hobbins 2005, 70). After Jargeau, French forces moved on to capture **Meung** (15 June 1429).

JARGEAU, MANIFESTO OF. *See* FRENCH CIVIL WAR.

JEAN DE SAINT-MICHEL. *See* KIRKMICHAEL, JOHN OF.

JEAN LÈFEVRE DE SAINT-REMY. *See* SAINT-REMY, JEAN LÈFEVRE DE.

"JESUS MARY." On one of Joan of Arc's **rings**, on her **standard**, and atop several of her surviving **letters** were the names "Jesus Mary" ("Jhesu Maria" in Latin). What may appear today as a simple religious devotion to the son of God and his virgin mother was a controversial subject in the fifteenth century. A contemporary of Joan's, Bernardine of Siena (1380–1444), faced a trial in Rome in 1427, charged with **idolatry** for preaching the holy name of Jesus. Although **Pope** Martin V found in his favor, the subject was still debated among theologians. Thus the assessors at Joan's **condemnation trial** (1431) questioned her on her use of the names in four different sessions (27 February and 1, 3, and 17 March).

When questioned on her letters and the use of "Jesus Mary" with a cross (1 March), Joan clarified that she did this in some of her letters, but not all. When asked their purpose, she explained she understood the use of "Jesus Mary" to be customary and that the cross was sometimes "a signal to someone in her party not to do what her letter said" (Hobbins 2005, 72). When pressed again on the purpose of the names on her letters, Joan again explained that someone told her it was customary (17 March). The implication from the line of questioning on Joan's ring, standard, and letters was to uncover superstition or magical thinking on the part of Joan when evoking the names.

Among Joan's surviving letters, she stopped using "Jesus Mary" on them after August 1429. The sole exception is the **letter to the Hussites (23 March 1430)**, written by **Jean Pasquerel**. Did someone explain to Joan that it was not as customary as she was led to believe in her first six months of letter writing? There is no evidence of this, but Joan managed to avoid any culpability in her answers at the trial. Regardless, Article 24 of the initial **seventy articles** of accusation brought against Joan claimed she abused the names by using them in her letters.

During the **nullification proceedings** (1450–1456), multiple eyewitnesses, including **Isembard de La Pierre**, **Jean Le Fèvre**, **Jean Favé**, and **Pierre Miget**, testified that Joan's last words during her **execution** were her calling out to Jesus repeatedly.

JOHN THE FEARLESS, DUKE OF BURGUNDY. *See* FRENCH CIVIL WAR.

JOHN OF LANCASTER. *See* BEDFORD, JOHN, DUKE OF.

JOURNAL DU SIÈGE D'ORLÉANS. Commissioned by **Orléans** officials in 1467, the *Journal du siège d'Orléans* provides a detailed account of the military operations between the **English**, **French**, **Scots**, and **Burgundians** between September 1428 and September 1429. Relying on an anonymous daily journal kept during the siege and augmenting it with details from later chronicles and the records of the **nullification proceedings** (1450–1456), the *Journal* provides extant details on fortifications, gunpowder **artillery**, logistics, planning, and events surrounding the sieges and battles of Orléans, the **Loire Campaign**, the **march to Reims**, and the siege of **Paris**. The information is presented in a chronological fashion, naming key players in a day-by-day, sometimes hour-by-hour, account, making it invaluable for understanding the military events of Joan of Arc.

A Latin translation of the *Journal* came to print in 1560 before another version in the original French was published in 1576.

Today, it remains a key source for historians researching the military campaigns of Joan of Arc. *See also* BOUVIER, GILLES LE; CHARTIER, JEAN.

JUDGE. *See* ROLES AND RESPONSIBILITIES.

JUVÉNAL DES URSINS, JEAN (1388–1473). Jean Juvénal des Ursins came from a large, wealthy, and well-connected family in Paris. Among his siblings were Guillaume (1401–1472), who served two terms as Chancellor of France; Michel (1409–?), who was **bailiff** of **Troyes**; and Jacques (1410–1457), who served as archbishop of **Reims** and later bishop of **Poitiers**. Jean Juvénal achieved his licentiates in **canon law** and **civil law** by 1410 and would go on to become doctor in both laws (*See* EDUCATION). The family fled Paris in 1418 after the Burgundian capture of the city, abandoning considerable wealth and property (*See* FRENCH CIVIL WAR).

Jean Juvénal remained loyal to **Charles VII** and worked in Poitiers, often as the king's personal lawyer. He held numerous roles throughout his life including bishop of Beauvais (1432–1444), bishop of Laon (1444–1449), and, finally, archbishop of Reims (1449–1473). Throughout this time, Jean Juvénal wrote histories and treatises on military matters and diplomacy, often with direct praise *and* criticism for both enemies, allies, and the king himself.

Most historians believe that Jean Juvénal was among those who questioned Joan of Arc during the Poitiers examination, as he was stationed there at the time (March 1429). He was one of the three officials that **Pope** Calixtus III appointed to judge during the **nullification proceedings** in 1455. In this role, he oversaw much of the process, which included writing personal letters to the **duke of Alençon** and **Jean d'Aulon** to acquire their testimonies on Joan. It was also in the palace of Jean Juvénal on 7 July 1456 where the verdict of Joan's original **condemnation trial** was nullified.

Historians believe that Jean Juvénal held an antagonistic view of Joan for several reasons. First, in all his histories, he never mentioned her existence. When writing about the sieges of **Orléans** or **Compiègne**, or the **coronation of Charles VII**, he often describes the events as miraculous or divine, but he never writes Joan's name. He goes so far as to describe an unnamed companion who suggested a strategy to Charles on how to lift the siege of Orléans, omitting Joan's well-known role. Another piece of evidence for Jean Juvénal's supposed antagonism toward Joan comes from the nullification proceedings. He was emphatic in surviving letters to **Isabelle d'Arc**, the duke of Alençon, and Jean d'Aulon that his goal was to determine the validity of the original trial and ultimately clear the name of Charles VII, not to sanctify Joan. Thus the final verdict only rendered an opinion on the trial, not on Joan.

Some historians have theorized that he wrote *Chronique de la Pucelle*, but no one has convincingly confirmed his authorship.

KATHERINE, SAINT. *See* CATHERINE, SAINT.

KATHERINE OF VALOIS. *See* CATHERINE OF VALOIS.

KIRKMICHAEL, JOHN OF. John of Kirkmichael was a Scot and **bishop** of Orléans from 1426 to 1435, serving in the court of **Charles VII**. Kirkmichael was part of the negotiations of the 1428 treaty between France and Scotland (*See* FRANCO-SCOTTISH ALLIANCE). He was present at the siege of **Orléans** (1428–1429) but left after the battle of the **Herrings** (12 February 1429) to plead with Charles for more assistance in the siege. The bishop returned to Orléans after its relief. After the French victory at **Patay** (18 June), Kirkmichael helped establish the yearly celebration of Orléans (8 May). Kirkmichael participated in the **coronation of Charles VII**, and he continued to serve Charles and represented France at the **Council** of Basel. *See also* CHRONIQUE DE L'ÉTABLISSEMENT DE LA FÊTE DU 8 MAI (C. 1456).

KNIGHT. Although there were knights sporting the most advanced armor and weapons on horseback during the time of Joan of Arc, the notion of a knight rising from an undistinguished lineage and protecting the castle of his lord had faded from Western Europe. During the late thirteenth century, the noble class took over the knight title, conferring it to other nobles through pomp and ceremony when they turned twenty-one. However, during the fourteenth century, a combination of cost and changes in warfare made the pursuit of knighthood too costly for the nobles, and many opted to delay or forego the official knighting ceremony altogether. Instead, these unknighted men, still somewhat armored in the latest equipment and always on horseback, became known simply as **squires**, a term that had lost its connotation of servant or attendant. As a result, there were still armored nobles on horseback, but the numbers of official knights in medieval France had dwindled dramatically from tens of thousands in the twelfth century to possibly one thousand by the mid-fifteenth century.

Those in the highest levels of nobility were sure to pay for the equipment and ceremony necessary to be called a knight. For example, virtually any duke or king was knighted, including **Henry V**, **Henry VI**, **Philip the Good**, and the dukes of **Bedford**, **Orléans**, and **Alençon**. The latter knighted **Charles VII** at his **coronation**.

Outside of the upper echelons of nobility, Joan of Arc encountered numerous knights in military campaigns, and the title carried weight among her peers and enemies. For example, Joan's **letter to the English (22 March 1429)** directly addressed the **earl of Suffolk**, **John Talbot**, and **Thomas Scales**, all knights. During the assault on **Jargeau** (12 June), Suffolk supposedly knighted a French squire to avoid what he believed was the shame of surrendering to someone of lesser stature. The capture of Talbot, Scales, and **Thomas Rempston** at **Patay** (18 June) was so prestigious that all three received honorable mention by Charles VII in his letters bragging about his army's success during the **Loire Campaign** (10–18 June).

L'ARBRE DES FÉES / L'ARBRE DES DAMES. *See* FAIRY TREE.

LA CHAMBRE, GUILLAUME DE. *See* PHYSICIANS IN THE CONDEMNATION TRIAL.

LA CHARITÉ, SIEGE OF (24? NOVEMBER–23? DECEMBER 1429). La Charité was a small yet strategic and well-fortified town on the Loire River with a bridge leading into **Berry**. It featured thick outer walls, large towers, and a set of interior walls. The walls had been refortified in 1365 by Charles V and again by its captain, **Perrinet Gressart**, who occupied the town almost uninterrupted from 1423–1438.

A warlord and mercenary, Gressart had played the English and the Burgundians off each other to maintain and expand his power. By the winter of 1429, he was firmly in the English camp while the duke of Burgundy (*See* PHILIP THE GOOD) had forbidden any assistance to Gressart. Meanwhile, **Jean d'Aulon** tells us through his testimony during the **nullification proceedings** that the council of **Charles VII** had determined that La Charité must be taken. Charles had attempted to hold the town through force in 1423, the terms of the truce of **Chambéry** (1424), and, finally, trading directly with Gressart (1427), all of which failed to dislodge the warlord from his base of operations. **Gilles le Bouvier** clarified that it was **Georges de La Trémoille** who made the decision to capture La Charité (after all, he had been captured and held for **ransom** by Gressart). The army was led by **Charles d'Albret**, half-brother of La Trémoille.

The army, which included Joan of Arc, captured **Saint-Pierre-le-Moutier** on 4 November, another of Gressart's strongholds. However, they spent most of their supplies. Joan's surviving **letter to the people of Riom (9 November 1429)** details how they needed gunpowder ingredients and other war materials, or they would not be able to capture their next target. A similar letter survives from Albret. Both **Bourges** and **Orléans** are recorded as having responded with money and supplies.

However, it was not enough. The siege lasted a month, possibly from 24 November to 23 December. This was atypical of Joan's other sieges, the longest of which was less than a week. The chroniclers are vague about the details, and we do not know the number of defenders or attackers. Gilles le Bouvier indicated it was a rough winter, and Joan and Albret were understaffed for about a month before abandoning the siege and leaving their artillery. This may have been because the army had lost some **horses** and could not transport their equipment. **Perceval de Cagny** blamed Charles VII for not sending any money or supplies. The only action described in the siege came from Joan's testimony during her **condemnation trial** (1431) when she said she had made an attempt to cross the moat but failed. Thus, through conjecture, we can imagine the army surrounding the town and bombarding it until they ran out of supplies. Their decision to leave may have been after failed attempts to scale the outer walls. We can also imagine a well-fortified town where Gressart simply sat back with passive resistance. He only had to wait out his enemy until they were too cold or hungry to continue. Albret and Joan left the region, ending the campaign entirely.

Gressart remained captain of La Charité until 1435 when Charles made peace with the warlord, recognizing him as royal captain of the town for life. Gressart held the role until his death in 1438.

LA FAYETTE, GILBERT MOTIER DE (C. 1380–C. 1463).

Gilbert Motier de La Fayette was a noble and military commander from Bourbon. Having served the dukes there throughout the 1410s, he joined the cause of the **dauphin** (See CHARLES VII) in 1420. He served as governor of Dauphiné and as **marshal of France**. Most notably, he was one of the French leaders in the victory at **Baugé** (1421). He was captured at, but released shortly after, the battle of **Verneuil** (1424).

La Fayette was present at the siege of **Orléans** (1428–1429), and he avoided capture at the battle of the **Herrings** (12 February 1429). When Joan of Arc arrived at the siege (29 April), he participated in its relief, followed by the **Loire Campaign** (10–18 June) and the battle of **Patay** (18 June). At the **coronation of Charles VII** (17 July), he did not hold the ceremonial position for the marshal of France, and **Gilles de Rais** took the role instead. Historians have theorized this may have been for the loss at the Herrings. Others have pointed out that during the 1420s, before **Georges de La Trémoille** joined the king's court in 1427, La Fayette was tasked with seizing some of the would-be advisor's estates. Did La Trémoille have a hand in demoting La Fayette, as he did with **Arthur de Richemont**? Regardless, La Fayette was back in favor with the king after the expulsion of La Trémoille in 1433. He continued to serve the king, joining the delegation for the negotiation of the **Treaty of Arras** (1435). In 1439, he became **seneschal** of Beaucaire and Nîmes. He continued campaigning for Charles, and he captured **Rouen** in 1449, his last military activity.

La Fayette died around 1463. He is an ancestor of Marquis de Lafayette (1757–1834), famous for his participation in the American Revolutionary War.

LA FONTAINE, JEAN DE (C. 1381–?).

Jean de La Fontaine served as examiner during the **condemnation trial** of Joan of Arc (1431), responsible for questioning the accused (See ROLES). He achieved a master of arts from the **University of Paris** in 1403, which would put his age as at least twenty-two based on average ages of academics, but this is not always certain (See THOMAS BASIN). He acquired his licentiate in **canon law** in 1424 (See EDUCATION). La Fontaine was active for the university, working to secure privileges for the university first from the **duke of Bedford** and **Henry VI** in 1422, and then from **Charles VII** in 1436.

As the examiner at Joan's trial, La Fontaine served alongside **Pierre Cauchon** in questioning Joan initially, but then La Fontaine led most of the questioning during her prison sessions between 10 and 17 March while Cauchon was away. He is on record as agreeing with **Jean d'Estivet** on 27 March that if Joan refused to submit to the **Church Militant**, then she should be excommunicated.

A broader perspective of La Fontaine is possible through testimonies from the **nullification proceedings** (1450–1456), especially from **Isembard de La Pierre, Jean Massieu, Guillaume Manchon, Nicolas de Houppeville**, and **Guillaume Duval**. From them, we learn that La Fontaine was among those advising Joan, recommending to her that she appeal directly to the **pope**. Duval claimed that he along with La Pierre and La Fontaine were threatened by the **earl of Warwick** and forbidden from seeing Joan again. Cauchon purportedly learned of La Fontaine's involvement and threatened him as well. Most of these witnesses tell us that La Fontaine and others fled **Rouen** after this, but Houppeville goes so far as to claim Cauchon had La Fontaine imprisoned. Either way, La Fontaine's name no longer appears among the attendees after 28 March.

LA HIRE (C. 1390–1443).

Étienne de Vignolles, more commonly known as "La Hire," is one of the most celebrated companions in arms of Joan of Arc, present at every single battle, siege, and march between her arrival at **Orléans** (29 April 1429) through the siege of **Paris** (8 September).

Born around 1390 in Gascony, La Hire was not from nobility, and he found a career as a mercenary. It is possible he sold his services to Count Bernard VII of Armagnac in the 1410s during the **French Civil War**, but the earliest confirmed mention of him is in 1418 in the service of the **dauphin** (*See* CHARLES VII). From then on, he had a lengthy career capturing towns and castles, as well as surrendering them along with himself, typically fighting against the English or the Burgundians. He was at the victory at **Baugé** (1421) and the defeat at **Verneuil** (1424). Throughout his career, he was often mentioned in tandem with **Poton de Xaintrailles**, and as early as 1427, he fought alongside the **bastard of Orléans**, both also companions in arms of Joan of Arc.

On 25 October 1428, La Hire joined the garrison at Orléans during the English siege, and he seemed to be present in nearly every development, as described in the *Journal du siège d'Orléans*. He was present for the defeat at the battle of the **Herrings** (12 February 1429), and he supported the retreat. The bastard of Orléans tells us that he and La Hire first met Joan of Arc at **Blois** en route to the siege. They escorted her to the city, arriving on 29 April. On 4 May, the bastard once again returned to Orléans with more reinforcements, and Joan and La Hire were at the head of a force that greeted their return and guarded his flank. After the relief of Orléans on 8 May, the bastard tells us that Joan instructed the army not to attack the English who had left their boulevards and deployed for battle. She wanted to give them an opportunity to leave peacefully. However, La Hire led the cavalry charge that attacked the English fleeing toward **Meung** and **Beaugency**, killing many of them. This annoyed Joan, according to **Louis de Coutes**, which is one of the few recorded moments when La Hire was not working in concert with Joan. La Hire then joined Joan and the **duke of Alençon** for the **Loire Campaign** (10–18 June). At the battle of **Patay** (18 June), La Hire was one of the leaders mentioned explicitly among the initial cavalry force that surprised the unprepared English. La Hire was also with the royal army during the **march to Reims** (29 June–16 July), the battle of **Montépilloy** (15 August), and the failed siege of Paris (8 September).

With the disbandment of the royal army, Joan and La Hire parted ways for separate campaigns. Still, they appear to have had a special bond, and numerous chroniclers and eyewitnesses attested to how she openly admonished him for swearing, encouraging him to instead swear by his staff. Joan was also able to convince La Hire, who was by no means a religious man, to make confession before battle. There were also several instances where La Hire deferred to Joan's direction on how to conduct campaigns, battles, and sieges. After Joan's capture at **Compiègne** (23 May 1430), there is a romanticized theory that La Hire attempted to rescue her. This is supported by La Hire's attack of Louviers, near **Rouen**, but no rescue attempt was made, and no surviving record exists with details of his plan, if there ever was one.

After Joan's **execution** (30 May 1431), La Hire continued his campaigns, often alongside Poton de Xaintrailles. One of their raids encroached into Burgundian territory in 1435, temporarily halting the Congress of Arras (*See* ARRAS, TREATY OF). La Hire received recognition and positions from Charles VII, including **squire** of the king's stable, captain of Beauvais, and lieutenant of Île-de-France. In 1436, he was made baron of Montmorillon. Like many active military men during this age, La Hire was captured and **ransomed** on numerous occasions, spending months and sometimes years in captivity (1422, 1424, 1431, 1437, and 1440). Charles supported or directly intervened in paying La Hire's ransoms, and even exchanged the town of Clermont-en-Beauvaisis to free him in 1437. La Hire's last military activity was alongside the **duke of Orléans** at the siege of La Réole. La Hire became ill with fever, which killed him on 11 January 1443. Historians lament La Hire's premature death before he could testify at the **nullification proceedings** (1450–1456) about his experiences with Joan of Arc.

La Hire's nickname is often attributed to his fiery temper, but the translation of "anger" is *la ire*, and historians are unsure of the exact origin. It is possible the nickname was associated with one of his family's estates.

LA PIERRE, ISAMBARD DE (C. 1392–?). Isambard de La Pierre (also spelled as Isambart or Ysambard) was a Dominican friar in Rouen, a bachelor of theology (*See* EDUCATION), and an assessor at Joan of Arc's condemnation trial (*See* ROLES). According to the trial transcripts, his first session at the trial was on 10 March 1431, and he was recorded at fourteen sessions total. On 12 May, he voted against using torture on Joan. On 22 May, he believed that Joan was heretical, but needed another admonishment. After she resumed wearing men's clothes (*See* RELAPSE), La Pierre voted to abandon Joan to secular authorities (29 May).

La Pierre lived to participate in the nullification proceedings, providing multiple testimonies in 1450 and 1452. Through these statements, a completely different picture of La Pierre emerges. Although he believed the judges followed the rule of the law, he also believed Pierre Cauchon sought to please the English and the entire trial was aimed at discrediting Charles VII. La Pierre tried to help Joan throughout the trial, explaining the Council of Basel and encouraging her to appeal to it. Cauchon purportedly refused to record her request in the trial transcripts, and the English threatened to drown La Pierre. Joan was kept in chains, and access to her was limited. He also attested that Joan said she resumed wearing men's clothes because the English tried to rape her (*See* SEXUAL ASSAULT AND RAPE). La Pierre, along with Martin Ladvenu, accompanied and comforted Joan on the day of her execution (30 May). Like several of the other assessors, La Pierre painted himself as sympathetic to Joan and merely one of many caught up in a rigged trial against her. Both Guillaume Duval and Nicolas de Houppeville attested that La Pierre was threatened with drowning for trying to help Joan. We do not know when he died, but La Pierre did not provide any further testimony after 1452.

LA POLE, WILLIAM DE. *See* SUFFOLK, WILLIAM DE LA POLE, EARL OF.

LA PUCELLE. *Pucelle* translates from French to "virgin," but is more often translated to "maid" in an attempt to catch its more nuanced meaning. In fifteenth-century France, *pucelle* was a common term used to denote a young, virgin girl who had not yet entered womanhood. This was a temporal phase in the life of a woman who was expected to one day become a wife and mother. It transcended class. Joan of Arc, who burst onto the public stage as an ignoble girl with no title, successfully adopted *la Pucelle* as her moniker, capturing the imagination of her contemporary supporters and detractors.

Virginity has been a powerful image and topic in Christianity, starting with the virgin birth of Jesus Christ, and in medieval Europe, the cult of the Virgin Mary was strong. Romance works often featured knights defending or defiling the chastity of maidens. Thus, when Joan called herself *la Pucelle* and professed divine revelations on military strategy and tactics, the status of her virginity became a focal point. Her enemies and some tepid allies forced her to undergo physical examinations to prove her virginity, with a negative outcome sure to ruin her credibility. Her supporters seized on her gender and virginity, reinterpreting prophecies about a maiden who would save France.

Joan used the *la Pucelle* title regularly when speaking to friends and foes, as she did in her letter to the English (22 March 1429). Her enemies attacked her virginity directly, calling her "whore" or similar names, as William Glasdale did at the siege of Orléans, and Jean d'Estivet did while she was imprisoned during her condemnation trial (1431). Her virginity was also a focal point during the nullification proceedings (1450–1456) where numerous eyewitnesses provided strong affirmation of her chastity. Some went so far as to stress that even while sleeping in close proximity or seeing her change clothes, they had no carnal desire toward her. Thus, Joan's status as *la Pucelle* promoted and maintained a divine and mythical quality that supporters revered and enemies chastised.

Medieval chroniclers and modern-day historians use the title as they would for a count or duke. Joan becomes Jeanne la Pucelle, Joan the Maid, La Pucelle, or the Maid, sometimes all interchangeably within the same text. At different stages in her story, she may be referred to as the "Maid of Lorraine," focusing on her home and the prophecies, or the "Maid of Orléans" after the relief of the city. Although Joan and her family were **ennobled**, she never adopted the associated title "*du Lys*" and neither have historians. Her enemies and the **transcripts** of her condemnation trial acknowledged that she and others referred to her as *la Pucelle*, but they do not use the title to refer to her.

LA ROCHELLE, CATHERINE DE. *See* CATHERINE DE LA ROCHELLE.

LA ROSE, PHILIPPE DE. Philippe de La Rose was a priest, the treasurer of the church in **Rouen**, master of requests for the hotel of **Henry VI**, and a supporter of English claim to the French throne at least until 1449 when the French retook the city. On 6 May 1452, Cardinal **Guillaume d'Estouteville** appointed La Rose to act in his stead for the **nullification proceedings** alongside **Jean Bréhal**, and he continued in this role through the nullification of Joan of Arc's **condemnation trial** (7 July 1456).

LA TRÉMOILLE, GEORGES DE (C. 1385–1446). Georges de La Trémoille was an advisor to the dukes of Burgundy and the kings of France. Often vilified by chroniclers and historians, he played a direct role in negotiating the **Franco-Burgundian Truce** (1429–1430) and the direction of Joan's military activities in October through December 1429.

Born around 1385, La Trémoille served under Duke John the Fearless of Burgundy as well as **Charles VI**. In 1415, he was captured at Agincourt, but released shortly after (*See* HUNDRED YEARS WAR). He rose to prominence through his marriage to the widow of the sonless duke of **Berry** in 1416, and when she passed in 1422, La Trémoille gained her territories. Brought into the court of **Charles VII** in July 1427, La Trémoille favored diplomacy over war, especially in the dealings with Burgundy (*See* FRENCH CIVIL WAR). His past service for Burgundy and his brother's presence in the court of the duke of Burgundy (*See* PHILIP THE GOOD) both played roles in his attitude. This diplomatic strategy conflicted with **Arthur de Richemont** who was aggressively waging wars for Charles. Later in 1427, La Trémoille was successful in banishing him from the king's court, after Richemont's brother, the **duke of Brittany**, signed a treaty with the English on 8 September. That same year, La Trémoille became the grand **chamberlain** for the king.

La Trémoille provided loans to Charles, typically in return for more territory. Chroniclers often depicted him as taking advantage of the king and overindulging in the royal coffers. Surviving records support this narrative. For example, after the relief of Montargis (5 September 1427), La Trémoille received payment for the siege, even though his days of campaigning were well behind him, and he did not participate at all.

When Joan of Arc arrived at **Chinon** (March 1429), the **duke of Alençon** tells us that La Trémoille was present when she spoke to the king, but there is no indication that he objected to her. He likely agreed with the advice to have her examined by theologians (*See* POITIERS). He is mentioned again in the **Laval Letter (8 June 1429)** as being present among other nobles who were ready to march alongside Joan. After the victory at **Patay** (18 June), **Jean Chartier** tells us that numerous soldiers came to join the king's army. However, La Trémoille was angry and fearful of the growing movement, turning away some of the new arrivals. During the **march to Reims** (29 June–16 July), **Gilles le Bouvier** tells us that it was La Trémoille who convinced the king to dismiss Arthur de Richemont who had joined the royal army during the **Loire Campaign**, arguing that Richemont would not remain loyal to the king. La Trémoille was present for the **coronation of Charles VII** (17 July) and the standoff at **Montépilloy** (15 August), riding beside the king.

La Trémoille was among the delegates of Charles in the negotiations with Philip the Good for a truce, which had started since the coronation, continuing through August and September before solidifying into the Franco-Burgundian Truce that would begin on 28

September. After the failed assault on **Paris** (8 September), the king called off the siege and later disbanded the royal army for other campaigns. Historians often point to La Trémoille as the key advisor pushing against the attack on Paris and then for its abandonment to avoid upsetting the new truce. Gilles le Bouvier cites La Trémoille as the one who ordered the army to leave the siege.

Joan of Arc was wounded at Paris (*See* INJURIES); after she had recovered in October, the duke of Alençon wanted her to join him on a campaign in **Normandy**. **Perceval de Cagny** tells us it was a combination of La Trémoille, **Regnault of Chartres**, and **Raoul de Gaucourt** who opposed pairing the two together, but Gilles le Bouvier lists only La Trémoille. However, Joan was not sidelined entirely, and she was instead sent along with **Charles d'Albret**, half-brother of La Trémoille, to combat **Perrinet Gressart** along the Loire River (*See* SAINT-PIERRE-LE-MOUTIER). Although contemporary sources do not provide La Trémoille's reasoning, he was clearly determined to deal with Gressart, a mercenary who served his own purposes, typically with the support of Philip the Good and at the cost of Charles VII. Gressart had captured and **ransomed** La Trémoille around 1427 while he was en route to meet with Philip. Thus, the assignment appears to have been an effort to channel Joan's eagerness for war, not stifle it.

After Joan was captured at **Compiègne** (23 May 1430) and through her **execution** (30 May 1431), there was complete silence and lack of action on the part of Charles VII. Historians often blame La Trémoille for this approach, but there survive no details in any records of his involvement. It is easy to envision him convincing the king that Joan had served her purpose and her aggressiveness led to her own capture. Regnault of Chartres, often allied with La Trémoille, later criticized Joan for following her own desires and not God's will, and thus he would have supported such an attitude toward the captive warrior.

La Trémoille's time with Charles was coming to an end, though. Arthur de Richemont reconciled with the king in 1432 and began making moves against his enemy. In the end, La Trémoille's track record of greedy finances led to his downfall, as he often received larger payments for campaigns than his counterparts including those in which he did not participate. Banished in 1433, he offered his services to Philip the Good and was successful in convincing the duke to abandon the English in 1435 for the **Treaty of Arras**. La Trémoille lost all hope of reconciliation with Charles in 1440 when he received the lion's share of the blame for convincing the **dauphin** (*See* LOUIS XI) to join the **Praguerie** rebellion. La Trémoille died in 1446, having served two dukes of Burgundy and two kings of France.

LADDER. The ladder, used for scaling walls, was one of the world's earliest **siege** weapons and was still in use during the time of Joan of Arc. Medieval illustrations of warfare depict ladders, but they were so common that chroniclers rarely mentioned them explicitly unless some unique event occurred (DeVries and Smith 2012, 168), as was the case in several of Joan's sieges. While some besiegers opted to build them from scratch at the site of a siege, this required time, materials, and expertise that were not always readily available. As such, armies carried them piecemeal to a target and then reconstructed them. Among the list of skilled laborers in **Salisbury's 1428 expedition** in France was one ladder-maker (Spencer 2005, 186). While the concept of a ladder is simple, modifications were often made such as **Christine de Pizan**'s instructions for adding wheels on one end to help push a ladder up a wall and a heavy weight at the base to help prevent tipping.

The height of ladders varied as ladders too short would be insufficient for scaling a wall and ladders that were too tall would be easier for defenders to knock over. Too much height was an issue for French attacking defensive positions outside of **Orléans**, as an English defender reportedly knocked down ladders with scalers on them. **Vegetius** provided several crude methods for measuring the height of a wall using an arrow and rope, as well as examining the shadow cast by a wall. In addition, surveying tools such as astrolabes made this task possible. Pizan called for ladders measuring as high as twenty-six feet. Ladders have their limits though, becoming unwieldy at thirty feet and the longest recorded functional ladder was thirty-six feet (Nossov 2005, 75).

Carrying ladders to the wall required coordination with teams of up to twelve to sixteen troops moving quickly in unison while exposed to projectiles. Joan of Arc, and later the **bastard of Orléans**, testified that she was the first to plant a ladder on the wall of the Tourelles bastille at Orléans. It was at this moment that Joan was first wounded in battle with a bolt to the neck (*See* INJURIES). Climbing up the ladder also required skill, as scalers needed to move quickly and often with a shield. The experienced were vulnerable, as one of **Henry V**'s knights was knocked from a ladder during the siege of Caen (1417), and French defenders were able to burn him alive in his armor with lit straw while he laid in a ditch. Joan herself was recorded as scaling a ladder carrying her **standard** at **Jargeau** before she was hit in the head with a rock, fell from the ladder, and lost her helmet. She was able to get to her feet and continue to rally the troops to victory.

LADIES' TREE. *See* FAIRY TREE.

LADVENU, MARTIN (C. 1398–1456). Martin Ladvenu was a Dominican **friar** based in **Rouen**, and virtually all we know about him comes from Joan of Arc's **condemnation trial** (1431) and testimonies from the **nullification proceedings** (1450–1456). At the condemnation trial, Ladvenu is first recorded on 20 February, but does not appear again until Joan's **abjuration** (24 May). After her resumption of male **clothing**, he voted to abandon Joan to secular authorities (29 May). On the day of her **execution** (30 May), he heard her last confession and administered her last communion. According to testimony recorded after the trial (7 June) and appended to the **transcripts** of the trial, Lavendu along with **Pierre Maurice**, **Nicolas Loiseleur**, and **Jean Toutmouillé**, visited Joan after she resumed wearing men's clothing. She purportedly admitted at this time that her visions and angels were fictitious, but she heard voices. Pressed further, she admitted she was deceived.

Ladvenu lived to testify during the nullification proceedings, providing statements in 1450, 1452, 1455, and 1456. His testimonies contain a bounty of details, some of which conflict with the 7 June 1431 details appended to the condemnation trial transcripts. His opinion of Joan was glowing, describing how without any representation, Joan answered difficult questions wisely. Ladvenu tells us that no one dared help Joan for fear of the English, and that those who did were threatened. Similarly, he believed **Pierre Cauchon** was a partisan of the English, insisting on holding Joan in a secular prison (*See* CAPTIVITY). When assessors pushed Cauchon to move Joan to an ecclesiastical prison, he refused for fear of upsetting the English. That Joan was in danger in the secular prison was clear to Ladvenu, who tells us that Joan only resumed wearing men's clothing after her abjuration because the English tried to rape her (*See* SEXUAL ASSAULT AND RAPE). He asserted that Joan maintained that her **voices, visions, and revelations** were all from God, and her actions were all done by His command. She admitted to no deception. After the inquisition determined that she was a relapsed **heretic**, they handed her over to secular authorities who immediately escorted her to the stake for execution without any deliberation. She requested Ladvenu bring a cross to her, which he held up for her to see while she burned. Ladvenu believed Joan died a true Christian.

LAGNY, BATTLE OF (29 MARCH 1430). Lagny is located roughly thirty kilometers east of Paris, on the south bank of the Marne River. After the **coronation of Charles VII**, the town was one of several that declared their loyalty to the king on 12 August 1429. Joan of Arc was recorded passing through the city on 13 September after her failed assault on **Paris** (8 September).

Joan was again at the city on 29 March 1430, seeking to aid Parisians sympathetic to Charles VII. The battle of Lagny was Joan's last major military victory before being captured at **Compiègne** (23 May 1430). Although recorded by **Perceval de Cagny**, **Jean Chartier**, **Georges Chastellain**, and **Monstrelet**, none of them were eyewitnesses to the battle, and the details are scant.

Upon receiving intelligence that there were three hundred to four hundred Burgundians nearby, Joan left Lagny with commanders from the town, and a force of at least four hundred. Joan made several assaults but appears to have been repulsed by Burgundian archers. However, Joan sent for reinforcements from Lagny and nearby towns, eventually overwhelming the enemy with multiple cavalry charges, killing or capturing the entire force.

Among Joan's prisoners was their commander, Franquet d'Arras, whose **sword** she also took and carried with her until her capture. She sought to exchange him for captured Parisians (*See* RANSOM), but upon learning that some of the Parisians were executed, Joan handed Arras over to the **bailiff** of Senlis who hanged him after a two-week trial. At her **condemnation trial** (1431), the assessors questioned Joan on his execution, blaming her for his death. However, Joan responded that during his trial, he confessed to murder, stealing, and treason. Since the prisoners she sought to free with her captive were dead, she said she had no qualms handing him over for justice.

While in Lagny, Joan purportedly prayed over a dead infant, after which the baby seems to have lived again long enough for a baptism before dying again. Joan left Lagny on 13 May for Compiègne.

Anglo-Burgundian forces made further attempts to capture Lagny in March 1431 and May and August 1432, but all were unsuccessful.

LANCASTER, HOUSE OF. The House of Lancaster or the Lancaster Dynasty refers to kings that ruled England beginning in 1399 with King Henry IV. Descending from the dukes of Lancaster, Henry IV deposed English King Richard II, his cousin. His son, King **Henry V** invaded France in 1415, allied with **Philip the Good**, and signed the **Treaty of Troyes** (1420). The treaty led to the marriage between Henry and **Catherine of Valois**, daughter of French King **Charles VI**. The treaty also disinherited the **dauphin** (*See* CHARLES VII) from the French throne and made the future son of Henry and Catherine, **Henry VI**, the king of France. With the death of Henry V followed by Charles VI in 1422, the infant Henry VI was too young to rule and his uncle, the **duke of Bedford**, acted as **regent** of France.

Historians often refer to Henry V's brothers by their house name. So the duke of Bedford can appear as John of Lancaster; Thomas, duke of Clarence, as Thomas of Lancaster; and Humphrey, duke of Gloucester, as Humphrey of Lancaster. Joan of Arc's **mission** to expel the English from France and secure the French throne for Charles VII can be referred to as her war against Lancastrian rule. The English control of Normandy is typically referred to as Lancastrian Normandy.

LAVAL, ANDRÉ DE (1406–1485). André de Laval and his older brother, **Guy XIV**, were well-connected nobles from **Brittany** and experienced soldiers. André was knighted in 1423 at the battle of La Gravelle. In 1428, he was captured alongside his brother at Laval by **John Talbot**. They had to pay hefty **ransoms** to secure their release. André and Guy joined the French army after the relief of **Orléans** just before the **Loire Campaign** in early June 1429. They were present in the army until the siege of **Paris** (8 September).

André de Laval later served as admiral of France (1437–1439) and then **marshal of France** (1439). In 1450, he married the daughter of **Gilles de Rais**. His last known military action was relieving the siege of Beauvais in 1472. *See also* LAVAL LETTER (8 JUNE 1429).

LAVAL, GUY XIV DE (?–1486). Guy XIV de Laval and his younger brother, **André**, were well-connected nobles from **Brittany** and experienced soldiers. In 1428, he was captured alongside his brother at Laval by **John Talbot**. They had to pay hefty **ransoms** to secure their release. André and Guy joined the French army after the relief of **Orléans** just before the **Loire Campaign** in early June 1429. They were present in the army until the siege of **Paris** (8 September). At the **coronation of Charles VII**, Guy was made **count** of Laval. *See also* LAVAL LETTER (8 JUNE 1429).

LAVAL LETTER (8 JUNE 1429). The 8 June 1429 letter from brothers **Guy XIV** and **André de Laval** to their mother and grandmother is an often-quoted source, as they chronicle their first encounter with Joan of Arc. It is a useful eyewitness account of Joan at an early point in her military career when she already had success in relieving the siege of **Orléans** (8 May), but had not yet begun the **Loire Campaign** (10–18 June). In the letter, the Laval brothers speak favorably of her. Upon meeting them, she provided them with wine, commenting that they would soon drink wine in **Paris**, indicating that she had full intention of bringing the city under the domain of **Charles VII**. They describe how Joan ordered that an unruly charger be brought in front of a church where she successfully mounted it. The brothers depict this as a divine moment, but it also demonstrates Joan's skill with **horses**. They also describe how men joined the royal army in preparation for the eventual **march to Reims**, which they planned on attending.

The original letter is now lost, but its contents have persisted in several histories from the sixteenth and seventeenth centuries.

LAVENU, MARTIN. See LADVENU, MARTIN.

LAXART, DURAND (C. 1396–?). Durand Laxart was Joan of Arc's cousin, but she referred to him as her uncle, likely because he was roughly seventeen years older than her. He lived near **Domremy**, on the road to **Vaucouleurs**. At the **nullification proceedings**, he attested to Joan's character, describing her as well-behaved, pious, patient, and gladly going to church, confessing, helping the poor, and performing chores.

In 1428, Joan left to meet with Laxart under the pretext of assisting her cousin in childbirth. Laxart tells us that Joan was explicit with her intensions to venture to **France** to crown the **dauphin** (See CHARLES VII). She was able to convince Laxart to escort her in May 1428 by evoking a well-known prophecy (See PROPHECIES FORETELLING JOAN OF ARC). He took her first to see **Robert de Baudricourt**, captain of Vaucouleurs, who instructed Laxart to beat her and take her back to her father (See ARC JACQUES D'). Laxart escorted her on her journey to meet with the **duke of Lorraine**, as well as on all three of her trips to meet with Baudricourt in Vaucouleurs. Laxart contributed to the purchase of Joan's **horse**, which Baudricourt reimbursed him for after he finally agreed to send her to meet Charles in **Chinon** in February 1429.

Laxart was at **Reims** for the **coronation of Charles VII** where he proudly shared his story with the king and others.

L'ÉCRIVAIN, ROLAND. See PHYSICIANS IN THE CONDEMNATION TRIAL.

LE COMTE, DENIS. See NOTARIES AT THE NULLIFICATION TRIAL.

LE FÈVRE, JEAN (C. 1394–1463). Jean Le Fèvre held a doctorate in theology from the **University of Paris** (See EDUCATION). Like most of his counterparts at the university, he supported the **Treaty of Troyes** (1420), but he continued his support well past the **Treaty of Arras** (1435). He was very active in English-controlled **Rouen**. In 1439, he is recorded leading prayers for troops fighting against the French. He also preached in favor of **Henry VI**'s rule in France that same year and in 1440. His support of the English was rewarded with a bishopric. He was an assessor, present for most of Joan of Arc's **condemnation trial** (1431) where he supported the decision to hand Joan over to the secular authorities.

In his 1452 and 1456 testimonies during the **nullification proceedings**, Le Fèvre was favorable to Joan, but he was not awestruck like some of his counterparts. Thus, he tells us he was impressed by Joan's answers while detailing how the assessors grilled her for long periods of two to three hours that left everyone exhausted. Furthermore, the assessors asked difficult questions and quickly changed subjects to trick Joan. Le Fèvre tells us that he tried to help Joan when he believed the notaries were not capturing her statements accurately (See ROLES). Concerning her imprisonment in a secular jail (See CAPTIVITY), he believed it was wrong and he complained about it, but no one truly dared raise it as an issue.

When Le Fèvre expressed concern over one of the questions, he claimed **Pierre Cauchon** rebuked him. Le Fèvre believed she died a true Christian and tells us that she requested a last Mass before her **execution**. She wept and cried out "Jesus," and others cried too. However, Le Fèvre tells us he could not stay until the end. In his testimony, he admitted that for about three weeks during the trial, he thought she was divinely inspired, but she ultimately relied too heavily on her revelations. Furthermore, the English hated and feared Joan, leading to a much harsher **inquisition** than Le Fèvre thought normal. Thus, Joan was more of a poor, young victim instead of a divinely inspired hero or martyr.

Even with his history of support for the English and his less than enthusiastic support of Joan, he was appointed as a substitute judge during the nullification proceedings (30 May 1456), and he was present for the ultimate nullification (7 July). Le Fèvre died in 1463.

LÈFEVRE, JEAN, DE SAINT-REMY. See SAINT-REMY, JEAN LÈFEVRE DE.

LE MAISTRE, JEAN (?–C. 1452). Jean Le Maistre (Lemaître or Le Maistre) was the inquisitor for the **condemnation trial** of Joan of Arc (1431). Le Maistre held a bachelor's in **theology** from the University of Paris (*See* EDUCATION), was a Dominican **friar**, served as **prior** for a convent in **Rouen**, and was the vice-inquisitor of **Jean Graverent**, a role that Le Maistre had held since 1424.

By 19 February 1431, Bishop Pierre Cauchon and his assessors determined there was enough evidence to proceed with an **inquisition** of Joan. As Cauchon made appointments for promoter, examiner, executor of mandates, and notaries (*see* ROLES), he needed an inquisitor, but Le Maistre argued whether he could legally serve in the role. He reasoned that while he was the local inquisitor for Rouen, Cauchon was bishop from Beauvais, operating in Rouen as a refugee. This was technically a Beauvais trial, not a Rouen trial. While Cauchon and Le Maistre debated, Cauchon agreed to write Jean Graverent, grand inquisitor of France, on the matter while Le Maistre agreed to at least attend the proceedings going forward in an unofficial capacity. The debate came to a head on 12 March when Cauchon received a letter from Graverent explicitly appointing Le Maistre to serve as inquisitor. Le Maistre asked to review Graverent's letter and the transcripts of the proceedings thus far, which Cauchon agreed to share while also reminding Le Maistre that he had been present for most of the sessions already. On 13 March, Le Maistre arrived wholly dedicated to the trial. He reaffirmed Cauchon's previous appointments for official roles in the trial, adding one notary, **Nicolas Taquel**.

Part of what we know of Le Maistre comes from those who knew him personally, testifying at the **nullification proceedings** (1450–1456). His fellow friars—**Isembard de La Pierre, Jean Massieu, Nicolas de Houppeville,** and **Guillaume Manchon**—all described him as a man acting under duress, afraid of Cauchon and the English. For example, Massieu acknowledged Le Maistre's attempts to get out of the trial, but he ultimately participated because he was afraid for his life. Still, Le Maistre was not a mere lapdog of Cauchon on all topics. For example, Manchon described how Cauchon wanted to punish **Jean de La Fontaine** and others for suggesting to Joan that she appeal to the **council** forming in Basel, but Le Maistre forbid Cauchon from taking any action against them and he threatened to quit the trial.

As a result, historians have downplayed Le Maistre's involvement, some claiming he played but a small, reluctant role. This may be true when compared to the eager Cauchon, but Le Maistre's name is all over the trial. As the cojudge with Cauchon, Le Maistre was present for much of the proceedings after his official appointment. If he was afraid of the English, he was also paid for his services by them, according to surviving records. When Cauchon asked for some of the assessors to chime in on the question of **torture** for Joan (12 May), Le Maistre only said that she should be questioned again on submitting to the **Church Militant**. After Joan's **abjuration** (24 May), Le Maistre led the delegation to Joan's prison cell, giving her women's **clothing** and shaving her head (*See* HAIR). He was also among the group that visited Joan's cell on 28 May to see her once again wearing men's clothing. His name was also on the final sentence read to Joan on 30 May, declaring her a relapsed **heretic**. She was then handed over to secular authorities who **executed** her. In addition, when **Pierre Bosquier** was imprisoned for speaking out against the trial and execution of Joan, Le Maistre's name was recorded alongside Cauchon's in accepting the public recantation of Bosquier.

Unfortunately, Le Maistre did not participate in the nullification proceedings, perhaps because he was too close to the final sentence. He was at least alive during the initial investigations in 1450 and 1452, but his whereabouts in 1455 are lost to history and he was perhaps dead by then. The result is a mixed picture of the inquisitor. He was a stickler for rules and ultimately condemned Joan as a heretic, but his fellow friars, who by the 1450s had all become sympathetic to Joan, were prepared to explain away his culpability.

LE ROYER, CATHERINE (C. 1402–?). Known simply as the wife of Henri Le Royer, Catherine lived in **Vaucouleurs** and provided testimony during the **nullification proceedings** (1450–1456) concerning Joan of Arc's time there (1428–1429). Catherine tells us Joan stayed in their home off and on for a total of three weeks, and that she was pious yet impatient to go meet with **Charles VII**. **Robert de Baudricourt**, the captain of the city, refused to send her. He eventually confronted Joan with a priest who attempted to exorcise her. Joan admonished the priest for not hearing her confession. Then she dropped to her knees in front of Baudricourt and said, "Have you not heard this prophecy, that France will be destroyed by a woman, and restored by a virgin from the marches of Lorraine" (Taylor 2006, 275).

Catherine last saw Joan when she left Vaucouleurs for Chinon, with male **clothing**, a **horse**, and an entourage, provided by the town. *See also* PROPHECIES; METZ, JEAN DE; POULENGY, BERTRAND DE.

LE ROYER, HENRI. *See* CATHERINE LE ROYER.

LEAGUE OF THE PUBLIC WEAL (1465). The *Ligue du Bien Publique*, or League of the Public Weal, or Public Good as it is sometimes translated, was a brief noble rebellion against **Louis XI**. Led by Louis's brother, Charles, it featured relatives or descendants of those who previously fought against Joan of Arc including Charles the Bold, son of **Philip the Good**, and Louis of Luxembourg, nephew of **John of Luxembourg**. It also featured some of the nobles who had been companions in arms with Joan including the count of Dunois (*See* ORLÉANS, BASTARD OF) and **Charles d'Albret**. Although this latter group had supported **Charles VII**, they joined the rebellion when Louis cleaned out his father's court upon becoming king in 1461. Louis was able to end the rebellion through compromise and changed his approach with the nobles, choosing to work closely with them through the rest of his reign.

LEPARMENTIER, MAUGIER (C. 1396–?). Maugier Leparmentier was an unmarried cleric whom we know very little about outside his 1456 testimony during the **nullification proceedings** (1450–1456). He was present in the tower of **Rouen** when Joan was threatened with **torture** during her condemnation trial (9 May 1431), but she remained defiant. He was also present for the **execution** of Joan (30 May). There, he tells us that as soon as **Pierre Cauchon** read the verdict, Joan was immediately escorted to the pyre and burned without any verdict from a secular judge. During her burning, he tells us she loudly cried "Jesus" six times while almost everyone wept.

LETTERS OF JOAN OF ARC. There is no complete list of every letter dictated by Joan of Arc quite simply because most of them have not survived. Attempts to compile such a list over the past seventy years have resulted in seventeen, twenty-five, and twenty-seven letters, with each curator admitting that it is not exhaustive.

Six original letters survived at least until the twentieth century, but Joan's letter to the people of Tournai (25 June 1429) was lost during German bombings that destroyed the

Tournai archives in 1940. Joan's letters to Philip the Good (17 July 1429), the people of Reims (5 August 1429), the people of Riom (9 November 1429), and two more letters to the people of Reims (16 and 18 March 1430) have survived. The latter three letters all bear her signature, and all of them are now preserved in archives.

The three letters to Reims were discovered in a private collection after the French Revolution. Although they remained in a private collection, facsimiles were published in 1911. Today, the letters reside in French archives.

There are also five copies of letters in various archives, chronicles, and the **condemnation trial** and **nullification proceedings**, including Joan's letters to the English (22 March and 5 May 1429), to the people of Tournai (25 June 1429), to the people of Troyes (4 July 1429), and to Jean IV, count of Armagnac (22 August 1429). There is also a copy of Joan's letter to the Hussites (23 March 1430), but her contribution to this letter remains disputed.

The surviving letters and copies of letters, assuming they were dictated (*See* LITERACY), provide us with a glimpse of how Joan spoke, as well as her monarchist views on Charles VII, her perspectives of the French and English peoples, and her understanding of military logistics, including the need for money, equipment, and ingredients for gunpowder.

There are references to additional lost letters found within both the condemnation trial and nullification proceedings, local city registers, and within other surviving letters. Any list of letters and allusions to letters are incomplete. For example, during her condemnation trial, Joan references several letters that are lost, including a letter to Charles VII with her opinion of **Catherine de La Rochelle**, a letter to the clergy of Sainte-Catherine-de-Fierbois asking for the **sword** behind the altar, and a letter to her parents. Each of these letters is lost, and we only know of their existence based on Joan's recollections, one to two years after each was written.

LETTER TO THE ENGLISH (22 MARCH 1429).

Although the original did not survive, the contents of Joan of Arc's first letter to the English has persisted through numerous copies, with slight variations, found in the **condemnation trial**, the **nullification proceedings**, and *Mistere du siege d'Orléans*, as well as French, Burgundian, and German chronicles including *Journal du siège d'Orléans* and *Chronique de la Pucelle*. Written on Tuesday of Holy Week (22 March 1429) and sent from **Blois** between 24 and 27 April 1429, the letter is addressed explicitly to **Henry VI**, the **duke of Bedford**, the **earl of Suffolk**, **John Talbot**, and **Thomas Scales**, but it was transmitted widely for greater effect. This was during the **Poitiers** examination and was likely the same letter referred to by **Gobert Thibault** during the nullification proceedings, which he claimed was transcribed by **Jean Érault**.

In the letter, Joan of Arc outlined some of what modern scholars refer to as her **mission**. Specifically, she wanted the English to lift the siege of **Orléans**, return all occupied cities including **Paris** to the kingdom of France, for all English troops to be expelled from France, and for **Charles VII** to be recognized as the king of France. Multiple times in the letter, Joan threatened to visit the English and their French allies, bring them harm, and even kill them. Joan switched from third to first person throughout the letter, proclaiming that she and Charles VII came in the name of God.

The letter is the most-cited of Joan's surviving **letters**, and it often appears in literature and cinema, likely owing to its provocative language that storytellers find atypical of a seventeen-year-old woman from fifteenth-century France. More remarkable is the clarity Joan presented at the time it was written. While she had just finished the Poitiers examination, Charles VII had not yet officially committed to back her mission. Still, she was confident in her demands and that she would be the one to see them through.

Modern scholars sometimes refer to the letter as a "declaration of war" that demonstrated hints of chivalry by giving the recipients the option to leave their holdings in France before she brought about their destruction. When she declared she would confront them personally, she said she would give them the option to comply before meeting their demise.

That it was intended for a wider audience as propaganda is attested to by some of its more poetic proclamations, such as threatening the English with a "war cry greater than any that there has been in France for a thousand years" (Taylor 2006, 75), and her multiple statements that she was sent by God.

The assessors at her condemnation trial produced a copy of the letter and questioned her on its contents (22 February 1431). She contested only a few of the words and phrases. The letter was also attached to Article 22 of the original **seventy articles** brought against her, highlighting what they saw as pride, presumption, and cruelty in her statements and threats.

Mathieu Thomassin included the letter in his *Registre delphinal*, but as four separate letters, each addressed individually to the king of England, Bedford, Bedford's commanders, and finally, the troops then besieging Orléans. No version of these individual letters survived by the time of the nullification proceedings, and Joan herself did not clarify this point when questioned by her assessors. It is possible that the letters were merged as a propaganda piece, which represented what Joan intended, or her memory had simply merged them together by the time of her condemnation trial, two years after she originally wrote them among the rigors of campaigning. It is also possible that Thomassin divided the original letter on his own initiative.

LETTER TO THE ENGLISH (5 MAY 1429). The contents of Joan of Arc's 5 May 1429 letter to the English come from the 1456 testimony of **Jean Pasquerel** during the **nullification proceedings**. The original letter is lost, but the contents, provided by Pasquerel, are persisted in Latin.

Written during the siege of **Orléans**, it was brief. Addressed to the English occupying the Tourelles bastille, Joan warned them that if they did not abandon the fortifications and return home, she would "make a war cry that will be remembered forever" (Taylor 2006, 84). She concluded by stating it was the third and last time she would write to them. A postscript includes details of how she was sending the letter by arrow, because the English had detained one of her messengers. For his safe return, she offered to exchange some captured English troops from Fort Saint-Loup, clarifying that they were not all dead. Pasquerel tells us that after sending the letter, the English called her a "whore," causing her to weep.

This letter is sometimes referred to as the "Ultimatum to the English," most likely to distinguish it from Joan's other surviving **letter to the English (22 March 1429)**. However, both letters possess clear ultimatums. In addition, some historians have taken Joan's words at face value and concluded that this was her "third" letter to the English. Further, they conclude that the lost "second" letter was what **Pierre Milet** and the **bastard of Orléans** testified separately about at the nullification proceedings. They each described Joan sending a letter to the English upon arriving at Orléans (29 April). However, it is possible that Joan's claim in her 5 May letter being the third in a series was simply her third sent to the English outside Orléans, whereas her 22 March letter is much broader in scope and audience. In addition, **Mathieu Thomassin's** claim that the 22 March letter was originally four separate letters further muddies the water on how many letters Joan sent to the English, while besieging Orléans or otherwise.

If this letter is the same one that the bastard of Orléans testified to having read, he attributed divine power to her words and believed it empowered the French defenders against the English.

LETTER TO THE PEOPLE OF TOURNAI (25 JUNE 1429). We can confidently refer to four letters from Joan of Arc to the people of **Tournai** due to the city's record keeping. These records were mostly consistent, providing details such as the date the letter was written, arrival date at its destination, the courier's name, and how much the city paid the courier. However, only Joan's first letter to the city (25 June 1429) had survived the medieval period, as the rest were only surmised or simply referenced in the city's register. There is little chance another letter will turn up because historians have scoured the city's register for this period, transcribing the contents in print in the nineteenth century. In addition, the register itself, including Joan's first letter, was destroyed with the rest of the Tournai archives from German bombing in 1940.

In this first letter, written one week after the battle of **Patay** (18 June), Joan provided details of the **Loire Campaign**, proclaiming that she had chased the English from the region. She explicitly named captured commanders including the **earl of Suffolk**, his brother John de La Pole, **John Talbot**, and **Thomas Scales**. **John Fastolf** managed to evade capture at Patay, but the initial reports from the battle were that he was captured, and Joan includes him in her list. In addition, Joan listed another of Suffolk's brothers, Alexander de La Pole, as well as **William Glasdale** among the English commanders killed during the campaign. She then asks the people of Tournai to join the **coronation of Charles VII** in **Reims**. Tournai sent a delegation to the coronation.

Joan's second and third letters, received August and September 1429, respectively, were listed in the city's register, but no summary survives. Based on when they were received, they likely provided details on the **march to Reims**, the battle of **Montépilloy**, and the impending siege of **Paris**, as well as requests for money and support.

Joan's fourth letter to Tournai was sent from **captivity** in August or September 1430. She requested twenty to thirty gold crowns from the city for supplies she needed while imprisoned. The city provided twenty-two.

LETTER TO THE PEOPLE OF TROYES (4 JULY 1429). During the **march to Reims**, Troyes remained in the path of Joan of Arc, **Charles VII**, and the royal army. Not only was the city the site of the signing of the **Treaty of Troyes** (1420), but it had prospered under the **Anglo-Burgundian Alliance** for nearly a decade. During the march, Charles sent messengers to the city as his army approached. Joan of Arc wrote her own letter on 4 July 1429 and likely put it in the hands of **Friar Richard** the next day when she arrived at the walls of Troyes with the royal army. Richard was acting as a sort of ambassador for the city, seeking to determine the validity of Joan.

The letter addresses the people of Troyes as friends, emphasizing that she was sent by God and that King Charles would march to **Reims** and **Paris**, gathering all the cities of France under him. She emphasizes that they should recognize Charles as king and doing so would ensure the safety of their lives and property. Unlike her letters to the English, her threat was more nuanced, stating that she would enter all cities in France and establish peace there, regardless of whom she faced.

The letter did not have an immediate effect, and the royal army remained outside Troyes until 9 July when Joan led an assault that resulted in a quick capitulation (*See* TROYES, SIEGE OF).

Although the original letter did not survive, the content survives in a register of Reims, compiled and transcribed in the early seventeenth century. The same register reveals there were two more letters sent from Joan to Troyes. The originals are lost, and we only have a summary for the third letter. The second letter was sent on 5 July, probably containing similar content as Joan's letter from the day before. A third letter was sent from Gien on 22 September 1429. It was read on 2 October, giving details on the assault of **Paris** (8 September) and Joan's **injury** there.

LETTER TO THE DUKE OF BURGUNDY (17 JULY 1429). Written on the day of the **coronation of Charles VII**, Joan of Arc's letter to **Philip the Good**, the duke of Burgundy, is the oldest of her surviving original **letters**. Today, it resides in the Departmental Archives at Nord, France. It is unsigned.

The letter is a firm, but heartfelt appeal to the duke to end the **Anglo-Burgundian Alliance** and make peace with Charles. She emphasizes that the duke would win no more battles against the French. Joan closes by revealing that she sent a letter three weeks prior, entreating the duke to attend the coronation, but no reply was sent nor had she heard from her courier at that point. It is unknown if the duke received either letter, let alone how he reacted to them. The duke had been in **Paris** until the day before the coronation and was at Arras by 31 July. If the courier was to deliver the letter personally, he would have had to find the duke on his travels.

Although the contents of the letter did not make it to Joan's **condemnation trial** (1431), she did evoke her correspondence to the duke in response to hearing Article 18 of the original **seventy articles** brought against her. This article argued that Joan always pushed Charles and his men toward making war instead of peace. Joan responded that she tried to make peace through letters with the duke of Burgundy, but she conceded the only way to peace with the English was for them to leave France.

LETTER TO THE PEOPLE OF REIMS (5 AUGUST 1429). This unsigned letter from Joan of Arc to **Reims** is the first of her three original letters to the city that have survived. The letter remained in the city's town hall until it was purchased in 1630 by Charles du Lys, who claimed direct lineage from Joan's brother (*See* ARC, PIERRE D'). The letter's contents were published in the nineteenth century, a facsimile was published in 1911, and the original was later sold and is now housed in the Archives Municipales at Reims.

Written from Provins, the letter addresses the people of Reims and the city's role as the recent site of the **coronation of Charles VII**. The proximity of the city to Burgundian territory certainly gave the people alarm, and Joan sought to quell their concerns while addressing the fifteen-day truce between the **French** and **Burgundians** (*See* FRANCO-BURGUNDIAN TRUCE). Joan tells the citizens to remain steadfast, emphasizing she would not abandon them. She shares the terms of the truce, which included **Philip the Good** handing over **Paris** to Charles, and then continuing to negotiate for a more permanent peace in the **French Civil War**. Joan explains she did not trust such truces and admitted she would struggle to maintain it. Regardless, she planned to keep the royal army together if Philip did not go through with the terms. He ultimately did not. Joan further instructs the city to remain guarded, look for traitors, and report any news to her.

LETTER TO JEAN IV, THE COUNT OF ARMAGNAC (22 AUGUST 1429). The letter from Count Jean IV of **Armagnac** to Joan of Arc, along with her response, both survive as copies in her **condemnation trial** (1431). A courier of the count presented the letter to Joan in August 1429 while she was still campaigning, on her way to assault **Paris**. The courier himself was not welcome among the army, as the count was estranged from **Charles VII** as well as excommunicated by the **pope** at the time. Still, Joan heard the letter, which asked her which of the three popes he should follow. Her response, recorded by the courier, is inconclusive and claims that she will provide a more definitive answer when she is in Paris. The trial transcript describes the original letter bearing her signature. For Joan's part, she argued that the surviving letter did not contain her full answer and was by no means meant to indicate that she would select a pope, as she maintained the true pope was in Rome. Still, the count's letter and her response were presented in Articles 26 to 30 of the **seventy articles** of accusation originally brought against her. Article 30 accused her of casting doubt on the true pope and setting herself above the church by implying she would select a pope at a later date. *See also* GREAT SCHISM.

LETTER TO THE PEOPLE OF RIOM (9 NOVEMBER 1429). Joan of Arc's letter to the people of Riom is the earliest surviving letter that bears her signature. Written from Moulins, Joan proclaims her intention to push out all enemies who oppose **Charles VII**. She then informs the town of the recent capture of **Saint-Pierre-le-Moutier** (4 November). Although successful, Joan and the army had depleted necessary supplies and equipment. She explicitly asks them for gunpowder and for ingredients of gunpowder: saltpeter and sulfur (*See* ARTILLERY). She also requests arrows, crossbows, and other military equipment.

The contents of the letter are nearly identical to a letter from **Charles d'Albret**, the commander of the force, to the people of Riom at the same time. They likely targeted Riom with the knowledge that the town had sent supplies to **Orléans** during its defense against the English siege. It is unknown what, if any, supplies Riom sent to Joan and Albret, but their month-long siege of **La Charité** (24? November–23? December) was unsuccessful. They sent similar letters to other towns during this period, but none have survived. For example, there is a record in the archives of Clermont where the town responded with saltpeter, sulfur, and two cases of arrows, as well as a personal gift to Joan that included a **sword**, two daggers, and an ax.

Joan's letter was rediscovered in the archives of Riom in July 1844 during a period of renewed interest in her. Its contents made it into newspapers and several books of collected documents. Jules Quicherat examined the letter and claimed that there were remnants of a red wax seal that included a single strand of black **hair**. Although now lost, the hair has been theorized to have been Joan's and has led to the belief that Joan did indeed have black hair. Today, the original letter resides in the Archives Communales of Riom.

LETTER TO THE PEOPLE OF REIMS (16 MARCH 1430). A letter to the people of **Reims**, which contains the second known surviving signature of Joan of Arc, is one of the three surviving letters that Joan sent to the city. The letter remained in the city's town hall until it was purchased in 1630 by Charles du Lys, who claimed direct lineage from Joan's brother (*See* ARC, PIERRE D'). The letter's contents were published in the nineteenth century, a facsimile was published in 1911, and the original was later sold in 1970 and is now housed in the Archives Municipales at Reims.

Writing from Sully-sur-Loire, Joan was responding to a letter from Reims, which has not survived. However, she addresses the letter's contents directly, which included their expressed fear of attack. Given the difficult location of Reims in relation to Burgundian territory and the expiration of the regularly violated **Franco-Burgundian Truce**, this was an understandable concern. Joan instructs them not to fear a siege, as she would engage the enemy in battle soon. If a siege did occur, then she instructs them to resist and she would arrive to relieve them, surprising the enemy. Joan claims she had more to share but did not for fear that the letter would fall into the wrong hands.

LETTER TO THE HUSSITES (23 MARCH 1430). John Huss (c. 1370–1415) was a professor of theology at the University of Prague who pushed radical reforms in the Church. While at the **Council** of Constance, he was arrested, tried, and condemned for **heresy**, after which he was handed to secular authorities who executed him by fire (6 July 1415). The event sparked an uprising in Bohemia, and the followers were known as **Hussites**. Pope Martin V issued a bull against the Hussites, and multiple crusades were attempted between 1419 and 1431 without success. The Hussites also battled among each other with the moderate wing winning and ultimately reconciling with the Church in 1434.

Joan of Arc's supposed letter to the Hussites is unique in her correspondence mainly because historians are still split on to what degree she was involved with its contents. Although it professes to be a message from Joan, it was written in Latin and signed by **Jean Pasquerel**. Since its rediscovery in 1834 when a German translation was published, historians have debated its authenticity or whether Pasquerel took liberties with Joan's name. The original has not survived, but a copy was preserved in the register of Holy Roman Emperor Sigismund (1368–1437).

The letter is addressed directly to the Hussites—referred to as the "Heretics of Bohemia"—comparing them to Saracens and imploring them to abandon their heretical ways. Joan explains that if she were not occupied in a war with the English, she would have pursued them already. She then threatens to abandon her current war to turn them from their heresy or kill them.

Some historians choose to exclude this letter altogether in their narratives on Joan. Others have argued that Joan understood international politics and would have been aware of Martin V's bull against them. If this is plausible, then certainly Pasquerel aided with the rhetoric of the letter, but Joan was capable and possibly willing to target those who she would have learned were considered heretics. In addition, the letter was written during a time of imposed inactivity for Joan, and it is plausible she was seeking opportunities for battle, and especially a divine cause. Regardless, Joan moved onto other battles and sieges before her capture outside **Compiègne** (23 May 1430).

The letter was not mentioned during her **condemnation trial** (1431), which has led historians to conclude that the assessors were unaware of its existence. Otherwise, they would have used it to question her as they did with the other letters in their possession. Ironically, the **University of Paris** issued a similar letter of condemnation to the Hussites just over a year prior (28 March 1429).

LETTER TO THE PEOPLE OF REIMS (28 MARCH 1430). This letter to the people of **Reims** contains the third known surviving signature of Joan of Arc. It is one of the three original letters that Joan sent to the city, and it is the last surviving letter of Joan. The letter, like the other two to Reims, remained in the city's town hall until it was purchased in 1630 by Charles du Lys, who claimed direct lineage from Joan's brother (*See* ARC, PIERRE D'). The letter's contents were published in the nineteenth century, a facsimile was published in 1911, and the original was later sold in 1970 and is now housed in the Archives Municipales at Reims.

Like the previous **letter (16 March 1430)**, Joan was writing from Sully-sur-Loire. Joan was again responding to a letter from Reims, which has not survived. However, she addresses the contents directly. Unlike the previous letter from Reims, this follow-up letter appears to have contained specific details on a plot to turn the city over to the **Burgundians**. Joan commends Reims for remaining faithful to **Charles VII**, who she said was well aware of their report and pleased with their diligence to remain loyal. Joan again instructs them to fear no siege and resist any that may come, as Charles would send an army to relieve them. She further provides details on reinforcements that were acquired from **Brittany**.

Joan left Sully-sur-Loire, but never made it to Reims before her capture at **Compiègne** (23 May).

LIBELLUS D'ESTIVET. *See* SEVENTY ARTICLES.

LICENTIATE. *See* EDUCATION.

L'ISLE-ADAM, JEAN DE VILLIERS DE. *See* VILLIERS, JEAN DE.

LITERACY / ILLITERACY OF JOAN OF ARC. Traditionally, Joan of Arc is believed to have been illiterate, only learning to sign her name during her military career, a signature that survives on three letters. Such illiteracy would not be surprising for a girl from the **Lorraine** countryside who lacked the education of someone like **Christine de Pizan**. Joan is often quoted as not knowing "A from B" during the **Poitiers** examination (March 1429). During her **condemnation trial** (1431), she shared that she received her instruction from her mother without help from anyone else. Furthermore, Joan's lack of education was underscored continuously during the **nullification proceedings** (1450–1456) to account for her not understanding all the difficult questions thrown her way during her inquisition. Modern scholars tend to support the belief of Joan's illiteracy, and it is not uncommon to pick up any recent book on Joan that declares her illiterate without any qualification.

However, some exceptions to the assumption of Joan's illiteracy have arisen to varying degrees in the mid-twentieth century. These require a re-examination of the evidence. For example, Joan's supposed statement that she knew neither "A from B," as attested by **Gobert Thibault** more than twenty years after the statement, did not necessarily mean she could not read. This was a turn of phrase that could also refer to lacking proficiency in something such as scripture or theology, two things Joan was certainly grilled on during the Poitiers examination.

During Joan's condemnation trial, she demonstrated that she could identify "**Jesus Mary**," as it was written on her **ring**, her **standard**, and in her **letters**. On 12 and 13 March 1431, she was questioned as to whether she ever received letters from saints or angels. On 24 February, she demanded to have a list of questions in writing for which the assessors planned to question her. On 15 March and on 2 May, she told her assessors that she would provide further responses in writing. While being questioned over the three popes on 1 March, Joan answered that she never wrote anything concerning them. On the same date, she also explained that she sometimes included the sign of a cross near her signature as a code to the recipients to indicate that she did not want her instructions followed. Some scholars contend that the lack of any recorded contempt from the assessors about Joan's supposed illiteracy toward her answers indicates that they knew she read. However, the counterpoint is that she simply meant that in all these instances, she intended to have a clerk read and write for her.

Finally, Joan was prolific with her letters and there are surviving originals, copies, or records of nearly thirty letters, but there were obviously many more that have not survived. Some of these letters clearly indicate that she dictated them, and the common convention is that even if Joan managed to gain a rudimentary reading proficiency, she almost certainly dictated all these letters. Those arguing aggressively for or against Joan's literacy share similar motivations. The latter want to further emphasize the capability of a medieval girl that grew up outside of courtly life, while the former want to emphasize that the same girl was capable despite her lack of education.

LOHÉAC, ANDRÉ DE. *See* LAVAL, ANDRÉ DE.

LOIRE CAMPAIGN (10–18 JUNE 1429). The Loire Campaign refers to a string of battles and sieges between French and English forces in the Loire Valley in June 1429, which resulted in the expulsion of English forces from the region and paved the way for **Charles VII** to **march to Reims**.

After the relief of the siege of **Orléans** (8 May 1429), Joan of Arc wanted to give the English the opportunity to leave peacefully. Although **La Hire** violated this approach initially by attacking retreating English that day, the **earl of Suffolk**, commander of the English, still managed to spread his forces throughout the remaining strongholds along the Loire River including **Meung** and **Beaugency**, while stationing himself in **Jargeau**. Although the next phase of Joan's **mission** was the **coronation of Charles VII** in **Reims**, it was necessary to recapture these strongholds before beginning the march northeast into enemy territory.

After much debate, Charles agreed to focus military efforts on the Loire River, placing the **duke of Alençon** in command. Along with the duke were Joan and many of the original captains from Orléans, including La Hire, the **bastard of Orléans**, **Poton de Xaintrailles**, and **Gilles de Rais**. The army began its march on 10 June, arriving outside of Jargeau on 11 June. After an initial skirmish in the suburbs, the English retreated inside the walls of Jargeau. Although Suffolk attempted to negotiate a delay in hostilities as he had received news that **John Fastolf** was en route with English reinforcements, Joan convinced Alençon to offer Suffolk the opportunity to leave Jargeau immediately. When Suffolk refused, the city was assaulted, Suffolk was captured, and many of the English defenders were massacred.

On 15 June, the French forces captured the bridge at Meung. The French then moved to Beaugency and began an assault. The defending English retreated to the inner castle. **Arthur de Richemont** arrived on 16 June with reinforcements for the French, and although the other commanders were wary of his presence, he joined their efforts. **John Talbot**, the remaining commander of the English forces in the Loire Valley, negotiated a surrender of the town and withdrew his forces the morning of 18 June.

Later, John Fastolf attacked French troops at the bridge of Meung, but failed to capture it. He then moved north to meet with forces commanded by John Talbot. Upon learning of Talbot's general location, Joan of Arc convinced Alençon to attack. They caught Talbot's forces unprepared and engaged the English outside **Patay**. The French took numerous prisoners including Talbot, **Thomas Scales**, and **Thomas Rempston** (*See* RANSOM). The fighting started before Fastolf could meet up with Talbot, and Fastolf did not engage in the fighting, as he believed the French had already won. The remaining English retreated to **Janville** in the north, but the French inside closed their gates, refusing them entry. The Loire Campaign came to a close, and the Loire River was secured for Charles VII.

The relief of Orléans and the quick successes during the Loire Campaign undid much of **Salisbury's 1428 expedition**, and it provided the necessary credibility for Joan of Arc to convince Charles and his advisers that the next step should be a march to Reims for his coronation.

LOISELEUR, NICOLAS (C. 1390–?). Nicolas Loiseleur was a canon of **Rouen**, friend of **Pierre Cauchon**, and an assessor at Joan of Arc's **condemnation trial** (*See* ROLES). By the time of the trial (1431), he had acquired his master of arts from the **University of Paris** (*See* EDUCATION). Loiseleur was present for much of the trial, starting with the earliest pre-trial session on 9 January 1431. He was one of the three assessors who voted in favor of **torture** for Joan (12 May), and he voted to abandon her to secular authorities after her **relapse** (29 May). He contributed to the post-trial testimony (7 June), claiming Joan admitted there were no visions, and she believed her **voices** deceived her (*See* TRANSCRIPTS). Loiseleur eventually attended the **Council** of Basel in 1435. He was alive in the 1440s, but his fate is lost to history.

During the **nullification proceedings**, Loiseleur became notorious based on the testimonies by **Jean Massieu, Guillame Colles**, and **Guillaume Manchon**, who all claimed that while Joan was imprisoned in Rouen, he stayed in a nearby cell and pretended to be a prisoner from **Lorraine**. With this ruse, he elicited information from Joan that was then used against her throughout the trial, and he gave her bad advice. Manchon tells us there was another nearby room where some of the assessors and notaries listened to the conversations. **Pierre Miget** said he learned about the ruse and complained to Cauchon. **Thomas de Courcelles**, who had not softened his condemnation of Joan by the time of the nullification proceedings, confirmed the ploy in his 1452 testimony.

Although Loiseleur seemed to be wholly antagonistic and deceitful in his ruse and post-trial testimony, both Guillaume Colles and **Nicolas Taquel** described Loiseleur crying during the **execution** of Joan. His emotional response apparently outraged nearby English soldiers, and Loiseleur had to seek protection from the **earl of Warwick**, who advised him to leave town.

LONGUEIL, RICHARD OLIVIER DE (1406–1470). Born in Lisieux from a noble family, Richard Olivier de Longueil held benefices in Lisieux and **Rouen** during the English control of **Normandy** as well as after its reconquest by **Charles VII** (1450). In 1452, he declined the Archbishop of Rouen, which was taken by **Guillaume d'Estouteville**. In 1453, he became bishop of Lisieux. By 1454, Longueil had taken a loyalty oath to Charles VII. The next year, the **pope** selected him as one of the three judges for the **nullification proceedings** examining the **condemnation trial** of Joan of Arc. After the nullification verdict (7 July 1456), Longueil was made cardinal of Coutances (17 December). He then toiled to revoke the **Pragmatic Sanction of Bourges**, but only made progress after the coronation of **Louis XI** (1461). *See also* CHARTIER, GUILLUAME; URSINS, JEAN JUVÉNAL DES.

LORÉ, AMBROISE DE (C. 1395–1446). Ambroise de Loré was a French knight, military commander, and companion in arms of Joan of Arc.

Prior to the arrival of Joan, Loré fought at Agincourt (1415) and alongside **Gilles de Rais** and **La Hire** in the 1420s. He was part of the convoy of reinforcements and supplies that arrived with Joan at the siege of **Orléans** on 29 April 1429. He was then present throughout the relief of the siege (4–8 May), the **Loire Campaign** (10–18 June), and the **march to Reims** (29 June–16 July). After **Troyes** opened its gates to **Charles VII** (9 July), he remained outside, in command of the royal army. After the **coronation of Charles VII** (17 July), Loré was part of a scouting force that tracked the **duke of Bedford**'s movements leading up to the standoff at **Montépilloy** (15 August). Charles appointed Loré captain of Lagny prior to the siege of **Paris** (3–8 September), and he watched the royal army march back after the failed assault. In November, he led a failed attempt to capture **Rouen**.

After the **execution** of Joan of Arc, Ambroise de Loré continued to serve Charles VII in campaigns. The king appointed him *prévôt* (prevost) of Paris in 1436, in charge of royal administration and trying treason cases. He held the role and continued to campaign for Charles until his death on 24 May 1446.

In the testimony of **Jean d'Aulon** during the **nullification proceedings**, he cited Ambroise de Loré as one of the commanders being in awe of Joan's achievements at Orléans as an act of God.

LORRAINE. During the life of Joan of Arc, Lorraine was a duchy loyal to **Charles VII** in the northeastern frontier of France, between the Holy Roman Empire to the north and east, and Burgundy to the north and south. Lorraine included major towns such as Metz, Toul, Nancy, and **Neufchâteau**. The Meuse and Moselle rivers run through the duchy where many of the towns are situated.

Joan's story begins in Lorraine. She was born and raised in **Domremy**. Her family likely visited Neufchâteau regularly for its festivals and markets. Joan's family also sought refuge there in 1428 when Burgundians raided the duchy. **Vaucouleurs** was home to **Robert de Baudricourt**, the captain of the city and the man that Joan would seek out when she sought endorsement to meet with Charles VII. Joan also ventured to Toul or Nancy in early 1429 to meet with the **duke of Lorraine**. By February 1429, Joan had gained the support of Baudricourt, and he sent her to meet with Charles VII who was in **Chinon**.

LORRAINE, CHARLES II, DUKE OF (1364–1431). The highest-ranking noble Joan of Arc met before arriving at **Chinon** was Charles II, duke of Lorraine. In a precarious position with territory in both the **Holy Roman Empire** and France, and with **Burgundy** at his borders, the duke had spent much of his life in a state of war. In the 1390s, he was on crusade and allied with the dukes of Burgundy through the start of the **French Civil War** (1407–1435). In 1418, he helped Duke John the Fearless of Burgundy capture **Paris**, but upon the assassination of John the next year, Lorraine sought a policy of neutrality between the warring factions. In 1419, he gave his eldest daughter in marriage to **René of Anjou**, son of **Yolande of Aragon**, an avid supporter of the **dauphin** (*See* CHARLES VII). However, on 6 May 1420, at the behest of French King **Charles VI**, he recognized **Henry V** as **regent** of France, but with the deaths of both Charles and Henry later that year, Lorraine returned to a wait-and-see policy.

After **Robert de Baudricourt** admonished a persistent Joan of Arc several times in **Vaucouleurs**, he sent her to meet with Lorraine in Nancy or Toul, in late January or early February 1429. Some historians have theorized that Baudricourt's close friend, René of Anjou, possibly organized Joan's journey and exchanged letters with the captain throughout January 1429 about Joan. There are several versions of the encounter. During her **condemnation trial** (1431), Joan explained that the duke sought help with an illness, which aligns with stories floating around about Joan concerning her divinity already. However, she offered no help other than suggesting he abandon his mistress and take back his wife. Joan told him of her **mission** to go to France and meet with Charles VII. She requested that Lorraine send his son-in-law, René, with her. He did not. The duke sent her back to Vaucouleurs, after which Baudricourt sent her to **Chinon**. At the **nullification proceedings** (1450–1456), stories differed on how much aid the duke provided Joan, but several attested to providing her a **horse**. Others said he just paid for her trip to meet Charles VII.

René of Anjou broke with the English and traveled to join the royal army after the **coro-**

nation of **Charles VII**. Lorraine continued his smaller wars in the region with little impact and died 25 January 1431, advising René to side with the Burgundians. He did not.

LOUIS, SAINT. Louis IX (1214–1270) was a king of France who participated in several crusades. Revered for his strong devotion to the faith, he was canonized in 1297. Although Joan of Arc was never recorded as evoking Saint Louis, Jean Dunois (*See* ORLÉANS, BASTARD OF) testified during the **nullification proceedings** that she prayed to him along with **Saint Charlemagne**. The same exchange is found in the *Chronique de la Pucelle*. *See also* CATHERINE, SAINT; CHARLEMAGNE, SAINT; GABRIEL, SAINT; MARGARET, SAINT; MICHAEL, SAINT; VOICES, VISIONS, AND REVELATIONS.

LOUIS XI, KING OF FRANCE (1423–1483). Eldest son of **Charles VII** and **Marie of Anjou**, the **dauphin** and future Louis XI would have been only five years old when he purportedly met Joan of Arc in Loches, according to the **Laval Letter** (8 June 1429). The year prior, Charles had arranged a marriage contract for his son with Margaret of Scotland, daughter of Scottish King James I. The marriage was part of a treaty that called for more reinforcements for Charles's wars (*See* FRANCO-SCOTTISH ALLIANCE). Louis found himself used as a pawn in several noble rebellions against his father (*See* PRAGUERIE REBELLION), but as he came of age, he participated willingly and sought exile under the protection of **Philip the Good**.

Upon the death of Charles VII (1461), King Louis XI cleaned out his father's court, casting out many of the nobles who had been companions in arms of Joan of Arc. After facing his own noble rebellion during the **War of the Public Weal** (1465), Louis reconciled with many of the nobles. The last decade of his life (1468–1477) was spent acquiring and unifying territory in Burgundy, Maine, and Anjou.

There is no surviving record of Louis's perspective about Joan of Arc. Some historians have theorized that his silence was because Joan had not yet reached the cult status of saint, and she was more associated with the victories of his father, Charles. There was a longstanding claim that Louis had the body of **Pierre Cauchon** exhumed and fed to dogs, but an excavation in 1931 found the bishop's grave intact.

LOUNGUEVILLE, COUNT OF. *See* ORLÉANS, JEAN, BASTARD OF.

LOYALISTS. A generic term sometimes used to denote those loyal to **Charles VII**'s claim to the French throne, which directly challenged the **Treaty of Troyes**. Given the range of allies and mercenaries that Charles incorporated into his military, this could include French, Scots, Lombards, and Spanish. *See also* ARMAGNACS; DAUPHINISTS; ORLÉANAIS; ROYALISTS.

LOYSELEUR, NICOLAS. *See* LOISELEUR, NICOLAS.

LUXEMBOURG, DEMOISELLE OF. *See* LUXEMBOURG, JOHN OF.

LUXEMBOURG, JEANNE OF. *See* LUXEMBOURG, JOHN OF.

LUXEMBOURG, JOHN OF (1392–1441). John of Luxembourg (Jean de Luxembourg) was the commander of the Burgundian forces besieging **Compiègne** when Joan of Arc was captured (23 May 1430). She remained his captive until November, when he **ransomed** her to the English.

Throughout the 1410s, Luxembourg served Duke John the Fearless of Burgundy, especially in the **French Civil War**. He suffered a wound in battle that cost him an eye. He was knighted in 1412, became governor of Arras in 1414, and took part in the capture of **Paris** in 1418. He was the **chamberlain** of John the Fearless before the duke's assassination in 1419, after which Luxembourg was firmly in the camp of the new duke of Burgundy (*See* PHILIP THE GOOD), knighting the duke in 1421. Luxembourg supported the **Treaty of Troyes** (1420) and often worked in concert with English leaders such as **Thomas Rempston** during campaigns. He continued fighting against those allied with **Charles VII**, almost capturing **Vaucouleurs** in 1428 before a truce stopped his advance. The event possibly played into **Robert de Baudricourt**'s change of attitude when it came to hearing pleas from Joan of Arc to send her to meet with the king in **Chinon**.

During the military success of Charles's army in spring and summer of 1429, Luxembourg guarded outlying cities in some of Burgundy's frontier. While Charles was in Compiègne (20–28 August), Luxembourg met with the king to make overtures of peace between Burgundy and France. Although **Gilles le Bouvier** described these efforts as a ruse, the continued negotiations coalesced into the **Franco-Burgundian Truce**.

In early 1430, the dukes of **Bedford** and Burgundy agreed on an offensive against the towns captured by Charles in 1429. Luxembourg, under the command of Philip the Good, marched out with a force on 20 April and began besieging Compiègne on 22 May. Joan of Arc was captured the next day and transferred to the possession of Luxembourg, and he held her captive until November. Early in her **captivity**, Luxembourg approached Joan with an offer to ransom her to the French if she agreed to stop fighting. She aggressively rebuffed his offer, questioning his authority to release her. Luxembourg received letters from **Henry VI**, **Pierre Cauchon**, and the **University of Paris** requesting custody of Joan so that they could hold an **inquisition**. While in captivity in Beaurevoir, Joan was visited by Luxembourg's wife, Jeanne de Béthune, and his aunt, Demoiselle of Luxembourg. Joan of Arc testified during her **condemnation trial** that they offered women's clothing to her, which she refused to wear. Demoiselle also pleaded with John of Luxembourg not to deliver Joan to the English. It is unclear how much Demoiselle's pleas played any part in the events, but historians have noted that she died on 13 November 1430 and Joan was sent to the English at the end of the month.

Although lifting the siege of Compiègne on 25 October, Luxembourg continued to serve Philip the Good until the **Treaty of Arras** (1435), which he argued against and refused to recognize. By this time, Luxembourg held numerous titles and estates including Beaurevoir, Guise, and Ligny. The Burgundians and French mostly avoided confronting him overtly, but some commanders such as **La Hire** made encroachments into his territories. By 1440, Charles VII had determined to make an offensive, but Luxembourg died on 5 January 1441 before the campaign began.

Derided by French chroniclers for ransoming Joan of Arc to the English, Luxembourg was compared to Judas and a rumor spread that he committed suicide. Conversely, Burgundian chroniclers praised him as an upstanding knight.

LUXEMBOURG, LOUIS OF (C. 1390–1443). Louis of Luxembourg was the bishop of Thérouanne (1415), the chancellor of English-controlled France (1425), and the brother of **John of Luxembourg**. In 1431, he was present for the admonishment (23 May), **abjuration** (24 May), and **execution** of Joan of Arc (30 May). It is unclear if he followed the trial closely or if he was merely present in **Rouen** as part of the entourage of **Henry VI**. During the **nullification proceedings** (1450–1456), several witnesses including **Pierre Miget**, **Martin Ladvenu**, and **Jean Le Fèvre** testified that many wept during the execution of Joan, but they each evoked Louis of Luxembourg explicitly as one of the criers.

Luxembourg continued to serve the English, narrowly escaping Paris when the French retook it in 1436. In 1439, he was promoted to cardinal. He died in 1443.

M

MAÇON, ROBERT LE (C. 1365–1443). After a lengthy career serving several French courts including the queen of France (*See* ISABEAU OF BAVARIA), Robert le Maçon became chancellor to future **Charles VII** in 1416, before the latter became the **dauphin**. Maçon gained everlasting favor with Charles during the Burgundian capture of **Paris** in 1418 (*See* FRENCH CIVIL WAR), when he offered his horse for Charles's escape. As **chancellor** (1416–1422), he advised against the murder of John the Fearless (1419), and he lobbied for the release of the **duke of Brittany** (1420).

Maçon appears to have been favorable to Joan of Arc. His wife, Jeanne de Mortemert, was part of the team that confirmed Joan's **virginity** in 1429. He introduced Joan to the **Laval** brothers. During the **march to Reims**, Maçon rode alongside Charles. At the **siege of Troyes** (5–9 July), when all of Charles's advisers suggested he abandon the effort, it was Maçon who suggested they consult Joan who immediately began preparations for an assault. The next day, the city capitulated. Maçon also signed the **ennoblement** document for Joan and her family.

Maçon remained in the king's council until 1436, likely retiring due to old age.

MACY, HAIMOND DE (C. 1400–?). Haimond (also spelled Aymon or Aimon) de Macy was a knight in the service of **John of Luxembourg** during the prominence of Joan of Arc. By the **nullification proceedings** (1450–1456), his admiration of her had grown and he provided several unique stories that are quoted often in histories. When Joan was still imprisoned by Luxembourg, Macy **sexually assaulted** her by grabbing her breasts on several occasions. He presented this as evidence of her purity, emphasizing that she aggressively pushed him away each time.

Before John of Luxembourg **ransomed** Joan to the English, he offered to free her if she agreed to never take up arms against him again. Joan spurned the offer, declaring that he did not have the power to release her and that the English would rather see her dead. They went back and forth until Joan referred to the English as *goddams*, spurning **Humphrey Stafford** to pull a knife on her before the **earl of Warwick** prevented him from harming her.

Macy also recalled the day of Joan's **abjuration** (24 May 1431). After she initially resisted, she finally agreed to abjure to avoid the fire. He identified **Laurent Calot** as the one who presented the paper for her to sign. Joan said she was illiterate and mockingly drew a circle. Calot then took Joan's hand and forced her to make a different mark, but Macy could not recall what it was.

MAID. *See* LA PUCELLE.

MANCHON, GUILLAUME (C. 1396–1456). On 9 January 1431, **Pierre Cauchon** selected Guillaume Manchon and **Guillaume Colles** to serve as notaries on Joan of Arc's **condemnation trial** (*See* ROLES). They were later joined by **Nicolas Taquel** on 14 March. At the time, Manchon was an official notary for the archbishop of **Rouen**. Manchon's signature and seal appears throughout the trial **transcripts** along with the other notaries.

After the trial, Manchon and **Thomas de Courcelles** were responsible for translating the trial record into Latin and collecting relevant documentation for distribution. They produced five copies, four of which made it to the **nullification proceedings** (1450–1456), one of them thanks to Manchon. After the nullification verdict, one transcript was ceremonially burned and only three survive today. In addition, Manchon provided his own notes from the condemnation trial, often referred to as the "French Minutes." That he kept his notes as well as a copy of the Latin transcript attests to Manchon's general interest in court procedures. He would serve as a promoter later in life.

Manchon's role in the trial and responsibility for producing, translating, and collating its documentation makes his testimonies during the nullification proceedings valuable. Like his fellow notaries, he claimed that he was pressured to withhold or change statements made by Joan during her trial. The pressure came from others present on behalf of **Henry VI**, contributing their own notes to the process. Where there were conflicts, Manchon made notes and pushed for Joan to clarify her meaning on the disputed topics. Regardless, Manchon was emphatic that he and his fellow notaries would not budge on recording Joan's statements or what they believed was her general meaning in the final record. This matches with an anecdote shared by **Jean Le Fèvre** who said that at one point during the trial, Joan asked the notaries to reread how they recorded one of her responses. She admonished them for recording the exact opposite of her meaning. Manchon corrected the record and promised to be more diligent in the future. After the trial was finished and Joan purportedly **relapsed**, there were further examinations of Joan. However, Manchon was not present, and he resisted pressure from Cauchon to sign the record of them.

Manchon adds more anecdotes to the numerous controversies surrounding the condemnation trial, including attempts by **Nicolas Loiseleur** to portray himself as an ally of **Charles VII** in order to gain the confidence of Joan, and how the summarized **twelve articles** were never officially read to Joan before the assessors and the **University of Paris** could render their opinions. Concerning the twelve articles, Manchon would not defend their validity or accuracy in capturing Joan's meaning, only that he was asked to include the articles in the record, and his signature on them in the trial transcripts was only meant to confirm including them as instructed. He also revealed that Joan had complained on more than one occasion that the English guards had attempted to rape her, which led to an intervention by the **earl of Warwick** who replaced at least two of the guards (See SEXUAL ASSAULT AND RAPE).

By the nullification proceedings, Manchon portrayed himself as someone sympathetic to Joan, as he did not wish to defend the condemnation trial, claiming it was political in nature and failed to prove Joan was a **heretic**. He claimed he later used his notary earnings to buy a missal to pray for Joan. Although there was no indication that he was so sympathetic at the time of the trial, **Jean Favé** testified that at some point the English became dissatisfied with Manchon due to his favorable disposition to Joan.

Manchon died on 9 December 1456, having lived long enough to see the original verdict against Joan nullified.

MARGARET, SAINT. Saint Margaret dates to the third century. As the daughter of a pagan priest, she was driven out when she converted to Christianity. After refusing to marry a Roman prefect, she survived being dropped in boiling water, but not her beheading. The following of Margaret grew in eleventh-century France, along with **Saint Catherine**. At the Church of St. Rémy in **Domremy**, Margaret was the patron saint, and Joan of Arc would have been exposed to a statue of Margaret there.

During her **condemnation trial**, Joan mentioned Margaret always in tandem with Saint Catherine, but it was Catherine who would further appear to Joan alone to comfort her. *See also* CHARLEMAGNE, SAINT; GABRIEL, SAINT; LOUIS, SAINT; MICHAEL, SAINT; VOICES, VISIONS, AND REVELATIONS.

MARGARET OF SCOTLAND. See FRANCO-SCOTTISH ALLIANCE.

MARIE OF ANJOU, QUEEN OF FRANCE (1404–1463). Born in 1404, Marie was the daughter of **Yolande of Aragon** and Duke Louis II of Anjou. Louis died in 1417, but not before Marie became engaged to the young future **Charles VII** in 1413. When Charles became **dauphin** in 1417, he and Marie moved to Paris. During the Burgundian capture of the city the next year, Charles made a hasty escape, leaving Marie behind to witness the subsequent massacres (*See* FRENCH CIVIL WAR). Marie made it out unharmed, and they were married in 1422, the same year Charles became the disputed king of France. In 1423, they had their first of fourteen children, future **Louis XI**.

We know very little of Marie's character and nothing concrete concerning her views on Joan of Arc. If Yolande of Aragon was as supportive of Joan as historians have theorized, it is possible Marie shared the same enthusiasm. There was an indication that the queen would join the **march to Reims** (29 June–16 July), but she ultimately did not, perhaps out of safety concerns. On 3 March 1431, Joan was questioned during her **condemnation trial** on whether the queen had commented on her male **clothing** or if the queen asked her to change her attire, but Joan refused to answer.

Although the king and queen had many children, Charles eventually took Agnès Sorel (1422–1450) as an official mistress, a well-documented relationship that resulted in an additional four children. Marie died on 29 November 1463, two years after Charles died and two years into the reign of her son, Louis XI.

MARRIAGE CONTRACT. During Joan of Arc's **condemnation trial** (1431), the assessors questioned her on a case in Toul about a marriage contract. The details of the marriage contract and subsequent case survive only through the condemnation trial. She clarified that she made no promise to marriage and had been summoned to Toul to make her case when the unnamed man pushed for fulfilment. Although the date is not known, historians sometimes date the event in January or early February 1429, possibly between her meeting with the **duke of Lorraine** and her third meeting with **Robert de Baudricourt**. No further details have survived from Toul, not even the man's name, and no one mentioned the contract during the **nullification proceedings** (1450–1456). However, **Jean d'Estivet** crafted a lengthy story in Article 9 of the initial **seventy articles** of accusation presented against Joan, claiming she summoned the man to Toul because he refused to marry her. Joan referred to her previous testimony and denied the rest of the article's claim. There was no further mention of the topic in the condensed **twelve articles**. *See also* LA PUCELLE.

MARSHAL OF FRANCE. By the fifteenth century, the marshal of France had evolved from an administrative role to one of the highest-ranking military positions. Appointed by the king, the responsibilities were fluid, but typically included recruiting, promoting, inspecting, organizing, disciplining, and paying troops. The marshal also organized the payments and prices of **ransoms** and participated in diplomatic discussions. The extent to which this power was wielded consistently and effectively varied greatly and like many royal appointments, it was sometimes honorary in nature.

Joan of Arc knew several marshals and would-be marshals of France during her military campaigns. **Gilbert Motier de La Fayette** and **Jean de Brosse** were both marshals when Joan first met them in 1429. **Gilles de Rais**, who had fought at the siege of **Orléans** and in the **Loire Campaign**, was appointed marshal during the **coronation of Charles VII**. Both **André de Laval** and **Poton de Xaintrailles** were appointed marshal in 1439 and 1454, respectively.

MARTIN V. *See* POPE.

MASSIEU, JEAN (C. 1405–1456?). Jean Massieu was a priest in **Rouen** at the time of Joan of Arc's **condemnation trial** (1431). At the beginning of the trial, **Pierre Cauchon** selected him to be the executor of mandates, responsible for escorting Joan, as well as the judges and assessors, to and from her prison cell (*See* ROLES). Thus, Massieu was present at every session alongside Joan, even when the trial **transcripts** do not list him explicitly. Because of this, post-medieval histories in English sometimes list his role as usher. Since Massieu served in this role until Joan's execution, he gained an intimate and unique perspective of the prisoner, which he shared in multiple testimonies during the **nullification proceedings** (1450–1456).

For example, early in the trial, Massieu claims after he allowed Joan to hear Mass in a local chapel, he was threatened by **Jean Beaupere** who would later block Joan's entrance to hear mass. Massieu said he became a mediator of sorts between Joan and Cauchon, delivering messages between the two regarding Joan's desire to hear Mass. This all hinged on her refusal to stop wearing men's **clothing**.

Concerning Joan's **abjuration** (24 May 1431), Massieu provides details on the sermon preached to Joan and how Massieu was responsible for reading the abjuration to Joan, which he believed she did not understand. He also believed she then only signed it after **Guillaume Érard** threatened to burn her.

Massieu provided details on Joan's prison before and during the trial, claiming that there were five Englishmen on guard, expanding on the three listed in the transcripts of the condemnation trial (*See* CAPTIVITY). Three of them remained in her cell with her. After her abjuration and her new commitment to wear women's clothing, Massieu tells us the guards ripped off and confiscated her clothing and dumped men's clothing on the floor. Although she argued and pleaded with them, they would not return the women's clothing.

On the day of her **execution** (30 May), Massieu paints a dramatic, detailed scene. He attended her last confession and communion before leading her, under the guard of eight hundred English soldiers, to the marketplace in Rouen. There, the judges condemned her as a relapsed **heretic** and handed her over to the secular authorities. Joan piously prayed and lamented, and asked people in the marketplace to pray for her while a final sermon was preached. Massieu describes how he attempted to comfort Joan on the scaffold, providing her with a cross, which she pressed to her chest. He then made sure another cross would be made visible to her during her execution per her request. Massieu's efforts went on for some time before he was pressed by eager Englishmen to execute Joan. From there, the executioner tied Joan to a stake and set the fire without any formal verdict read from the secular authorities. Her final word was "Jesus."

Although rich in detail, some of which can be corroborated with other eyewitnesses, critical historians remain suspect of Massieu's testimony for a combination of reasons. First, he is clearly in awe of his subject. Second, he obviously exaggerates in his details, sometimes to a fanciful degree (e.g., Joan's heart full of blood somehow survived her burning). Finally, several recorded fines and punishments against Massieu during his career demonstrate that he had a track record of impropriety. Some historians believe he testified often and in length during the nullification proceedings partly to whitewash his own past. Regardless, many of his details have captured the post-medieval image of Joan that has perpetuated along with its subject.

MASTER OF ARTS. *See* EDUCATION.

MAURICE, PIERRE (1393–1436). By the time of Joan of Arc's **condemnation trial** (1431), Pierre Maurice had recently become **canon** of **Rouen** (1430), held a doctorate in theology (*See* EDUCATION), and was the former rector of the University of Paris. He was brought in as an assessor to Joan's trial on 13 February 1431, and he was present at roughly two dozen sessions. On 23 May, Maurice led the presentation to Joan of the condensed **twelve articles** of accusation against her. These had already been reviewed by the university who had returned an opinion, but Joan was hearing them for the first time. The **transcripts** of the trial capture Maurice's concern for Joan, as he pleads with her to submit to the **Church Militant**, using lengthy analogies he hoped would reach her. Joan, however, refused to abandon men's **clothing** or change her previous statements from the trial. After Joan's **execution** (30 May), Maurice provided testimony (7 June) that was appended to the trial transcripts where he claimed that upon visiting Joan in her cell on that day, she admitted her visions were fictitious and her **voices** were imagined from small events.

Maurice died in 1436, but his fellow assessors evoked him in their testimonies during the **nullification proceedings** (1450–1456). **Guillaume Colles** noted Maurice's sadness when Joan resumed wearing men's clothing. **Richard de Grouchet** tells us that Maurice faced antagonism and threats from the English for his attempts to warn Joan during the presentation of the twelve articles. Historians tend to view Maurice sympathetically, as he appeared to genuinely care for Joan's soul, lacking any discernible desire to destroy her.

MEHUN. Located fifteen kilometers northeast of **Bourges**, Mehun was another estate of Duke Jean of Berry (1340–1416). The duke gave his estates to his great nephew, future **Charles VII**, and Mehun quickly became one of Charles's favorite residences. From this city, Charles learned of the death of his father (*See* CHARLES VI), after which he was proclaimed king (30 October 1422). Joan of Arc stayed in Mehun at the end of September 1429 after the failed assault on **Paris**, and again at the end of December, after the failed siege of **La Charité**. Charles spent the last three months of his life in Mehun, dying there on 22 July 1461.

MEN-AT-ARMS. In fifteenth-century France, the term men-at-arms was somewhat fluid and could refer to any mounted soldier such as a **knight** or **squire**. In other instances, it refers to an unknighted mounted soldier and was interchangeable with squire (or esquire in England). Yet it did not always indicate class, and so men-at-arms could be ennobled knights and squires, as well as paid soldiers. England's muster rolls were often explicit that an archer was different from a man-at-arms.

Historians are not always precise or consistent with their usage of men-at-arms, and they could simply be referring to a group of soldiers.

METZ, JEAN DE (C. 1399–?). Jean de Metz, also known as de Novelonpont or Novelompont, is one of the earliest characters in Joan of Arc's story, yet we know little about him outside of his interactions with Joan. Based on his testimony and verified by the testimonies of others at the **nullification proceedings** (1450–1456), he first encountered Joan while she was at **Vaucouleurs**. He would later receive an ennoblement from **Charles VII** in 1448 for distinguishing himself in war, but when he first met Joan in 1429, he was a mere commoner under the service of **Robert de Baudricourt**.

In Metz's testimony, he claimed to have sworn allegiance to Joan from the beginning and he provided **clothing** from his own servants after Joan said she preferred male attire. His admiration of Joan is evident, as he recounted several of their interactions in which she won him over with a combination of charm, sarcasm, confidence, and divine inspiration. Baudricourt entrusted a small group of men led by Metz and **Bertrand de Poulengy** to escort Joan from Vaucouleurs to **Chinon** in order to meet Charles VII. Metz testified that for eleven days, they traveled through enemy territory, mainly at night, between 13 and 23 February 1429. When they slept, he was emphatic that Joan remained clothed, and he never had attraction toward her. Outside of these anecdotes from Metz, other testimonies and royal records tell us Metz paid for the travel expenses on this journey, after which the scant surviving evidence suggests he was a constant companion in arms of Joan's and was with her throughout most, if not all, of her campaigns.

MEUNG, BATTLE OF (15 JUNE 1429). Meung is located sixteen kilometers southwest of **Orléans** with a bridge crossing the Loire River. The English captured the town during **Salisbury's 1428 expedition**. The **earl of Salisbury**, who was wounded on 24 October at the beginning of the siege of **Orléans**, was transported to Meung where he died (3 November).

After the relief of Orléans (8 May 1429), English troops retreated toward Meung, pursued by **La Hire** who forced them to abandon their prisoners and artillery. **Thomas Scales** then remained stationed in Meung. After the capture of **Jargeau** (12 June) during the **Loire Campaign**, the French, led by the **duke of Alençon** with Joan of Arc, marched to Meung and captured the bridge (15 June). While the French were negotiating the surrender of **Beaugency** (17–18 June), English forces arrived outside Meung and began a brief assault on 18 June. However, upon learning of the capture of Beaugency, they withdrew to meet up with **John Fastolf**'s army in the north. The French then moved to attack the English before they met up with Fastolf, defeating them at **Patay** that same day.

Charles VII and Joan of Arc later passed through Meung in September after the failed assault on **Paris** (8 September).

MICHAEL, SAINT. Michael is an archangel prominent in texts associated with Judaism, Christianity, and Islam. He had grown in importance among the kings of France beginning in the fourteenth century, as they transitioned from Saint Denis. This transition seemed to culminate with the English capture of the town of **Saint-Denis** in 1419 followed by the dauphin (*See* CHARLES VII) depicting Saint Michael on his standard in 1420. In 1469, King **Louis XI** created the order of Saint Michael.

Saint Michael would have been well-known to Joan of Arc, as there were at least forty-six sanctuaries dedicated to the saint in Lorraine alone. **Christine de Pizan** tells us that Michael along with **Saint Gabriel** appeared to Joan and led her to the king (*See THE TALE OF JOAN OF ARC*). The two saints purportedly were depicted on her **standard**, but Joan would tell the assessors at her **condemnation trial** (1431) that the angels on her standard were only there to glorify God, without identifying them. The assessors honed in on Joan's claim to see and talk to Michael. She explained that he was the first among the saints to appear to her when she was around thirteen years old. They asked her for specific details about his appearance like if he was naked or if he had hair. Joan famously responded with her own questions, "Do you think God can't find him clothes?" And "Why would it be cut off?" (Hobbins 2005, 75–76). Not only could she understand Michael, even though he spoke the language of the angels, but he also comforted her.

During the **nullification proceedings** (1450–1456), Pierre Boucher, a priest who visited Rouen to witness some of Joan's trial, claimed that after praying to Saint Michael, Joan agreed to her **abjuration** (24 May 1431). He also said she cried out to Michael while tied up on the scaffold for her **execution** (30 May). **Jean Massieu** claimed that she commended herself to God and Saints Michael and Catherine. Guillaume de La Chambre (*See* PHYSICIANS) said she cried out to Jesus and Saint Michael. Thus, Saint Michael bookends Joan of Arc's story, being the first of her revelations and the last among the names she called out before her death. *See also* VOICES, VISIONS, AND REVELATIONS; SAINTS.

MIDI (MIDY), NICOLAS. Nicholas Midi held a doctorate in theology from the **University of Paris** (1424), and he was an avid participant in Joan of Arc's **condemnation trial** (1431). During the trial, he received an appointment as **canon** of **Rouen** by the **duke of Bedford**. Midi had two major roles during the trial. **Thomas de Courcelles** tells us that Midi was responsible for narrowing down the original **seventy articles** of accusation presented against Joan down to the **twelve articles** that were then shared with the University of Paris. He then gave Joan her last sermon on 30 May 1431, after which the judges abandoned her to secular authorities, who **executed** her. **Jean Massieu** tells us that at the end of the sermon, Midi told Joan they could no longer help her and to go in peace.

After the trial, Midi, who was still firmly in the camp of the **Anglo-Burgundian Alliance**, was present for the entry of **Henry VI** into **Paris**, giving a speech on behalf of the university. Throughout the 1430s, he was very active, attending the **Council** of Basel in 1432, teaching at the University of Louvain in Burgundy (1432–1433), and welcoming **Charles VII** to Paris in 1437 with another speech. The latter event indicates that he switched sides in the **Hundred Years War**, likely after the **Treaty of Arras** (1435). Also, his sermon to Joan on the day of her trial and his two speeches to the kings demonstrate that he was appreciated for his oratory skills. We do not know the exact date of his death, and **Guillaume Colles**'s claim that he died from leprosy shortly after the trial is inaccurate. However, he very well may have died from the disease in the late 1430s or early 1440s.

MIGET, PIERRE (C. 1385–?). Pierre Miget was a **prior** of Longueville-Giffard in **Normandy** with a doctorate in theology from the **University of Paris** (*See* EDUCATION). In the earliest stages of the **French Civil War**, he sided with the Burgundians, backing the claim of John the Fearless that his assassination of Duke Louis of Orléans was justified (1407). During Joan of Arc's **condemnation trial**, he acted as an assessor (*See* ROLES) and frequently attended the sessions starting on 9 January 1431. On 9 May, he agreed with the recommendations from the University of Paris regarding Joan and on 29 May, he voted to abandon her to secular authorities.

During the **nullification proceedings**, Miget provided testimony in 1452, 1455, and 1456, each time emphasizing the same points. He believed the trial and thus the verdict were unjust, driven by the English who feared and hated Joan, and sought to discredit **Charles VII**. He told of how they feared Joan more than one hundred men and they believed she wielded magic. Miget believed she was a sincere Catholic but needed guidance on the role of the Church (*See* CHURCH MILITANT). He further believed that wearing men's **clothing** was not enough to condemn her as a **heretic**. However, he believed her claims of talking to saints were suspect (*See* VOICES, VISIONS, AND REVELATIONS). When she was taken by the English to be executed, Miget painted a scene of Joan crying and calling out "Jesus" over and over. He said he was moved to tears and could not witness the **execution**.

MISSION OF JOAN OF ARC. Historians have attempted to define the strategy of Joan of Arc in what is often described as her "mission" or "military mission," as directed by her **voices**. Cobbling together statements from her **letters**, statements at her **condemnation trial**, and eyewitness accounts, the mission of Joan of Arc becomes a shorthand to answer *why* Joan thrust herself into the **Hundred Years War**. This is complicated by the fact that the goals evolved and seemed somewhat fluid, depending on *when* and with *whom* Joan discussed the details.

The first part of Joan's mission was to lift the siege of **Orléans**. She is recorded professing it to or in front of people such as **Robert de Baudricourt, Simon Charles, Seguin de Seguin**, the **duke of Alençon**, and **Charles VII**. The latter sent her to be examined in **Poitiers** for eleven days of questioning by the theologians and scholars there (March 1429). They concluded that she could prove the divinity of her mission by lifting the siege. Joan then aggressively declared her mission to lift the siege in a **letter to the English (22 March 1429)**, threatening **Henry VI** and the **duke of Bedford** with violence if they persisted. With the siege lifted on 8 May, Joan gained much-needed collateral with Charles VII, his nobles, and her companions in arms.

The second part of Joan's mission was the **coronation of Charles VII** at **Reims**. Joan supported this goal from the earliest moment by always insisting on referring to the king as "dauphin" until he was crowned at Reims, and she received criticism from those who had already been referring to Charles as the king. Charles had gone so far as to pass the dauphin title on to his son in 1423 (*See* LOUIS XI). However, in order to hold the ceremony at Reims, it would mean marching through enemy-controlled territory. A month after Orléans, Joan and the royal army conducted the **Loire Campaign** (10–18 June 1429), recapturing cities held by the English along the Loire River. The campaign concluded in an open-field victory at **Patay** (18 June) and the capture of several key English nobles. Next came the **march to Reims** (29 June–16 July) where the royal army reclaimed city after city, often without firing a single shot, as French towns opened their gates and swore loyalty to Charles. Finally, on 17 July 1429, Charles VII was officially crowned.

After the coronation, the support for Joan's mission was strong, but not infallible. As Joan pushed the next aspects of her mission to free Paris from the English and ultimately expel the English from France, Charles and the duke of Burgundy (*See* PHILIP THE GOOD) began discussions for a possible truce (*See* FRANCO-BURGUNDIAN TRUCE). Still, Joan was empowered to pursue her mission, getting as far as the gates of Paris. After an unsuccessful assault on 8 September that included Joan's wounding (*See* INJURIES), Charles called off the siege entirely the next day. From here, support for Joan began to fade.

The question of the capture of Paris being part of her mission is still debated. Seguin de Seguin and Alençon both claimed Paris was always part of her professed mission, but these are based on recollections made several decades later during the **nullification proceedings** (1450–1456). However, Joan mentioned reclaiming Paris early and often, as attested to in the **Laval letter (8 June 1429)** and her **letter to the count of Armagnac (22 August 1429)**. It is also logical to conclude that if she was to expel the English from France, as she claimed in her letters to the English and attested by Alençon and the **bastard of Orléans**, then reclaiming Paris for Charles was naturally part of that mission. Still, Joan admitted during the condemnation trial that she did not have explicit instructions from her voices to attack Paris, at least not that day. Thus, historians begin to split hairs between what Joan professed was a divinely inspired action versus her continuing the general cause against the English.

Finally, there was her cause of freeing the captive **duke of Orléans**, prisoner of the English since Agincourt (1415). Seguin de Seguin and Alençon claimed they heard her profess this goal, and during her condemnation trial, she said she had instructions to trade prisoners for him (*See* RANSOM). If that failed, she planned to cross the English Channel to free him by force in what would be a one- to three-year endeavor.

As Joan demonstrated during her trial, she was not initially forthcoming with everything she heard from her voices. Thus, Joan's military career, including her **captivity**, can be defined by her continual effort to convince others of the divinity and/or plausibility of her mission while people chose to join, aid, ignore, or thwart her. As her mission progressed and evolved, people chose different reactions. For example, Joan attempted to convince Robert de Baudricourt of her mission on three occasions, but it was not until February 1429 that he decided to send her to **Chinon** to meet with Charles VII. It was not evident that he was entirely convinced of the divinity of her mission, but he was at least willing to aid instead of ignore her.

Historians sometimes use a combination of these professed goals to grade Joan's success in her military career, claiming that she was at least successful in two of them, and had started the progress for a third. Joan's other actions, such as the sieges of **Saint-Pierre-le-Moutier** (4 November 1429) and **La Charité** (24? November–23? December), as well as relieving the siege of **Compiègne** where she was captured (23 May 1430), were all actions she admitted were not specifically from her voices. The question then becomes whether Joan would have ever returned to civilian life upon completing her "mission." However, the mission was clearly fluid. She gave indications that she was interested in eventually pursuing a crusade, hopefully with the help of pacified English, or also pursuing the heretical Hussites. Had Joan lived, it is plausible that she would have continued her military career. *See also* LETTER TO THE HUSSITES.

MISTERE DU SIEGE D'ORLEANS. Mystery plays were large-scale religious productions of varying sizes and scope featuring music and hundreds of speaking roles that were prominent throughout France in the fifteenth and sixteenth centuries. Of the two hundred–plus mystery plays that have survived, they typically occurred over three to four days, but some were as long as twenty-five or more days. The plays required makeshift stages, as there were no permanent stages in medieval France. The cost was often so extraordinary that funding came directly from the cities where they were performed.

One such mystery play, *Mistere du siege d'Orleans*, tells the story of Joan of Arc and existed as early as 1429 with possibly other performances, or at least intentions to perform, in the 1440s, 1460s, and around 1500. At twenty thousand verses, it features as many as 160 characters at once and would have taken several days to perform. However, the version that has survived was a later version, clearly evolving with each iteration. Among other characters, there is the **bastard of Orléans**, referred to as the count of Dunois, a title he did not have until 1440. The play also uses the *Journal du siège d'Orléans* and the *Chronique de l'établissement de la fête du 8 mai* (c. 1456) as sources, sometimes word for word, or at least versified.

The play maintains a religious theme, focusing heavily on saints and the intervention of prayer on the part of characters such as **Charles VII** and Joan of Arc. It includes Joan meeting Charles in **Chinon**, the **Poitiers** examination, the lifting of the siege of **Orléans**, and the **Loire Campaign**. Joan is portrayed as divinely inspired and full of wit, as she leads French soldiers to victory. It does not include Joan's **execution**. That such a play would resonate with Orléans at this time is clear, especially since the citizens recognized the lifting of the siege as part of a yearly celebration.

The production of one of the versions of *Mistere du siege d'Orleans* is often associated with **Gilles de Rais** as an example of one of his many monetary indiscretions, but the evidence is not conclusive.

MOAT. *See* SIEGE.

MONSTRELET, ENGUERRAND DE (C. 1390–1453). Enguerrand de Monstrelet fought under the command of **John of Luxembourg** during the siege of **Compiègne** (1430), a city where Monstrelet would later serve as **bailiff**. He claims to have briefly met Joan of Arc after her capture, but he admits he cannot remember what words were exchanged. In the 1440s, he began work on his ambitious *Chronique*, covering the history of France and its neighboring countries throughout 1400 to 1444. He explicitly sought the continuation of Jean Froissart's *Chroniques* that covered 1327 to 1400, but Monstrelet is often criticized for lacking the same flair as his predecessor. Conversely, he has been praised for his straightforward storytelling, reproduction of letters and documents, detail, and accuracy.

Presented to **Philip the Good** in 1447, *Chronique* sometimes exhibits anti-**French** tendencies, especially against Joan of Arc, and he was obviously in favor of the **Anglo-Burgundian Alliance**. However, his work is invaluable for reconstructing the diplomatic and military activities at the time including **Salisbury's 1428 expedition**, the siege of **Orléans**, negotiations between Philip the Good and Charles VII, and numerous battles and sieges including **Herrings, Jargeau, Patay, Paris, Lagny**, and Compiègne. His presence at the latter has resulted in extensive details that are invaluable in understanding the ebb and flow and eventual abandonment of the four-month siege.

Also concerning Joan, Monstrelet describes from a Burgundian perspective Joan's arrival to **Chinon**, the **march to Reims** and **coronation of Charles VII**, and the capture (and recapture) of numerous cities by all sides throughout this period. He explicitly questions whether Joan was truly the leader in her battles, emphasizing that she had experienced commanders in her army, especially for relieving Orléans. Also useful are his reproductions of letters from **the duke of Bedford** and **Henry VI**. Although Froissart overshadows Monstrelet today in terms of transmission and study, his work was extremely popular in the sixteenth century and historians today use *Chronique* extensively when writing about Joan of Arc.

MONTAGU, THOMAS. *See* SALISBURY, EARL OF.

MONTÉCLAIR, JEAN DE. Jean de Montéclair, also known as Jean le Cannonier or le Couleuvrinier, was originally from **Lorraine**, but was living in Angers when the siege of **Orléans** started (1428). He was one of numerous gunners hired on behalf of **Charles VII** to help defend the city, but Montéclair was specifically remembered in several chronicles and by **Jean d'Aulon** for his exploits and idiosyncrasy. He was skilled with gunpowder **artillery**, especially culverins, hitting targets from as far away as four hundred yards. The *Journal du siège d'Orléans* tells us how he would play wounded or dead out in the field. He would then be carried back into Orléans, only to return to the fighting. Jean d'Aulon tells how one of the English defenders of the Tourelles bastille at Orléans was causing trouble for the French, and Montéclair targeted and killed him with one shot from a culverin. The *Chronique de la Pucelle* tells a similar story during the assault on **Jargeau** (11–12 June 1429) when the **duke of Alençon** ordered Montéclair to take down a specific defender and he did with a single shot.

Records still survive for the payment of services for Jean de Montéclair along with other gunners who came to the service of Charles in 1428 and 1429, but Montéclair is the most renowned of the lot. Unfortunately, we only know these few anecdotes about his exploits and even less about other hired gunners who were typically not from nobility. It is clear that commanders such as Alençon relied on him, and it is likely that Joan learned from gunners such as Montéclair as she studied how to use guns.

MONTÉPILLOY, BATTLE OF (15 AUGUST 1429). After the **coronation of Charles VII** at Reims (17 July 1429), towns continued to forsake the **Treaty of Troyes** and switch their loyalties to the French king, as others did during the **march to Reims**. The **duke of Bedford** sought to blunt the momentum of **Charles VII** by issuing a challenge, asking the king to pick a time and place for a battle of their two armies. The challenge, sent by letter on 7 August, survives in **Monstrelet**, and includes insults toward Charles, Joan of Arc, **Brother Richard**, and the king's allies.

The resulting battle of Montépilloy was recorded by numerous chroniclers including **Perceval de Cagny**, who was an eyewitness. Bedford's army included troops from Lancastrian **Normandy**, Burgundy, and recently recruited English that were en route to join **Henry Beaufort**'s crusade against the Hussites. Although numbers vary in the medieval chronicles, most historians believe the armies were numerically matched between six thousand to ten thousand. On the evening of 14 August, the royal army camped near Montépilloy, roughly four kilometers from Senlis. The Anglo-Burgundian force camped roughly two kilometers from Senlis, between the royal army and the city. The chroniclers agree that the site was an open field. There were minor skirmishes that resulted in ten to twelve English captured, but nightfall ended the fighting. Throughout the night, Bedford fortified his position, using similar techniques to what had been successful at the battles of **Cravant** and the **Herrings**.

The next morning (15 August), the troops confessed and heard Mass. The royal army arrayed in three groups within a gunshot's distance of Bedford's army. One group was led by the **duke of Alençon** and the **count of Vendôme**, another by **Rene of Anjou**, and the third by Charles VII, the **count of Clermont**, and **Georges de La Trémoille**. The wings were covered by **Jean de Brosse** and **Gilles de Rais**. In reserve was the **bastard of Orléans**, **Charles d'Albret**, and **La Hire**, along with Joan of Arc.

The armies remained stagnant, refusing to fully commit an attack on each other. **Jean Chartier** tells us that dust obscured the view of the armies. Joan pushed for an attack. Alençon made an offer to Bedford to withdraw his army back, allowing Bedford to bring his army into the open away from their defenses, but this was declined. Joan is described as approaching the English lines with her **standard**, enticing them to attack. There were also skirmishes initiated by the royal army that resulted in three hundred deaths according to Monstrelet, but Bedford refused to move. By nightfall, the royal army withdrew from the field and retired to their camp. The next morning (16 August), the royal army withdrew in an orderly fashion, anticipating an attack that never came. By noon, Bedford withdrew his army as well. The standoff at Montépilloy was over.

On 17 August, the king received the keys to **Compiègne**; he visited the city the next day. However, the battle had seemingly curbed the momentum of the royal army. Negotiations were in progress for a **Franco-Burgundian Truce** that would come to fruition on 28 August. The idea of splitting the Burgundians and the

English without bloodshed was too enticing for Charles and his advisors.

MONTIGNY, JEAN DE. Jean de Montigny held a doctorate of **canon law** and served as bishop of **Paris** (1440) and the dean of the **University of Paris** (1446). In 1454 or 1455, he was one of the experts who answered the call of **Jean Bréhal** to provide an opinion on the **condemnation trial** of Joan of Arc. He found overwhelmingly in favor of Joan, arguing that the trial's process, accusations, **abjuration**, **relapse**, and verdicts were suspect. He found the line of questioning and the summations of Joan's responses unfair, vague, imbalanced, and inconsistent (*See* SEVENTY ARTICLES; TWELVE ARTICLES). He also found that the original accusations against her regarding her **voices** or her pursuit of war did not mean she erred in the faith. Furthermore, Joan was mistreated. Access to her and attempts to advise her were hindered, her appeals to the **pope** were ignored, and she should have been permitted to hear Mass and receive communion even while in men's **clothing**.

In his assessment, Montigny recommended a new trial be held on neutral ground such as Rome, and those holding the offices of the **roles** of Joan's original trial should be represented. He even recommended seeking counsel from **Henry VI**. Although his recommendations for what became the nullification trial were not followed precisely, his opinion was recorded, and it influenced those reviewing and judging the trial.

MONT-SAINT-MICHEL. *See* NORMANDY.

MOREL, AUBERT. Aubert Morel was a **Rouen** lawyer with a licentiate in **canon law** from the **University of Paris** (*See* EDUCATION). He had several **benefices**, some of which he obtained from the English. He was present for at least twelve sessions during Joan of Arc's **condemnation trial** (1431), starting with the first public session on 21 February until her **relapse** on 28 May.

When it came time to render an opinion on the **twelve articles** formally brought against Joan, Morell signed a joint declaration with **Jean Duchemin**, arguing that Joan's revelations were not real and her refusal to wear women's **clothing** was wrong. After spurning the admonishments from the judges and assessors, she deserved excommunication. They hedged their statement that it was *possible* her revelations could be real, but she provided no evidence aside from her own word. Thus, they deferred to the theologians on the validity. Their final recommendation was that if she did not **abjure**, she deserved prison for life.

Morel was one of the assessors present when Joan was threatened with **torture** on 9 May, and he later recommended torture to expedite the trial on 12 May. When the University of Paris submitted their opinion on the twelve articles, he agreed with the other assessors that Joan should abjure or be condemned as a **heretic** and handed over to secular authorities.

N

NAME OF JOAN OF ARC. The name of Joan of Arc, as she is known today by English speakers, is Jeanne d'Arc among French speakers. However, these were not her names during her lifetime. When asked for her name and surname during the first interrogation of her **condemnation trial** (20 February 1431), "She answered that she was called Jeannette in her region, and Joan [Jeanne] after she came to France. But of her surname she said she knew nothing" (Hobbins 2005, 50). Joan more commonly referred to herself as Jeanne la Pucelle or simply **la Pucelle**, the literal anglicized version being "Joan the Maid." Of the three surviving **letters** that bare her signature, she signed them as "Jehanne." Her supporters referred to her with versions of Jeanne, Jeanne la Pucelle, or la Pucelle. Her detractors followed suit, but typically added qualifiers such as "the so-called" or "the one who calls herself." It was not until 1455 during the **nullification proceedings** that a version of "Jeanne d'Arc" appears in writing. Similarly, Joan's family all bear versions of the surname Darc with no apostrophe, adopting the surname because of her fame. Although methods have varied over time, historians since the twentieth century have consistently employed "d'Arc" as the family's surname. Histories written in English can vary, featuring either Jeanne d'Arc or Joan of Arc, but almost always "d'Arc" when referring to members of her family. *See also* ENNOBLEMENT.

NEUFCHÂTEAU. Neufchâteau is a town in **Lorraine** on the banks of the Meuse River, roughly ten kilometers south of Joan of Arc's home, **Domremy**. Since the battle of Agincourt in 1415 (*See* HUNDRED YEARS WAR), the town had been under the rule of **the duke of Lorraine**, and, like other towns in the region, it was loyal to **Charles VII**. Uniquely, it was known for its active markets and itinerant **friars** that often passed through. Historians have theorized that Joan and her family visited there regularly, exposing Joan to the fiery preaching and prophecies known to accompany the friars.

When Burgundian forces raided Lorraine and besieged **Vaucouleurs** in the north (22 June 1428), Joan's family and the citizens of Domremy were forced to seek refuge in Neufchâteau. During her **condemnation trial** (1431), Joan said she was there for fifteen days, confessing to Franciscan friars three times. Historians have theorized that this experience may have been the final impetus for Joan to embark to Vaucouleurs to meet with **Robert de Baudricourt** and begin her **mission**. It is also likely Joan heard news and rumors of the English expedition force led by the **earl of Salisbury** into the Loire Valley that would culminate in the siege of **Orléans** (*See* SALISBURY'S 1428 EXPEDITION).

Article 8 of the initial **seventy articles** of accusation brought against Joan at her trial seem to mix up Joan's testimony related to seeking refuge in Neufchâteau and embarking to Vaucouleurs, emphasizing that Joan left her mother and father to go to Neufchâteau. During the **nullification proceedings** (1450–1456), inhabitants in Domremy were asked explicitly if Joan was always in the company of her father and mother while in Neufchâteau, something several of them were able to confirm.

NICHOLAS V. *See* POPE.

NORMANDY. A northwestern duchy in France, Normandy had been part of the French crown since 1204. Throughout the **Hundred Years War**, attempts to capture the duchy by England were weak and unsuccessful until **Henry V**. On 1 August 1417, Henry arrived with an invasion force and spent the next two years capturing towns and fortifications including Caen (19 September 1417) and Falaise (16 February 1418). Henry began a lengthy siege of the duchy's capital, **Rouen**, on 29 July, focused on starving the inhabitants into submission, and the town finally surrendered on 19 January 1419. Historians traditionally use the capture of Rouen to mark the end of Henry's conquest of Normandy, but more towns and fortifications in the region surrendered throughout the rest of the year. Mont-Saint-Michel, with its natural defense as an island, managed to remain defiant against multiple attempts at capture via force, deceit, and bribery throughout the English occupation of Normandy. Historians refer to the duchy as Lancastrian Normandy over the next two decades.

Henry's hold on the region strengthened with the signing of the **Treaty of Troyes** (1420), which officially recognized him as the heir of France, and explicitly included Normandy. Henry then toiled to secure the duchy by collecting loyalty oaths from nobility and clergy, garrisoning the towns and redistributing property to his relatives. With the deaths of Henry V (13 August 1422) followed by **Charles VI** (22 October), the future **Henry VI** was too young to rule his inherited kingdoms, and the **duke of Bedford** served as **regent** of France. Those still loyal to **Charles VII** sought to undo the Treaty of Troyes and reclaim the land possessed by the English over the next three decades. In 1424, Bedford soundly defeated a Franco-Scottish force at **Verneuil** that blunted the progress of Charles into Normandy.

By the arrival of Joan of Arc, Lancastrian Normandy was a decade-old reality for the geopolitical landscape, and Charles's leaders and advisors were intent on reclaiming it. However, Joan's **mission** called for marching to **Reims**, far east of Normandy, for the **coronation of Charles VII** (17 July 1429), and the mission was given priority. Joan continued to focus the efforts of the royal army well outside of Normandy, but after the signing of the **Franco-Burgundian Truce** and Joan's failed assault on **Paris** (8 September), Charles again turned his attention to Normandy. The **duke of Alençon** was tasked to lead a campaign into the duchy, and he unsuccessfully lobbied for Joan to join him. The rest of Joan's military campaigns were focused in the southeast (*See* SAINT-PIERRE-LE-MOUTIER) and northeast (*See* COMPIÈGNE).

Rouen, the traditional capital of Normandy, became a central focus of the English in 1429 and 1430, with the arrival of **Henry Beaufort** and the duke of Bedford in October 1429 and then Henry VI on 29 June 1430. Henry VI's presence on the continent was part of a plan to undermine Charles VII by holding a separate coronation ceremony in Paris for Henry as king of France. However, with concerns over security, Henry was initially taken to Rouen instead of Paris. After **John of Luxembourg** ransomed Joan of Arc to the English, she was taken to Rouen (23 December) where an exiled Bishop **Pierre Cauchon** would conduct her **inquisition** in 1431 (*See* CONDEMNATION TRIAL).

Rouen continued to remain in focus with a failed attempt to capture the city by French in 1432 followed by public executions of those implicated in the plot. Rouen again became the capital of English-controlled France after Charles VII's reclamation of Paris in 1436. Lancastrian Normandy would slowly be retaken by the French, including Harfleur in 1441, Rouen in 1449, and Caen and Falaise along with the rest of Normandy in 1450. This same year, Charles made his official inquiry into the original trial of Joan of Arc, asking for a review of the available documents in Rouen (*See* TRANSCRIPTS). This kicked off what became known as the **nullification pro-**

ceedings (1450–1456), which ended with a nullification of Joan's trial and its verdict, read publicly in Rouen.

NORWICH, BISHOP OF. *See* ALNWICK, WILLIAM.

NOTARY. *See* ROLES AND RESPONSIBILITIES.

NOTARIES OF THE NULLIFICATION TRIAL. Among the official roles of the **nullification trial** that began on 17 November 1455 were three notaries: François Ferrebouc, licentiate in **canon law**; Denis Le Comte, priest of Coutances with a bachelor in canon law; and Jean de Cruisy, priest of Auxerre. Like the notaries at Joan of Arc's **condemnation trial** (*See* ROLES), they were responsible for recording the minutes of the proceedings, transcribing the articles presented to witnesses along with responses, and vouching for the authenticity of the record. After the verdict (7 July 1456), Ferrebouc and Le Comte were responsible for producing an official register of the trial in Latin, producing six copies. Three of these copies have survived. There are also surviving records of payments from **Charles VII** to Le Comte and Ferrebouc for their services.

NOVELOMPONT, JEAN DE. *See* METZ, JEAN DE.

NULLIFICATION PROCEEDINGS / TRIAL. The nullification proceedings occurred between 1450 and 1456, focusing on the validity of the 1431 **inquisition** of Joan of Arc (*See* CONDEMNATION TRIAL). The process had several false starts, but eventually culminated in a papal-sanctioned nullification trial (1455–1456) that rendered null and void the original verdict of the trial that condemned Joan as a relapsed **heretic**. The beginning of the process was not arbitrary, and it started after **Rouen** was finally brought under the rule of **Charles VII** who officially entered the city on 10 December 1449. Rouen, the location of the original trial, housed the documents of the trial (*See* TRANSCRIPTS), and it was home of many of the surviving participants who could shed light on the process (*See* ROLES).

In February 1450, **Guillaume Bouillé** initiated an inquiry into the condemnation trial on behalf of Charles. He interviewed seven of the original participants: **Guillaume Manchon, Jean Massieu, Jean Beaupere, Martin Ladvenu, Isambard de La Pierre, Guillaume Duval,** and **Jean Toutmouillé**. The general theme of the testimonies was that the trial was a sham orchestrated by the English to discredit Charles. After reviewing the results of the 1450 inquiry with others, Bouillé believed that the condemnation trial should be nullified. However, this effort was secular in nature, initiated by the king, not the Church or the **pope**. The process went no further, and no official declarations were made.

On 1 May 1452, Cardinal **Guillaume d'Estouteville**, cousin of Charles, began another inquiry, alongside Guillaume Bouillé and **Jean Bréhal**, grand inquisitor of France. They interviewed twenty-one witnesses from 2 to 9 May. Estouteville was only present on 2 and 3 May, appointing **Philippe de La Rose**, treasurer of the church in Rouen, to fill in for his duties. Estouteville sent Bouillé and Bréhal to report their progress to Charles on 22 May. In July, the cardinal and the king met, and determined to continue the effort. Meanwhile, Bréhal drafted his so-called *Summarium*, a brief document that examined some of the accusations and Joan's responses, which he then shopped around to scholars and experts for their opinion.

Although much of the new testimony supported the 1450 inquiry's conclusions, official papal support was not forthcoming. Historians are split on the reasons why. One theory is that Pope Nicholas V feared upsetting English sensibilities. There was also contention between the pope and the king over the **Pragmatic Sanction** that challenged papal authority in France. However, other historians have argued that crises, such as the fall of Constantinople on 29 May 1453, preoccupied the pope. Further still, some argue that overturning an inquisition's verdict for such a high-profile defendant simply took time, and the process was well underway when Nicolas V died on 24 March 1455. How else could the new pope, Callixtus III (20 April), so quickly issue a bull to take up a reexamination of Joan's inquisition on 11 June 1455?

Regardless, the papal bull made the proceedings official and appointed three judges: **Richard Oliver de Longueil**, bishop of Coutances; **Guillaume Chartier**, bishop of **Paris**; and **Jean Juvenal de Ursins**, archbishop of **Reims**. Jean Bréhal, who had been involved in the process since 1452, was also listed explicitly, as the grand inquisitor would be required to review and undo the work of his predecessor (*See* GRAVERENT, JEAN). The bull was in response to a petition, which has not survived, from Joan's family, especially her mother, **Isabelle d'Arc**, to annul the original trial's verdict and restore honor to Joan. The pope's bull said he was moved by the request. A formal plea from Isabelle was presented on 7 November 1455 at the Notre-Dame in Paris. The proceedings began on 17 November and accusations were made against **Pierre Cauchon**, **Jean Le Maistre**, and **Jean d'Estivet**, the two judges and promoter, respectively, during Joan's trial (*See* ROLES). Cauchon and Estivet were both dead, and Le Maistre was missing from the historical record, possibly dead as well. The heirs and successors of the accused stated they did not wish to defend the actions of their predecessors, and the trial moved forward. The judges selected **Simon Chapitault** as the promoter who was then responsible for building the case by examining witnesses and documents.

The approach of the nullification trial involved drafting articles that were presented to witnesses to illicit their testimony. The inquiries began in 1456, much broader than all previous efforts, interviewing 115 witnesses. First in Lorraine, thirty-four witnesses testified (28 January–11 February), then forty-one in Orléans (22 February–16 March), twenty in Paris (2 April–11 May), and finally, nineteen in Rouen (12–14 May). **Jean d'Aulon** was interviewed separately (28 May). Among those interviewed were multiple participants from the original inquisition, other clergy, nobles, companions in arms, and family and friends, all who knew or had at least interacted with Joan of Arc. Some of them provided few details, simply unable to answer the presented articles. Although the general theme of the testimonies was overwhelmingly positive toward Joan, historians have questioned the validity of some of the witnesses who may have lapsed memories after two to three decades. With some of those involved in the original inquisition, there is the possibility that they tried to cover up their own culpability in Joan's demise. There was also a strong momentum to sanctify Joan, and it is possible some were caught up in the moment. Charles VII was funding the proceedings, after all. Still, some, such as **Thomas de Courcelles** and **Jean Beaupère**, remained unconvinced of Joan's innocence, or at least her claims of divine inspiration.

Present throughout the entire process was Jean Bréhal, who produced what has become known as his *Recollectio*, a lengthy document that examined and picked apart all the accusations against Joan including the initial **seventy articles** of accusations and the surmised **twelve articles**, as well as the partiality of the judges and validity of the process. The results were handed to the three judges who then deliberated.

On 7 July 1456, the nullification trial's sentence was read aloud by Jean Juvenal de Ursins. Although the trial is often described as a "retrial of Joan of Arc," the judges rendered their verdict against the original condemnation trial, not Joan. The ruling states that the original inquisition and its sentences contained "deceit, slander, contradiction and manifest error of law and of fact," and thus, Joan's **abjuration**, **relapse**, and **execution** were "null, invalid, without effect or value" (Taylor 2006, 349). Contrary to much of the testimony, recorded opinions from experts, and Bréhal's *Recollectio*, the nullification did not render any verdict or official opinion on the original accusations against Joan such as her male **clothing** or the authenticity of her **voices**. Those responsible were not explicitly condemned. Nevertheless, upon concluding the nullification of the 1431 trial, a ceremony was held in the Old Market Square of Rouen where Joan had been executed, and a copy of one of the condemnation trial transcripts was burned.

The surviving transcripts of the nullification proceedings have provided extensive details on the life and habits of Joan of Arc and the process of the condemnation trial including tasks handled during the trial, as well as encounters outside the trial's record. The transcripts are predominantly in Latin with the exception of Jean d'Aulon's testimony, which was recorded and maintained in French.

The process has held numerous names including "retrial" and "rehabilitation," but since the 1970s, historians have referred to it as the nullification proceedings or nullification trial. *See also* NOTARIES.

ORDER OF FRIARS PREACHERS. *See* FRIAR.

ORLÉANS. The location of Orléans has ancient roots, including the site of the Gallic stronghold of Cenabum that was destroyed by Julius Caesar in 52 BC. In the late third century, Roman Emperor Aurelium rebuilt the city. By the fourth century, a bishopric of Orléans had been established, and the city was successfully defended against Attila in 451. In 498, Clovis I captured the city, and it eventually became the capital of the duchy of Orléans. The city's location on the Loire River made it a major trade route with continued importance. Philip I (1052–1108) built a royal mint in the city, and in 1108, Louis VI (1081–1137) was crowned there, as opposed to **Reims**. In 1308, Pope Clement V established the University of Orléans, focusing on **civil law** with students from all over Europe.

By the time of Joan of Arc, Orléans remained a prominent city in France, second only to **Paris**. Duke Louis of Orléans (1372–1407) led the **Armagnac** faction in the **French Civil War** until his assassination. Louis's son, Charles, became the new **duke of Orléans** and was captured at Agincourt (*See* HUNDRED YEARS WAR) and another son, the **bastard of Orléans**, remained steward of the city through Charles's captivity (1415–1440). The English began the lengthy siege of **Orléans** on 12 October 1428. Joan of Arc arrived on 29 April 1429 with reinforcements and supplies, eventually rallying the French to relieve the city on 8 May.

The Orléanais have remained grateful to Joan, celebrating the liberation of the city nearly every year since 1429. Two letters of indulgence from the 1450s that have survived alongside the *Chronique de l'établissement de la fête du 8 mai* encourage citizens to participate in the yearly festivities. Although the memory of Joan has ebbed, flowed, and evolved over the centuries, it has remained strongest in Orléans where she became known as the "Pucelle d'Orléans" ("Maid of Orléans"). This perhaps explains why the city, like others, was duped in 1440 by **Claude des Armoises**, claiming to be Joan of Arc. Joan's mother, **Isabelle d'Arc**, and her brother, **Pierre d'Arc**, both resided near the city, receiving donations as recognition for their familial ties with Joan. *See also* KIRKMICHAEL, JOHN OF.

ORLÉANS, CHARLES, DUKE OF (1394–1465). Although Charles, duke of Orléans, never met Joan of Arc, his presence loomed large before, during, and well after her prominence.

Charles was the son of Duke Louis of Orléans and a cousin of **Charles VII**. Charles became the new duke of Orléans when his father was murdered at the beginning of the **French Civil War** (1407–1435). He was captured at the battle of Agincourt (1415) and would remain a captive of the English for twenty-five years until his release in 1440. During that time, he remained heavily involved with the affairs in France, providing direction to the lands technically under his possession. During that time, his half-brother became the **bastard of Orléans**, managing the city's affairs and its defense during the English siege (1428–1429). After the **Loire Campaign**

(10–18 June 1429), the duke financed **clothing**, including a tabard, for Joan of Arc.

During the negotiations for the **Treaty of Arras** (1435), the English transferred Orléans to Calais as a possible bargaining chip, but after they abandoned the negotiations, his hopes of release waned. He was finally released for a hefty **ransom** in 1440 when he returned to France. There, he knighted Joan's brother, **Pierre d'Arc**. Upon remarrying, Orléans had a son who would eventually become King Louis XII of France in 1498. His daughter from his first marriage, Jeanne, married the **duke of Alençon**.

Joan knew of and spoke fondly of the duke of Orléans, proclaiming that his release, either through ransom or force, was part of her **mission**. It is unclear how much or when Orléans knew of Joan's story (*See* ASTESAN, ANTOINE).

Throughout his life, Orléans wrote poetry, and much of his work survives today.

ORLÉANS, JEAN, BASTARD OF (C. 1402–1468). Jean, the bastard of Orléans, was a companion in arms of Joan of Arc, a fervent supporter of her **mission**, and a supporter of **Charles VII**. His lengthy 1456 testimony during the **nullification proceedings** provides intimate details about Joan's activity between her arrival at the siege of **Orléans** (29 April 1429) and the battle of **Montépilloy** (15 August), as well as an assessment of her character and habits.

Born around 1402, Jean was the bastard of Duke Louis of Orléans. Upon the duke's assassination that sparked the **French Civil War** (1407–1435) and the death and imprisonment of his older half-brothers (1412–1420), Jean became known as the **bastard** of Orléans. Accepted and raised by Valentina of Milan, the widow of Louis, the bastard would strive to see the release of his older half-brother, Charles, the new **duke of Orléans**. He entered the service of the **dauphin** (*See* CHARLES VII) in 1417 and was very active in campaigns throughout the 1420s including the victory at **Baugé** (1421). The *Journal du siège d'Orléans* tells us he arrived at Orléans on 25 October 1428 to take command of the defense of the city against the besieging English. He and **La Hire** led several failed attacks on the English, and the bastard was wounded at the battle of the **Herrings** in an attempt to disrupt the English supply lines (12 February 1429).

At the nullification proceedings, the bastard testified that news of Joan of Arc reached Orléans, and he sent messengers to inquire more about her, probably in March 1429. The messengers were present for Joan's arrival in **Chinon**, bringing back news to the besieged city. The bastard met Joan in Blois and escorted her along with reinforcements and supplies to Orléans on 29 April where she complained about the route he chose, away from the English. The bastard then traveled back to Blois and returned with more reinforcements on 4 May. He describes in detail how she was wounded with an arrow between the neck and shoulder on 7 May, recovered, and then led an assault to capture the Tourelles outside Orléans (*See* INJURIES). The next day, when the English abandoned their defenses and deployed for battle, Joan forbid the army from attacking, preferring to give the English the opportunity to leave peacefully.

Between the relief of Orléans (8 May) and the **Loire Campaign** (10–18 June), the bastard provides several snapshots of Joan's encounters with Charles VII. In these meetings, she emphasized that God wanted Charles to go to **Reims** for his coronation. She convinced him at least to recapture the English-occupied strongholds along the Loire River. During the campaign, the king put the **duke of Alençon** in charge of the army. The bastard and Joan are often depicted in the decision-making in chronicles and eyewitness testimonies. The bastard was present for each siege and assault, and he testified that Joan aggressively pushed the army to pursue the English on 18 June, leading to the victory at **Patay**.

After the Loire Campaign, the advisors and military commanders of Charles VII believed they should take their success into Lancastrian **Normandy**. The bastard tells us that Joan aggressively pushed the king to march to Reims instead. She told him that once he was crowned there, all who opposed him would fall and no one could take France from him. She convinced everyone, and Charles joined the royal army on the **march to Reims** (29 June–16 July). The bastard described how they captured numerous cities, many without firing a single shot. However, **Troyes** refused to surrender, and the leaders were split on what to do, some pushing to just bypass the city entirely. The bastard describes how Joan pushed to besiege the city. She set up her tent next to the city's moat and spent the night deploying **artillery**. The next morning, the city saw the cannons and immediately surrendered. The bastard attributed the victory to Joan's efforts, emphasizing her skill in deployment. The bastard attended the **coronation of Charles VII** (17 July) but did not hold a special role in the ceremony.

After the coronation, the bastard was present for the standoff at **Montépilloy** (15 August), but he was not listed in the royal army during the failed assault on **Paris** (8 September). There are romanticized notions that the bastard attempted to rescue Joan after her capture, but these are based on a recorded payment for an expedition into Normandy on 14 March 1431. No details of the expedition survived, if they were ever recorded. It is also difficult to imagine the bastard or others not bragging about their attempted efforts to rescue Joan.

Still, the bastard of Orléans remained loyal to Charles, even during most of the noble revolts, and the king rewarded him. Although he temporarily sided with participants in the **Praguerie** (1440), he returned to the king's side before the fighting began. In 1433, Charles made him his grand **chamberlain**. In 1439, Jean became the count of Dunois and in 1443, the count of Longueville, and was therefore no longer referred to as the bastard of Orléans. Now known as Dunois, he participated in the campaigns to recover Normandy (1449–1450) and Gascony (1451). He remained in the king's service until the death of Charles (1461), after which the rebellious son and new King **Louis XI** dismissed Dunois. However, the two reconciled and the count served as a councilor from 1465 until his passing on 23 November 1468.

The bastard of Orléans remained awestruck by Joan of Arc from 1429 through his testimony during the nullification proceedings on 22 February 1456. **Thomas Basin** claimed that the bastard was instrumental in convincing Charles to at least meet with Joan. The bastard's testimony of Joan is centered around the belief that she was sent from God and all her actions and words were divinely inspired up to the coronation of Charles, including the periods she was recovering from her wound at Orléans, pushing for actions that led to success, and influencing the king. He described her daily habit of prayers and songs at dusk while she encouraged others to join her. When it came to military matters, Dunois emphasized that Joan never joked or took them lightly.

ORLÉANS, LOUIS, DUKE OF. *See* FRENCH CIVIL WAR.

ORLÉANS, SIEGE OF (12 OCTOBER 1428–8 MAY 1429). The siege of Orléans was the culmination of **Salisbury's 1428 expedition**. The relief of the siege marked the first military victory of Joan of Arc and the completion of the first part of her **mission**.

After the **earl of Salisbury** had captured cities and fortifications north of and along the Loire River in August through October 1428, he settled in for the siege of Orléans on 12 October. His force was predominantly English, but also included Burgundian troops supplied by **Philip the Good**. Salisbury's army was modest for the task, and based on surviving records, he started his campaign with roughly five thousand troops, which, after the campaign and occupation of other cities, would have been fewer. There were about fifteen hundred Burgundian troops to augment his force. Orléans sat north of the Loire with a 350-meter bridge crossing south into the Tourelles bastille, a large stone fortification with two towers acting as a gate. Built in the fourteenth century, the Tourelles had recently been refortified. Modern-day estimates put the city's population in 1428 at approximately thirty thousand.

The first major victory for the English came with the capture of the Tourelles on 24 October. However, Salisbury was wounded by a cannon that same day, losing part of his jaw. The **bastard of Orléans** arrived on October 25 with reinforcements and assumed command of the defense. The French destroyed part of the bridge between Orléans and the Tourelles, preventing any attack there. Meanwhile, Salisbury was transported to **Meung** where he died on 3 November. The **earl of Suffolk** then assumed command of the siege.

Orléans posed a major challenge for the besiegers because of its size. They were unable to establish a complete blockade, and supplies made it to both the besiegers and the besieged over the next six months. Instead, the English built and occupied a network of boulevards, which were makeshift forts meant to house troops and withstand assaults. Through February 1429, both sides continued to bombard each other with cannons, and they made concerted attacks on each other that did not change the situation. In addition, the French destroyed suburbs outside the city's walls. In December, **John Talbot** and **Thomas Scales** arrived and joined Suffolk in leadership. **William Glasdale** was established as commander of the Tourelles.

The siege turned desperate for the defenders when their plan to disrupt the English supply lines from **Paris** was repulsed at the battle of the **Herrings** (12 February 1429). The city's inhabitants made an appeal to Philip the Good, offering to surrender directly to him. However, this notion was vetoed by the **duke of Bedford** (17 April). In response, Philip withdrew his troops from the siege (*See* ANGLO-BURGUNDIAN ALLIANCE).

Joan of Arc's arrival on 29 April occurred without incident, as she traveled from the east, bypassing the Saint Loup boulevard. Joan's entrance into the city was met with enthusiasm. The bastard of Orléans left for **Blois** on 1 May, returning on 4 May with more reinforcements and supplies. That same day, the French attacked and captured Saint Loup. On 5 May, the French ventured to the Saint Jean le Blanc boulevard on the southeast side of the Loire, but discovered it was abandoned; they occupied it. On 6 May, the French captured the Augustins boulevard south of the Tourelles. On May 7, the French made an aggressive assault on the Tourelles where Joan of Arc was wounded with an arrow between her neck and chest (*See* INJURIES). After a quick recovery, Joan returned to rally the French troops attacking from the south while more French troops crossed a makeshift bridge to attack from the north. Many of the English defenders fled into the Loire and drowned, including William Glasdale.

On 8 May, the remaining English lined up for battle, but Joan held the French back in order to give the English the opportunity to leave peacefully, which they did. The siege of Orléans was over. The remaining English troops spread their forces across other fortified towns along the Loire including Suffolk in **Jargeau**, Talbot in **Beaugency**, and Scales in **Meung**. These cities would remain occupied by the English until the **Loire Campaign** (10–18 June).

With the relief of Orléans, Joan of Arc had achieved the first part of her mission and completed the necessary requirement presented by those who examined her at **Poitiers**. She had gained clout with **Charles VII**, his advisers, his nobles, and the French people who still supported the king. It is often listed as the greatest of her achievements. *See also* ARTILLERY; *JOURNAL DU SIÈGE D'ORLÉANS*; LETTER TO THE ENGLISH (22 MARCH 1429); SIEGE.

ORLÉANAIS/ORLÉANISTS. Depending on the period in which a historian uses this term in their narrative on Joan of Arc, Orléanists can represent different groups. Leading up to the **French Civil War** (1407–1435), it would denote those who sided with Duke Louis of Orléans in his disputes with Duke John the Fearless of Burgundy. Upon the assassination of Louis in 1407, it would represent those who sided with his son, Charles, the new **duke of Orléans**. In 1410, the marriage of Charles and Bonne, the daughter of Count Bernard of Armagnac, led to the formation of the League of Gien. Due to the strong influence of Armagnac, the political faction became known as the **Armagnacs**, but some historians will still emphasize that the war started over an Orléanist grievance.

Elsewhere, the term simply means someone living in Orléans, just as *Parisian* means someone living in **Paris**. Thus, it is common to see the term in narratives on the siege of **Orléans** (1428–1429) or to describe the inhabitants of the city, who have held yearly celebrations on 8 May to commemorate Joan of Arc and her lifting of the siege.

P

PAGE. *See* COUTES, LOUIS DE.

PARIS. Like many large cities in France, Paris has ancient roots pre-dating the Romans. It began as a Celtic settlement on an island in the Seine River. The Romans occupied it in 52 BC initially as a military base but expanded it over the centuries. Fending off a series of invasions in the third through fifth centuries, eventually the Franks overtook the city and their leader, Clovis (c. AD 466–511), converted to Christianity and established Paris as his capital. The power and influence of Paris ebbed and flowed through different groups and rulers, but it became the capital of France under Philip II (1165–1223). During his reign, he surrounded the city with walls, established hotels for princes, paved streets, and centralized the royal archives. The establishment of the **University of Paris** (1150) and its growth made the city an intellectual capital of Europe. The Parlement of Paris was established in the mid-thirteenth century, and by the fourteenth century it had evolved into the king's tribunal arm that could intercede in all parts of France. Under Charles V (1338–1380), the size of the city doubled when the king built a wall on the north bank. The population estimates of the city vary, but at the beginning of the **Hundred Years War**, it was as much as 120,000. However, plagues and civil war had dwindled those numbers by the time of Joan of Arc.

Paris was hotly contested during the **French Civil War** (1407–1435) with several rebellions and attempts to capture the city for the opposing factions. In 1418, Burgundians successfully seized the city with help from **Jean de Villiers** and co-conspirators. While opponents were massacred, the **dauphin** (*See* CHARLES VII) and numerous supporters including nobles and clergy escaped south to **Bourges** and **Poitiers**. The duke of Burgundy (*See* PHILIP THE GOOD) eventually ceded the city to **Henry V** on 8 May 1420, two weeks before the signing of the **Treaty of Troyes**.

Two attempts were made by Joan of Arc to capture the city. On 8 September 1429, Joan assaulted the Saint-Honoré gate, was wounded, and eventually forced to abandon the siege (*See* PARIS, SIEGE OF). In the spring of 1430, Joan made another concerted effort to capture the city, this time with help from citizens inside. However, the leader of the plot was discovered and after he sold out his co-conspirators, 150 people were executed on 15 April.

Although the English controlled the capital in 1430, the **duke of Bedford** decided to escort **Henry VI** to **Rouen** upon his arrival in France due to security concerns. Similarly, Bedford pushed to conduct Joan of Arc's **inquisition** in Rouen, even though the University of Paris was directly involved in initiating and participating in the **condemnation trial**. Henry VI was eventually coronated in Paris on 16 December 1431.

After the signing of the **Treaty of Arras** (1435), public opinion in Paris turned against the English. Thus, it was possible for **Arthur de Richemont** to claim the city for Charles VII on 13 April 1436, again with the help of Jean de Villiers. Charles officially entered the city on 12 November 1437, but he did not make it his home. He remained itinerant, spending more time in cities south of the Loire River. Future kings followed suit, and it was not until Henry II (1519–1559) that kings made their home in Paris.

The **nullification trial** to reexamine Joan of Arc's inquisition began in Notre-Dame de Paris on 7 November 1455. It was an ironic location as it was home to the same university that was so instrumental in condemning Joan.

PARIS, SIEGE OF (8 SEPTEMBER 1429). After the relief of the siege of **Orléans** (8 May 1429) and the **coronation of Charles VII** at **Reims** (17 July), the capture of **Paris** was the next part of Joan of Arc's **mission**. The series of military victories accrued since Orléans, all at the behest of Joan, had given her the clout necessary for the siege. Although negotiations between **Charles VII** and **Philip the Good** for a truce explicitly excluded Paris (*See* ANGLO-BURGUNDIAN TRUCE), there was still concern among Charles and his advisers of upsetting the truce. Perhaps this explains why Charles was not eager to begin the assault.

Joan of Arc arrived at **Saint-Denis**, north of Paris, on 26 August, and she began examining its massive defenses for weakness through a series of daily skirmishes and bombardments with cannons (*See* ARTILLERY). The city was far too large for the royal army to surround it. Its walls were eight meters high with towers every 100 to 120 meters. Joan eventually identified the Saint-Honré gate, one of the six gates of the city, as the best option for an assault. It too was formidable, measuring roughly 18.5 meters by 8.34 meters. In front of it was a moat, 3 meters deep and 32 meters wide, that ebbed and flowed throughout the year (DeVries 1999, 147–49).

However, Joan did not yet have the whole royal army with her, and she could not commit a full attack without the king's approval. The **duke of Alençon** reached out to the king on 1 September and again, personally, on 5 September. The king finally arrived at Saint-Denis with the army on 7 September. Joan and the army marched to the Saint-Honré gate the next day. The army began a steady bombardment while filling the moat with bundles of sticks for a crossing. During an assault, Joan was wounded by a crossbow bolt in the thigh, and one of her pages was killed. She hid in a ditch until she was recovered later that night.

The next day, Joan and the army were prepared for another assault, but messengers from the king arrived to tell them that the siege was over. There are numerous theories about why Charles made the decision, but according to **Jean Lèfevre de Saint-Remy**, once Charles saw the defenses of Paris, he determined they were too strong for the siege. The royal army marched south and was disbanded by the king. The duke of Alençon was sent on campaign in Lancastrian **Normandy**, and after Joan recovered from her wound, she was sent to the southeast against **Saint-Pierre-le-Moutier**.

Paris marked a turning point in the military career of Joan of Arc. Although she achieved other successes before her capture at **Compiègne** (23 May 1430), none were as grand as the achievements prior to Paris. Chroniclers agree that her air of divinity had dissipated with Charles, his advisers, and some of the French people (*See* LA PUCELLE). Joan would never again be among such a large army or be able to influence military policy in the king's court.

PASQUEREL, JEAN (C. 1400–?). Most of what we know of Jean Pasquerel comes from his 4 May 1456 testimony during the **nullification proceedings**. He was a **friar** of the St. Augustine Order. At some point, he was a **prior** in **Chinon**, and in 1439, he was teaching theology at the University of Angers. Based on his testimony, he learned of Joan of Arc in late March or early April 1429, meeting her mother while she was on a pilgrimage (*See* ARC, ISABELLE D', ROMMÉE). Pasquerel traveled to Chinon and then Tours where he met Joan in April. There, she had her **standard** constructed. Upon meeting the friar, she claimed she had heard of him and quickly asked him to become her confessor. Pasquerel then followed Joan in all her campaigns until she was captured at **Compiègne** (23 May 1430). Pasquerel unfortunately provided no military details, but he did grant us a view into her religious habits. According to

Pasquerel, Joan confessed almost daily and took communion often. She also pushed for the army to confess and participate in Mass while Pasquerel acted as the army's chaplain. Pasquerel attributed several prophecies to Joan. For example, she admonished one man for **blasphemy** and the man died the following day. She also predicted her wounding at **Orléans** (*See* INJURIES). Pasquerel was the author of the **letter to the Hussites (23 March 1430)**, written in Joan's name.

PATAY, BATTLE OF (18 JUNE 1429). The battle of Patay was the final engagement in the **Loire Campaign**, which had already resulted in the French recapture of **Jargeau**, **Meung**, and **Beaugency** along the Loire River.

During the preceding days, English leaders **John Fastolf** and **John Talbot** had been at odds at how to proceed. Talbot wanted to retake Meung while Fastolf urged a withdrawal, but Talbot won the debate. After a relief army failed to recapture the Meung bridge during a halfhearted assault on the morning of 18 June, he marched his army north to meet up with Talbot, who was marching toward Patay.

Once Joan of Arc learned of the retreating English, she urged the French army's commander, the **duke of Alençon**, to attack. He later recalled her stating, "In the name of God, we must fight them! [Even] if they were hanging from the clouds, we would have them, because God wants us to punish them" (Taylor 2006, 309). Alençon agreed and sent a cavalry vanguard ahead of his army, led by **La Hire** and **Poton de Xaintrailles**, to find the English. Medieval accounts and modern historians agree that the English, although spread out, numbered upwards of five thousand. However, medieval numbers for the French vary wildly from six thousand to thirteen thousand, with modern historians putting their numbers between three thousand and eight thousand. Regardless, the cavalry force led by La Hire and Xaintrailles numbered no more than a few hundred.

Upon learning that the French were pursuing, Talbot determined to establish a defensive ambush with five hundred archers behind stakes, similar to approaches that had been successful at **Cravant** and **Herrings**. This was a delaying tactic to give time for the rest of the army under Fastolf to arrive to the battlefield. French scouts learned of the English position when a horse got loose and ran into Talbot's archers, causing them to yell with excitement. La Hire and Xaintrailles charged and caught the archers unprepared, capturing Talbot and **Thomas Scales**. As they sent the English into disarray, the main French army arrived with Joan of Arc. The French suffered few casualties, but the English suffered around twenty-five hundred killed and captured. Fastolf moved toward the fighting, but the battle was already lost, and he retreated toward **Janville** where the French inside had closed their gates. Fastolf continued to flee north, and the French decided not to pursue.

The repercussions of Patay and the Loire Campaign were numerous. Fastolf was temporarily banished from the Order of the Garter, the most exclusive order for knights in England, on the charge of cowardice. Upon Talbot's release in 1434, he revived the charge, and Fastolf was fighting to clear his reputation until 1442. More importantly, the campaign undid the English successes from **Salisbury's 1428 expedition**. Joan of Arc continued to gain clout with **Charles VII**, his nobles, and his advisers, and she was able to convince them to conduct the **march to Reims**.

The location of the battlefield has been debated and theorized for the past few hundred years, based on conjecture, old Roman road networks, and, more recently, promising archeological discoveries. Although the debate is not wholly settled, all theorized locations feature a large, open field. **Monstrelet** tells us the name of the battle comes from the town where the French leaders slept later that night.

Among **Orléans**, **Paris**, and **Compiègne**, Patay is one of the most recorded military actions in which Joan of Arc participated. There are surviving eyewitness accounts from both sides including the duke of Alençon and **Jean de Wavrin**, the latter being from among the ranks of John Fastolf. In addition, numerous chronicles provide accounts of the battle (*See* JOURNAL DU SIÈGE).

PAVIA-SIENA, COUNCIL OF. *See* COUNCILS.

PENNON. *See* STANDARD.

PHILIP THE BOLD. *See* BURGUNDY.

PHILIP THE GOOD, DUKE OF BURGUNDY (1396–1467). Philip the Good became the new duke of Burgundy and the count of Flanders upon the assassination of his father, John the Fearless in 1419. With the dauphin (*See* CHARLES VII) implicated in the murder, Philip was open to negotiations with English King **Henry V** who sought to exploit the **French Civil War** (1407–1435). Although wanting revenge for his father's murder, Philip ultimately signed the **Treaty of Troyes** (1420) after weighing the pros and cons, and deciding that if he refused Henry's offer, then the dauphin would accept it. The treaty recognized Philip's current territory held in France; in return, he no longer recognized the dauphin as the rightful heir to the French throne and instead would recognize Henry V and his descendants as the heirs (*See* HENRY VI).

Philip's military coordination with the English was inconsistent (*See* ANGLO-BURGUNDIAN ALLIANCE). He joined Henry on campaign in the summer of 1420, but the death of Henry on 31 August 1422 followed by the death of French King **Charles VI** on 21 October created a potential crisis for the infant Henry VI. Although Henry V wanted Philip to act as **regent** of France, Philip declined, leading Henry V's brother, **the duke of Bedford**, to take up the burden. Philip's focus was on the Low Countries, where he sought to extend his territory and rule. However, Bedford was able to negotiate the **Treaty of Amiens** (1423) with Philip and Jean V, **duke of Brittany**, in which the three dukes recognized Henry VI as king of France. To solidify the treaty, Bedford married Philip's sister, **Anne of Burgundy**, on 13 May. In addition, Jean V's brother, **Arthur de Richemont**, would marry Margaret of Burgundy, another sister of Philip, on 10 October.

The apex of Anglo-Burgundian military coordination came at their overwhelming victory at **Cravant** (31 July 1423) over the army of Charles VII. However, Bedford dismissed Burgundian soldiers before his victory at **Verneuil** (17 August 1424), a move that offended Philip who then signed the **truce of Chambéry** with Charles VII (28 September). In moments such as these, Anne of Burgundy was instrumental in repairing the relationship between the dukes. However, from 1425 through 1433, Philip focused heavily on conquering Holland in the east. Still, during the siege of **Orléans** (1428–1429), Philip sent troops to aid the English. In April 1429, Philip met a delegation from Orléans, led by **Poton de Xantrailles**, to negotiate a surrender of the city explicitly to the duke. The proposed terms allowed Philip to install his own leadership with half the income from the city going to **Henry VI** and the other half going to Philip. The duke was open to the concept, but Bedford refused, causing Philip to withdraw his troops from the siege before the arrival of Joan of Arc (29 April).

After the relief of Orléans (8 May) and the **Loire Campaign** (10–18 June), the army of Charles VII began its **march to Reims**, which encroached into Burgundian territory. Joan of Arc's **letter to Philip the Good (17 July 1429)**, sent the same day as the **coronation of Charles VII**, still survives, and she revealed that she was disappointed he did not attend the ceremony as she had requested in a prior letter, now lost. Joan's efforts to reconcile Philip and Charles were for naught. Bedford had modified his will in June to leave his possessions in France to his wife Anne and any prospective children, but since there were no offspring, Philip was added as the next in line. In addition, Bedford promised to compensate Philip to rekindle the Burgundian war with Charles.

Philip, however, bought time by negotiating a truce with Charles (*See* FRANCO-BURGUNDIAN TRUCE), which lasted through 16 April 1430, although both sides found ways around it to attack each other's cities. It was because of these negotiations that Charles halfheartedly supported Joan's attempts to capture **Paris**, but after a day of failed assaults (8 September), he abandoned the siege and disbanded his royal army.

By May 1430, Philip was once again fully invested in a war with Charles, besieging **Compiègne** on 22 May. The next day, Joan of Arc was captured outside the city trying to relieve it. **Monstrelet** tells us that Philip and Joan met briefly, but no details of their conversation survive. The Burgundians ultimately **ransomed** Joan over to Bedford who orchestrated her **condemnation trial** and **execution** (30 May 1431). However, Anglo-Burgundian relations were further strained as promises of compensation fell short and Burgundians abandoned the siege of Compiègne on 25 October 1430.

By 1432, Philip sought to bring peace in France through a conference between the English, French, and Burgundians with papal mediation. Anglo-Burgundian relations were further strained with the death of Anne of Burgundy (14 November 1432) followed by Bedford's choice to marry Jacquetta of Luxembourg (22 April 1433), a territory that Philip sought to conquer. By 1435, Philip had found a loophole in the Treaty of Troyes, arguing that since Henry V died before Charles VI, he never inherited the French throne from Charles and thus, Henry V could not then pass it on to Henry VI. By summer, the Congress of Arras had begun. The English abandoned negotiations in September, Bedford died on 14 September, and the **Treaty of Arras** was signed on 21 September between Philip and Charles, officially ending the French Civil War and the Anglo-Burgundian Alliance.

Although Arras was a turning point in the **Hundred Years War**, it was not a smooth alliance between Charles and Philip, the latter of which did not take part in the reconquest of English-controlled territory. Instead, Philip continued to focus on the expansion of his territory in the Low Countries. With the conquest of Luxembourg in 1443, Philip had doubled the territory of Burgundy since 1419. In 1447, he failed to gain recognition from the **Holy Roman Empire** as king of an independent Burgundy. In 1467, he provided sanctuary to Charles's rebellious son, the current dauphin (*See* LOUIS XI). Philip helped negotiate the release of the **duke of Orléans** in 1440, but this was a political move, as Philip saw the duke as a potential ally.

During the prominence of Joan of Arc, Philip was a major player in the political landscape, more often allied against Charles VII with convenient moments of truces that hindered Joan's **mission** to see the English expelled from France. The Peace of Arras did not bring France and Burgundy into harmony, and Philip's role became that of a neutral party, sometimes mediator, but always with Burgundy's best interests at heart. To Joan, Philip was a direct descendant of French King John II (1319–1364), and thus a member of the same **House of Valois** as Charles. However, Philip never fully subscribed to Joan's monarchist view that Charles VII was the divine king of all of France, including Burgundians.

Philip died on 15 June 1467, earning the moniker "the Good" for being a patron of the arts; numerous tapestries, paintings, and works of literature are dedicated to him. Most notable among those who benefited was **Georges Chastellain**, official historian of Burgundy. Philip's son, Charles the Bold (1433–1477), died in battle, leaving no male heirs. Much of the original Burgundian territory that Philip inherited in 1419 was ultimately absorbed back into France.

PHYSICIANS IN THE CONDEMNATION TRIAL. By the fifteenth century, the medical field had been successfully incorporated into the **University of Paris**, where men could train as a bachelor, licentiate, and doctor in medicine. A licentiate in medicine was authorized to teach, and a doctor was considered a master of the field. Along with training, degrees required teaching, theses defenses, and hands-on practice.

There were at least seven assessors with degrees in medicine who treated or gave an opinion on Joan of Arc during her **condemnation trial** (1431). The **University of Paris** reviewed the **twelve articles** presented against Joan, and in their ranks were two physicians—Henri Thiboust and Simon de La Mare, both doctors of medicine. At the trial in Rouen, there were two doctors of medicine—Gilles Canivet and Roland L'Écrivain—who were present for a single session on 3 March 1431.

More pertinent to the story of Joan of Arc were the three physicians who attended multiple sessions, treated Joan for illness, and voted along with everyone else on 29 May to hand Joan over to the secular authorities: Guillaume Desjardins, Guillaume de La Chambre, and Jean Tiphaine.

Guillaume Desjardins (1370–1438) attended seven sessions. Trained at Paris, his **benefices** included canons in **Paris** and **Rouen**.

Guillaume de La Chambre (c. 1407–?) attended five sessions. On 15 March 1436, he swore an oath to uphold the **Treaty of Troyes** (1420), well after the signing of the **Treaty of Arras** (1435) and the collapse of the **Anglo-Burgundian Alliance**. The oath was initiated by **John of Luxembourg** and the first to swear it was **Pierre Cauchon**, which has led some historians to brush the incident off as a moment of pressure, not genuine loyalty to England. This theory is lent credibility by the fact that La Chambre would become the dean of faculty teaching medicine in Paris (1448–1450) well after the city came under control of **Charles VII**.

Finally, Jean Tiphaine (1395–1469) attended four sessions. He was a Norman priest who had taught medicine at Paris. He had also served as physician for **Catherine of Valois** after her marriage to **Henry V**. In 1432, after the trial, he became canon of Rouen.

Although Desjardins did not survive to participate in the **nullification proceedings** (1450–1456), both La Chambre and Tiphaine provided corroborating testimony. In April 1431, Joan fell ill, and the physicians were summoned by the **earl of Warwick** and **Henry Beaufort** to treat her. La Chambre tells us that the English were emphatic that they did not want Joan to die outside of an execution. So, when they found her with a fever and vomiting, and they decided to treat her with bloodletting, Warwick cautioned them not to overdo it. As for the source of the illness, Tiphaine tells us that Joan believed it was bad fish fed to her by Cauchon. Although she was recovering, both the physicians described a verbal altercation between Joan and **Jean d'Estivet** that resulted in Joan's fever returning.

As for their participation in the trial, La Chambre tells us he was forced to vote as he did on 29 May by Cauchon and the English. Tiphaine claimed he never voted.

One further detail from La Chambre was that he had heard that Joan was determined to remain a virgin. According to his medical opinion she was a virgin, as he saw her almost naked, and she was quite thin. *See also* EDUCATION; INJURIES; VIRGINITY.

PIUS II. *See* POPE.

PIZAN, CHRISTINE DE (C. 1364–C. 1430). Christine de Pizan demonstrated that if women in history had been afforded just a taste of the privilege reserved predominantly for men, they were more than capable of rising to the top of a field and achieving critical acclaim across medieval Europe. Originally born in Florence, Pizan grew up in the French court while her father served as the astrologer to King Charles V. From a young age and with the encouragement of her father, she took advantage of the classical education in the court.

A pivotal year for Pizan was 1380, as she married Étienne du Castel, a royal clerk, but also saw the passing of Charles V and, along with it, her access to the royal court. Over the next decade, she would have three children. With the passing of her father in 1387 and then her husband in 1390, Pizan found herself solely responsible for three children and her mother. Pizan picked up her pen to start her writing career to support her family, becoming one of the most prolific and well-known writers of her time. Her works cover a wide range of styles and genres, including what we would today categorize as history, politics, military theory and logistics, literary criticism, and feminism.

Always writing in Middle French, Pizan was able to find patrons by dedicating her works to various leaders and by accepting commissions from them. For example, Duke Philip the Bold of Burgundy commissioned a biography on his brother, King Charles V, which resulted in *Livre des fais et bonnes meurs du sage roy Charles V* (c. 1404), a work that remains a primary source to this day. Throughout the 1400s and early 1410s, she wrote letters to French nobles, seeking their help in ending the disputes between each other that had eventually boiled into the **French Civil War**, but her efforts dissipated with the large swath of noble leaders who were casualties at Agincourt in 1415 (*See* HUNDRED YEARS WAR).

Among the works most relevant to Joan of Arc is *Livre des fais d'armes et de chevalerie* (c. 1410), a detailed military treatise that continued the transmission of classical works such as **Vegetius**, Valerius Maximus, and Frontinus. This was no mere recycling by Pizan, as she incorporated criticism and logistics from contemporary military experts, most likely those within the court of **Burgundy**. For example, when discussing defenses, she incorporated details on gunpowder **artillery**, including necessary supplies and manpower.

Pizan's last work, *Ditié de Jehanne d'Arc* (*The Tale of Joan of Arc*), was a poem celebrating the exploits of Joan, written after the **coronation of Charles VII** (17 July 1429). The poem has the distinction of being the first literary work on Joan and the only surviving literary work written during her lifetime. Through Joan of Arc, Pizan had finally found the leader that she believed would unite France. It is likely that Pizan passed before Joan's capture outside **Compiègne** (23 May 1430).

POITIERS. After the Burgundians seized **Paris** in 1418, the **dauphin** (*See* CHARLES VII) and those still loyal to him fled south (*See* FRENCH CIVIL WAR). Charles then spread out the administrative functions of his government in various cities including **Bourges** and Poitiers. The latter housed the Parlement of Poitiers, the king's judicial arm, that remained active in the city until 1436 when its members were reintegrated with the Parlement of Paris. The members of the Parlement of Poitiers included numerous scholars and theologians, many of whom were responsible for examining Joan of Arc in March 1429. The examination is traditionally dated to 11 to 22 March 1429, but historians have argued for different days of arrival for Joan at Poitiers including as early as 1 or 3 March, based on extant records of other officials who arrived in the city. However, Joan was in Poitiers at least until 22 March, the date of her first **letter to the English**, and she left as early as 23 March.

All the original records of the examination are lost, and historians are left with testimonies of participants, as well as a summary of the examination's conclusions that has survived in chronicles in Scotland and Germany, indicating the document was widely distributed. Based on testimonies of those present, there were roughly eighteen theologians involved with the examination. The so-called Poitiers Conclusions have been suspected of being a propaganda tool, which is likely an accurate description, but their contents match with testimonies of those who were present. The conclusions also reveal an earnest attempt by the theologians to flesh out any ill intent on the part of Joan of Arc, and they do not provide complete approval. Instead, the conclusions reveal that "no evil has been found in her, only goodness, humility, virginity, devotion, honesty and simplicity" (Taylor 2006, 73). Such examinations of prophets or those claiming divine authority from God involved asking for a **sign**. Joan, however, refused to provide one, claiming that by giving her soldiers, her sign would be the relief of the siege of **Orléans**. The examiners determined that the king should not prevent Joan "from going to Orléans with his men-at-arms . . . in order to show the sign of divine aid there" (Taylor 2006, 74).

Historians have inferred the contents of the examination based on testimonies of those present who provided numerous anecdotes. According to these testimonies, Joan harped on her **mission** to relieve Orléans, see the king crowned at **Reims**, and drive the English from France. When asked why God would not just deliver France Himself, Joan responded "In the name of God, the men-at-arms will fight and God will give victory" (Taylor 2006, 337). When a theologian asked what language her **voices** spoke, "she replied that it was a better language than his" (Taylor 2006, 337).

Joan evoked Poitiers during her **condemnation trial** in **Rouen** on 27 February and 3 March 1431, affirming that the assessors at Rouen were asking similar questions posed at Poitiers. At her trial, **Nicolas de Houppeville** argued that the questioning at Poitiers should be consulted, but he was promptly removed from the proceedings. The so-called Poitiers book that Joan referenced was possibly just minutes that she saw someone recording, but without any surviving record, historians are unsure. By the **nullification proceedings** (1450–1456), the details were lost. Some historians have theorized they were purposefully destroyed perhaps after Joan's **execution** to limit the king's culpability in not intervening in her **captivity**, but there is no evidence of this.

The Poitiers examination was a turning point for Joan of Arc in convincing the king to support her mission, and prominent people such as **Christine de Pizan** cited the examination as proof of her validity. She returned to **Chinon** before being sent with troops and supplies to the siege of Orléans.

Poitiers continued to be an important city in the administration of Charles VII, and he established the University of Poitiers in 1431. *See also* VIRGINITY.

POLE, WILLIAM DE LA. *See* SUFFOLK, WILLIAM DE LA POLE, EARL OF.

POPE. Although Joan of Arc never met any popes, they played prominently during her lifetime, at her **condemnation trial** (1431), and at the **nullification proceedings** (1450–1456). She was born during the climax of the **Great Schism** (1378–1417) that eventually saw three different concurrent popes claiming legitimacy, going so far as to excommunicate each other. With support for the three popes falling mainly along regional lines, the Schism threatened to become a permanent break. However, at the **Council** of Constance (1414–1418), one pope was forced into retirement and the two others deposed, after which Martin V was elected the sole, legitimate pope in 1417. He would hold office until his passing on 20 February 1431, before the last few months of Joan's life. Eugene IV was elected pope on 3 March 1431 and served until his death in 1447.

Although the Great Schism was settled across most of Western Europe, there were still some nobles, such as **Jean IV, count of Armagnac**, who held allegiance to one of the deposed popes and his successor. Armagnac pushed the issue until he was declared a **schismatic** on 4 March 1429, which was not as severe as **heresy**, but still caused trouble for the count. Before he was whole with the church again, he wrote a letter to Joan of Arc after the battle of **Montépilloy** (15 August), asking which of the three popes was the legitimate pope. The response in her **letter (22 August 1429)** was inconclusive, claiming she would answer him later when she was not busy with the campaign. She never did.

Given the sensitivity of the authority of the pope, which had just recently been debated and argued for decades and only recently settled during the Council of Constance, the question of the pope's authority weighed heavily in the questions posed to Joan at her condemnation trial. When Martin V passed on 20 February 1431, the assessors took the opportunity to present the exchange between the count of Armagnac and Joan on declaring who was the legitimate pope. Without knowing there was not yet an elected successor, Joan remained elusive in her responses, simply saying the pope in Rome was the legitimate pope. The judges eventually dropped that line of questioning.

On 1 May 1431, three of Joan's assessors informed her of the newly elected Pope Eugene IV and explained that she was within her right to appeal to him at any point during the trial. When Joan appealed to the pope the next day, Bishop **Pierre Cauchon** responded by threatening those that helped Joan, and her request never made it to the pope.

Throughout the trial when Joan refused to reveal details of what her **voices** told her or what occurred during her meeting with **Charles VII**, her assessors often invoked the pope's authority. Joan always insisted she would share her personal revelations with the pope directly.

On 26 May 1431, Joan was sentenced and threatened. She appealed directly to the pope but was told he was too far away and that she should accept the decision by the judges.

Well after Joan's passing and after a few false starts, it was Pope Calixtus III who authorized the nullification proceedings that began in earnest in 1455.

Finally, in 1461, thirty years after her execution, Pope Pius II reflected on Joan of Arc, dedicating an entry of his *Commentaries* to her life. Although Pius was not convinced of her divine mandate, he was emphatic on her military prowess, describing in detail her success at **Orléans** and crediting the success to her. He dismissed the condemnation trial as a sham, believing that her male **clothing**, which did not bother him, was an excuse to execute her for the English and their allies who did not feel safe with her alive.

PORTE DE FRANCE. *See* VAUCOULEURS.

POULENGY, BERTRAND DE (C. 1392–?). Little is known about Bertrand de Poulengy outside his 1456 testimony during the **nullification proceedings**, at which point he was still a **squire**. He claimed to know Joan's parents, visiting their house often, at least as early as 1417. He also testified that he had visited the **fairy tree**, which was a point of contention at Joan's **condemnation trial** (1431).

Like **Jean de Metz**, he first met Joan in **Vaucouleurs** in 1428 where he witnessed some of Joan's interactions with **Robert de Baudricourt**. Poulengy encountered Joan again when she returned to Vaucouleurs in 1429. He claimed that in addition to the male **clothing** that Metz provided to Joan, the citizens provided her with armor and a **sword** for her journey. Poulengy and Metz led the company that escorted Joan, between 13 and 23 February 1429, from Vaucouleurs to **Chinon** to meet **Charles VII**. Poulengy's testimony is like that of Metz, as he was struck by her confidence and what he believed was a divine inspiration. He claimed he was not attracted to her and that, during their travels, she never removed her clothing. Poulengy remained a companion in arms of Joan's; based on the scant evidence, he was likely with her through most of her campaigns.

POULNOIR, HAVES. *See* STANDARD.

PRAGMATIC SANCTION OF BOURGES (1438). The Pragmatic Sanction of Bourges was a royal decree from **Charles VII** that changed the relationship between France, the local church, and the **pope**. The decree declared independence from papal authority, which included the suppression of taxes from Rome, subjecting church courts to royal courts, and asserting the right to approve, veto, or appoint potential local clergy such as bishops. The decree became a sticking point between France and Rome. Some historians believe it may have contributed to Pope Nicholas V's lack of interest in reexamining Joan of Arc's **condemnation trial** (1431). Regardless, in 1451, Nicholas sent Cardinal **Guillaume d'Estouteville** to France with the explicit purpose of abolishing the Pragmatic Sanction. This effort was a failure, but the cardinal did pick up the languishing **nullification proceedings** to reexamine Joan's condemnation trial during his trip.

PRAGUERIE, THE (1440). The Praguerie was the most concerted of several brief noble rebellions against **Charles VII**. Although it was well after the **execution** of Joan of Arc, it demonstrates how several of her companions in arms did not remain loyal to the king.

On 2 November 1439, the king issued an order that nobles could no longer raise private armies. Orders then went out to nobles on campaign to return to **Paris** with their armies. The duke of Bourbon (See CLERMONT, COUNT OF) followed such an order, but only by marching through Burgundian territory in February 1440, violating the **Treaty of Arras** (1435). He then began an effort to recruit other nobles to his side including the **duke of Alençon**, the count of **Vendôme**, the estranged **Georges de La Trémoille**, and the dauphin (*See* LOUIS XI). The nobles modeled their rebellion after the Hussites, referring to their cause as the Praguerie. The count of Dunois (*See* ORLÉANS, BASTARD OF) briefly joined the cause but switched sides before the fighting started. The king responded swiftly, leading armies against various strongholds of the nobles. Charles gained the upper hand, and the nobles were prepared for peace talks, which the king refused until they released the captive **Raoul de Gaucourt**. Most of the nobles were pardoned but were forced to relinquish their holdings. The king refused to pardon La Trémoille who was seen as the prime instigator in convincing the dauphin to join the rebellion.

It is impossible to know where Joan of Arc would have sided in such a rebellion. Some of her closest companions, such as Alençon, would likely have tried to sway her to their cause. She was no stranger to recruiting soldiers to her armies, but most often under the banner of the king whom she was loyal to until her death.

PRÉVOSTEAU, GUILLAUME. Licentiate in **civil law**, Guillaume Prévosteau was appointed promoter of the **nullification proceedings** in May 1452 by **Guillaume d'Estouteville**. In this role, he expanded the initial twelve articles used for questioning witnesses to twenty-seven articles. On 17 November 1455 when the trial officially began, he changed his role to representing the Arc family as their principal lawyer, replaced by **Simon Chapitault** as promoter of the trial. Prévosteau represented the Arc family through the final verdict on 7 July 1456.

PRIOR. The prior was typically the second in command of a monastery, appointed by the **abbot**. There were at least three priors present at Joan of Arc's **condemnation trial** (1431) including **Pierre de Miget**, prior of Longueville-Giffard, along with priors of Saint-Lo and Signy, all three local monasteries in **Rouen**. Although the priors of the latter two are not explicitly named in the trial transcripts, records show that Petrus de La Crique was the prior of Signy and trained in both **canon law** and **civil law**.

PRISON. *See* CAPTIVITY.

PRISONER OF WAR. *See* RANSOM.

PROMOTER. *See* CHAPITAULT, SIMON; ESTIVET, JEAN D'; ROLES AND RESPONSIBILITIES.

PROPHECIES FORETELLING JOAN OF ARC. In the fifteenth century, prophets and prophecies were examined seriously but viewed with suspicion by theologians who were concerned about the validity of the messenger as well as the message. Prophecies often outlived prophets, and nobles and chroniclers were aware of, regurgitated, and reinterpreted them for their own political purposes. With the rise, fall, and rehabilitation of Joan of Arc, prophecies purportedly foretelling her arrival and mission were regularly invoked.

The three most common prophecies mentioned in tandem came from the wizard Merlin of Arthurian legend, the Sybil, and the Venerable Bede (?–735), often merged and enhanced, a practice pre-dating the arrival of Joan of Arc. When **Christine de Pizan** wrote *The Tale of Joan of Arc*, she evoked all three prophets, telling us

> But it was found in histories that she was destined to accomplish her mission; for more than five hundred years ago, Merlin, the Sibyl and Bede foresaw her coming, entered her in their writings as someone who would put an end to France's troubles, made prophecies about her, saying that she would carry the banner in the French wars and describing all that she would achieve. (Quoted in Taylor 2006, 103)

Merlin's prophecy found prominence in fifteenth-century France through Geoffrey of Monmouth in his *History of the Kings of Britain*, which was interpreted to foretell the arrival of a young girl riding on horseback, performing miracles. Multiple chroniclers had cited Sibyl, the term referring to the broader prophecies from unnamed women dating back to Ancient Greece. However, the exact prophecy relating to Joan from the sibyls remains lost and was most likely reinterpreted for the moment. Bede found prominence through the work of John of Bridlington (c. 1320–1379) who told of a young virgin girl carrying a banner. Supporters of Joan such as Pizan merged these prophecies together to give Joan credence and add a divine element to the rule and conquest of Charles VII. Together, the interpretations called out a young virgin girl from

Lorraine who would smite the English and save France. It is common to find one or all of these prophets mentioned in works about Joan of Arc.

Historians are often in agreement that Joan knew *something* of these prophecies, but nothing survives that quotes her directly concerning them, not even during her **condemnation trial** (1431). Historians are split on the validity of testimonies from **Durand Laxart** and **Catherine Le Royer** during the **nullification proceedings** (1450–1456) that Joan was finally able to convince **Robert de Baudricourt** to send her to meet **Charles VII** in **Chinon** by telling him, "Have you not heard this prophecy, that France will be destroyed by a woman, and restored by a virgin from the marches of Lorraine?" (Taylor 2006, 275). The ruiner was supposedly Queen **Isabella of Bavaria**, mother to Charles VII, who, along with **Charles VI**, signed the **Treaty of Troyes** (1420) and disinherited their son. Similarly, during the nullification proceedings, both **Jean Bréhal** and **Jean Érault** evoked Marie Robine d'Avignon (?–1399), astrologer to Charles VI, who they claimed was quoted during the **Poitiers** examination. Her prophecy foretold of an armed maiden that would save France.

Joan did adopt the *la Pucelle* ("the virgin") moniker in letters and statements such as in her **letter to the English (22 March 1429)**. Thus, she was often depicted as the *la Pucelle* foretold in prophecies. *See also* BOWER, WALTER; VOICE, VISIONS, AND REVELATIONS.

PROSTITUTES. *See* CAMP FOLLOWERS.

PUCELLE. *See* LA PUCELLE.

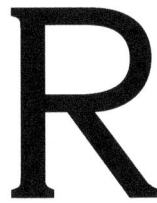

RABATEAU, JEAN (1370–1453). Jean Rabateau was a lawyer in the court of **Charles VII**. Prior to that, he represented Duke Jean of Berry (1340–1416), great-granduncle of Charles, in the Parlement of Paris from 1399 to 1416. During the Burgundian takeover of **Paris** in 1418 (*See* FRENCH CIVIL WAR), Rabateau resettled in **Poitiers**, and by 1427, he was representing the king in criminal cases in the Parlement of Poitiers. After Charles reclaimed Paris in 1436, Rabateau became president of the Parlement of Paris, serving in that role until his death while also remaining an advisor to Charles.

Upon the arrival of Joan of Arc in 1429, Charles determined to send Joan to be examined by theologians in Poitiers, and it was Jean Rabateau and his wife who provided Joan with lodging for about three weeks. While there, Joan was visited often by theologians and other curious residents who questioned her. She was said to pray on her knees after dinner and in a nearby chapel. When Joan visited **Orléans** on 19 January 1430, Rabateau was accompanying her. He died before interviews were conducted in Paris for the **nullification proceedings** (1450–1456), and no record of Rabateau's opinion on Joan has survived.

RAIS, GILLES DE LAVAL, BARON OF (1404–1440). Gilles de Laval, baron of Rais, commonly referred to as Gilles de Rais, was a companion in arms of Joan of Arc between her arrival at **Orléans** (29 April 1429) until the failed assault on **Paris** (8 September). He later became the most notorious rapist and mass murderer of children during this period, and was tried and executed for his crimes.

Born in **Brittany** in 1404, Gilles de Rais lost his mother and father by 1415, after which he was raised by his violent grandfather, Jean de Craon. In 1420, Rais took part in freeing the captive **duke of Brittany**. Later that year, he kidnapped his future wife, Catherine de Thouars, forcing a monk to marry them. The rich heiress was in high demand, and Rais managed to convince **Pope** Martin V to legitimize the marriage in 1422 with the belief that Catherine was with child. The marriage further expanded the estates of Gilles de Rais, which now resided in Brittany, Poitou, Maine, and Anjou. While still a teenager, Rais had become one of the richest men on the continent.

In October 1425, Gilles de Rais first met **Charles VII**, and he remained loyal to the king even though the duke of Brittany did not (*See* AMEINS, TREATY OF). In 1427, chroniclers record how Rais waged war against the English and their French allies. He captured several towns and massacred the French soldiers within them.

In 1428, Gilles de Rais joined the court of Charles VII by way of his cousin, **Georges de La Trémoille**. He was likely present in **Chinon** during the arrival of Joan of Arc in March 1429. Historians typically dismiss the claim that he was the one who posed as Charles to trick Joan, as it came from two testimonies from the **nullification proceedings** (1450–1456), made by men who were not present for the event. After Joan made it through the examinations and questioning at **Poitiers**, Charles decided to send her with reinforcements and a supply convoy to Orléans. Gilles de Rais led the operation. After arriving at the city on 29 April, Rais left with the **bastard of Orléans** for Blois to gather more reinforcements, returning on 4 May. Joan rode out to meet them on their return and guarded their flank.

Gilles de Rais was then present for Joan's campaigns, battles, and sieges during the **Loire Campaign** (10–18 June) and the **march to Reims** (29 June–16 July). He is often mentioned among the leaders, including the moments of debate for the next move. Surviving records show that he was given an award for his service, specifically at the battle of **Jargeau** (11–12 June). Historians often accept his loyalty to Charles VII and his continued presence in Joan's campaigns in a positive light. However, there is no indication if he favored Joan or deferred to her in any of the debates.

At the **coronation of Charles VII** (17 July), Gilles de Rais held a prominent position, carrying the sacred oil used to anoint the king. Afterward, he was promoted to **marshal of France**, a position he held until his death.

After the failure at Paris and the disbanding of the royal army (September), Gilles de Rais never interacted with Joan again. There are romanticized theories that he contemplated a rescue attempt of Joan after her capture at **Compiègne** (23 May 1430), but the evidence is slim. In late 1430, there is a record of him recruiting troops, and then in early 1431, he can be found in the same city as **La Hire**, but nothing came of these developments. After Joan's **execution** (30 May 1431), Rais remained active in the royal army, most notably during the relief of **Lagny** (August 1432). Rais forced the **duke of Bedford** to redeploy his besieging army for a possible battle, which distracted the duke long enough to slip reinforcements and supplies into Lagny. After this, Bedford abandoned the siege.

In November 1432, Jean de Craon, grandfather of Gilles de Rais, died. Rais withdrew from military life and began lavishly spending and trading away his riches for parties while maintaining a large entourage. In 1433, he began work on the Chapel of the Holy Innocents, a project that took several years of labor and materials, and upon its completion in 1435, the chapel employed roughly thirty people. Rais's spending involved not only money, but trading away property, often for less than its value to people who did not pay on time or in full.

Another project typically attributed to Gilles de Rais is a production of *Mistere du siege d'Orleans* in Orléans, which also included a massive advertising campaign in 1435.

That same year, relatives attempted the first of several interventions, seeking help from dukes and Charles VII, by having them swear not to buy anymore property from Rais. Around this time, Rais also realized his fortune was dwindling and he began dabbling in magic to seek its recovery, which led to a train of grifters swindling him for the next five years. One such example came in the form of **Claude de Armoises**, claiming to be Joan of Arc having survived execution. Rais was one of several people who knew Joan personally to welcome Armoises and support her claims until she was revealed a fraud.

It was not until 15 May 1440 that Gilles de Rais went too far. After raising a group of armed men and kidnapping a priest during a Mass, he held the priest captive for two months over payments for yet more sold property. In July, Rais was arrested. He then faced an **inquisition** from an ecclesiastical trial that ran until 25 October and a concurrent civil trial that finished on 8 October. The surviving accusations, testimonies, and confessions are horrifying in their contents and unfathomable in their scale. Rais admitted to kidnapping, raping, and murdering scores of children, mostly boys, ages eight to eighteen. Some were for pleasure and others as part of magic rituals involving human sacrifice in hopes of regaining his fortune. In his confession, the first murder occurred in 1432, but the forty-seven-point indictment dated them as far back as 1426. Historians vary on their estimates, but based on those who came forward, the number of victims were possibly as many as 150.

At the beginning of the trials, Gilles de Rais was defiant. However, after an excommunication, he was repentant and began confessing. There are a small group of historians who believe the whole trial was a ruse, employed by those who wanted to put an end to Rais's haphazard spending, but they are in the minority. They theorize that his testimony was elicited through **torture**, not uncommon during an inquisition. However, the surviving testimonies from roughly one hundred witnesses are too graphic and overwhelming for most historians to accept as conspiracy. At the end of the trials, the ecclesiastical court found him guilty of **heresy**, sodomy, and violating church immunity. The civil court found him guilty of kidnapping, torture, and raising an army without permission. Gilles de Rais was hanged on 26 October 1440, having squandered most of his fortune.

Historians struggle with the dichotomy of a marshal of France who fought alongside Joan of Arc between Orléans and Paris, and who always remained loyal to Charles VII, only to become the worst known mass murderer of children during this period. Some narratives of Joan simply omit this latter part of Gilles de Rais's story, only focusing on his rank and his part in Joan's campaigns. Others provide a brief sentence or two to his later crimes. If the accusations were real, then the question of when the crimes started seems paramount. If they started in 1426, then Joan was allied with a monster. If his crimes against children started in 1432, was it somehow related to the death of his grandfather? If so, had he previously found an outlet for his violent tendencies through the socially acceptable means of war? He was present for numerous massacres after battles and sieges, including Jargeau (1429). Did Joan and his involvement in war somehow reign him in at times? These questions may never be answered.

RAMPSTON, THOMAS. See REMPSTON, THOMAS.

RANSOM. The ransom of a prisoner of war during the time of Joan of Arc has undergone considerable examination over the past half-century by historians. The general consensus is while there were guidelines on how to handle valuable prisoners, particularly nobles, the ultimate decision lay with the captor. Still, in England and France, the kings had the right to take cuts from ransoms or claim dibs at buying a prisoner. Thus a prisoner could not expect protection, especially if a ransom could not be paid. Some prisoners were so valuable that their ransom was outright denied or simply too high, as in the case of the **duke of Orléans** from 1415 to 1440. Although Joan of Arc made threats to kill all her enemies, as she did in her **letter to the English (22 March 1429)**, she also understood the general rules of ransoms, knew when to break them, and was prepared to utilize them.

When besieging a fortification, there were often periods of negotiations if the defenders believed their position was untenable (*See* SIEGE). The besiegers typically set the terms though, and if negotiations fell through and the besiegers breached the defenses, the defenders could expect no mercy. This was the situation when the **duke of Alençon** led the king's army against **Jargeau (11–12 June 1429)**. The defenders were offered the chance to abandon the city, but they instead requested more time. The French denied the request, captured the city, and killed many of the defenders, but they still managed to capture the **earl of Suffolk** and his brother, both valuable prisoners. When questioned about the massacre at Jargeau during Joan's **condemnation trial** (1431), the assessors asked why she did not grant the defenders' request for a treaty. Joan explained that the defenders wanted an extra fifteen days before they would abandon the city. She instead gave them an hour to leave with their horses and armor. Otherwise, the city would be assaulted.

Suffolk was not the only valuable prisoner of war Joan encountered. At **Patay (18 June 1429)**, the famous prisoners included **Thomas Rempston, Thomas de Scales**, and **John Talbot**, all three of which were bragging points for **Charles VII**. They were all eventually ransomed for their freedom albeit through different paths. Suffolk was first under the custody of the **bastard of Orléans** before the king took possession of him. Suffolk was released in 1431 after selling off all his estates in France to pay his ransom. Rempston remained in captivity until 1435 when he could secure a portion of his ransom with a promise to pay the rest later. The details of Scales's captivity and release are unknown, but he was at least free by April 1430. Talbot had possibly the most complex path to freedom. First, he was under **Poton de Xaintrailles** who apparently asked for an exorbitant amount. Then Xaintrailles sold Talbot to Charles VII in 1431 where he remained prisoner until 1433, in an ironic exchange for the release of a then captive Xaintrailles.

Although Joan did not survive to see the release of each of these prisoners, she understood their value. For example, with her own prisoner, Franquet d'Arras, captured at **Lagny** (1430), Joan hoped to trade him for some captives in Paris. However, upon learning that some of the Parisians were executed, Joan handed Franquet d'Arras over to the **bailiff** of Senlis who hanged him after a two-week trial where he confessed to murder, stealing, and treason. Arras had quite simply lost his value as a prisoner, and Joan had no qualms about handing him over for justice. When questioned about part of her **mission** to free the captive duke of Orléans, the assessors at Joan's condemnation trial wanted to know *how* she planned to free him. One of her approaches was to secure enough English prisoners for an exchange. *See also* RANSOM OF JOAN OF ARC.

RANSOM OF JOAN OF ARC. Outside of **Compiègne** (23 May 1430), Joan of Arc was captured by soldiers of **John of Luxembourg**, a vassal of the duke of Burgundy (*See* PHILIP THE GOOD). Joan was arguably the highest profile prisoner of the **Hundred Years War** since the capture of French King John II in 1356. The **University of Paris** recognized this and immediately began sending letters to the duke of Burgundy and then John of Luxembourg, congratulating them on their acquisition, but also imploring them to hand Joan over for an **inquisition**. The university then sent **Pierre Cauchon**, bishop of Beauvais, to make the case in person on 14 July. In each letter, the university asserted the need to avoid losing Joan as a prisoner whether through escape or ransom, and the need to try her for her crimes. This was not a foregone conclusion, though, and testimony from the **nullification proceedings** (1450–1456) reveals that Luxembourg offered to ransom Joan if she agreed to stop fighting. Joan was defiant, doubting his authority to release her (*See* MACY, HAIMOND DE).

As with many **ransoms** at this time, the captive's fate was the prerogative of the captor, and it took the intervention of **Henry VI** to secure Joan as a prisoner from the Burgundians. A tax was levied in **Normandy** in August 1430 to pay what amounted to ten thousand *livres tournois*, the maximum the king was required to pay for acquiring a prisoner of war from his subjects. The process was lengthy, and the university sent a letter to Cauchon on 21 November, chastising him for taking so long. Still, the English had secured the prisoner in November and by 23 December, Joan was in **Rouen**, the site of her **condemnation trial**. Joan was not officially transferred to the Church for an inquisition until 3 January 1431. Even then, she remained in a secular prison, guarded by the English. In addition, the terms were explicit that if Joan were found innocent in the inquisition, she would go back to the English for a separate trial. *See also* CAPTIVITY.

RAPE. *See* SEXUAL ASSAULT AND RAPE.

RAYMOND. *See* COUTES, LOUIS DE.

RÉCIT DU HERAULT BERRI. *See* BOUVIER, GILLES LE.

REGENT. In the fifteenth century, a regent was an officially appointed ruler in the event that the king, duke, or other ruling monarch was a minor or simply incapable of ruling due to illness or absence. In France, however, the king was such an integral role that they were less apt to appoint a regent. For example, even though King Charles V wished there to be a regent in the event his heir was too young, the royal court still coronated **Charles VI** as king when he was only eleven years old (1380). In addition, while Charles VI became incapable of ruling during bouts of mental illness, France never declared a regent in his stead. Charles eventually gave authority to Queen **Isabeau of Bavaria** in 1402, but her ability to lead still relied on the cooperation of the king's brothers and uncles who were dukes and counts in the royal court. This resulted in politicking and maneuvering between these dukes and counts that ultimately led to and propagated the **French Civil War** (1407–1435).

On 26 December 1418, while still **dauphin**, future **Charles VII** declared himself regent of France. After the signing of the **Treaty of Troyes** (1420), **Henry V** began styling himself as "heir and regent of France." The **duke of Bedford** served as the regent of English-occupied France upon the death of his brother, Henry V, in 1422, who left behind a nine-month-old son. Bedford served in the role until the official coronation of **Henry VI** in Paris (1431).

REHABILITATION. *See* NULLIFICATION PROCEEDINGS.

REIMS. The site of Reims was inhabited as far back as the Roman era. The city gained prominence in the Middle Ages for hosting the baptism of Clovis I, king of the Franks at the end of the fifth century, following his conversion to Christianity. The office of **bishop** in Reims was raised to **archbishop** in the eighth century and the city played host to seven ecclesiastic **councils**. Future kings would be coronated at Reims, but it was not until 1129 with the coronation of King Philip that it became the permanent site associated with the ceremony. The city successfully held out against English King Edward III who besieged the city in the winter of 1359 and 1360 in hopes of coronating himself king of France there.

Reims is located 130 kilometers northeast of Paris, well within Burgundian territory in 1429; it had been under Burgundian control since 1417. Thus, when Joan of Arc arrived at the court of **Charles VII** (1429), claiming that she would lead his army to Reims to see him coronated there, it was difficult to fathom. Still, after several months' worth of military victories against the English and Burgundians, promises of clemency from Charles and Joan, and the fair treatment demonstrated at **Troyes** (5–9 July), the city cleared out those opposing Charles and opened its gates to his army on 16 July (*See* REIMS, MARCH TO). The **coronation of Charles VII** was successfully hosted on 17 July and the town remained loyal to the king.

In March 1430, the city wrote several letters to Joan, expressing concerns over possible treachery from within and sieges from nearby Burgundians. Joan responded with her own letters, encouraging them to remain diligent, resist any siege, and be ready for her arrival in the event of an attack. Although Reims foiled several plots, the city was never directly threatened for the rest of the Hundred Years War.

Today, the Reims Cathedral that hosted the coronation of Charles VII still stands. Archives in Reims host three original **letters** from Joan to the city (5 August 1429 and 16 and 28 March 1430). In addition, a register in the city preserved records of two lost letters that Joan sent to Troyes (5 July and 22 September 1429).

REIMS, MARCH TO (29 JUNE–16 JULY 1429). After the relief of **Orléans** (8 May 1429) and the success of the **Loire Campaign** in recapturing fortified towns along the Loire River (10–18 June), the next step for the growing momentum from Joan of Arc's presence needed to be settled. For Joan, her **mission** was clear that **Charles VII** should be coronated at **Reims**, held within Anglo-Burgundian territory. Although many historians today follow Joan's lead in referring to Charles as the **dauphin**, meaning the uncrowned heir to the French throne, Charles and his allies had seen him as king since 1422. Charles's enemies would not even call him the dauphin, instead recognizing **Henry VI** as the king of France based on the **Treaty of Troyes** (1420).

Charles, along with his nobles and advisers, debated their next move and they were leaning toward a push into Lancastrian **Normandy**. However, Joan of Arc burst into one of the meetings and implored the king to march to Reims for his coronation. According to the **bastard of Orléans**, she argued that "once the King had been crowned and consecrated, the power of his enemy would steadily decline, until in the end they would not be able to harm either the King or the kingdom" (Taylor 2006, 283). Joan had her way, as she still carried the clout of the military successes from the preceding month.

The royal army, numbering upwards of twelve thousand, began its march from Gien on 29 June. Joan is described as marching alongside the king for much of the journey. Numerous towns that had previously sworn loyalties to Henry VI and the **Anglo-Burgundian Alliance** opened their doors to the army and switched allegiance to Charles VII.

The first obstacle was Auxerre. The army camped outside its gates on 1 July. Negotiations lasted until 3 July when the town surrendered without any fighting. Charles forgave the inhabitants, and the army was resupplied. The army then arrived at **Troyes** on 5 July. Camped outside, negotiations began that included Joan hand-delivering her **letter to the people of Troyes**. The town remained defiant, and by 8 July, Charles was contemplating whether he should bypass Troyes entirely. However, Joan again intervened and personally took command of preparing for a siege of the city that night. The next morning, after the king's cannons fired a single shot, the town capitulated (*See* TROYES, SIEGE OF). From there, the march continued with more cities opening their gates to the king, and the royal army arrived at Reims on 16 July. The next day there was the official ceremony for the **coronation of Charles VII**.

Afterward, more towns continued to surrender to Charles. The **duke of Bedford** formed an army and challenged the king to battle. The result was a standoff at **Montépilloy** (15 August). Although negotiations were underway for a truce with the Burgundians (*See* FRANCO-BURGUNDIAN TRUCE), Joan's summer of military successes increased her clout, and the next part of her mission was capturing **Paris** (*See* PARIS, SIEGE OF).

RELAPSE OF JOAN OF ARC. On 24 May 1431, Joan of Arc had signed an **abjuration**, denouncing her interactions with **saints** and agreeing to wearing women's **clothing** while spending the rest of her days in prison. On 28 May, the judges and a small group of assessors visited Joan in her cell upon hearing rumors that she had resumed wearing men's clothing. Although the **transcripts** of the **condemnation trial** are meant to support the case against Joan, the recorded interactions reveal her mistreatment, and they support much of the elaborations made by witnesses during the **nullification proceedings** (1450–1456).

Upon visiting Joan, the assessors first focused on her clothing, but then turned to her **voices, visions, and revelations**. She still believed in them and she was still communicating with them, and therefore they told her that she was wrong to have abjured. Joan ultimately said she would not turn against her voices again, but she was willing to wear women's clothing in order to hear Mass and receive communion. Furthermore, she claimed she was told she would have been released from her current prison and that she never understood what she signed.

Joan's claims are portrayed as her relapsing, but several testimonies reveal that the version of the abjuration she signed was much shorter than what appears in the transcripts of the trial. Guillaume de La Chambre (*See* PHYSICIANS) claimed that **Guillaume Érard** convinced her to sign by promising that she would be released. No one else claimed to have heard this interaction. Was Joan's claim that she was promised to be released recorded in the trial transcripts referring to release from imprisonment altogether or simply being moved to a Church prison, no longer guarded by English (*See* CAPTIVITY)? Regardless, the transcripts do record that the assessors visited Joan later in the day of her abjuration to ensure she understood the terms. It is possible that Joan signed an abbreviated document that was then expanded for the transcripts.

After the assessors met with Joan on 28 May, they met on 29 May and agreed to hand Joan over to secular authorities. The next day, they read the new sentence for relapse, and she was immediately **executed**.

REMPSTON, THOMAS (?-1458). Based on what survives from muster rolls, Thomas Rempston's military experience dates as far back as 1415 when he joined **Henry V**'s expedition force, already a knight. After fighting at Agincourt (*See* HUNDRED YEARS WAR), Rempston would go on to experience much of the English expansion firsthand. This enabled him to acquire estates and wealth through war and conquest while his hereditary wealth was tied up with long-living widows in his family. He participated in the conquest of **Normandy** (1417–1419), entered **Paris** with Henry V in 1420, served as captain of at least three castles, captured cities such as Guise (1424) and Le Mans (1428), and fought at major battles such as **Caravant** (1423) and St. James (1426), the latter at which he defeated a much larger French force under the command of **Arthur de Richemont**. Throughout this period, he served under major English military leaders including the **duke of Bedford**, the **earl of Suffolk, John Fastolf**, and **John Talbot**.

Thus, by the time Rempston joined **Salisbury's 1428 expedition** on 8 August, he was already an experienced military leader with all sorts of success in France. The expedition force captured major cities and fortifications north of the Loire River and settled in for the siege of **Orléans** (12 October). His last taste of success during the time of Joan of Arc came at the battle of the **Herrings** (12 February 1429). He was present at Orléans for Joan's arrival (29 April) and the lifting of the siege (8 May). Worse, he was among the English leaders captured at **Patay** (18 June). Chroniclers such as **Fauquembergue** and **Monstrelet** cited Rempston's name among the captured at Patay, demonstrating the prestige of his name.

Although Rempston would continue to fight in the war, his days of success were behind him. He eventually secured part of his **ransom** for release in 1435. He was imprisoned in 1439 for financial misconduct, and he would again be captured in battle in 1442, not securing his ransom again for several years, at least until 1445. He eventually returned to England in 1449, his military days behind him. With the loss of Lancastrian **Normandy** in 1450, he lost his last possessions in France. When his mother passed in 1454, he finally gained access to hereditary wealth that had eluded him for decades. He died in 1458, survived by three daughters.

RENÉ OF ANJOU (1409–1480). Born on 16 January 1409, René of Anjou was the son of **Yolanda of Aragon** and cousin of **Charles VII**. His older sister, **Marie of Anjou**, married Charles in 1422 and became queen of France. In the 1420s, René lost his counties of Anjou and Guise to the English and Burgundians, finding refuge with his father-in-law, the **duke of Lorraine**. It is here where he met Joan of Arc in late January or early February 1429, summoned by the duke. He was close with **Robert de Baudricourt**, and historians have theorized that René may have intervened in convincing Baudricourt to send Joan to meet with the duke. Joan requested that the duke send René with her to meet with Charles VII in **Chinon**, but the duke refused. Given her monarchist zeal, Joan would have been impressed by René's lineage from French King John II (1319–1364).

René, like his father-in-law, struggled with his geographical position in France with lands bordering or conquered by English and Burgundians. Between April and June 1429, René went through the process of pledging allegiance to the **duke of Bedford** and recognizing the **Treaty of Troyes** (1420). However, after the **coronation of Charles VII** (17 July 1429), René broke with his oath and marched to meet up with the royal army in time to participate in the battle of **Montépilloy** (15 August). After the failed siege of **Paris** (8 September), René was among the king's troops that arrived to call off the siege the next day.

These are the only confirmed interactions that René had with Joan of Arc. After which, he went on to hold numerous titles including duke of Bar (1430), duke of Lorraine (1434–1453), and king of Naples (1435–1442). After the death of Duke Charles II of Lorraine in 1431, René was captured at the battle of Bulgnéville (2 July), fighting over his father-in-law's duchy. He was released on 1 May 1432 with a promise to pay his **ransom** to the duke of Burgundy (See PHILIP THE GOOD). On 16 January 1435, he mediated between diplomats of Charles VII and Philip the Good for the initial steps to what led to the Congress of Arras (See ARRAS, TREATY OF). However, Philip ordered René back to prison for failing to pay his ransom in full and he was not released until 1437. René was present for the Truce of Tours (1444) between England and France, and in 1445, he gave his daughter, Margaret of Anjou, in marriage to **Henry VI**. With the death of Charles VII (1461) and the rise of King **Louis XI**, René lost both Bar and Anjou to the new king. He died on 10 July 1480.

His moniker "the good" was a nineteenth-century addition, added in recognition for his support of literature and art. He exchanged poetry with the **duke of Orléans**. Other works, including paintings, have been attributed to René as well.

RETRIAL. See NULLIFICATION PROCEEDINGS.

RICHARD, FRIAR (BROTHER). In 1429 to 1431, a mendicant, Franciscan **friar** simply known as Friar Richard stirred up towns throughout France to extreme acts of devotion with his fiery preaching. He was ultimately discredited and labeled an **apostate** and **heretic**. Joan of Arc's contemporary detractors strove to associate her with the friar.

The earliest surviving mention of Friar Richard has him arriving from Jerusalem and Syria to **Paris** in April 1429. The author of the *Journal d'un bourgeois de Paris* tells us that the friar started preaching atop a platform for up to ten hours a day. He claimed that the Antichrist was alive in Babylon and events on par with the Apocalypse were imminent by the next year. Preaching daily for a week and a half, the friar's audience reached five thousand to six thousand at its peak. The friar convinced listeners to burn all forms of gambling, as well as expensive headpieces worn by women, which resulted in one hundred spontaneous bonfires around the city. When he finally left Paris (late April or early May), everyone purportedly wept, and the city had never shown such pious devotion. If his departure was a mystery to the Parisians at the time, **Monstrelet** later claimed his sermons favored the French loyal to **Charles VII**. From Paris, he eventually settled in **Troyes** and continued to preach.

It was outside the walls of **Troyes** where Friar Richard was sent by the city's inhabitants to assess Joan of Arc while the royal army besieged the city (5–9 July). This task indicates that he had won over the inhabitants as he had in Paris. Joan testified during her **condemnation trial** (1431) that the friar approached her, splashed the area with holy water, and made signs of the cross. Joan, who had experienced similar behavior during her third encounter with **Robert de Baudricourt**, instructed the friar to "approach boldly—I won't fly away" (Hobbins 2005, 81). It was likely that Joan handed her **letter to the people of Troyes (4 July 1429)** directly to Richard. Joan was questioned about whether the friar preached upon her entry to the city and whether he later held her **standard** during the **coronation of Charles VII** (17 July), but she could not recall either.

Richard continued to follow Joan in her military campaigns, and it was during the siege of **Paris** in September 1429 when he finally returned to the city that he had so moved the previous spring. The knowledge that he was now firmly in the camp of Joan and Charles sent Parisians into a tizzy. According to the *Journal d'un bourgeois de Paris*, they cursed Richard, destroyed medallions they had made as part of their devotion from his teaching, and they picked up all the old games they had abandoned.

From there, the friar's whereabouts become scarcer. He is recorded as being in **Jargeau** at the same time as Joan in Christmas 1429. The next year, he preached for thirty-three days during Lent in **Orléans**. He was still in the city when the queen, **Marie of Anjou**, passed through on 16 May. The last mention of the friar had him imprisoned in **Poitiers** on 23 March 1431 on suspicion of being a heretic.

During her condemnation trial, Joan claimed she had a falling out with Richard, because she refused to believe the visions of **Catherine de La Rochelle**, one of the friar's devotees, and she claimed to have sent Charles a letter saying as much.

Given Friar Richard's infamy throughout Paris, Troyes, Orléans, and Poitiers, he became an easy guilt-by-association tool for Joan's detractors. Article 52 of the initial **seventy articles** of accusation brought at Joan's trial mention the friar and his sermon in Troyes, even though Joan could not recall him preaching it. When the **duke of Bedford** publicly wrote Charles VII (7 August 1431) in an attempt to convince the king to give up his claims, the duke lumped Joan and the **apostate** friar together as the king's company. Similarly, **Jean Graverent** preached a sermon in Paris that same year (9 August) where he described Joan as being under the friar's direction. Both Monstrelet and **Jean de Wavrin** later described Charles as always being in the company of Joan and the friar.

Whatever became of Friar Richard is a mystery, but his unfulfilled apocalyptic predictions for 1430 likely did not help his cause. Joan appears to have been unimpressed with the friar's preaching and his most dedicated followers.

RICHEMONT, ARTHUR DE (1393–1458). Arthur de Richemont was a prominent and often controversial noble and military commander, fighting in the **French Civil War** and the **Hundred Years War**, and briefly a companion in arms of Joan of Arc.

Born on 24 August 1393 as the younger son of the duke of Brittany, Arthur's mother married English King Henry IV in 1403. He became count of Richemont in England, but this was solely a title, as he never possessed the county. When the French Civil War broke out (1407), he sided with the **Armagnacs**, predominantly because of his close friendship with Louis of Guyenne, the **dauphin**, and older brother of future King **Charles VII**. In 1414, he was knighted, and in 1415, he fought alongside the French at Agincourt where he was wounded and captured. Treated well in captivity in England, he was released in 1420 with the assignment of bringing **Brittany** to the side of the English. Richemont was instrumental in convincing his brother, the **duke of Brittany**, to sign the **Treaty of Troyes**. The **duke of Bedford** rewarded Richemont's efforts, making him count of Touraine and earl of Ivry in 1422. In 1423, Richemont married **Margaret of Burgundy**, sister of the duke of Burgundy (*See* PHILIP THE GOOD), seemingly solidifying the **Anglo-Burgundian Alliance**. However, Richemont came to the camp of Charles VII in 1424 when Bedford refused to give him a military command. In 1425, the king made him constable of France, and Richemont campaigned against the English. However, by 1427, he came at odds with **Georges de La Trémoille**, an advisor of the king who favored diplomacy over war, and La Trémoille was successful in banishing Richemont from the king's court. Outcast, he still spurned overtures from Bedford to side with the English.

Richemont was not present for the arrival of Joan of Arc in 1429, but during the **Loire Campaign** (June 10–18), he arrived outside of **Beaugency** on 15 or 16 June with at least one thousand troops. The **duke of Alençon**, commander of the campaign, testified during the **nullification proceedings** (1450–1456) that Joan and the other commanders were not happy to see him, and Alençon threatened to leave if Richemont stayed. Joan appeared to tepidly welcome him regardless. Historians have theorized she put aside concerns because they needed the reinforcements. The point was moot, as the army quickly mobilized to confront the English army outside **Patay**, where Richemont participated (18 June). While it appears that Richemont initially joined the **march to Reims** (29 June–16 July), **Gilles le Bouvier** tells us that La Trémoille convinced the king to dismiss him outside the gates of **Troyes** (5–9 July) on the basis that he would not remain loyal.

Richemont strove to make amends with Charles, making progress in March 1432. With the fall of Georges de La Trémoille in 1433, Richemont was back in the king's court in April 1434. From there, he was present and active in campaigns and diplomatic efforts. He helped negotiate the **Treaty of Arras** (1435), and he entered Paris on behalf of the king on 13 April 1436. During the noble rebellions against Charles, Richemont remained loyal to the king. In 1449, he was the primary architect of the reconquest of **Normandy**. With the death of his brother, he became Duke Arthur III of Burgundy on 22 September 1457 until his death on 26 December 1458.

Historians have theorized that Richemont's brief moment in the military career of Joan of Arc and her acceptance of him inflamed La Trémoille's antagonism toward her, as both Richemont and Joan favored war over diplomacy.

RINGS OF JOAN OF ARC. Rings were common among people in fifteenth-century France, and Joan of Arc was known to have worn at least two rings. Joan was also recorded gifting a ring to the grandmother of the Laval brothers (*See* LAVAL LETTER). During her **condemnation trial** (1431), the assessors attempted to associate her rings with sorcery in the same vein they portrayed her fondness of her **standard**. There was precedence for this, and historians often evoke the case of Jean de Bar who, in 1398, was executed in **Paris** after his confession that included enchanting rings with devils that he hoped would fulfill his wishes upon kissing the rings.

When first questioned about her rings on 1 March 1431, Joan was recorded turning to **Pierre Cauchon** and saying, "You have one of mine, give it back to me" (Hobbins 2005, 74). Joan revealed that one of her brothers gave her this ring, but ultimately told the assessors to donate it to the church.

She claimed another ring was taken by the Burgundians, which she asked to at least see if possible. This ring was given to Joan by her mother or father in **Domremy**. Through several rounds of questioning, we learn that the ring was made of brass or gold but certainly not fine gold, there was no stone, and there were the names Jesus and Mary on it, and possibly three crosses.

When asked if people tried to touch the ring after the **coronation of Charles VII** (17 July 1429), Joan admitted people touched her hand, but she did not know their intent. Later, the assessors seized on Joan's affection for this ring by asking why she looked at it before going into battle, an informed question. Joan said it brought her joy, and she did it "in honor of her father and mother" (Hobbins 2005, 133), which ended the questioning about the rings.

In Article 20 of the **seventy articles** of accusation brought against Joan, she was accused of casting a spell on her ring among other items, but Joan refuted the charge, adding that there was "no sorcery or any black art in anything she did" (Hobbins 2005, 133). The ring did not make it into the condensed **twelve articles** brought against Joan. There was also no mention of the ring during the **nullification proceedings** (1450–1456).

Historians often evoke **Walter Bower** who, while pondering Joan's successes, recounted how she purportedly looked at her ring regularly, and that the Burgundians took the ring after her capture at **Compiègne** (23 May 1430). This demonstrates that the story of the ring had spread, and that Bower either questioned the ring's power or at least noted that the Burgundians saw power in it.

On 26 February 2016, an auction was held in London for what was claimed to be Joan's ring, and it sold to Philippe de Villiers for £297,600, after the buyer's premium. The ring's provenance, based solely on documentation from the twentieth century, includes supposed owners such as **Henry Beaufort** and Henry VII before eventually falling into the hands of private collectors, but always remaining in England after 1431. The ring has engravings of "IHS" and "MAR" on the face, common abbreviations for "Jesus" and "Mary." It is, however, lacking the three crosses that Joan believed were on it. Still, no one has been able to rule out that the ring comes from fifteenth-century France. The abbreviations and gothic lettering are consistent with other rings from the period and region. In addition, tests reveal that the ring is silver with traces of yellow metal in the engravings. Since there is no oxidation or greening, this metal is indeed gold, meaning this was a gold-plated silver ring, a technique used during this period.

The ring is currently on display in Puy du Fou, a historical-themed park in France. *See also* "JESUS MARY."

RIQUIER, JEAN (C. 1410–?). Jean Riquier was a priest from Heudicourt, roughly forty-three kilometers southeast of **Rouen**. Although he was not present for the sessions of the **condemnation trial** of Joan of Arc (1431), he attended both her **abjuration** (24 May) and her **execution** (30 May). Concerning the latter, he provided oft-quoted, gruesome details during his testimonies in the **nullification proceedings** (1450–1456). He stated that once the judges delivered their verdict and Joan was handed to secular authorities, she was immediately taken to be executed with no further deliberation. Upon seeing the fire, she cried "Jesus" over and over again. After her burning, the executioner kicked at the pyre to expose her charred body to confirm she was dead for the crowd.

ROLES AND RESPONSIBILITIES IN JOAN OF ARC'S CONDEMNATION TRIAL. Historians often refer to judges, assessors, and "judges and assessors" present at Joan of Arc's **condemnation trial** (1431). They are not always precise with these terms, and they can refer to anyone present during the **inquisition**, but they can also include the students and professors from the **University of Paris** who submitted their opinion in writing after reading the **twelve articles** formally brought against Joan.

Given the infamy of Joan in the Anglo-Burgundian world, the trial attracted a lot of attention. **Pierre Cauchon** also invited numerous experts to attend the process, which many did if only for a day. The surviving **transcripts** of the trial attempt to list the names, degrees, and benefices of every man present at the beginning of each session. However, there are conflicts between the surviving copies, and the transcribers were not always diligent in the effort. Thus, the modern attempts to reconcile the exact number of men present during at least some portion of the inquisition range from 126 to 193, but the most common estimate is 131.

If we are forced to be precise with the terminology, the only judges were Cauchon, as the local bishop, and the assigned inquisitor, **Jean Le Maistre**—the two roles responsible for conducting an inquisition. **Jean de La Fontaine** was assigned as the examiner or counselor, responsible for questioning Joan, but others, such as **Jean Beaupère**, may have interjected with or submitted their own questions. **Jean d'Estivet** was the promoter or prosecutor, responsible for building the case against the accused, and he compiled the initial **seventy articles** of accusation brought against Joan. **Jean Massieu** was the executor of writs or mandates, responsible for escorting Joan to and from her cell. As such, he is sometimes labeled an usher. Finally, there were the notaries, initially **Guillaume Colles** and **Guillaume Manchon** who were later joined by **Nicolas Taquel**, responsible for transcribing the meeting minutes in French shorthand, comparing notes, and compiling an official record in Latin. The notaries are sometimes referred to as "scribes," which should not give the impression that they were capturing word-for-word statements by the assessors or Joan. While they sometimes captured supposed direct quotes, they more often captured the general meanings of statements.

Historians sometimes lump all of these roles together as "clerks." And while everyone in attendance or submitting an opinion may be considered an assessor or adviser, the final judgment came from Cauchon and Le Maistre.

Outside of these roles, there were three named English guards appointed to guard Joan starting on 22 February, but Guillaume Manchon would later testify at the **nullification proceedings** (1450–1456) there were four of them, and Jean Massieu would testify there were at least five. John Grey, John Berwoit, and William Talbot are listed by name in the trial transcripts, but little is known about any of them. Manchon also said two of the guards were replaced after the **earl of Warwick** learned of attempts to rape Joan (*See* SEXUAL ASSAULT AND RAPE). Several of these guards purportedly slept in Joan's cell, and multiple people testified that the guards would not let anyone see Joan in her cell without explicit permission from the judges after some assessors tried to coach her (*See* CAPTIVITY). Finally, there was Geoffroy Thérage, the executioner in Rouen responsible for building the scaffold and pyre and lighting the fire for Joan's **execution**.

There were other active participants who had no official title or role in the process. For example, **Thomas Courcelles** presented the seventy articles to Joan, translating them into French for her. **Nicolas Midi** condensed the initial seventy articles down to **twelve articles** that were distributed for opinion from assessors and the University of Paris, and formally presented against Joan. **Jean de Châtillon** and **Pierre Maurice** both preached lengthy sermons at Joan in their attempt to get her to submit to the **Church Militant**. After the trial, Thomas Courcelles worked with Guillaume Manchon to compile the official Latin record, generating and distributing five copies (*See* TRANSCRIPTS).

There was no representation or defense for Joan outside of her own testimony and her responses to the initial seventy articles presented to her. *See also* EDUCATION.

ROMAN LAW. *See* CIVIL LAW.

ROUEN. The capital of Lancastrian **Normandy** (1419–1449) and the capital of English-controlled France after the fall of Paris (1436), Rouen was the city where Joan of Arc was imprisoned (23 December 1430–30 May 1431), subjected to an **inquisition**, and **executed** (*See* CONDEMNATION TRIAL). After the city returned to French control in 1449, **Charles VII** initiated an official inquiry into Joan's original trial, an effort which has become known as the **nullification proceedings**. Interviews with participants in the trial were conducted in Rouen in 1450, 1452, and 1456. The nullification judges rendered their official verdict in Rouen, nullifying the original condemnation trial and verdict. *See also* CAPTIVITY.

ROUEN TRIAL. *See* CONDEMNATION TRIAL.

ROUSSEL, RAOUL (?–1452). Doctor of both **canon law** and **civil law** (*See* EDUCATION) by 1416 and **canon** of **Rouen** by 1420, Raoul Roussel was one of the most assiduous assessors during the **condemnation trial** of Joan of Arc (*See* ROLES). By the time of the trial (1431), Roussel was an avid supporter of the **Treaty of Troyes** and had served directly on behalf of the **duke of Bedford** on several occasions, most recently by inspecting fortresses in **Normandy** in 1428.

During the condemnation trial, Roussel attended all but one of the public sessions (he was there on 22, 24, and 27 February, and 1 March 1431). After reviewing the transcript on 30 April, Roussel declared that Joan's statements were false and invented to support **Charles VII**. He was present for **Jean de Châtillon**'s passionate attempt to push Joan to submit to the **Church Militant** on 2 May. When **Pierre Cauchon** called for a vote on whether to use **torture** on Joan, Roussel voted no, but only on the grounds that it would tarnish what he saw as a well-conducted trial. After reviewing the opinion of the **University of Paris** on the trial, Roussel believed that if Joan did not abjure, then she should be declared a **heretic**. He was present for Joan's **abjuration** (24 May), but not for the vote on her **relapse** (29 May).

After witnessing the **execution** of Joan (30 May), Roussel continued to serve the English, becoming an advisor to King **Henry VI**. He was part of delegations that negotiated with Charles VII in at least 1435 and 1438. In 1444, he became the new **archbishop** of Rouen. After serving the English in Rouen for thirty years, he swore an oath to serve Charles when the king officially entered the city in 1449.

With this as his background, historians have been left to theorize on what sort of role Roussel played during the **nullification proceedings** that began with a general inquiry from the king in 1450 and then with a concerted ecclesiastical effort in 1452 by Cardinal **Guillaume d'Estouteville** and **Jean Bréhal**, inquisitor of France. The record of the condemnation trial makes plain his high attendance and opinion at the time (*See* TRANSCRIPTS). By 1450, he was the highest-ranking living participant that was on record supporting the trial against Joan. Roussel did not testify during the nullification proceedings even though they were taking place in his city. There is no evidence that he volunteered, nor was he called. Did he impede the work of Estouteville and Bréhal? Again, there is no evidence or contemporary commentary, but historians point to Roussel's death on 31 December 1452 as a turning point, or at least the removal of a barrier in the nullification proceedings.

Regardless, Guillaume d'Estouteville was nominated as the new archbishop of Rouen while in Rome in 1453, and he assumed the role in July 1454.

ROUVRAY, BATTLE OF. *See* HERRINGS, BATTLE OF THE.

ROYALISTS. Historians often employ this term to refer to the supporters and armies of French King **Charles VI**. This is meant to differentiate the king from the feuding factions of the **Armagnacs** and **Burgundians** in the **French Civil War**, as both sides strove to sway the king to side with their claims and military campaigns.

The term is sometimes used to denote those loyal to **Charles VII**'s claim to the French throne after the **Treaty of Troyes** (1420). Given the range of allies and mercenaries Charles VII incorporated into his military, this could include French, Scots, Lombards, and Spanish. This term especially applies to Joan of Arc who continually stated that the **coronation of Charles VII** was part of her **mission**. *See also* DAUPHINISTS; LOYALISTS; ORLÉANAIS.

ROYER, CATHERINE LE. *See* LE ROYER, CATHERINE.

S

SAINT-DENIS. Saint Denis, the first bishop of **Paris**, was beheaded in AD 272 during the reign of Roman Emperor Diocletian. He purportedly picked up his head and carried it north before resting in the spot where he was buried, later named Saint-Denis. Over the centuries, the site became one of pilgrimage for many, including rulers, and abbeys and churches were built to commemorate the saint along with a local town that benefited from yearly festivities. By the thirteenth century, the saint had evolved to become the protector of the kingdom, but this view had diminished somewhat due to setbacks early in the **Hundred Years War**. By the fifteenth century, Saint Denis was still prominent among the French, and in 1422, the **duke of Bedford** organized the funeral of **Charles VI** who was buried at the town like many kings before him.

Joan of Arc arrived at Saint-Denis on 26 August 1429 en route for her siege of **Paris** (8 September). After the siege was abandoned, Joan and **Charles VII** stayed in the town from 9 to 13 September. Before leaving, Joan left her armor and a **sword** in one of the churches. After the departure of the royal army, the English reclaimed Saint-Denis and confiscated Joan's armor.

Joan's act of leaving her armor received attention from her assessors during her **condemnation trial** (1431). On 12 March, they asked if Denis was among the **saints** that appeared to Joan. She told them no, perhaps alleviating concerns that the saint might be on the side of Charles VII. On 17 March, they asked why she left her armor, to which she responded she did it "out of devotion, according to the custom of soldiers when they are wounded." Further, she offered her arms "to Saint Denis, because that is the battlecry of France" (Hobbins 2005, 111). This response demonstrates that Joan understood the local customs and beliefs surrounding the saint. However, the assessors followed up by asking if she left the armor to be worshipped. Even though she said no, they listed the act in Article 59 of the **seventy articles**, accusing her of leaving relics for the people. Although the armor was gone, a local historian claimed seeing Joan's sword in a church there at the beginning of the sixteenth century.

SAINT-PIERRE-LE-MOUTIER, SIEGE OF (1–4 NOVEMBER 1429). Saint-Pierre-le-Moutier was a fortified town between the duchy of Bourbon and the town of Nevers. At some point, likely during **Salisbury's 1428 expedition** and the siege of **Orléans** (1428–1429), **Perrinet Gressart**, a local warlord based out of **La Charité**, took the opportunity to seize Saint-Pierre. By May 1429, the **duke of Bedford** had appointed François l'Aragonois, one of Gressart's men, as **bailiff** of the town.

In late October 1429, a war-hungry Joan of Arc had healed from her wound at the siege of **Paris** (8 September) and was sent to combat Pierre Gressart, starting with Saint-Pierre. The details of *why* she was sent there are lost, but **Gilles le Bouvier** tells us that it was **Georges de La Trémoille** who made the decision to capture La Charité. Furthermore, **Charles d'Albret**, half-brother of La Trémoille, was placed in charge of the army.

Much of what we know about the campaign and siege comes from 1456 testimony during the **nullification proceedings** by **Jean d'Aulon**, a **squire** who was on the campaign. Joan and Albret headed to **Bourges** where they assembled their force before marching to Saint-Pierre. We are not sure when they left Bourges or when the siege began exactly, but it was certainly before 1 November, as news reached Charles on that day that the siege was underway. The town was surrounded by a wall, a deep moat, six towers, and three gates. Though the town was old, the fortifications had been reinforced as recently as 1421.

The siege lasted for days and by 4 November, the order was given to assault the walls, likely by Joan's insistence, given her approach at other sieges (*See* JARGEAU). The defenders put up a strong resistance and the first assault failed, according to Aulon who was wounded in the attack. He described a scene where Joan had not fled far from the walls, standing with but four or five men. Aulon rode to her position and implored her to retreat. Instead, she ordered another attack, specifically calling for bundles of wood and withies. The troops came rushing, filling up the moat and making a bridge before successfully scaling the walls of Saint-Pierre, which seems to have given little resistance at this point. The successful approach indicates that the first assault might have been against one of the gates or perhaps too close to one of the towers. Joan's second assault may have focused on a spot of the wall susceptible to **ladders**. Reginald Thierry, a surgeon in the army, testified that, once in the town, the troops attempted to loot the church, but Joan stopped them, refusing to let them take anything.

The victory took its toll, and whatever the army invested in the siege seems to have left them ill-supplied. Joan's surviving **letter to the people of Riom (9 November 1429)** requested gunpowder and other supplies, lamenting that they did not have enough for another siege. Albret sent a similar letter. They would receive supplies from Bourges and Orléans before beginning their lengthier siege of La Charité (24? November–23? December), which they failed to capture.

Saint-Pierre remained in French hands until Perrinet Gressart retook it on 14 May 1431. The French reclaimed it in 1432 or 1433, installing their own bailiff, seemingly for good this time. *See also* ARTILLERY; SIEGE.

SAINT-REMY, JEAN LÈFEVRE DE (1396–1468). Jean Lèfevre de Saint-Remy was the king-of-arms for **Philip the Good**, a chronicler writing in French, and an eyewitness to some of the events involving Joan. One of his works, *Chronique ou Mémoire sur l'institution de la Toison d'Or* (Chronicle and Dissertation on the Institution of the Golden Fleece), covers the period 1408 to 1436. He provides a pro-Burgundian perspective while remaining antagonistic toward Joan of Arc and other allies of **Charles VII**. Although he uses other chroniclers such as **Monstrelet** as sources, Saint-Remy also provides his own details. Concerning Joan, Saint-Remy covers **Orléans, Jargeau, Patay,** the **march to Reims, Montépilloy,** the **coronation of Charles VII, Paris,** and **Compiègne.** Also of interest is his spin on the **prophecies foretelling the arrival of Joan of Arc**, which he depicts as finding relevancy among the English during the siege of Orléans, causing them to abandon it. Among her soldiers, he states that Joan had a commanding presence that the French followed eagerly.

SAINTE-SÉVÈRE, MARSHAL DE. *See* BROSSE, JEAN DE.

SAINTS. In fifteenth-century France, saints were a prominent part of Christianity. These holy people who had entered heaven were revered by a part of the populace for their courageous lives, martyrdoms, and miracles. With recognition by some ecclesiastical authority, they became known as saints. The rigorous process employed by the Catholic Church today was not in place by fifteenth-century France. Thus, the list of those deemed to be saints and revered by believers in medieval France varied between regions and periods. Even as the Catholic Church attempted to be stricter about who was deemed a saint and revoke the saintly status of some, local groups continued to recognize saints on their own accord. The people celebrated saints through feasts, naming churches after them and hosting their relics. The saints were thought to intercede on behalf of believers to God, heal them of diseases, and protect them against enemies.

When pressed on the nature of her **voices** during her **condemnation trial** (1431), Joan of Arc claimed to interact with saints **Michael**, **Catherine**, and **Margaret**. From these saints, Joan learned that **Catherine de La Rochelle** was fabricating her visions and they announced Joan's capture, but not the date. The saints told Joan to don men's **clothing**, and they encouraged her to seek forgiveness after her attempted **escape**. The assessors seized on Joan's claims of interacting with saints, asking her questions about their appearance, whether they wore clothes, what language they spoke, and whether Joan touched them (she said she did). Joan said the saints told her she would be rescued, which she interpreted as a physical rescue from the English. After she signed her **abjuration** (24 May), it was the saints who told her she was wrong. Throughout their initial **seventy articles** of accusation and then their shortened **twelve articles** presented against Joan, the assessors used these claims of communing with saints to accuse Joan of fabrication and pride. After her **execution** (30 May), some of the assessors gave sworn statements that Joan claimed her envisioned saints deceived her (7 June). These statements were appended to the trial **transcripts**, but later disputed by those who contributed to them.

During the **nullification proceedings** (1450–1456), the list of saints purportedly evoked by Joan expanded to include **Charlemagne**, **Gabriel**, and **Louis**. *See also* VOICES.

SALAZAR, JEAN DE (C. 1410–1479). A Spanish knight and mercenary, Jean de Salazar was involved in numerous campaigns for **Charles VII**, and later **Louis XI**, from the late 1420s to early 1470s. He is absent from surviving chronicles and eyewitness testimony during the **nullification proceedings** (1450–1456), yet a 1471 trial of Salazar by the Parlement of **Paris** records his service to the kings as part of his defense, including **Orléans**, **Herrings** (where he was wounded), **Jargeau**, **Beaugency**, **Patay**, **Compiègne**, and the **march to Reims**. No surviving perspective of this Spanish knight survives concerning Joan.

SALISBURY, THOMAS MONTAGU, EARL OF (1388–1428). Thomas Montagu, the earl of Salisbury, was the English leader of the expedition force that captured cities along the Loire River and initiated the siege of **Orléans** (1428–1429).

Born the first son of the earl of Salisbury in 1388, Thomas Montagu's father died in 1400 during a plot to assassinate English King Henry IV. Although Montagu began styling himself the earl of Salisbury as early as 1401, he did not gain recognition of his title until 1409, but even then, without his father's estates.

In 1412, he joined the duke of Clarence's expedition to France to aid the **Armagnacs** (*See* FRENCH CIVIL WAR). In 1414, he became a knight of the Garter, the most exclusive order in England. He joined **Henry V**'s campaigns in France, participating in Agincourt (1415), the **duke of Bedford**'s naval expedition (1416), and the conquest of Normandy (*See* HUNDRED YEARS WAR). In 1419, he was appointed lieutenant-general in **Normandy** and became count of Perche. In 1420, he began serving as governor of multiple regions including Alençon. In 1421, with the backing of Parliament, Henry V restored all of Salisbury's estates in England.

In 1421, the overeager duke of Clarence advanced without waiting for Salisbury's forces, dying in the battle of **Baugé**. Salisbury arrived to claim Clarence's body. Throughout the 1420s, under Henry V and then under the duke of Bedford, Salisbury served as captain and governor of numerous towns and regions, and received numerous lands throughout France. He was present for the victories at **Cravant** (1423) and **Verneuil** (1424). In February 1426, he resigned all his duties for a pilgrimage to Jerusalem, but he changed his mind and received clearance from the **pope**.

He returned to England in April 1427 and began raising reinforcements for the war in

France. He arrived with an expedition force in July 1428 (*See* SALISBURY'S 1428 EXPEDITION). After meeting briefly with Bedford in **Paris**, Salisbury began his march to the Loire River, capturing numerous strongholds before settling in for the siege of **Orléans** (12 October). Salisbury was mortally wounded on 24 October from cannon fire and died in **Meung** on 3 November. Several chronicles, including *Journal du siège d'Orléans*, treated the event as miraculous, but *Chronique de l'établissement de la fête du 8 mai* treated it as an accident. With the death of Salisbury, the **earl of Suffolk** took command of the siege.

Salisbury was instrumental in creating the situation along the Loire River in which Joan of Arc arrived with reinforcements and supplies (29 April 1429). All progress made by Salisbury was completely upended with the lifting of the siege of Orléans (8 May) and the **Loire Campaign** (10–18 June). Bedford later derided the strategic rationale for Salisbury's campaign, defending himself from the deteriorating situation in France.

SALISBURY'S 1428 EXPEDITION. Salisbury's 1428 expedition refers to the English campaign conducted by the **earl of Salisbury** into the Loire Valley and along the Loire River, culminating in the siege of **Orléans**.

Although the **duke of Bedford** was the **regent** of English-controlled France, his strategy was at odds with his brother, duke of Gloucester, who held influence in England. While Bedford wanted to finish conquests of the duchies of Anjou and Maine, Gloucester successfully lobbied in England to fund an expeditionary force that would attack further south into the Loire Valley. The earl of Salisbury, an experienced commander, was selected to lead and was provided with men and funds. He commissioned a massive artillery train and oversaw transportation across the English Channel. After arriving in Paris, he started his march south in August, capturing numerous cities including **Janville** that month. He then captured **Meung** (5 September), **Beaugency** (25 September), and **Jargeau** (5 October) before arriving outside of **Orléans** on 12 October. Salisbury was mortally wounded early in the siege on 24 October, dying on 3 November. The **earl of Suffolk** took over command of the siege.

A 1434 memorandum from the duke of Bedford defending his actions in France to that point, stated that the siege of Orléans was "undertaken by God knows whose advice" (Taylor 2006, 239), underscoring the conflict between Bedford and Gloucester. However, Bedford did not neglect the siege entirely at the time, as he is on record providing funds to aid in the fledgling siege. *See also* ARTILLERY.

SCALES, THOMAS, BARON OF (C. 1399–1460). Born around 1399, Thomas was an English noble and commander who became the baron of Scales upon the death of his older brother in 1419. Two years later, he was granted the associated estates and in 1422, he was campaigning in France, although muster rolls indicate he may have been there as early as 1417. He was certainly present for the victories at **Cravant** (1423) and **Verneuil** (1424), and in 1424, he was campaigning in Maine with **John Fastolf**. In 1425, he became a knight of the Garter, the most exclusive order in England.

In December 1428, Scales joined the siege of **Orléans** alongside **John Talbot** and the **earl of Suffolk**, the latter of which took command upon the death of the **earl of Salisbury** in October. In her **letter to the English (22 March 1429)**, Joan of Arc called out Scales, Talbot, and Suffolk together, commanding them to abandon the siege and leave France, or face violence. Joan arrived at Orléans on 29 April with supplies and reinforcements, and after several days of fighting, the English abandoned the siege on 8 May. On 18 June, Scales was captured at **Patay**, and **Charles VII** listed him along with Talbot and Suffolk as captives in a letter celebrating the success of the **Loire Campaign** (10–18 June).

The details of the release of Scales are scant (*See* RANSOM), but he was free by April 1430 in time to greet **Henry VI** when he arrived in France for his coronation. Over the next two decades, he continued to serve in France, serving in multiple roles including seneschal of **Normandy** (1434), captain of **Rouen** (1436), and lieutenant-general of western Normandy

(1435–1444). Scales was invested financially in the war, and records survive of Parliament paying him for loans he made to the war effort.

Back in England in 1449, Scales supported Suffolk's political hegemony, and when Suffolk was killed in 1450, Scales took over management of his estates. After the War of the Roses broke out in 1459, Scales was stationed in London in 1460, attempting to hold the city before falling back to the Tower of London. When he learned that Henry VI had been captured at the battle of Northampton (10 July), he made plans to escape by river. On 25 July, Scales was recognized by boatmen who killed him.

SCHISMATIC. A schismatic is someone who separates from the Church, which was a lesser charge than heresy. In addition, while a **heretic** is also a schismatic, a schismatic is not necessarily a heretic. For example, **Jean IV, count of Armagnac**, was declared a schismatic in 1429 for his continued support of a papal line rejected during the **Council** of Constance (1414–1418). However, he was able to recant and was pardoned the next year.

During Joan of Arc's **condemnation trial** (1431), the judges and assessors were willing to label her a schismatic while deeming her actions as heretical, indicating that she could correct her ways. In Joan's **abjuration** written up for her (24 May), she only confessed to being a schismatic, not a heretic. However, when she **relapsed** a few days later and was handed over to secular authorities for her **execution** (30 May), they placed a cap on her head that read "relapsed heretic, **apostate, idolater.**" *See also* GREAT SCHISM.

SCRIBE. *See* ROLES AND RESPONSIBILITIES.

SEGUIN, SEGUIN DE (C. 1386–?). Seguin de Seguin, who also appears as Seguin Seguin or Guillaume Seguin, was a Dominican **friar** with a doctorate in theology from the **University of Paris** (*See* EDUCATION). During the **French Civil War**, he had fled **Paris**, most likely in 1418 when Burgundians took control of the city. He was stationed in **Poitiers** when Joan of Arc arrived to be examined by the theologians there (March 1429). Seguin was among the theologians questioning Joan, and he lived to testify in 1456 during the **nullification proceedings**. By then, he was a professor and dean at the fledgling University of Poitiers, established in 1431. He provided a short but raw testimony of Joan at Poitiers and his general perception of her words and character.

Based on his testimony, we learn that Seguin first met Joan upon her arrival in Poitiers. During the examination, she told them that she had heard a voice that told her to go to the king in France. Further, the voice instructed her to go via **Vaucouleurs** where the captain there would ensure she made it to the king (*See* BAUDRICOURT, ROBERT DE). The theologians asked Joan for a sign before entrusting her with the king's army, to which she said she would provide a sign at the siege of **Orléans**. Seguin also spoke of four prophetic statements made by Joan, which he saw come true. These included the relief of Orléans (8 May 1429), the **coronation of Charles VII** at **Reims** (17 July), the submission of Paris to **Charles VII** (1436), and the release of the **duke of Orléans** (1440). The last two occurred well after Joan's **execution** (1431). However, by 1456, the story of Joan had coalesced around stories such as these to attribute posthumous events to her.

SENESCHAL. By the fifteenth century, the seneschal role in France had evolved into an administrative role, existing predominantly in the southern regions. Like the **bailiff**, a seneschal's duties could vary depending on the region and period, but often involved collecting revenues, administrating justice, and recruiting for the military, the latter of which was the more common role for seneschals. A seneschal could also act as the steward for a lord when he was not present.

Historians often use seneschal and bailiff interchangeably, which is not wholly misleading albeit imprecise, as regions in fifteenth-century France were often administered by bailiffs in the north and seneschals in the south.

SEVENTY ARTICLES OF ACCUSATION. During the **condemnation trial** of Joan of Arc

(1431), the assessors questioned Joan publicly in six sessions (21 February–3 March) and then privately in her prison cell in nine sessions (10–17 March). After reviewing the transcripts of the interrogations (18–21 March), the assessors decided to create a list of articles to present against Joan. This resulted in seventy articles of accusation generated by **Jean d'Estivet**, the promoter (*See* ROLES). This period is traditionally referred to as the "preparatory trial." When the assessors presented the seventy articles to Joan on 27 to 28 March, it is referred to as the "ordinary trial." The articles were composed in Latin, and each article was translated into French for Joan by **Thomas de Courcelles**. The assessors presented each article and allowed Joan to respond.

The theme of the articles is broad, aggressive, haphazard, and contradictory at times. Joan is described as a witch, false prophet, conjurer of evil spirits, **blasphemer**, seducer, **idolator**, **schismatic**, and a **heretic**. Furthermore, she was superstitious, sacrilegious, seditious, pro-war, and in violation of her gender role. The articles accuse her of fabricating her **voices** and interactions with **saints**, but Article 37 also accuses her of disobeying these same voices, which proves she went against direction from God. Joan methodically responded to each accusation, confirming or correcting her recorded statements, and in some instances refusing to say more.

Afterward, the assessors decided to generate a more concise list of articles with Joan's responses baked into them. According to Courcelles, this task was handled by **Nicolas Midi** who generated **twelve articles** (2–5 April) that were notarized on 12 April and distributed to the **University of Paris** for their review and opinion.

SEX WORKERS. *See* CAMP FOLLOWERS.

SEXUAL ASSAULT AND RAPE. For conflicting motives, some historians have conjectured that Joan was raped in her last days while others have argued aggressively that she was sexually assaulted, but not vaginally penetrated. The available evidence supports the latter, but it is not infallible.

Haimond de Macy, a knight and friend of **John of Luxembourg**, testified during the **nullification proceedings** (1450–1456) that he visited Joan while she was a captive of Luxembourg and tried to grab her breasts on several occasions (1430). Because of her forceful defense against him, he offered his testimony as evidence of her purity. One can imagine the terror of an eighteen-year-old prisoner of war being sexually assaulted. We are left to wonder how many times or how often Macy attempted this assault without success. Did she complain of her treatment? Did anyone offer to help her or keep Macy from her cell?

Once in English captivity, **Anne of Burgundy** had Joan examined to confirm her **virginity**. After which, she ordered that none of the guards were to touch Joan. Anne further tried to make female **clothes** for Joan. While a tailor was fitting Joan for a dress, he touched her breast causing her to slap him, according to **Jean Marcel**. Joan continued to wear male clothing as protection.

Guillaume Manchon also revealed at the nullification proceedings that while Joan was imprisoned in **Rouen**, she complained once or twice that one of the guards had tried to rape her. The guards were purportedly warned and replaced. Manchon also said that she refused to take off her male clothing for fear of the guards coming in her cell to assault her. **Martin Ladvenu** confirmed that he heard this directly from Joan as well.

After Joan's **abjuration** (24 May 1431), she wore women's clothing briefly before putting on male clothing again. Joan claimed that the English guards confiscated her female clothing, leaving only male clothing in her cell. When she needed to relieve herself, they refused to give her any other clothing. Finally, she put on the male attire, so that she could leave her cell and relieve herself.

Once Joan learned that she was to be put to death, **Jean Toutmouillé** claimed that Joan lamented that she was pure and unblemished, implying that she was still a virgin. He also shared how she reported that the guards violently assaulted her before leaving the male clothing in her cell. This is the point where some historians have conjectured that

Joan was possibly vaginally raped during the assaults. We are limited by the available testimony, but we also have to admit that those testifying sought to uphold Joan's purity.

Joan was certainly sexually assaulted to some degree on multiple occasions by Haimond de Macy, a tailor, and various guards during different phases of her captivity. It is possible she was vaginally raped, but we remain unsure. Those arguing for the plausibility of rape are often emphasizing the plight of Joan in these conditions. *See also* CAPTIVITY; CLOTHING.

SHREWSBURY, EARL OF. *See* TALBOT, JOHN.

SICILY, QUEEN OF. *See* YOLANDE OF ARAGON.

SIEGE. Although major battles such as Crécy (1346) and Agincourt (1415) have received the lion's share of attention in histories of the **Hundred Years War**, historians over the past thirty years have brought forth a renewed interest in sieges, and with good reason. The outcome of territorial possession was not decided by these battles, but by the control of fortified towns and cities. Thus, after the English victory of Agincourt, **Henry V** still had to invest heavily in sieges to conquer **Normandy** (1417–1419). The underlying effect of the Hundred Years War on French towns was to transform them into strong fortifications. This was accomplished through a combination of the king pushing towns to hire military experts to examine and help with fortifications, and empowering these towns to plan and tax for these projects. While a survey in 1335 revealed that most French towns had woefully inadequate defenses, by the mid-fifteenth century, most towns were well fortified.

The fortifications included a combination of walls made from brick and stone, as well as ditches and moats. Walls were expensive. **Paris** boasted the highest walls standing at twelve meters and **Orléans** had walls that reached eight meters, but most towns had walls around three meters. Moats and ditches expanded the defense through depth by pushing besiegers and their **artillery** further away from the walls. This distance affected both sides though. For example, at Paris, Joan of Arc and the besiegers stood outside its fortifications with few casualties until they began their assault. The walls included walkways for defenders to quickly move around on, as well as towers and positions for their own crossbowmen, archers, and gunners. Larger towns also featured bastilles made from brick and stone outside the walls to house artillery and protect gates and bridges, as found at Paris, Orléans, and **Compiègne**. The capture of a bastille did not necessarily lead to capturing the city, as the English captured the Tourelles early in the siege of **Orléans** (23/24 October 1428), but then lost it six months later (7 May 1429). The rise of gunpowder artillery brought evolutionary changes to these fortifications to house their own cannons, as well as continue to push attacks further away from the walls. In addition, walls began to wrap around earthen mounds built by the towns to better withstand bombardment from cannons.

Besiegers began investing heavily in gunpowder artillery, and surviving records of **Salisbury's 1428 expedition** reveal a massive artillery train. Still, while towns continued to resist, sieges became longer and more costly to supply the besiegers, who also had to worry about relieving armies that sought to lift the siege. Another concern came from besieged troops packing up against a gate and opening it for a retreat or attack, catching the besiegers unprepared. These threats gave rise to boulevards, which were makeshift camps fortified with earth mounds, wooden walls, and ditches. This was the tactic employed by the English during the siege of Orléans. Besiegers rarely let a town's citizens through their lines, tying their fate to that of the town. Boulevards introduced a new wrinkle to sieges where defenders and those relieving them were forced to make their own assaults on these makeshift fortifications. The defenders at Orléans made multiple attacks on English boulevards but were not successful until Joan of Arc arrived (29 April 1429).

Besiegers then had multiple options in capturing fortifications. If the defenders felt their situation untenable due to a lack of supplies, no hope for a relieving army, or starvation, they could negotiate a surrender as was done at **Beaugency**. The terms would vary, but often allowed the defenders to leave with their arms unmolested with the promise to avoid further fighting for a specified amount of time. If defenders did not agree with the terms, they could continue to resist, as was the case at Orléans and **Jargeau**.

Then there was treachery, which often took the form of convincing key figures within the fortification to help the besiegers gain access to the town. Due to the impenetrable nature of some of the strong fortifications, this was the only option, and this was how Paris was captured by the Burgundians in 1418 and then by **Charles VII**'s forces in 1436. Joan of Arc hoped to capture Paris in 1430 through similar means before the plot was discovered, and the conspirators were executed.

When besiegers lacked adequate artillery, time, or patience, an assault on the walls was necessary. This involved filling the ditches and moats with bundles of sticks or barrels of dirt, allowing the attackers to quickly make it to the walls. Then **ladders** would be used for scaling. During such an assault, defenders loosed arrows, fired guns, and hurled lime, chunks of wood, and rocks down at those on the ladders who had to make their climbs in full armor. Joan of Arc fell victim to a rock to the head that knocked her to the ground during the assault on Jargeau (*See* INJURIES). A besieged town was susceptible to a less defended portion of the wall, so walkways provided a means for defenders to quickly plug gaps. One tactic of besiegers was to attack multiple sides of a wall to overwhelm the defenders. Joan was successful in rallying assaults up walls at Jargeau and **Saint-Pierre-le-Moutier**, but she was unsuccessful at **La Charité**, after multiple assaults.

Although the battle of Castillon (1453) marks the traditional end of the Hundred Years War, the war was really won through a series of sieges and the capturing of fortified towns. Most of Joan of Arc's military engagements were sieges, meaning assaults on fortifications. Some historians quibble over the terms, and it is common to see a reference to Jargeau as a battle, not a siege, with the logic that it was short and ended with an assault on the town, but it was not won through artillery or starvation of the inhabitants.

In 1430, Charles VII made a renewed interest in fortifying towns and building a siege train capable of capturing towns with more costly gunpowder artillery that could only be maintained with royal funds.

SIGNS OF JOAN OF ARC. Joan of Arc claimed divine inspiration (*See* VOICES), and she adopted the title *la Pucelle*, causing doubters to naturally ask for proof or signs. These so-called signs appear often in histories of Joan, many of them evolving, and sometimes accepted at face value. For example, rumors circulated that Joan was able to convince **Robert de Baudricourt** to send her to meet with **Charles VII** after she told him of the defeat at the battle of the **Herrings** before news could have possibly reached **Vaucouleurs**, as recorded in the *Journal du siège d'Orléans* and the *Chronique de la Pucelle*.

When Joan of Arc was examined by theologians in **Poitiers** (March 1429), they asked her for a sign. Citing Isaiah 7:10–14 and Judges 6:36–40, they stated, "Thus God commanded Ahaz to ask for a sign, when God promised him victory . . . and the same with Gideon, who requested a sign" (Fraioli 2000, 206). However, Joan refused to conjure anything, only promising her sign would be the successful relief of the siege of **Orléans**. Since the theologians could not find any fault in her, they said that if she could fulfill her sign, then she was sent from God.

Yet the sign that has received the most attention is what she demonstrated to Charles VII to convince him of her **mission**, or at least to send her to **Poitiers** for further examination. The most common story is that Joan met with Charles in private and afterward, he was converted. As for what she may have said or shown to Charles, some have theorized that she referenced a prayer by the king that only he knew, concerning his legitimacy as heir. However, the question of Charles's legitimacy came from **Paris** in the 1420s as a means to discredit his mother, **Isabeau of Bavaria**, and was probably not given much credence. Historians have found no credible evidence to the rumor or that it was believed. Furthermore, the story of Joan dispelling Charles's concerns of his legitimacy originates from the sixteenth century.

During Joan's **condemnation trial** (1431), the assessors were relentless on the supposed sign she demonstrated to Charles. She initially refused to answer, claiming she was sworn to secrecy. However, in her prison cell, they pressed the issue and gained more details, which were fluid. Joan eventually described an angel walking through a door into the room and presenting a crown to Charles in front of witnesses. Joan offered to write to the witnesses for them to confirm that they saw the sign. During the questioning, Joan defiantly proclaimed, "The sign you need is that God will deliver me from your hands, and it is the most certain one he could send you" (Hobbins 2005, 89).

After the trial, testimony was recorded from some of the assessors who claimed that upon visiting Joan in her cell the morning of her **execution** (30 May 1431), she admitted the sign was made up. This testimony was appended to the trial **transcripts**, but not authenticated by the notaries (*See* ROLES) who refused to sign anything not part of the official trial. Some of those recorded in this post-trial testimony did not corroborate their own supposed words during the **nullification proceedings** (1450–1456). Thus, the proceedings disregard it, and modern historians often follow suit.

Since then, depictions of Joan of Arc in literature, art, and film have seized on this sign of an angel crowning Charles. However, some historians contend that Joan was possibly speaking metaphorically. Others believe she was confused by the continual questioning of the topic over the course of multiple days by different assessors. Concerning her claim that she would be delivered from the hands of the **inquisition** has been considered as a spiritual, not necessarily a physical, salvation. *See also* PROPHECIES; SEGUIN DE SEGUIN.

SQUIRE. The earliest surviving use of the title "squire" dates to the twelfth century, and by the time of Joan of Arc, it had evolved dramatically. Initially, the squire was a paid job, and they were employed by **knights** to provide an array of services such as preparing food, attending horses, and carrying a knight's arms and armor. By the thirteenth century, the noble class had absorbed the knightly class, and the more popular notion of squire became that of an apprenticeship for aspiring young nobles who had not yet reached twenty-one years of age. These noble squires focused mainly on carrying the knight's equipment while other servants handled the dirtier jobs like attending horses. As the pool of knights began to dwindle due to many nobles foregoing the cost and ceremony of knighthood altogether in the fourteenth century, the squire title slowly lost its lowly connotation entirely, and changed its meaning. Noblemen who served as cavalrymen, sporting some or all the latest arms and armor of knights, became simply known as squires, bearing the title possibly for life.

In narrative histories of Joan of Arc, the squire title appears often, and readers should not mistake it for some sort of attendant or servant. Thus, when **Jean de Metz** and **Bertrand de Poulengy** are described as squires at **Vaucouleurs**, they were not attendants or apprentices of **Robert de Baudricourt**; they were well-equipped cavalrymen. Similarly, **Jean d'Aulon** was a squire who fought alongside Joan throughout most of her campaigns and was captured alongside her at **Compiègne** (23 May 1430). Modern historians sometimes inaccurately describe Aulon as "Joan's squire." Instead, he was an equipped cavalryman from nobility who was in the thick of battle, with explicit instructions from **Charles VII** to protect her. It would be fair to describe him as a bodyguard, but not a page. Similarly, the **bastard of Wandomme**, the man who captured Joan and Aulon, was a man that some medieval histories identify as a squire, commanding nearly seventy troops.

William Glasdale was another famous squire, or esquire as they were called in England, who encountered Joan. English-speaking historians often refer to him as "Sir William Glasdale," but he was never knighted. Surviving muster roles explicitly list him as an "esquire."

This trend of erroneously knighting Glasdale dates back as far as Shakespeare, whose fictional portrayal of Sir William "Glansdale" in *Henry VI* was based on Glasdale. This may also be a case where the modern-day misinterpretation of the fifteenth-century squire as one who was subservient to a knight has unconsciously caused some people to believe that someone with so much martial and leadership experience as Glasdale could not possibly be a mere squire.

STAFFORD, HUMPHREY (1402–1460). More prominently known as the first duke of Buckingham (1444), Humphrey, earl of Stafford, was an English noble in the council of **Henry VI**. He arrived in France with the king in 1430 and was part of an English contingent that supported the Burgundian siege of **Compiègne** where Joan was captured (23 May). **Haimond de Macy** told a story during the **nullification proceedings** (1450–1456) where **John of Luxembourg** offered to ransom Joan to the French if she agreed to stop fighting. Joan was defiant, questioning Luxembourg's authority to release her. She further declared that the English would not conquer France with one hundred thousand more soldiers, referring to them as *goddams*. Macy tells us that Stafford was present for the exchange, drawing his sword to stab her, but the **earl of Warwick** stopped him. Some historians have theorized that Joan's use of "goddams" may have incensed him, but certainly the declaration as a whole was enough to fire up the noble.

Guillaume Manchon tells another story where someone—he could not recall who exactly—said something regarding Joan, and Stafford drew his sword, chasing the speaker into a sanctuary. If the would-be victim was an assessor at her **condemnation trial** (*See* ROLES), it was possibly someone defending Joan's innocence. If it was another soldier, it could have been someone who did not believe they could win until Joan was dead, a commonly recorded belief among English soldiers at the time.

Stafford would go on to serve in France in several roles including governor of **Paris** (1432–1434) and captain of Calais (1442). Stafford remained loyal to Henry VI, dying at the battle of Northampton while defending the king (1460).

STANDARD, PENNON, AND BANNER OF JOAN OF ARC. The earliest image of Joan of Arc depicts her in a dress, carrying a sword and a two-tailed flag with the initials JHS ("Jesus") on it (*See* FAUQUEMBERGE). The histories and legends of Joan are entwined with her standard, which found its way onto battlefields and processions, as recorded explicitly at **Orléans, Jargeau, Troyes, Reims, Paris,** and **Compiègne,** but it was most assuredly present at all her battles and sieges.

Although histories are not always precise in their usage, standards, pennons, and banners were three distinct types of flags carried on military campaigns in fifteenth-century France, and Joan had a version of each. The largest of the three was the *standard*, a long, tapering flag attached to a lance. Not every knight or commander carried one, and they were often reserved only for those in command of at least a dozen troops with few exceptions. A *pennon* was a smaller, triangular flag attached to a lance, typically depicting the coat of arms of the owner. These were much more common on the battlefield and records survive of the **dauphin** (*See* CHARLES VII) having 650 made in 1421. A *banner* was a square or rectangular flag attached to a lance, typically reserved for a **knight** or noble, including the king. Meant to rally the troops to their commander, standards were often carried by a bearer, but sometimes by the owner as well. Only the highest levels of nobility—**counts, dukes,** kings—carried both a pennon and banner into battle. Joan of Arc is the most prominent exception to these rules, as she had all three well before her **ennoblement**, which was far from anything resembling the ranking of even a count.

In April 1429, Joan requested a standard from the king, and he agreed to fund its creation. In Tours, Hauves Poulnoir painted the designs for her standard and pennon. It is unclear who was responsible for her banner. None of these flags have survived, and the descriptions of their designs vary between Joan and eyewitnesses, but her standard appears to have depicted God holding the world, flanked by two angels or **saints** who Joan later identified as **Catherine** and **Margaret**. On the flip side were the words "**Jesus Mary**" and possibly fleur-de-lis.

Joan's pennon depicted the Annunciation with Saint Gabriel presenting a lily to the Virgin Mary. In the *Journal du siège d'Orléans*, there was an incident where Joan's pennon caught fire among an excited crowd and she rushed to extinguish it. There is no further mention of the pennon after this incident.

Joan loved her standard, telling her assessors at her **condemnation trial** (1431) that "she was much fonder, indeed forty times fonder" of her standard than her **sword** (Hobbins 2005, 69). She explained that she carried her standard into battle to avoid killing anyone personally. However, her standard was often carried by others, very likely her pages (*See* LOUIS DE COUTES). Regardless, eyewitnesses described her holding her standard at Orléans, Jargeau, and during the **coronation of Charles VII**. There is no record of her standard becoming a trophy after her capture at Compiègne, and it is possible the bearer was able to escape capture.

Joan's assessors grilled her on her standard with questions implying she attached some magical power to it. Joan explained that its design came to her from her **voices**. When asked why she saw fit to hold it during Charles's coronation, she quipped that her standard "had been through perils; it made good sense that it should have the honor" (Hobbins 2005, 114). Articles 20 and 50 of the initial **seventy articles** of accusation brought against her claimed she attached magical power to the standard and that she wished to see it honored at the coronation, but these charges were not included in the **twelve articles**. A letter written on behalf of **Henry VI** after her **execution** highlighted her use of the standard, claiming she exuded "a very great insult, arrogance and presumption" (Taylor 2006, 225).

Sometimes medieval texts interchanged the use of standards and banners, and modern histories and translations often follow suit. Thus, a reference to Joan's banner is almost always referring to her standard.

STEWART, JOHN. *See* FRANCO-SCOTTISH ALLIANCE.

SUFFOLK, WILLIAM DE LA POLE, EARL OF (1396–1450). William de La Pole, the earl of Suffolk was an English commander at the siege of **Orléans** (1428–1429), later captured at **Jargeau** (1429).

The second son of Michael II de La Pole, earl of Suffolk, William was born in 1396. Little is known of his early life, but he joined **Henry V's** invasion of France in 1415 along with his father and older brother (*See* HUNDRED YEARS WAR). While on campaign, William's father died during the siege of Harfleur (September), and his brother died at Agincourt (25 October). Although also wounded at Agincourt, William survived to become the new earl of Suffolk.

Suffolk returned to France in August 1417 and continued to serve under Henry V and the **duke of Bedford**, gaining recognition, titles, lands, and responsibilities. His experiences included the siege of **Rouen** (1418–1419) and the battles of **Cravant** (1423) and **Verneuil** (1424). In 1419, he became admiral of **Normandy** and was captain of several towns. In 1421, he joined the Order of the Garter, the most exclusive order of knights in England. In 1424, he became admiral of France. He also became count of Dreux (c. 1425).

After the death of the **earl of Salisbury** (3 November 1428), Suffolk took over command of the siege of Orléans. The siege continued through 1429. By March, Joan of Arc was gaining support in her determination to lift the siege. She addressed Suffolk directly in her **letter to the English** (**22 March 1429**), threatening violence if he did not lift the siege and leave France. Joan first arrived at the city on 29 April with supplies and reinforcements. After several days of fighting and multiple setbacks, Suffolk abandoned the siege on 8 May.

His next step was to retreat to Jargeau, one of several strongholds captured during **Salisbury's 1428 expedition**. French forces arrived outside the town on 11 June, led by the **duke of Alençon** with Joan of Arc. After several attempts to negotiate dates and terms for leaving the city, the French attacked on 12

June, massacring many of the defenders. Suffolk surrendered along with one of his brothers while another brother died in the assault. According to the *Journal du siège d'Orléans*, he surrendered to Guillaume Regnault, an aggressive **squire**. Upon learning Regnault's status, Suffolk knighted him, not wanting to surrender to someone of lower stature. Suffolk went under the custody of the **bastard of Orléans** and then **Charles VII**, and he was not released until 1431, selling all his estates in France to pay the **ransom**.

Present for the coronation of **Henry VI** in **Paris** (16 December 1431), the earl of Suffolk eventually returned to England and pursued politics. He served as the master of the king's household from 1433 through 1447, a role that he used to enrich himself and his associates. He still remained involved in the war in France, diplomatically. He escorted the captive **duke of Orléans** to Calais in 1435 as a possible bargaining chip during the Congress of Arras (*See* ARRAS, TREATY OF). In 1444, he led negotiations for the Truce of Tours with France. In 1448, he was elevated to duke of Suffolk.

However, as Suffolk celebrated such successes, he also faced accusations of abusing his power. Rumors spread that Suffolk and his allies were making decisions on behalf of the king, and the titles and estates they continually gained supported this claim. Outrage and protest grew so much in Parliament that he was imprisoned on 28 January 1450. In February and March, he was charged with sixteen counts that included treason, corruption, and extortion. After answering the charges to a hostile Parliament, Suffolk believed his best option was to forego a trial and submit directly to the king. Henry absolved him of any treason, but for the other charges, he banished Suffolk for five years, beginning on 1 May. Until his sentence began, Suffolk was back at this estate; as news spread that he was "free," he caught wind of mobs seeking justice. Suffolk fled for the Low Countries on 30 April but was caught by privateers. On 2 May, they conducted a mock trial of the duke and beheaded him.

SUICIDE. *See* ESCAPE.

SUPER FACTO PUELLAE ET CREDULITATE SIBI PRAESTANDA (14 MAY 1429). Shortly after the lifting of the siege of **Orléans** (8 May 1429), **Jean Gerson** received word while in Lyons, and he responded with a short pamphlet in Latin on Joan of Arc (14 May). The earliest and most common title that appears on surviving manuscripts of the work is *Super facto puellae et credulitate sibi praestanda*, or "About the Feat of the Maid, and the Faith That Should Be Placed in Her" (Field 2012, 36). The work was composed quickly and in stages, as Gerson appended more thoughts over the following week, and the result was an aggressive support of Joan of Arc, her **mission** to restore the kingdom of France to **Charles VII**, and a defense of her male **clothing** and short **hair**.

Given Gerson's prominence as a scholar who had voiced strong opinions against divine **voices, visions, and revelations** of women such as Bridget of Sweden (1303–1373), the strong support of Joan was and is remarkable. In the pamphlet, he examines her life, those who followed her, and the results thus far, and Gerson concludes that she adhered to her voices without veering from their mandate. He compares Joan to Deborah from the Bible and Saint **Catherine**. Although he does not mention Orléans or **Poitiers** by name, he makes references to her victory and to theologians who had examined her thoroughly.

The work was quickly distributed, reaching Rome by June, and then Bruges and Venice by November. Upon reaching **Paris**, probably by the fall, an unknown canon lawyer appended a rebuttal against Gerson's work, arguing against Joan and her pro–**Charles VII** sentiments. When French poet Martin Le Franc wrote his *Champion des dames* (1440–1442), he referenced Gerson's work. The work also made it into **Jean Bréhal's** *Recollectio* that was compiled as part of the **nullification proceedings** (1450–1456).

Today, the work is more commonly known as *De mirabilia victoria* ("The wonderful victory"), as this was the title given to it in early printed editions of Gerson's works, and the title has stuck until the twenty-first century when Gerson scholars pushed to use the *Super facto puellae* title. In addition, there has been dispute over the centuries as to whether Gerson wrote this work, some theorizing it was by **Henry of Gorkum** or possibly forged. This confusion has been propagated by printed editions of Gerson's works from the sixteenth through eighteenth centuries questioning the authorship. However, by the mid-nineteenth century, historians were once again accepting it as an authentic Gerson work. This was challenged once again in 1957 by Dorothy Wayman, who questioned it based purely on style. From there, dozens of historians have accepted Wayman's critiques or simply referred to the author of the work as anonymous. However, Daniel Hobbins has demonstrated after examining seventeen extant manuscripts of the text that the work was indeed written by Gerson (Hobbins, "Jean Gerson's Authentic Tract on Joan of Arc," 2005).

SWORDS OF JOAN OF ARC. The earliest surviving depiction of Joan of Arc comes from **Clément de Fauquembergue** who had not seen Joan, but nonetheless depicted her holding a sword and a **standard** at the siege of **Orléans**. At her **condemnation trial** (1431), Joan claimed that she much preferred her standard over her sword. During the **nullification proceedings** (1450–1456), **Seguin de Seguin** claimed that Joan preferred to carry her standard instead of a sword, because she did not wish to kill anyone. Yet there is no question Joan owned and carried multiple swords throughout her military career. The number, timeline, and fate of each sword is convoluted, especially because of the imprecise testimony of Joan and other witnesses.

The first sword was a gift from **Robert de Baudricourt** when Joan left **Vaucouleurs** for **Chinon** (February 1429), as attested by **Bertrand de Poulengy** and **Catherine Le Royer** during the nullification proceedings. Joan tells us during her condemnation trial that she had no more use for it after she acquired her next, most-famous sword.

While Joan was at Tours or Chinon (she could not recall exactly where or when), she requested that a sword be retrieved from an altar at the church in Sainte-Catherine-de-Fierbois. The French minutes of the trial do not record her saying it was buried, but the Latin translation (*See* TRANSCRIPTS) provides this explicit detail, leading some historians to conclude that the assessors embellished. As to how she knew the sword was there, Joan claimed her **voices** told her, but historians often theorize it was possible she learned of its existence while in Sainte-Catherine-de-Fierbois on her way to Chinon. The discovery of the sword is also attested to in the *Journal du siège d'Orléans*. It describes **Charles VII** offering Joan a sword, which she declines and instead sends for the sword in Sainte-Catherine-de-Firebois, to the amazement of the king.

Regardless, the assessors pressed Joan on the sword on 27 February and 27 March 1431. She claimed that upon finding the sword, residents were able to rub the rust right off it. The sword bore five crosses, of which she did not know the significance. The citizens of Tours were impressed and made several scabbards for it, and she also had her own made. Joan's affection for the sword was clear, and she admitted it was because it came from a church of **Saint Catherine**, who was one of her voices. Joan carried the sword until she departed **Saint-Denis** after the defeat at **Paris** (8 September 1429). The assessors asked numerous questions about whether she blessed, prayed over, or placed the sword upon any altars, which she did not. Still, the assessors fixated on Joan's sword, evoking it in Articles 12, 19, 20, 33, and 63 of the initial **seventy articles** of accusation brought against her. They claimed she hid the sword herself to fake a divine revelation in knowing the sword's location. Against her own testimony, they also claimed she prayed over the sword. The surmised **twelve articles** evoked the sword in Articles 4 and 7, again emphasizing that Joan sought to claim divine revelation and predict the future.

The sword's fate is not entirely clear. The **duke of Alençon** said he saw Joan break it on the back of a sex worker she chased out of camp, although **Louis de Coutes** said she never struck these women (*See* CAMP FOLLOWERS). Still, the sword had a spiritual connotation, and **Jean Chartier** would later conclude that Joan drew her success from it. Sometime before the siege of Paris, Chartier believes she broke the sword, which is why she no longer experienced the same successes she had in her previous military campaigns. It was not until the seventeenth century that the romanticized story of the sword originally belonging to Charles Martel (c. 688–741) gained prominence, but Joan and her contemporaries never claimed this to be the case and modern historians typically dismiss it.

After Paris, Joan left behind a suit of armor and a third sword she won from the siege. Some historians have interpreted or mistranslated statements from Joan to mean that the armor and sword were worn by her, but this is not the case. This was a different sword than the ones mentioned previously. There is a record of the armor and sword still in the inventory of Saint-Denis in 1505. They were transferred to Paris in 1793 and then lost during the French Revolution.

Finally, there was a fourth sword that Joan said she won at the battle of **Lagny** (29 March 1430) and carried with her until her capture at **Compiègne** (23 May). She told her assessors that she won it from a Burgundian and that it was a good sword for striking, meaning not killing.

Descendants of Joan's family claimed to possess a sword of Joan's until at least 1793 as well, but it is unclear if this sword was any of the ones mentioned here.

Thus, we have testimonies and records of at least four swords that were given to or won by Joan, and she carried at least three of them. It is unclear if Joan always carried a sword, even if it remained sheathed, between Paris and Lagny, or if Joan simply relied on her standard. There were no shortage of swords in her campaigns, so it is entirely plausible she carried far more swords than those recorded.

Joan of Arc was in possession of other weapons. For example, the **duke of Alençon** testified to seeing Joan practice jousting and the authors of the **Laval letter** described her carrying a small ax. When Joan and **Charles d'Albret** reached out to nearby cities for supplies to aid them in the siege of **La Charité**, there is a record in the archives of Clermont that the town made a personal gift to Joan of a sword, two daggers, and an ax (*See* LETTER TO THE PEOPLE OF RIOM). What became of these gifts from Clermont are unknown. Of course, none of these other weapons received as much attention from Joan's contemporaries as her swords, which remains still the case today with modern historians.

T

TALBOT, JOHN (C. 1387–1453). John Talbot was an English commander captured at the battle of **Patay** (1429) who continued fighting against the French until his death at the battle of Castillon (1453).

As early as 1404, John Talbot was participating in military campaigns, beginning with the pacification of Wales (1404–1409) and then in Ireland (1414–1419). In May 1420, he arrived in France and was possibly present for the signing of the **Treaty of Troyes** that same month. He participated in the siege of Melun (July–November) and then returned to England with **Henry V** for the coronation of **Catherine of Valois**. In 1421, he became the baron of Talbot and returned to France to continue in Henry's campaigns (*See* HUNDRED YEARS WAR). Talbot was back in Ireland between 1424 and 1425 before returning to England. Also in 1424, he became a knight of the Garter, the most exclusive order in England. Talbot fought in local disputes over land and titles before being called back to France in 1427, where he led campaigns to recover and shore up English conquests. By 1428, he had held numerous positions in France including captain of Pont-del'Arche and Falaise, and governor of Anjou and Falaise.

Talbot joined **Salisbury's 1428 expedition**, but he was not present when Salisbury was killed in the early stages of the siege of **Orléans** (3 November). The **earl of Suffolk** took command of the siege, later bringing Talbot and **Thomas Scales** to join him in command. Joan of Arc addressed Talbot directly, along with Suffolk and Scales, in her **letter to the English** (22 March 1429), threatening violence if they did not lift the siege and leave France. After the relief of Orléans (8 May) and the capture of Suffolk at **Jargeau** (12 June), Talbot became the leader of the remaining English forces in the region, and he and **John Fastolf** argued over the next course of action. Fastolf pushed for a retreat to **Paris** while Talbot pushed for attacks against a victorious French army that continued to grow. After the French recaptured **Beaugency** (18 June), the last English-held stronghold on the Loire River, the point became moot, and Talbot agreed to take the remaining troops back to Paris. However, the French army, led by the **duke of Alençon** with Joan of Arc, was in pursuit. Talbot determined to set a trap for the French outside Patay, but the French arrived before he was ready, overwhelming the English and capturing Talbot and other prominent English leaders on 18 June. **Charles VII** mentioned Talbot by name in a letter he sent celebrating the success of Patay and the **Loire Campaign**.

Talbot remained in captivity until 1433, first under **Poton de Xaintrailles** before being sold to Charles VII in 1431. Negotiations ebbed and flowed for Talbot's **ransom**. However, with the capture of Xaintrailles in August 1431, negotiations focused on exchanging the two prisoners. Released in early 1433, Talbot was back on campaign in **Normandy**. In 1434, he was tasked with defending Paris, but by 1435 he had abandoned the city for refuge in **Rouen**. In 1436 he was appointed **marshal of France**, and in 1439 he became governor and lieutenant-general of France. In 1442, he achieved his highest rank of nobility, becoming the earl of Shrewsbury. With the death of Bedford in 1435, he was the highest-ranking English commander in France for the remainder of the war. Talbot continued his fight in France, bringing reinforcements in 1442, and winning enough victories to begin negotiations for a truce the next year that would become the Truce of Tours in 1444, set to last five years. After a brief stint in Ireland in 1446, he was back in France in 1448. In 1449, he encroached into **Brittany**, rekindling the war with Charles VII, which the king now waged aggressively. Talbot surrendered at Rouen in November 1449 but was released after the fall of Normandy in July 1450, exchanged for the town of Falaise. In 1452, Talbot sailed for Gascony to defend the last of the English-held territories in France. After some initial successes, he died charging cannons outside Castillon (17 July 1453), marking the traditional end of the Hundred Years War.

Talbot's fifty-year military career was dominated by his aggression and ruthlessness, traits that likely appealed to leaders such as Henry V and Bedford who gave him commands. Talbot was typically eager to attack, a trait he had in common with Joan of Arc. Throughout his life, he was captain of upwards of eighteen different towns. In addition to military experience, his library shows he was well read, as it contained several military treatises including works by **Christine de Pizan**. He has been celebrated and romanticized throughout history, including by Shakespeare. However, Talbot lost his arguably two most important battles—Patay and Castillon.

TALBOT, WILLIAM. See ROLES AND RESPONSIBILITIES.

THE TALE OF JOAN OF ARC (31 JULY 1429). At the height of Joan of Arc's success, between the **coronation of Charles VII** (17 July 1429) and her assault on **Paris** (8 September), **Christine de Pizan** wrote the lyrical poem *Ditié de Jehanne d'Arc* (*The Tale of Joan of Arc*). This was Pizan's last surviving work, and it is the earliest known literary work on Joan of Arc, written during Joan's lifetime. Compared to Pizan's lengthier histories and treatises, the poem is relatively short at sixty-one stanzas. Although there is no dedication, it directly addresses Charles, Joan, French troops, the English, and French allies of the English. Jubilant and patriotic in tone and rhetoric, the poem provides a cursory review of Joan's successes and is only explicit in **Orléans**, the coronation, and the impending attack on Paris, which Pizan was convinced would succeed. Her praise for Joan is overwhelming, comparing her to Biblical figures Moses, Joshua, Gideon, Esther, Judith, and Deborah, as well as Hector and Achilles from the *Iliad*. Although she never names any explicitly, Pizan ranks Joan above any ancient Roman. In Joan, Pizan found the leader to save and unite France that she had sought in nobles for decades, as well as the fulfillment of the famous prophecies (*See* PROPHECIES FORETELLING JOAN OF ARC).

Although the last stanza of the poem claims it was completed on 31 July 1429, some historians question this date. With the poem containing campaign details as recent as 29 July, it seems unlikely the news traveled so quickly to Pizan, well outside the French court by this time. Thus, later August or early September seems more appropriate for the completion of the poem.

Only two complete manuscripts survive, but the poem is well-known today because of its author and subject. However, this should not force us to draw conclusions on its popularity at the time, as historians believe this was a work meant to be read aloud at gatherings as opposed to transmitted through text. It is unknown if Joan was aware of its existence.

TAQUEL, NICOLAS (C. 1398/1400–1456?). Nicolas Taquel was a priest in **Rouen** brought into Joan of Arc's 1431 **condemnation trial** by **Jean Le Maistre** to serve as a third notary alongside **Guillaume Manchon** and **Guillaume Colles** (*See* ROLES). While he was part of the process of recording the trial starting on 14 March 1431, he later admitted that he did not personally record any of Joan's answers to questions and instead deferred to Manchon and Colles. Still, he recalled that some of the questions were too difficult for Joan to answer. She sometimes pushed the questions back on the assessors, to the approval of some of those present. Taquel recalled several key moments in the trial including Joan's **abjuration** (24 May) and her **execution** (30 May), which he said moved some of the crowd to tears. Unlike his fellow notaries, Taquel's testimony during the **nullification proceedings** (1450–1456) does not reveal any remorse toward Joan. He did, however, reveal that his payment received from **Jean d'Estivet** for his services was only half what he was originally promised. *See also* TRANSCRIPT.

TERMES, THIBAUT DE, D'ARMAGNAC (C. 1405–1457). A younger member of the Armagnac family, Thibaut de Termes was an experienced military commander who fought for **Charles VII** throughout the 1420s and alongside Joan of Arc in 1429. He was present at the beginning of the siege of **Orléans** (1428), and surviving records list payments to Termes as a captain, as well as to his men. He took part in the defeat at **Herrings** (12 February 1429), and he was present alongside the **bastard of Orléans** upon the arrival of Joan of Arc (29 April). Termes was then present throughout the relief of Orléans (4–8 May), the **Loire Campaign** (10–18 June), and the **march to Reims** (29 June–16 July). Termes became **bailiff** of Chartres in 1430, serving in the role until his death. After the fall of Joan of Arc, Termes continued to serve in battles for Charles including the final defeat of the English in 1453 (*See* HUNDRED YEARS WAR; TALBOT, JOHN).

Termes participated in the **nullification proceedings** (1450–1456) where he provided eyewitness accounts of Joan of Arc. He also corroborated the story that Joan encouraged **La Hire** and others to pursue the unprepared English at **Patay** (18 June 1429). He found Joan's actions and words to be brave and inspiring to the soldiers. He is also often quoted for describing Joan as simple in all matters except warfare, a common statement made by others (*See* CHARLES, SIMON; ORLÉANS, BASTARD OF). Termes also attributed Joan's success to divinity rather than human skill, as he watched her often confess, take communion, and hear Mass.

THEOLOGY. *See* EDUCATION.

THÉRAGE, GEOFFROY. *See* EXECUTION.

THÉROUANNE, BISHOP OF. *See* LUXEMBOURG, LOUIS OF.

THIBAULT, GOBERT (C. 1405–?). A royal **squire** of **Charles VII**, Gobert Thibault met Joan of Arc when she first arrived in **Chinon** (February 1429), and he accompanied her to **Poitiers** (March) where she was examined by theologians. In his 1456 testimony from the **nullification proceedings**, he provided some oft-quoted statements such as Joan claiming that she knew neither "A from B" when questioned at Poitiers (*See* LITERACY). He also tells us that when Joan dictated her **letter to the English (22 March 1429)**, **Jean Érault** transcribed it for her.

THIERRY, REGINALD. *See* SAINT-PIERRE-LE-MOUTIER, SIEGE OF.

THOMASSIN, MATHIEU (C. 1391–1463). Born in Lyons, Mathieu Thomassin studied civil law at the University of Orléans (*See* EDUCATION), and he went on to serve both **Charles VII** and his son, the **dauphin** (*See* LOUIS XI), predominantly in the Dauphiné region.

In 1456, during his service for Louis, the dauphin commissioned him to investigate the history of the dauphins and their rights. The result was the so-called *Registre delphinal*, a work that was never finished, nor officially presented to Louis, but survives today through late-fifteenth- and early-sixteenth-century compilations of Thomassin's other works. The *Registre* evokes a monarchist zeal for the king of France, and while determining that the dauphin holds the same rights as the king within Dauphiné, the king can revoke the region from the dauphin, as Charles VII did in 1456 and 1457.

With this perspective, Thomassin's interest in Joan of Arc is glowing, and within the *Registre* he evokes **prophecies** foretelling her arrival and quotes extensively from **Christine de Pizan**'s poem *The Tale of Joan of Arc*. The *Registre* also tells us that during the siege of **Orléans**, some of the king's men wanted to retreat south to Dauphiné before Joan lifted the siege, which he described as miraculous. Thomassin's most unique addition to the story of Joan is his treatment of her **letter to the English (22 March 1429)**, which he breaks down into four separate letters addressed to the king (*See* HENRY VI), the **duke of Bedford**, his captains, and their soldiers. Although some historians have explored the notion that Joan's letter was later compiled into a single work by chroniclers, the evidence is scant, and it is possible Thomassin was acting on his own initiative.

TIPHAINE, JEAN. *See* PHYSICIANS IN THE CONDEMNATION TRIAL.

TORTURE. In fifteenth-century France, torture could be used in all sorts of cases including criminal, civil, and ecclesiastical, often meant to extract a confession when the judges believed the accused was holding back the truth. **Gilles de Rais** avoided torture by confessing during his trial (1440), while the **duke of Alençon** escaped torture during his trial (1456–1458) because of his status. In 1431, there were limitations on what was permissible during an **inquisition** based on reforms from the early fourteenth century. First, the inquisitor had to partner with a local **bishop** during the entire process, the two men meant to keep each other in check. Second, the applied tortures had to be bloodless in nature. Thus, imprisonment or iron shackles were regularly used, as they were on Joan of Arc, even though the judges claimed it was so she would not try to **escape** again. In addition, the judges could employ starvation, rods, switches, and whips.

During Joan's 1431 **condemnation trial**, she was escorted to the tower of **Rouen** where she was shown torture devices (9 May). Present in the tower were **Pierre Cauchon**, soldiers, perhaps a dozen of her assessors, and **Maugier Leparmentier**, who was summoned to Rouen with the expressed purpose of torturing Joan.

In the tower, she was threatened with torture for not answering their questions truthfully, but Joan was defiant, telling them they could rip her limbs apart and tear out her soul, but she would not reveal anything else. She went further, claiming that any confession from her would be forced. The judges believed her and decided to deliberate on the topic further. Leparmentier later confirmed the events, that he was marveled by her wisdom, and he never laid a hand on her.

On 12 May, Pierre Cauchon and **Jean Le Maistre** met with thirteen of the assessors to debate the use of torture on Joan. The trial **transcript** records their responses in detail. Most believed it would be inexpedient, and **Raoul Roussel** went further to say that it would malign what he saw as a well-conducted trial thus far. **Guillaume Érard** believed they had enough evidence already. Only **Aubert Morel, Thomas de Courcelles**, and **Nicolas Loiseleur** were in favor of torture, but they were the clear minority. Cauchon's opinion was never recorded, but the majority ruled, and they determined torture of Joan was inexpedient and unnecessary.

TOURNAI. Tournai was a city loyal to the French crown throughout the **Hundred Years War**, even after the **Treaty of Troyes** (1420). Its location in Flanders left it in a tenuous position, like **Vaucouleurs**, surrounded by Burgundian territory. The duke of Burgundy (*See* PHILIP THE GOOD) was also the count of Flanders and supported Troyes. Tournai sent a delegation to the **coronation of Charles VII** seemingly without issue, which means that Burgundy was either not a threat any longer or did not maintain pressure on the city.

Although Joan of Arc never visited Tournai, she wrote four letters to the city, as recorded in its register. The register provided details such as the name of the courier, when he arrived, and how much he was paid for his services. Only one text, from her **letter to Tournai (25 June 1429)**, survives in its entirety, describing the victory at **Patay** and inviting the city to send a delegation to **Reims** for the coronation. The complete text of the three other letters were not recorded, but her final letter, sent sometime in August or September 1430, was written while she was in **captivity**. The register of the city indicated that she requested money for supplies, which the city provided.

The city's original register detailing the logistics around all four letters was lost when the Tournai Archives were destroyed in May 1940 from German bombing during World War II.

TOUTMOUILLÉ, JEAN. Jean Toutmouillé was a Dominican **friar** in **Rouen** during Joan of Arc's **condemnation trial** (1431). Although he did not attend any of the trial, he was present alongside **Martin Ladvenu** and **Pierre Maurice** in Joan's cell the morning of 30 May 1431. Toutmouillé provided two very different versions of the events, one recorded in the post-trial testimony on 7 June and appended to the **transcripts** of the trial, and the other in 1450 during the **nullification proceedings**. His age is wildly different between the two testimonies, as he is said to be about thirty-four years old in 1431, but then only forty-two years old in 1450.

In 1431, Toutmouillé tells us that upon visiting Joan's cell the morning of her **execution** (30 May), she confessed that her visions were fictitious and that although she heard **voices**, they deceived her. As to whether the voices were good or evil, she would leave that to them to decide. In 1450, Toutmouillé portrayed a defiant Joan. He tells us that in her cell that morning, they told her that she was going to be executed. She lamented her death while still being a **virgin**. She argued that she would not have resumed wearing men's **clothing** if she had only been kept in a Church prison. Instead, her enemies had been allowed to attack her (*See* SEXUAL ASSAULT AND RAPE). When **Pierre Cauchon** arrived, she claimed her death was his doing, but Cauchon blamed her for not keeping her promise. She again complained about not being kept in a Church prison. Toutmouillé then said Joan appealed directly to God against Cauchon. He also editorialized that the English sought vengeance against Joan, who believed that even while in captivity she held power, and therefore they refused to besiege Louviers until she was dead.

Toutmouillé is recorded as preaching in Rouen in 1458, but he did not provide further testimony during the nullification proceedings in 1452 or 1456.

TRANSCRIPTS OF JOAN OF ARC'S CONDEMNATION TRIAL. Ironically, one of the reasons Joan of Arc's story is so accessible to us today is because of the diligence of the men who toiled so hard to condemn her. During her **condemnation trial** (1431), an official register of events was maintained like any other **inquisition** at the time. Sessions typically occurred in the mornings, and after lunch, the three assigned notaries—**Guillaume Colles, Guillaume Manchon**, and **Nicolas Taquel**—compared notes and recorded attendees, questions, answers, and statements made by the judges, assessors, and Joan. All three men testified during the **nullification proceedings** (1450–1456), where they revealed that outsiders pressured them to change the meaning of her responses or exclude aspects that helped Joan's case. However, these men were emphatic that they did not succumb to such pressure. Manchon went so far as to claim that after reading back what he had recorded to Joan at one point, she corrected him. From there, he promised to be more careful in recording her words. Such attention in inquisitions was rare, but not unprecedented. Today, the original register is lost, which is not uncommon for documents of this era. However, the effort after the trial to create five Latin translations with supporting documentation was extraordinary.

After the trial, Guillaume Manchon and **Thomas de Courcelles** toiled to generate these five Latin translations using the now-lost register produced by the notaries along with Manchon's own notes known today as the "French Minutes." Historians have debated when these two men worked on this translation, and testimonies from the nullification proceedings do not clear up the dates. In earlier scholarship, historians argued for 1435, well after Joan's **execution** (30 May 1431). More recent scholarship argues for a date no later than 8 August 1432, because **Pierre Cauchon**'s seal on the Latin translations still listed him as bishop of

Beauvais, before he officially took over as bishop of Lisieux. Modern historians believe the Latin translations were produced between 1 July and 30 November 1431, because there are records for Pierre Cauchon receiving payments for producing the trial records on those dates. This also fits with the schedule of Courcelles, who left for Rome in mid-October 1431 and did not return until 1435. The date is important, because working on such a record immediately after the trial kept the events fresh in the minds of Manchon and Courelles. In addition, by 1435, Courelles had joined the camp of **Charles VII**.

At the nullification proceedings, four of the original five Latin translations had survived and were confirmed to be authentic by the notaries. At the conclusion of the proceedings, one of the Latin translations was ceremonially burned, and today, three survive in Parisian archives, referenced by historians as manuscripts A, B, and C.

Also, at the nullification proceedings, Guillaume Manchon provided his original notes or "French Minutes." A partial copy of his minutes survives today in a Parisian archive, known as manuscript U. Another copy of the minutes survives in an Orleanian archive known as manuscript O, but historians believe this is a later copy of manuscript U. What remains, then, are three Latin translations of the trial and two copies of the minutes from one of the notaries.

The Latin translations themselves include a slew of supporting documentation including letters from the **University of Paris**, **Henry VI**, and others regarding the establishment of the inquisition, securing Joan as a prisoner, and the validity of the trial and verdict. All of this had the intention of emphasizing that the trial was legitimate and to remove any doubt from would-be detractors. Although diligence was taken to record participants and their credentials, these are not always consistent or complete. Historians have reviewed the differences between the Latin translations and the French Minutes to determine what, if anything, was changed. The biggest differences are absent

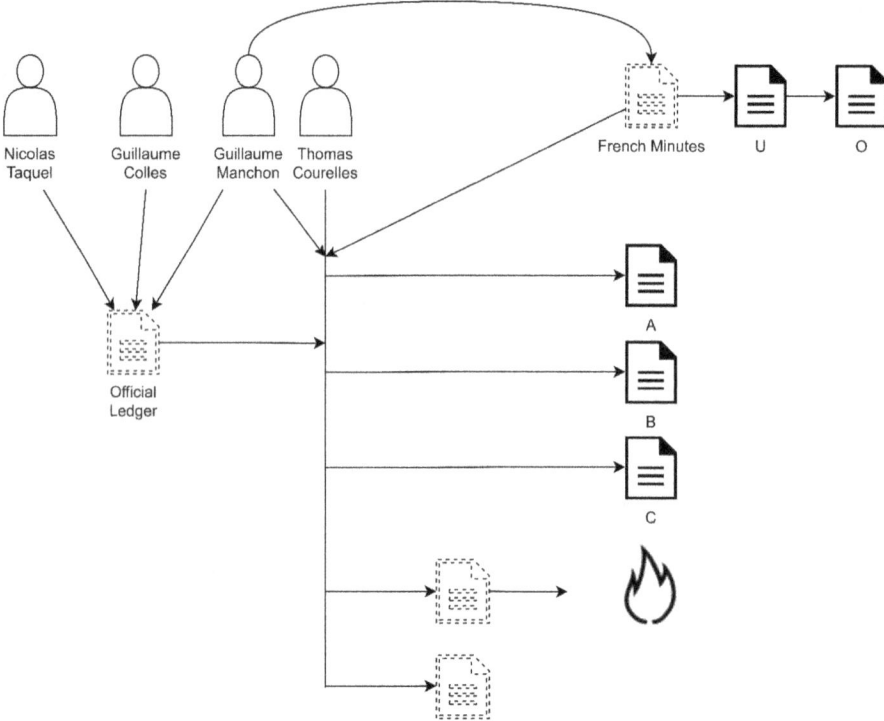

Sources and fate of the transcripts and minutes from Joan of Arc's condemnation trial.

supporting documents, such as letters, the initial **seventy articles** of accusation brought against Joan, as well as many of the recorded opinions from assessors and the University of Paris during the trial.

Although some historians have sought to establish a conspiracy, particularly by Thomas de Courelles, to whitewash his own implications in the trial, evidence is flimsy at best. For example, the French Minutes list opinions from individuals on whether to torture Joan, which included Courelles being one of the few men who were for it. However, the Latin translation does not name names. The exclusion of individual names appears to be more of an editorial choice consistent throughout the Latin translations.

One blatant addition to the Latin translation is the 7 June 1431 record of the events of 30 May, which detail Joan's supposed **relapse** and her purported confession that she was deceived by her **voices**. While Manchon agreed to add these details as instructed, he refused to sign them or add his seal, as they were not part of the original inquisition nor was he present for the events.

Historians have provided modern French and English translations of the Latin documents and French Minutes, analyzing the differences, and arguing for which document is more authentic to the events. What becomes apparent is that the records are solid and lack any grand conspiracy to change Joan's original words or cover up implication by the assessors and judges. The latter believed firmly in their work on the inquisition, and they kept thorough documentation with the intent that it should be shared with everyone far and wide.

TREBUCHET. See ARTILLERY.

TREE OF FAIRIES / LADIES. See FAIRY TREE.

TROYES. Troyes sits on a loop of the Seine River, roughly 150 kilometers southeast of **Paris**, a site that had been inhabited since before the Roman Era. By the fifteenth century, Troyes benefited from an intersection of roads that led to Flanders in the north and Italy to the south. During the **French Civil War**, it had been under Burgundian control since 1417. In 1420, it was the site of negotiations between diplomats of **Henry V**, **Charles VI**, and **Philip the Good**, leading to the **Treaty of Troyes** that resulted in the disinheriting of the **dauphin** (See CHARLES VII) as heir to the French throne. Afterward, the town benefited economically from the **Anglo-Burgundian Alliance**.

In July 1429, Troyes was in the path of Joan of Arc, Charles VII, and the royal army on their **march to Reims**. After a skirmish on 5 July followed by three days of unsuccessful negotiations, the city finally capitulated the morning of 9 July at the beginning of an assault by the royal army. Upon entering Troyes, Charles forgave the city's transgressions and in a widely distributed letter, asked other towns such as **Reims** to follow suit and receive the same clemency. The capture symbolically attacked the Treaty of Troyes in a town where many people had taken loyalty oaths to the treaty's terms. The royal army remained in Troyes until 12 July, when they left for Reims.

Joan wrote at least three letters to Troyes. The contents for her **letter to the people of Troyes (4 July 1429)** survive in a register in Reims. The same register also reveals that Joan wrote another letter from Gien on 22 September 1429. It was read on 2 October, giving details of the siege of **Paris** (8 September) and Joan's wounding there (See INJURIES).

TROYES, SIEGE OF (5–9 JULY 1429). Troyes was in the path of the royal army during the **march to Reims**. The town had ditches and high walls (See SIEGE), and Burgundian troops had occupied the city since 1417. When Joan of Arc arrived outside the city on 5 July, the *Chronique de La Pucelle* tells us there were five hundred to six hundred troops inside. Modern estimates for the royal army are as high as twelve thousand. After an initial skirmish in which the Anglo-Burgundian troops rushed to meet the approaching army, they were overwhelmed by the much larger approaching force and retreated into the city, closing its gates.

Joan presented a **letter to the people of Troyes (4 July 1429)**, requesting them to surrender to **Charles VII**. The letter was possibly delivered by **Friar Richard**, a then-respected spiritual leader in the city who also voiced his support of Joan to the town. Negotiations continued fruitlessly, even as Charles offered mercy. Joan's letter explicitly said the lives and property of the people would be safe if they surrendered. Troyes held out for reinforcements, which never came.

On the night of 8 July, Charles and his commanders debated whether to assault the town or march around it, as they were exhausting their supplies. **Robert le Maçon**, adviser to the king, suggested they consult Joan before making a decision. Joan entered the discussion, determined to attack, and took command of the preparations. After deploying the army throughout the night, Joan began the assault the morning of 9 July and the town immediately capitulated, as attested to by several chronicles and eyewitnesses including **Simon Charles**. The **bastard of Orléans** explicitly praised Joan's preparations for the assault.

Upon entering Troyes, Charles VII forgave the city's transgressions, and in a widely distributed letter, he called on other towns such as **Reims** to follow suit and receive the same clemency. The capture symbolically attacked the Treaty of Troyes in a town where many people had taken loyalty oaths to the treaty's terms. The royal army remained in Troyes until 12 July when they left for Reims.

TROYES, TREATY OF (1420). The Treaty of Troyes was the single most important document in France during the time of Joan of Arc, and understanding its origins, contents, and reception sets the stage for the political world in which she entered.

The treaty was the culmination of the **French Civil War** (1407–1435) and English claims to the French throne. Although the **Armagnac** and **Burgundian** parties had been in relatively open conflict since 1407, the success of **Henry V**'s conquest of **Normandy** in 1417 to 1419, and his imposing conditions for peace, had seemingly opened the door for reconciliation against a common enemy. However, the assassination of Duke John the Fearless of Burgundy on 10 September 1419 ended any chance for reconciliation. The blame for the assassination fell on the **dauphin** (*See* CHARLES VII), who was the last living son of French King **Charles VI**.

By 2 December, the new duke of Burgundy (*See* PHILIP THE GOOD) was openly willing to recognize Henry V as the heir of Charles VI. Negotiations between diplomats of Philip, Henry, and Charles ran from January to May 1420 in Troyes. On 20 May, the three met to officially seal the treaty.

Troyes established the so-called dual monarchy with four major acts. First, Charles VI would remain king of France until his death, but Henry would act as **regent**. In this new role, Henry would manage the government of France and continue to subdue those loyal to the dauphin. Second, Henry would marry the daughter of Charles, **Catherine of Valois**. Third, Charles would adopt Henry as his son. And lastly, the new heir to the French throne would be Henry and his heirs. Although the treaty did not state it explicitly, Charles VI later disinherited his son, the dauphin, on 3 January 1431.

The text of Troyes claimed its goal was to bring peace in the region by ending the civil war in France and the war with England, but the events over the next few years made it nearly impossible for that to be a reality. Henry and Catherine wed on 2 June 1420, and Catherine gave birth to a son on 6 December 1421 (*See* HENRY VI). Henry V died on 31 August 1422, after which the **duke of Bedford**, Henry's brother, took over as regent of France. Charles VI died on 21 October, leaving the infant son of Henry V as the future king of France. Bedford continued to act as regent.

The reception of the treaty was far from universal. While Burgundian cities accepted it in the north, the disinherited dauphin refused to recognize the treaty, and his territory south of the **Loire River** remained loyal to him and proclaimed him King Charles VII on 30 October 1422. Opinions throughout the rest of France remained mixed, some seeing the treaty as providential, while others saw its adherents as traitors. **Jean Juvénal des Ursins** described the treaty as shameful.

There was a massive effort to shore up support for the treaty. On 21 May 1420, the day after the treaty was sealed, Charles VI sent letters to multiple cities in support of the treaty, asking them to be posted widely. At Troyes, some fifteen hundred people swore loyalty to the treaty. That summer, leaders of the **University of Paris** made similar oaths. Some oaths were forced, as they were in January and February 1423 in Paris where numerous townsfolk were rounded up for ceremonies. These loyalty oaths varied over time, targeting Henry V, the duke of Bedford, or Henry VI. Even by June 1429, there were large ceremonies of the people of Paris and its university.

It is a fair assessment that during Joan of Arc's **condemnation trial** (1431), all of those with official roles, and most of the assessors, had taken some sort of oath regarding the terms of the Treaty of Troyes. Joan's continually stated **mission** of expelling the English from France and ensuring that Charles VII was the king of all of France directly challenged the terms of Troyes.

The Treaty of Troyes was officially replaced by the **Treaty of Arras** (1435), where Philip the Good recognized Charles VII as the king of France. The kings of England, and later Great Britain, continued to claim the throne until 1800 when King George III dropped France from his title.

TWELVE ARTICLES OF ACCUSATION. After reading the initial **seventy articles** presented against Joan of Arc during her **condemnation trial** and recording her responses (27–28 March 1431), the assessors decided to condense the articles. According to **Thomas de Courcelles**, **Nicolas Midi** handled this task (2–5 April). The result was the twelve articles, which were then read and commentated on by the judges and a small group of assessors (*See* ROLES) before being notarized and sent to the **University of Paris** for review on 12 April. The opinion of the university was received by the assessors on 19 May. They were read to Joan for the first time on 23 May. Unlike the seventy articles, Joan was never given the opportunity to respond to the twelve articles.

The theme of the twelve articles was more focused than the seventy articles. Joan is still accused of **blasphemy**, lying, erring in the faith, rashness, superstition, and being an **idolator**, **schismatic**, and **apostate**, but gone are the explicit accusations of being a **heretic**, or at least suspicion of heresy.

The first four articles focus on Joan's claims of interacting with **saints** since the age of thirteen, which the university determined were superstitious lies that Joan was rash to believe in.

The next three articles focus on Joan's interactions outside of saints. The fifth article attacks Joan for wearing men's **clothing**, accusing her of blasphemy, erring in the faith, prone to idolatry, worshipping herself, and transgressing divine law, Scripture, and **canon law**. The sixth article focuses on Joan's **letters**, such as her **letter to the English (22 March 1429)** in which she made violent threats while prefacing them with "**Jesus Mary**." The university believed such evocation was blasphemous while displaying eagerness for bloodshed and encouraging tyranny. The seventh article focuses on the early stage of Joan's story, lambasting her for leaving her parents against their will, convincing **Robert de Baudricourt** to send her to see the king (*See* CHARLES VII), and deciding to wear men's clothing.

The next four articles return to Joan's interactions with **saints**. The eighth article focuses on **Catherine** and **Margaret**, and Joan's claim that they warned her not to **escape** her captivity, leading to a severe **injury**. The university called her a coward, believing it was a suicide attempt. They further criticized her for disobeying the saints, and then claimed she was rash for believing that the saints forgave her. The ninth article saw Joan as rash for claiming she committed her **virginity** to the saints as well as for claiming she committed no mortal sin. The tenth article focuses on Joan's claims that the saints spoke French to her, which they saw as an indication that the saints had picked sides against the English. The eleventh article listed the sorts of interactions Joan had with the saints including touching, kissing their feet, and talking to them. Their concern here was Joan's claim that she knew they were real and good without consulting clergy, which they believed was, again, rash (*See* VOICES).

The final article focused on the **inquisition**, and Joan's refusal to submit to the **Church Militant**. This received the harshest condemnation from the university, labeling Joan a schismatic and an apostate. With the reading of the articles and the university's opinion on each point, Joan was warned to submit or face destruction of her soul and body. Joan simply said she stood by her previous statements. With that, the judges concluded the trial and said they would render their final verdict the following day on 24 May (*See* ABJURATION).

UNIVERSITY OF PARIS. During the time of Joan of Arc, the University of Paris was the most important educational institution in France. Founded in the twelfth century, it focused on **theology** and **canon law**, whereas the University of Orléans focused on **civil law**. The university men—students and professors—saw themselves as the intellectual center of Christianity. While a traditional view held that the university had a lineage dating as far back as the ancient Egyptians with autonomy granted by the pope, most university men understood that dukes and kings held the real power in France. Similarly, kings, dukes, and politicians were content to use the perceived prestige associated with the university to push their agendas.

Regardless of who was in power, university men had several motivations that influenced their actions and stated opinions on politics. First, there was a strong desire to protect and extend the privilege of the university, which usually meant appealing to the current political powers. Second, there was a desire to maintain and extend **benefices** bestowed to students and teachers from the political powers in the form of parishes and canons. Finally, during Joan of Arc's lifetime, there was a strong desire for peace, especially between Christians in what they viewed as an unjust war, but also to end the disruption that war brought to enrollment and the curriculum.

Understanding these motivations sheds light on the seemingly naïve and ever-changing political positions of the university between 1418 and 1446, a period that saw extreme power shifts in the region. Thus, when Duke John the Fearless of Burgundy captured **Paris** in 1418, the university issued a proclamation decrying the opposing **Orléanists** for propagating the war for power (*See* FRENCH CIVIL WAR). In 1420, the university participated in the **Treaty of Troyes** and issued several loyalty oaths to future king **Henry VI**, often with a grand show. In 1430 and 1431, their focus on Joan of Arc was not just for her perceived heretical acts, but for bringing the war to their doorstep outside Paris where the surrounding region had experienced relative stability for a decade. Then in 1432, they were incensed when the **duke of Bedford** established the University of Caen in **Normandy**, a move that was sure to affect enrollments in Paris. Later that year, they recommended that **Charles VII** be allowed to keep his territorial possessions south of the Loire River in hopes of ending hostilities, and they acted as ambassadors between Charles and Duke **Philip the Good** of Burgundy. In 1435, the university men enthusiastically participated in forming the **Treaty of Arras**, even when the English pulled out of the negotiations. The next year, most university men stayed in Paris and shifted their loyalties to Charles after the city returned to his domain. In 1439, they pressured Charles to end the war, arguing that recapturing the English-controlled territory was not worth the cost. From 1441 to 1446, the university men went on strike five times, bringing the university to a standstill roughly one-third of the time, culminating in retribution from Charles.

The University of Paris was actively against Joan of Arc from the beginning. In 1429, they sent a delegation to Rome to speak with the **pope** and accused Joan and her followers of heresy. When Joan was finally captured at **Compiègne** (23 May 1430), the university sent multiple letters to Philip the Good, **John of Luxembourg**, and Henry VI, demanding that she be tried in **Rouen** or in Paris by an **inquisition**. When their requests were unheeded, they sent more letters, claiming that Joan's allies were attempting to rescue her. When Henry agreed to hand Joan over (3 January 1431), most of the assessors came directly from or were at least educated by the university, including **Pierre Cauchon**, the **bishop** who had jurisdiction in the region where Joan was captured.

Throughout the process, the university chastised Cauchon, first for his inability to acquire the prisoner from secular authorities and then for the length of the trial. Finally, the university gave its opinion on the **twelve articles** formally brought against Joan and determined that if she did not abjure, then she should be handed over to secular authorities.

While historians have questioned how much political power the University of Paris wielded throughout 1418 to 1446 in general, they had clear influence over the **condemnation trial** and **execution** of Joan of Arc.

USHER. *See* ROLES AND RESPONSIBILITIES.

V

VALOIS, HOUSE OF. The House of Valois or the Valois Dynasty refers to the line of kings and their families who ruled France from 1328 to 1589. The name comes from King Philip VI, the first in the line, who was the son of the late Charles, count of Valois.

Ruling France throughout the **Hundred Years War**, the Valois kings faced many crises with varying degrees of success. Charles V, ruling 1364 to 1380, was successful at revitalizing the crown and undoing some of the setbacks that resulted from the war with England. His son Charles VI ruled until 1422, but his recurring bouts with mental illness paved the way for disputes between his brothers and cousins that led to the **French Civil War** (1407–1435).

Worse, during the reign of Charles VI, **Henry V** conducted his conquest of **Normandy**, and both Charles and Henry signed the **Treaty of Troyes** (1420), which disinherited the **dauphin** (See CHARLES VII). Charles VI continued to rule with Henry V acting as **regent** of France. Henry married Charles's daughter, **Catherine of Valois**, and according to the Treaty of Troyes their firstborn son was to be the next king of France. Meanwhile, the dauphin continued his claim to the French throne, diplomatically and militarily. Upon the deaths of Henry V and Charles VI in 1422, the infant **Henry VI** was too young to rule officially, so the **duke of Bedford** became the acting regent of France.

This was the state of the House of Valois when Joan of Arc came to prominence in 1429. Although Charles VII was calling himself king, she continued to refer to him as the dauphin until he was officially crowned in Reims, the traditional site for the ceremony (See CORONATION OF CHARLES VII). Joan was a staunch monarchist and challenged any progressive notions that the time of kings was fading. To her, Charles VII was the king of France by divine birthright and all parts of France, including independent **Brittany** and **Burgundy**, and Lancastrian Normandy should be his subjects. She expressed these thoughts often according to eyewitness statements, her testimony during her **condemnation trial** (1431), and through her own letters (See LETTER TO PHILIP THE GOOD).

Charles VII would continue to rule until his death in 1461. During his reign, he ended the French Civil War with Burgundy through the **Treaty of Arras** (1435), and he successfully undid most of the English territorial gains in France. After his death, his son, **Louis XI**, ruled until 1483, followed by his grandson, Charles VIII. With no surviving sons to inherit the throne upon the death of Charles VIII in 1498, the next king was Louis XII, son of the late **duke of Orléans**, a man whom Joan hoped to see released from English captivity during her lifetime. As the great-grandson of Charles V, Louis XII continued the Valois line.

VALPERGUE, THÉODORE DE (?–1461). Théodore de Valpergue was a Milanese noble that served **Charles VII** through nearly all his reign. In 1423, he arrived with some sixteen hundred troops in service to the cause of Charles. The next year, he was part of the disastrous defeat at **Verneuil**. Charles still valued Valpergue, dubbing him the king's chamberlain. He arrived at the siege of **Orléans** on 24 October 1428, and there is a record of his participation in the victory at **Patay** (18 June 1429). Valpergue was then in the company of **Poton de Xaintrailles** at **Compiègne** during the capture of Joan of Arc (23 May 1430), and he later took part in the relief of the city (25 October).

Valpergue continued to serve Charles both militarily and diplomatically. Military service included participation in the reconquest of **Normandy** (1449–1450) and Aquitaine (1451–1452). Diplomatic service included negotiating the **Treaty of Arras** (1435) and truces in Aquitaine, Burgundy, and Italy. Valpergue held numerous roles and titles, including **seneschal** of Lyon (1435–1458), count of Valperga (1436), and captain of Bayonne (1459). During his military actions, Valpergue was often in the company of Xaintrailles. He died shortly after the king on 7 October 1461.

VANDONNE, BASTARD OF. *See* WANDOMME, GUILLAUME.

VAUCOULEURS. Vaucouleurs was a fortified town in **Lorraine**, which Joan of Arc visited on three separate occasions at the beginning of her military **mission**.

Vaucouleurs sits on the bank of the Meuse River, which roughly marked the western-most border of the Holy Roman Empire. Vaucouleurs featured heavily fortified walls with twenty-two towers and the presence of Captain **Robert de Baudricourt**, who had been in the role at least since 1419. Throughout the 1420s, Lorraine was surrounded by Burgundian territory, but the **duke of Lorraine** remained loyal to **Charles VII**, as did Baudricourt who conducted raids, battles, and **ransom** negotiations through the decade. His hawkishness seems to have simmered by the summer of 1428 when the **duke of Bedford** ordered a siege of the town (22 June), but after a conditional surrender, Bedford ordered his troops to leave without disturbing the region in late July.

It was this same year that Joan arrived to meet with Baudricourt, asking him to send her to meet with Charles VII. The question inevitably arises as to why Joan selected Vaucouleurs to begin her mission. It is at least nineteen kilometers away from **Domremy** or twenty-five kilometers if walking along the Meuse River, which is much further than **Neufchâteau** (ten kilometers). Historians tend to settle on two answers. First, Baudricourt was the only captain of a royal city in Lorraine, a military rank as opposed to a noble title such as **baron, count,** or **duke**. Given the military nature of Joan's mission, she sought a military leader. Second, Joan's father (*See* ARC, JACQUES D') met with Baudricourt in 1423 when the captain helped negotiate the ransom of some prisoners. Jacques certainly shared his impressions of the captain with his family.

Joan arrived under the escort of her cousin, **Durand Laxart**. The timeline of Joan's visits to Vaucouleurs is still disputed. **Bertrand de Poulengy** placed her there on 13 May 1428, but since Joan arrived claiming she was supposed to help relieve the siege of **Orléans**, which did not start until October, it is quite possible he misremembered the date during his 1456 testimony at the **nullification proceedings**, twenty-eight years after the encounter. Joan's second visit came in December 1428 or January 1429 when the duke of Lorraine requested to meet with her, and Joan passed through Vaucouleurs on the way to meet him. Upon her return in February, Baudricourt was finally convinced to send her to meet with Charles VII. The city equipped her with a **sword**, a **horse**, and male **clothing**. Baudricourt sent Joan with an entourage that included Poulengy and **Jean de Metz**. During Joan's time in Vaucouleurs, she stayed with Henri and **Catherine Le Royer**, possible relatives of Thevenin Le Royer, one of her godfathers.

Vaucouleurs had four gates, and the porte de France, which points toward the Kingdom of France and through which Joan and her companions passed on their way out, still stands in the city. Although the porte de Neuville, through which Joan would have entered the city, no longer stands, a local museum has preserved a plaque of the Virgin Mary and child that was hanging on this gate before its demise.

VEGETIUS. Publius Flavius Vegetius Renatus, more commonly known simply as Vegetius, was the Roman author of *Epitoma rei militaris* (*Epitomes of military matters*), often shortened to *De re militari*. Written in the third or fourth century AD, the work was copied, translated, rewritten, updated, and adapted throughout medieval Europe and was immensely popular during Joan of Arc's time among her fellow combatants, allies, and enemies. Today, there are hundreds of surviving manuscripts in French and Latin. With approximately 150 of these manuscripts originating from the fifteenth century alone, it was the most prevalent secular book of medieval Europe.

There is evidence that versions of Vegetius were in the libraries of military commanders, politicians, and theorists, including **Charles VII**, **John Fastolf**, and the **earl of Warwick**. Focused on the military matters of Romans, the work spoke authoritatively on training, logistics, weapons, equipment, battles, and sieges, including defense and assault. Surviving manuscripts were often updated with commentary or modernized with technology and tactics from the period. For example, **Christine de Pizan** relied heavily on Vegetius when discussing sieges, but updated the logistics with necessary supplies and manpower for gunpowder weaponry (*See* ARTILLERY). **Jean Juvénal des Ursins** borrowed heavily from Vegetius in his military treatise *Verba mea* (1452), a work that focused on incorporating discipline, training, and leadership in the armies of Charles VII. In addition, notes on surviving manuscripts indicate a strongly engaged readership. Although Joan of Arc was supposedly illiterate (*See* LITERACY) and there is no direct connection between her and Vegetius, the work helps inform modern-day interpretations of the strategy and tactics of Joan's companions in arms and her enemies.

VENDÔME, GUILLAUME, BASTARD OF. *See* WANDOMME, GUILLAUME.

VENDÔME, LOUIS DE BOURBON, COUNT OF (1376–1446). Member of the court of **Charles VII**, Louis de Bourbon, the count of Vendôme, was identified by **Jean Pasquerel** as the one who escorted Joan of Arc to the room in **Chinon** where she first met the king.

Up until then, Vendôme participated in both sides of the **French Civil War** before being captured at Agincourt in 1415 (*See* HUNDRED YEARS WAR). Released in 1424, he immediately sided with Charles. In 1429, he participated in **Patay** (18 June), the **march to Reims** (29 June–16 July), the **coronation of Charles VII** (17 July), and **Montépilloy** (15 August). Although he supported the **Franco-Burgundian Truce**, he was also in favor of continuing the **siege of Paris** after its failed assault (8 September). In 1430, he was at **Compiègne** during Joan's capture (23 May) and the relief of the city (25 October). Vendôme continued to serve Charles and was present for the signing of the **Treaty of Arras** (1435). Although he fell out of favor with Charles for participating in the **Praguerie** (1440), he returned to court in 1443.

VERNEUIL, BATTLE OF (17 AUGUST 1424). Verneuil was an overwhelming victory by the English over the army of **Charles VII**, featuring some prominent **companions in arms** that fought alongside Joan of Arc. The battle had major repercussions for Charles's military strategy throughout the rest of the 1420s and to the **Anglo-Burgundian Alliance**.

The **duke of Bedford** led an Anglo-Burgundian army that besieged the town of Ivry in August 1424. Among his forces were upwards of eight thousand troops according to some medieval sources, as well as the **earl of Salisbury** and the would-be chronicler **Jean de Wavrin**. The town agreed to capitulate on 15 August if no relief army arrived. Although Charles's army arrived, they did not attack Bedford who was positioned outside the town. Instead, they attempted to draw Bedford outside of Verneuil where there were open fields conducive to the cavalry in their army.

The French army was as big as eighteen thousand troops according to **Monstrelet**, but historians tend to place the number around fourteen thousand to sixteen thousand. Led by the **duke of Alençon**, the force was made up of French, Lombard, Scot, and Spanish troops. Among Alençon's force were **La Hire** and **Poton de Xantrailles**. Upon arriving at Verneuil, Alençon's army convinced the town that they had already defeated Bedford, and the town opened its gates.

Before engaging Alençon's army, Bedford dismissed his Burgundian troops, as many as two thousand. They would not participate in the battle, and much has been written and theorized about this move. The common belief among modern historians is that Bedford was wary of treachery, having heard rumors that Duke **Philip the Good** of Burgundy was in negotiations with Charles for a truce. Regardless, the English were victorious, killing some six thousand men and taking two hundred prisoners, including Alençon. The Scots, including their nobles, were slain, as Bedford believed them to be in violation of the recently signed **Treaty of Durham**. The English suffered sixteen hundred casualties according to medieval sources. The victory of a much smaller force was so impressive to Wavrin that he compared it to Agincourt (*See* HUNDRED YEARS WAR).

Verneuil marked the last time Charles was willing to pursue an open battle against the combined forces of the Anglo-Burgundians before the arrival of Joan of Arc (1429). Instead, he focused on the reinforcement of towns and strongholds. In addition, although Bedford's concerns over a possible truce between Philip and Charles were accurate, Philip took the moment as a personal slight, ensuring that he agreed to the **truce of Chambéry** (24 September). The result was the English and Burgundians waged predominantly separate wars against Charles, the latter off and on, through the rest of the decade. *See also* FRANCO-SCOTTISH ALLIANCE.

VEUGLAIRE. *See* ARTILLERY.

VIGNOLLES, ÉTIENNE DE. *See* LA HIRE.

VILLIERS, JEAN DE (C. 1380–1437). Born around 1380 in **Paris**, Jean de Villiers came from a military family. After the death of his father in 1400, he became lord of L'Isle-Adam, and his earliest military activity is recorded in the defense of Harfleur (1415) during the campaign of **Henry V** (*See* HUNDRED YEARS WAR). During the **French Civil War** (1407–1435), he initially sided with the **Armagnacs**, but he switched to the **Burgundians** upon the death of Dauphin Louis in 1417. He held numerous military offices throughout the rest of his life including **marshal of France** twice (1418–1422 and 1432–1435), and captain of Pontoise (1418), Compiègne (1427), Louvre (1428), Saint-Denis (1433), and Bois de Vincennes (1433). He served in multiple sieges and battles including the standoff at **Montépilloy** (1429). His most renowned activity was around his hometown of Paris. He was part of the Burgundian force that captured it in 1418. He took command of the city's defenses in July 1429 and staved off the assault of Joan of Arc (8 September), and alongside **Arthur de Richemont**, he was part of the force that retook it for **Charles VII** in 1436.

Jean de Villiers served Burgundy loyally from 1417 until his death in 1437, and as the **Anglo-Burgundian Alliance** formed and dissolved during his service, he found himself fighting against, alongside, and, again, against the English during that twenty-year period. Although he did not seem to connect with Henry V, the **duke of Bedford** employed his services often, finding favor in a French lord who supported the **Treaty of Troyes**. The duke supported his second stint as marshal of France, and as marshal he continued to fight against the armies of Charles VII, alongside **John Talbot**, until the signing of the **Treaty of Arras** (1435), after which he once again fought against the English.

Jean de Villiers died on 22 May 1437 during a riot in Bruges.

VIRGINITY. Because Joan of Arc came onto the public stage proclaiming herself *la Pucelle* (the Virgin), the topic of her virginity was constant through her **condemnation trial** (1431) and during the **nullification proceedings** (1450–1456). Her physical status as a virgin was tested multiple times, promoted by her supporters, and derided by her enemies.

From the earliest phases of Christianity, virginity and chastity were valued and encouraged, as emphasized in the virgin birth of Christ, the cult of the Virgin Mary, and proclamations by Apostle Paul (1 Cor. 7:25–38). While some women in fifteenth-century

France achieved new status through marriage, the most common stages in a woman's life were virgin, wife, mother, and widow. There are several exceptions, such as the author and military theorist **Christine de Pizan** who achieved renown through her works. The virginity and chastity of women were common topics among theologians and in Arthurian romances where knights defended and violated the chastity of women.

Joan of Arc's adoption of the *la Pucelle* moniker asserted her physical integrity, as well as her status. Joan claimed that she dedicated her virginity to God at the age of thirteen (*See* VOICES). Coupled with the reinterpretations of **prophecies** foretelling her arrival and saving France, her virginity was put to the test, often. Between her arrival at **Chinon** and the **Poitiers** examination (March 1429), she was tested possibly three times. **Jean Pasquerel** claimed that two different women examined and confirmed her virginity. **Jean d'Aulon** claimed that **Yolande of Aragon** supervised an examination, possibly with the same two women. Pasquerel also claimed that the theologians at Poitiers confirmed her virginity, but this could have been the same examination under Yolande. Finally, while in **captivity**, there was at least one more examination and confirmation. **Guillaume Colles** tells us that while in **Rouen**, this was done under the supervision of **Anne of Burgundy** while the **duke of Bedford** secretly watched. **Thomas de Courelles** said he was unaware of any examination during the trial, but Bedford told him that Joan was a virgin. Courelles also conceded that if Joan had failed such a test, it would have been used against her during her condemnation trial.

The methods for testing virginity in the Middle Ages are unclear. The understanding of the hymen is a post-medieval development, and it remains an unreliable indicator. Women are born without hymens, grow them back, and break them through activities outside of sex such as horseback riding, which Joan did excessively (*See* HORSES). Historians have revealed that such tests varied and were a matter of exposing what the examiners expected. For example, a **physician** later claimed he believed Joan was a virgin because of her small frame.

During the nullification proceedings, the topic of Joan's virginity and chastity were a focal point. Those who knew her in **Domremy** attested to her purity. Her companions in arms had no anecdotes or rumors of her engaging in sexual activities. They even claimed that while she was sleeping near them or changing clothes while on campaign, they had no carnal thoughts toward her, further adding to her mystique of purity. While some historians have theorized that she was raped after her **abjuration** (24 May 1431), this is purely conjecture. The *Chronique de la Pucelle* claims she stated at the Poitiers examination that part of her reasoning in sporting men's clothing was for protection around the soldiers who were surely lustful. **Guillaume Manchon** tells us that she resumed wearing the clothing after her abjuration, because she was trying to protect herself from the guards (*See* SEXUAL ASSAULT AND RAPE).

Also coupled with her virginity is the claim from **Jean d'Aulon** that she never menstruated. While there is no way to confirm this claim, it was certainly possible. High stress through campaigning and then captivity, as well as her diet, could have affected her cycles even if she was someone who had then consistently menstruated in the first place. **Louis de Coutes** commented on her light eating, seeing her eat only a piece of bread on a day of battle and other times only eating two meals. Similarly, after she was treated for a wound, the **bastard of Orléans** saw her eat five pieces of toast soaked in heavily watered wine. She also fasted, at least during Lent in 1431. A lack of menstruation coupled with her virginity would add to her divine mystique as *la Pucelle*, the virgin who dedicated her body to God and remained in that state until her **execution** (30 May). The physical confirmations of Joan's virginity added to her validity as *la Pucelle* in the minds of her supporters. Her enemies attacked her virgin status, calling her names such as "whore" (*See* ESTIVET, JEAN D'; GLASDALE, WILLIAM).

VISCOUNT. Derived from the Latin word for "vice-count," the viscount role in fifteenth-century France was the representative of a **count** while he was away. In some instances, it could be hereditary or honorary. Joan of Arc encountered few notable viscounts during her mission, but several of her companions in arms acquired viscount titles, such as **Poton de Xantrailles**.

VOICES, VISIONS, AND REVELATIONS. Voices, visions, and revelations from God after the Ascension of Jesus Christ into heaven date back to the early Christians as recorded in Acts in the Bible. Believers ever since have toiled with how to develop a reliable, critical approach to suss out who genuinely experienced such a divine interaction, as opposed to someone who was a false prophet that was making it up or being misled by demons. By the fifteenth century, the Church had developed multiple tactics to deal with someone claiming divine experiences or knowledge. The first approach was to push the person to share and vet the experiences with local clergy. Often a priest could quickly identify misalignment with Church doctrine and quell the excitement on a local level before self-declared prophets started marching into throne rooms. Another strategy was time, believing that the longer you delay such a person, the harder it would be for them to maintain a ruse or for a demon to deceive. This was often coupled with interrogations by multiple theologians and scholars who would ask questions to expose inconsistencies in her stories or misalignment with Church doctrine. Finally, when the person still seemed genuine and no fault could be found, the person was asked to produce a sign, often citing Isaiah 7:10–14 and Judges 6:36–40. The person's ability to produce a sign or predict an event determined their credibility.

Each of these tactics comes into play with the theologians siding with or against **Charles VII** when it came to challenging Joan of Arc. Often, how Joan's contemporaries interpreted her visions and her intentions depended on their viewpoint. A theologian in **Poitiers** may see Joan seeking to restore the kingdom of France, whereas a theologian in **Paris** may see Joan as a warmonger. After she spent nearly two weeks of interrogation in Poitiers (March 1429) by theologians and scholars loyal to Charles VII, they told the king that he "should not turn away from, or reject, the Pucelle, who says that she has been sent by God, but should give her help, even though her promises are human" (Taylor 2006, 73). Joan's first promise was to relieve the siege of **Orléans**, which happened on 8 May. From there, she was able to influence the strategy and tactics in the court of Charles VII by pushing for the **Loire Campaign** (10–18 June), embarking on the **march to Reims** (29 June) for the **coronation of Charles VII** (17 July), and attacking Paris (8 September). Testimony from eyewitnesses tell how she aggressively pushed for these actions, often evoking her voices. However, she could not prevent negotiations for the **Franco-Burgundian Truce**, which, coupled with the failure to capture Paris, diminished her ability to influence the king's court.

Joan's voices, or at least the contemporary understanding of them, evolved over her three years in the spotlight. With hindsight, we know that Joan claimed they came from physical manifestations of the archangel **Michael** and Saints **Catherine** and **Margaret**. However, the early record does not indicate that Joan named or described these deities until she was pressured for days during her **condemnation trial** (1431). Prior to then, the descriptions of Joan's interactions are simply "voices" or, in one instance, a voice from a cloud (*See* BOULAINVILLIERS). Those who knew her and later testified during the **nullification proceedings** (1450–1456) did not, for the most part, identify the deities. **Seguin de Seguin**, the **duke of Alençon**, **Jean d'Aulon**, and **Jean Pasquerel** all referred to her "counsel" from God. Jean Dunois (*See* ORLÉANS, BASTARD OF) claimed she evoked saints **Louis** and **Charlemagne** prior to lifting the siege of Orléans, but this was far too early in her story to name names, and he is the only source that lists these two deities.

During Joan's condemnation trial, the assessors pushed her on the identity, appearance, content of their messages, frequency, and absence of her voices. When pressed, Joan revealed they wore clothes, had hair, and spoke good, clear French. Joan talked to them and touched them. She did not always agree with them, or even obey, as she indicated with her failed **escape** attempt, which they warned her against, but they forgave her. The assessors wanted to know what side the voices were on, asking her questions like whether God hates the English or Burgundians. She said she did not know who God loved or hated, but knew that He wanted to see the kingdom of France restored, which meant Charles VII ruling over all of France.

In the end, the bulk of the **twelve articles** of accusation brought against Joan dealt with her voices. The **University of Paris** declared Joan's voices to be "false, misleading, and harmful stories; or that these revelations are superstitious, and they proceed from evil and diabolical spirits" (Hobbins 2005, 184). Thus, Joan was either a liar or she was deceived by demons. In her **abjuration** (24 May), Joan declared her voices to be false. However, during her **relapse**, she revealed that she had only abjured "from fear of the flames," and since then, both Saints Catherine and Margaret had admonished her for the act (Hobbins 2005, 197). The final verdict that condemned Joan as a relapsed **heretic** emphasized her claims to interact with saints.

According to testimony recorded after the trial (7 June) and appended to the transcripts of the trial, a group of assessors visited Joan the day of her **execution** (30 May). She purportedly admitted at this time that visible saints were fictitious, but she *heard* voices. Pressed further, she admitted she was deceived. The validity of this testimony was disputed almost immediately (*See* TRANSCRIPTS), and some historians have theorized that if Joan did make these statements, it might have been to receive communion one last time. Regardless, Joan's voices and her supposed recantation of them the day of her execution became prominent talking points for her enemies including the author of the *Journal d'un bourgeois de Paris*, **Henry VI**, and **Jean Graverent**. Each of them evoked Joan's three main voices—Saints Michael, Catherine, and Margaret—emphasizing that she either made them up or was misled by demons.

Joan of Arc was not the first woman who claimed to hear voices, see visions, or share revelations, and historians often evoke notable examples prior to Joan such as Angela of Foligno (1248–1309), Bridget of Sweden (1303–1373), Julian of Norwich (1342–1406), and Catherine of Siena (c. 1347–1380). Prominent theologian **Jean Gerson** wrote extensively on examining so-called prophets and those claiming to commune directly with God and His saints, especially when it came to women whom he saw as imperfect vessels for such messages. He strongly questioned the revelations of Bridget of Sweden and argued against her canonization. Thus, Gerson's aggressive support of Joan in 1429 is surprising (*See* SUPRA FACTO PUELLAE). When viewed in a purely political, perhaps cynical, context, of course, the support Joan received from Gerson and others in the world of Charles VII is understandable in that she told them what aligned with their politics. She claimed a mandate from God to restore the kingdom of France under the rule of Charles. People such as Gerson and his counterparts at Poitiers, who were all refugees from Paris, could lend support to a teenage girl who seemed genuine, demonstrated no ill intent, and produced results. Would the assessors at **Rouen** have accepted Joan if she claimed her voices told her to support Henry VI as king of France? Some contemporaries of Joan suggested this would have been the case.

In **Jean Bréhal**'s *Recollectio*, compiled for the nullification proceedings, he admitted it was not easy to determine if Joan's voices were good or evil. This implies that he had determined they were at least real. Having examined her accounts of how, when, and where she encountered the voices, her reactions to them, and the content of their messages, Bréhal found no suggestion of deceit or intentional alterations on the part of Joan. Many of those testifying during the nullification proceedings may not have had direct opinions on her voices, but numerous eyewitnesses to her on the battlefield believed that her accomplishments were divine.

W

WANDOMME, GUILLAUME, BASTARD OF. Guillaume, the bastard of Wandomme (or Wandonne), was the man credited with capturing Joan of Arc outside **Compiègne** (23 May 1430). That day, Joan was among a cavalry group leading hit-and-run attacks across the bridge from the town into Burgundian lines, before retreating back to the town. During her **condemnation trial** (1431), Joan described making two of these attacks, successfully driving back the Burgundians. After a third charge, her return to Compiègne was impeded by English troops who blocked her entrance to the gate of the bridge. Joan and her company attempted to flee elsewhere, but she was knocked from her horse. Others captured included **Poton de Xaintrailles**, **Jean d'Aulon**, and Joan's brother, **Pierre d'Arc**. Burgundian chroniclers such as **Monstrelet** claim that Joan "surrendered and pledged her faith" to Wandomme (Monstrelet, 1:572), meaning she was entrusting her life to her captor and agreeing to be **ransomed**. However, during her trial, Joan was clear that she would escape if given the opportunity.

Surviving records of the bastard of Wandomme reveal military service as early as 1414, and he became attached to **John of Luxembourg**, leading several hundred soldiers in various campaigns and sieges. Wandomme is mentioned by name by multiple chronicles, as well as in a letter sent by **Pierre Cauchon** to secure possession of Joan for an **inquisition**.

Aside from his capture of Joan of Arc, Wandomme's career was unremarkable.

WARWICK, RICHARD BEAUCHAMP, EARL OF (1382–1439). Richard Beauchamp, earl of Warwick, was an English military commander and advisor to kings Henry IV, **Henry V**, and **Henry VI**, as well as the **duke of Bedford**. During Joan of Arc's **condemnation trial** (1431), he was the captain of **Rouen**, directly intervening against those who tried to physically harm her as well as against those who tried to advise her.

Born in 1382 as the eldest son of Earl Thomas Beauchamp of Warwick, Richard became the new earl of Warwick upon his father's death in 1401. In 1399, he was knighted and served in campaigns in Wales and France. In 1408 to 1410, he made pilgrimages to Rome and the Holy Land. In 1413, he gained power with the coronation of Henry V. In 1414, he became captain of Calais, and in 1415, he joined Henry's campaign in France, participating in the siege of Harfleur, the conquest of **Normandy**, and the siege of Rouen (*See* HUNDRED YEARS WAR). He traveled back to England for the coronation of **Catherine of Valois** (1421) and returned to France with Henry later that year, participating in and leading more sieges. He was present for the death of Henry (31 August 1422) and became the executor of the late king's will. In December, he joined the council of Henry VI.

Warwick continued to serve in France, becoming captain of Rouen in 1423 and serving as **regent** of France in 1425 while Bedford was in England. He continued campaigning and was defeated at Montargis by the **bastard** of Orléans in 1427. He returned to England in 1428, becoming the tutor of Henry VI. He participated in the coronation of Henry as king of England in 1429, and he returned to France in 1431 for Henry's coronation as king of France. It was during this time, as captain of Rouen, that he interfered with the trial of Joan of Arc according to testimonies recorded from multiple sources in the **nullification proceedings** (1450–1456). Like **Pierre Cauchon**, Warwick had not survived, and he became a scapegoat for the assessors still around for the nullification proceedings. From their testimonies, Warwick's interventions appeared to be twofold. First, he wanted to protect Joan from excessive physical harm during the trial. Second, he wanted to ensure that Joan was found guilty.

Concerning her protection, **Haimond de Macy** tells us that Warwick stopped **Humphrey Stafford** from stabbing Joan in her cell. **Guillaume Manchon** tells us that Warwick first warned and then replaced two English guards who attempted to rape Joan (See SEXUAL ASSAULT AND RAPE). During Joan's illness in April 1430, he sought help from **physicians**, but instructed Guillaume de La Chambre to be careful not to overdo the bloodletting. After Joan was better, La Chambre tells us that **Jean d'Estivet** was verbally abusive toward her and she became ill again. Warwick once again intervened and admonished Estivet for the exchange.

Warwick's concern for Joan's physical wellbeing extended only as far as it served to allow them to finish the trial with a guilty verdict. Several of the assessors tried to help Joan with her answers and her approach to the trial. When **Isembard de La Pierre** offered advice to Joan, **Guillaume Duval** tells us that Warwick threatened him. **Nicholas de Houppeville** takes it further, claiming Warwick threatened to drown him. Guillaume Manchon tells us that Warwick similarly threatened **Jean de La Fontaine** and **Martin Ladvenu**, and the former fled the city out of fear. At the end of the trial when Joan signed an **abjuration** and was sentenced to life in prison (24 May), Warwick complained that the result was not beneficial to the king. However, when Joan was again found wearing men's **clothing** and she withdrew her abjuration, he rejoiced loudly to a crowd, according to Ladvenu.

Warwick's involvement in Joan's condemnation trial was never official, and there is no documentation of his actions except for testimonies from men who, for the most part, adored Joan and loathed Warwick. In his entry in the *Oxford Dictionary of National Biography*, there is no mention of Joan of Arc, which tells us he was only present in France that same year for the coronation of Henry VI. After her **execution** (30 May), Warwick continued to serve England, conducting more sieges and campaigns throughout the 1430s and eventually dying on 30 April 1439 in Rouen.

WAVRIN, JEAN DE (C. 1400–C. 1475). Jean de Wavrin was an experienced soldier who became a diplomat, bibliophile, and chronicler for the Burgundian court. At age fifteen, he witnessed the battle of Agincourt (1415) from the French camp, and later fought at the battles of **Cravant** (1423) and **Verneuil** (1424) under the command of the **duke of Bedford**, the battle of **Patay** (1429) under **John Fastolf**, and then served under **Philip the Good** until 1436. Staunchly pro-Burgundian and in favor of the **Anglo-Burgundian Alliance**, Wavrin was against the **Treaty of Arras** (1435). Still, Philip legitimized Wavrin in 1437, as he was the bastard of a Flemish nobleman. In addition, Wavrin served in numerous roles in the Burgundian court including diplomat, chamberlain, and counselor, the former of which led to trips to England and Rome to meet with the **pope**.

Wavrin maintained an extensive library of works, some of which have survived today. Using this library in the 1440s, Wavrin began work on the *Collection of the chronicles and ancient histories of Great Britain, now called England*, a French chronicle that borrowed heavily from other writers such as **Monstrelet**, even for events he witnessed. However, the collection does provide some extant perspectives throughout, especially related to Joan of Arc. He was the earliest chronicler to claim **Charles VII** and his court never truly believed Joan but opted to use her merely as a political instrument. Still, he believed Joan was effective at weakening English resolve, and he goes so far as to admit that her involvement turned the tide of the war. He also concedes that French leadership outmatched English leadership during the **Loire Campaign** (10–18 June 1429). His detail regarding Patay, a battle that he experienced firsthand, is remarkable from the English perspective. However, it is clear his extensive narrative serves the purpose of clearing the then-tarnished reputation of John Fastolf.

WEDDING. *See* MARRIAGE CONTRACT.

WESTERN SCHISM. *See* GREAT SCHISM.

WILLIAM DE LA POLE. *See* SUFFOLK, WILLIAM DE LA POLE, EARL OF.

WINCHESTER, BISHOP OF. *See* BEAUFORT, HENRY.

WOUNDS. *See* INJURIES OF JOAN OF ARC.

XANTRAILLES, POTON DE (1400–1461). Poton de Xantrailles was an experienced mercenary and military commander, companion in arms of Joan of Arc in most of her campaigns, and loyal to **Charles VII**.

Born in Gascony, Xantrailles entered the royal army in 1418 where he met **La Hire**, another soldier he is often mentioned in tandem with in medieval chronicles. Throughout the 1420s, Xantrailles gained experience through victory and defeat, fighting alongside **Charles VII**'s army and the Burgundian army. He was present at both the disastrous defeats at **Cravant** (1423) and **Verneuil** (1424), the former at which he was captured and **ransomed**. In the mid-1420s, he served under the duke of Burgundy (*See* PHILIP THE GOOD), but never in battles against Charles VII.

Xantrailles rejoined Charles's army during the siege of **Orléans** (1428–1429), and he was present at the defeat at the **Herrings** (1429). Because of his positive relationship with Philip the Good, the citizens of Orléans sent him to negotiate a possible surrender with the duke. The proposed terms allowed Philip to install his own leadership with half the income going to **Henry VI** and the other half going to Philip. Although the duke favored the surrender, it was rejected by the **duke of Bedford** (*See* ANGLO-BURGUNDIAN ALLIANCE).

After the arrival of Joan of Arc at Orléans (29 April), Xantrailles became a constant presence in most of her campaigns in 1429 including the **Loire Campaign** (10–18 June), **Patay** (18 June), the **march to Reims** (29 June–16 July), and **Paris** (8 September), mentioned by numerous chronicles. He was captured alongside Joan in her attempt to relieve the siege of **Compiègne** (23 May 1430). After his release, Xantrailles took part in the relief of the siege (25 October), seeing the completion of Joan's last military act.

Xantrailles continued to serve Charles against rebellions and through the end of the **Hundred Years War** (1453), winning numerous battles and capturing cities. When the king officially reentered Paris in 1436 and **Rouen** in 1449, Xantrailles was there with him. During the **Praguerie** rebellion (1440), he remained loyal to Charles and negotiated the surrender of the **bastard of Orléans**, the **duke of Alençon**, and the **dauphin** (*See* LOUIS XI). He was captured at the battle of the Shepherd in an unsuccessful attempt to capture the duke of Bedford (12 November 1431). Held in **Rouen**, he was treated well, eating meals with the **earl of Warwick** and meeting **Henry VI**. He was again ransomed as part of a trade to release **John Talbot** who was captured at Patay (1429). Although successful at other battles and sieges, he was captured again in 1453 by John Talbot, but released in time to take part in the battle of Castillon (17 July) where Talbot was killed.

In the latter half of his life, Xantrailles held numerous positions including **seneschal** of Limousin (1433–1437), **bailiff** of Berry (1437–1452), and **marshal of France** (1454). When he died on 7 October 1461, Xantrailles was rich but had no descendants.

Although alive during the **nullification proceedings** (1450–1456), there was no recorded testimony from Xantrailles.

Y

YOLANDE OF ARAGON (C. 1384–1442). Yolande of Aragon was the titular queen of Sicily, duchess of Anjou, and the mother-in-law of **Charles VII**. Historians have theorized that she played an instrumental role in the introduction and support of Joan of Arc in the king's court in 1429.

Born around 1384, Yolande was the daughter of Louis I of Aragon (1350–1396). Her husband became Louis II of Aragon (1377–1417) with their marriage in 1400, but she did not remarry after his death in 1417. After the **Treaty of Troyes** (1420), Yolande determined to side with Charles VII who married her daughter, **Marie of Anjou**, in 1422. The duke of Burgundy (*See* PHILIP THE GOOD) asserted his own title of duke of Anjou acquired through the **Anglo-Burgundian Alliance**, and he made conquests against Yolande's territories in Anjou and Maine in the 1420s. She toiled diplomatically to dismantle the English hold in France by luring the somewhat neutral **duke of Brittany** to the camp of Charles VII. The duke's brother, **Arthur de Richemont**, joined the court of Charles and became constable of France in 1425. However, the rise of **Georges de La Trémoille** soured the relationship, and he managed to expel Richemont from the king's court in 1427.

After Joan of Arc met with the **duke of Lorraine** and convinced **Robert de Baudricourt** to send her to meet with Charles VII in **Chinon** in 1429, Yolande appears to have been in support of Joan. **Jean d'Aulon** tells us that Yolande oversaw the efforts to confirm Joan's professed **virginity**, which were necessary to support her claims of being *la Pucelle* ("the virgin"). Yolande then provided funds for the supplies and reinforcements sent with Joan to the siege of **Orléans**. This, however, is the extent of Yolande's recorded support of Joan.

Beginning in the nineteenth century, historians began theorizing that Yolande had a more integral, undocumented role in the rise of Joan. Did Yolande correspond with her son, **René of Anjou**, who was also the son-in-law of the duke of Lorraine? After all, Joan did request that the duke send René with her for her journey to Chinon (the duke refused).

Joan's **mission** to see the siege of Orléans lifted, Charles VII crowned in Reims, and the English expelled from France matched perfectly with Yolande's anti-Burgundian policy. However, there are no further recorded details of her having a hand in the promotion of Joan, not even in the chronicles that would have certainly seized on such rumors. Upon Joan's capture at **Compiègne** (23 May 1430), there are no recorded reactions from Yolande, as perhaps Joan had served her purpose.

Yolande lived to see the crumbling of the **Anglo-Burgundian Alliance** and died in 1442.

Appendix A

Roles and Responsibilities for the Condemnation Trial

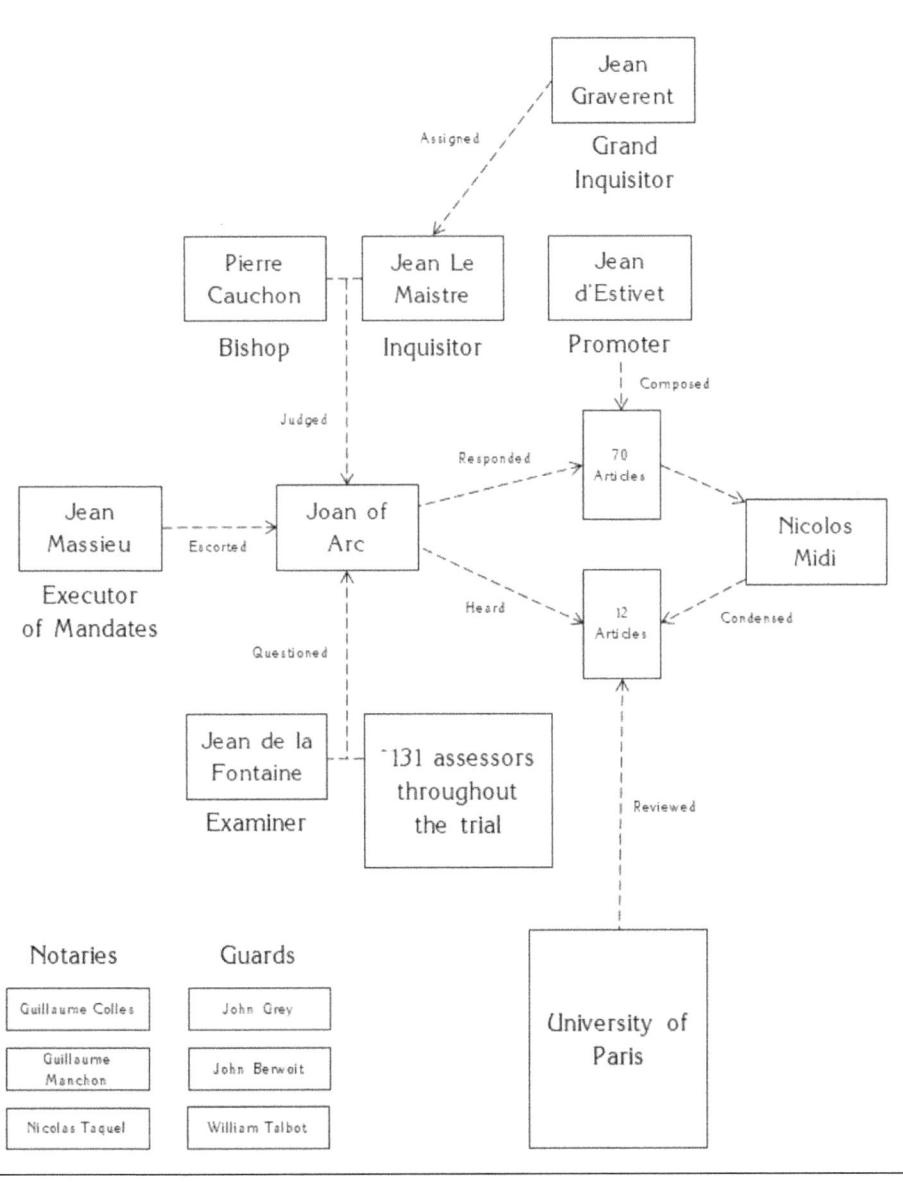

Appendix B

Key Battles, Sieges, and Captured Cities

1428
    12 October: Siege of Orléans begins

1429
    12 February: Battle of the Herrings
    4 May: French capture Saint Loup outside Orléans
    7 May: French capture Tourelles bastille outside Orléans
    8 May: English abandon siege of Orléans
    11–12 June: Battle of Jargeau
    15 June: Battle of Meung
    15–17 June: Battle of Beaugency
    18 June: Battle of Patay
    29 June–16 July: French army marches to Reims
    5–9 July: Siege of Troyes
    15 August: Battle of Montépilloy
    8 September: Siege of Paris
    1–4 November: Siege of Saint-Pierre-le-Moutier
    24? November–23? December: Siege of La Charité

1430
    29 March: Battle of Lagny
    22 May–25 October: Siege of Compiègne
    11 June: Battle of Anthon.

1431
    2 July: Battle of Bulgnéville

Appendix C

Selected Treaties and Truces during the Time of Joan of Arc

Treaty of Bourges
Date: 18 May 1412
Signatories: England, Orléans

Treaty of Auxerre
Date: 22 August 1412
Signatories: Berry, Burgundy, Orléans

Treaty of Buzançais
Date: 14 November 1412
Signatories: England, Orléans

Treaty of Arras
Date: 4 September 1414
Signatories: Burgundy, Orléans

Treaty of Troyes
Date: 21 May 1420
Signatories: England, France, Burgundy

Treaty of Amiens
Date: 13 April 1423
Signatories: Bedford, Brittany, Burgundy

Truce of Chambéry
Date: 24 September 1424
Signatories: France, Burgundy

Treaty of Durham
Date: 28 September 1424
Signatories: England, Scotland

Treaty of Saumur
Date: 7 December 1425
Signatories: Brittany, France

Auld Alliance Renewal
Date: 1428
Signatories: France, Scotland

Franco-Burgundian Truce
Date: 28 August 1429
Signatories: France, Burgundy

Treaty of Arras
Date: 21 September 1435
Signatories: France, Burgundy

Appendix D

Joan of Arc's Immediate Family

Isabelle d'Arc, Romée (1380?–1458), mother of Joan

Jacques d'Arc (?–c. 1439), father of Joan

Jacquemin d'Arc (c. 1392–c.1450), brother of Joan

Jean d'Arc, du Lys (?–c. 1476), brother of Joan

Pierre d'Arc, du Lys (?–c. 1478), brother of Joan

Catherine d'Arc, sister of Joan

Appendix E

Surviving Letters of Joan of Arc

The contents of the following letters of Joan of Arc survive in their original form in a copy found in transcripts of the condemnation trial (1431), the nullification proceedings (1450–1456), or city registers.

To the English (22 March 1429)
To the English (5 May 1429)
To the People of Tournai (25 June 1429)
To the People of Troyes (4 July 1429)
To the Duke of Burgundy (17 July 1429)
To the People of Reims (5 August 1429)
To Jean IV, the Count of Armagnac (22 August 1429)
To the People of Riom (9 November 1429)
To the People of Reims (16 March 1430)
To the Hussites (23 March 1430)
To the People of Reims (28 March 1430)

Appendix F

Popes during the Time of Joan of Arc

Martin V (1417–1431)
Eugene IV (1431–1447)
Nicholas V (1447–1455)

Callixtus III (1455–1458)
Pius II (1458–1458)

Appendix G

Selected Monarchs and Rulers

Burgundy
    Philip the Bold (1363–1404)
    John the Fearless (1404–1419)
    Philip the Good (1419–1467)
    Charles the Bold (1467–1477)
England
    Henry IV (1399–1413)
    Henry V (1413–1422)
    Henry VI (1422–1461, 1470–1471)
France
    Charles V (1328–1350)
    Charles VI (1380–1422)
    Charles VII (1422–1461)
    Louis XI (1461–1483)
    Charles VIII (1483–1498)
    Louis XII (1498–1515)
Holy Roman Empire
    Sigismund (1410–1437)
    Albert II (1438–1439)
    Frederick III (1440–1493)
Scotland
    James I (1406–1437)
    James II (1437–1460)

Appendix H

Constables and Marshals of France

Constables
  Bernard VII, count of Armagnac (1415–1418)
  Charles, duke of Lorraine (1428–1425)
  John Stewart, earl of Buchan (1421–1424)
  Arthur de Richemont (1425–1458)
Marshals
  Jean de Villiers (1418–1437)
  Jacques de Montberon (1418–1422)
  Gilbert Motier de La Fayette (1421–1464)
  Antoine de Vergy (1422–1439)
  Jean de la Baume (1422–1435)
  Jean de Brosse (1426–1433)
  Gilles de Rais (1429–1440)
  André de Laval (1439–1486)
  Philip de Culant (1441–1454)
  Poton de Xaintrailles (1454–1461)

Bibliography

CONTENTS

Printed Medieval Sources	247
Condemnation Trial	247
Nullification Proceedings	247
Chronicles and Journals	247
Collected Works	247
Commentary on Joan of Arc	248
Military Treatises	248
Bibliographies and Source Analyses	248
Joan of Arc	249
Biographies	249
Military Career, Battles, and Sieges	250
Spirituality	250
Examinations, Condemnation Trial, Nullification Proceedings	251
Appearance, Clothing, Armor, and Weapons	252
In the Footsteps of Joan of Arc	252
Special Topics	252
Post-Medieval Depictions	253
Biographies	253
Key Personalities	253
Collections	254
Hundred Years War	254
General Narratives and Overviews	254
The War from 1400 to 1428	255
France	255
Burgundy	256
England and the English in France	257
Brittany	258
Other	258
Armies, Soldiers, Ransoms	258
Fortifications and Artillery	259
Alliances, Treaties, and Peace Conferences	260
Propaganda	261
French Civil War (1407–1435)	261
Medieval	262
General	262
Dictionaries and Encyclopedias	262
Warfare and Technology	262
Military Writings and Theory	263
Nationalism	263
Universities	263
Church History, Heresy, Inquisition	264
Online Resources	265
Non-English Sources	265
Printed Medieval Sources Focused Primarily on Joan of Arc	265
Medieval Chronicles and Journals	265
Biographies	265
Dictionaries and Encyclopedias	265
Online Sources	265

INTRODUCTION

The vast amount of literature from the past six centuries regarding Joan of Arc can be daunting for those new to Johannic scholarship, especially English speakers. One only needs to look at the more than fifteen hundred select entries in Nadia Margolis's *Joan of Arc: in History, Literature and Film* (1990) to get a taste of what is out there in archives and in print. Most English speakers will start with translated works by the late Régine Pernoud, which are still in print and readily available in libraries. Those interested in Joan of Arc today owe a great debt to Pernoud for her extensive work. However, terminology and accuracy in some of her works have come into question over the past few decades. For example, historians have moved away from referring to the process that examined Joan of Arc's original inquisition as a "Retrial" and instead refer to it as the "Nullification Process," as established by Pierre Duparc in his five-volume *Procés en Nullité de la condemnation de Jeanne d'Arc* (1977–1989). In addition, the biographies found at the end of Régine Pernoud and Marie-Véronique Clin's *Joan of Arc: Her Story* (1998) are a regurgitation of those originally written by Pierre Champion in *The Trial of Jeanne d'Arc* (1931), complete with misleading or inaccurate statements.

The two books any English speaker should start with are Daniel Hobbins's *The Trial of Joan of Arc* (2005) and Craig Taylor's *Joan of Arc: La Pucelle* (2006). Both authors provide lengthy contextual information to the period and culture as well as translated documents with further analysis. Taylor's is especially useful for its fifty-plus medieval documents including letters, chronicles, contemporary commentary, and selections from the condemnation trial and nullification proceedings. He also includes translations of all of Joan's surviving letters. There are other sources for medieval texts, some of which date back to the nineteenth century. Sometimes the relevant texts are buried within larger works, and I have attempted to narrow down the useful sections, such as those found within DeVries and Livingston's *Medieval Reader* (2019).

The number of biographies on Joan of Arc is vast, but historians continue to find fresh approaches to Joan of Arc: by Kelly DeVries (1999), Deborah A. Fraioli (2005), Juliet Larissa Taylor (2010), and Helen Castor (2015). These are all superb starting points for the uninitiated, and the biographical section of this bibliography focuses predominantly on those published in the past twenty years. Since Joan spent most of her time campaigning while in the spotlight, there are endless works focusing on her military career. Kelly DeVries has been the most prolific in this arena, but the reader should also consider Gail Orgelfinger's first chapter in her *Joan of Arc in English Imagination* (2019) for a superb analysis of how Joan viewed the English.

For narratives on the larger context of the Hundred Years War and world of Joan of Arc, Juliet Barker's *Conquest* (2012) is a gripping read. In "The War from 1400 to 1428" section are works focusing on the war before Joan of Arc arrived on the scene. There are further sections focusing on "Burgundy" and the "French Civil War" to provide more context to the complex geopolitical landscape in which Joan fought. Over the past decade, historians have delved deep into aspects of the conflicts in France, and Emily J. Hutchison and Tracy Adams have both published fascinating studies on the civil war and propaganda between the feuding parties. There are further sections focusing on "Fortifications and Artillery" and "Warfare and Technology" for a deeper understanding of how these wars were fought.

Three invaluable sources to understanding gunpowder artillery at the time of Joan of Arc are Smith and DeVries's *The Artillery of the Dukes of Burgundy* (2005) and Spencer's "The Provision of Artillery for the 1428 Expedition to France" (2015), along with his *Royal and Urban Gunpowder Weapons in Late Medieval England* (2019). While these narratives do not cover all of Joan's wars, they do cover the expedition to Orléans and the siege of Compiègne. More importantly, these works have cobbled together a vast array of documentary evidence on the evolving world of gunpowder artillery in fifteenth-century France, providing logistical details on their funding, construction, transportation, maintenance, and usage. The appendices in each of these works provide extensive details on varying shapes, sizes, and names of guns.

Finally, although much about Joan of Arc has been translated or written in English, there is a massive amount of work in French and Latin that remains inaccessible to the English speaker. The "Non-English Sources" section contains works related to Joan of Arc that do not have a sufficient English equivalent. Jules Quicherat's five-volume work in the mid-nineteenth century (1841–1849) was the first to aggregate all the known source material. Although the portions focusing on the condemnation trial and the nullification proceedings have since been superseded by Duparc (1977–1989) and Tisset and Yvonne (1960–1971), Quicherat is found in virtually all major works on Joan, even today. Contamine, Bouzy, and Hélary's *Jean d'Arc: Histoire et dictionnaire* (2012) provides an extensive historical narrative coupled with the most reliable encyclopedic work on Joan in any language.

PRINTED MEDIEVAL SOURCES

Condemnation Trial

Barrett, W. P., ed. and trans. *The Trial of Jeanne d'Arc Translated into English from the Original Latin and French Documents.* London: George Routledge, 1931. Reprint, New York Routledge, 2014.

Champion, Pierre. *The Trial of Jeanne d'Arc.* Translated by Coley Taylor and Ruth H. Kerr. New York: Gotham House, 1932. Reprint, Aeterna Press, 2015.

Douglas, T. Murray, ed. and trans. "The Trial." In *Jeanne d'Arc: Maid of Orleans, Deliverer of France,* 1–154. New York: McClure, Phillips & Co., 1902.

Geary, Patrick J. "*The Trial of Joan of Arc.*" In *Readings in Medieval History,* 602–15. Fifth edition. Ontario: University of Toronto Press, 2016.

Hobbins, Daniel, trans. *The Trial of Joan of Arc.* Cambridge: Harvard University Press, 2005.

Scott, W. S., trans. *The Trial of Joan of Arc: Being the Verbatim Report of the Proceedings from the Orleans Manuscript.* London: Folio Society, 1956.

Taylor, Craig, trans. and ed. "The Trial of Condemnation (February-May 1431)." In *Joan of Arc: La Pucelle,* 137–224. Manchester: Manchester University Press, 2006.

Nullification Proceedings

Douglas, T. Murray, ed. and trans. "The Rehabilitation." In *Jeanne d'Arc: Maid of Orleans, Deliverer of France,* 157–320. New York: McClure, Phillips & Co., 1902.

Pernoud, Régine. *The Retrial of Joan of Arc: The Evidence for Her Vindication.* Translated by J. M. Cohen. San Francisco: Ignatius Press, 1955.

Taylor, Craig, trans. and ed. "The Nullification Trial (1455–1456)." In *Joan of Arc: La Pucelle,* 262–349. Manchester: Manchester University Press, 2006.

Chronicles and Journals

Monstrelet, Enguerrand de. *The Chronicles of Enguerrand de Monstrelet.* Volume 1. Translated by Thomas Johnes. London: William Smith, 1845.

Shirley, Janet, trans. *A Parisian Journal, 1405–1449.* Oxford: Clarendon Press, 1968.

"Siege of Orléans." In *Medieval Warfare: A Reader.* Edited by Kelly DeVries and Michael Livingston, 217–26. Toronto: University of Toronto Press, 2019.

Wavrin, John de. *A Collection of the Chronicles and Ancient History of Great Britain, Now Called England.* Volume 3. Translated by Edward L. C. P. Hardy. London: Eyre and Spottiswoode, 1891.

Collected Works

Calendar of Patent Rolls, Henry V, Vol. II., A.D. 1416–1422. London, 1911.

Curry, Anne, ed. *The Parliament Rolls of Medieval England, 1275–1504.* Volume 10, *Henry VI: 1422–1431.* Woodbridge: Boydell Press, 2012.

———. *The Parliament Rolls of Medieval England, 1275–1504.* Volume 11, *Henry VI: 1432–1445.* Woodbridge: Boydell Press, 2012.

Fraioli, Deborah A. "Primary Documents." In *Joan of Arc and the Hundred Years War,* 113–60. Westport: Greenwood Press, 2005.

Given-Wilson, Christopher, ed. *The Parliament Rolls of Medieval England, 1275–1504.* Volume 9, *Henry V: 1413–1422.* Woodbridge: Boydell Press, 2012.

Margolis, Nadia, ed. and trans. "The Mission of Joan of Arc." In *Medieval Hagiography: An Anthology.* Edited by Thomas Head. New York: Routledge, 2001.

Pernoud, Régine. *Joan of Arc: By Herself and Her Witnesses.* Translated by Edward

Hyams. Lanham: Scarborough House, 1994.

Quintal, Claire, and Daniel Rankin. *Letters of Joan of Arc*. Pittsburgh: Pittsburgh Diocesan Council of Catholic Women, 1969.

Stevenson, Joseph. *Letters and Papers Illustrative of the Wars of the English in France during the Reign of Henry the Sixth, King of England*. Volume 1. London: Longman, Green, Longman, and Roberts, 1861.

Taylor, Craig, trans. and ed. *Joan of Arc: La Pucelle*. Manchester: Manchester University Press, 2006.

Commentary on Joan of Arc

Field, Sean L. "A New English Translation of Jean Gerson's Authentic Tract on Joan of Arc: *About the Feat of the Maid, and the Faith That Should be Placed in Her*." *Magistra* 18, no. 2 (2012): 36–54.

Gragg, Florence Alden, trans. "Book VI: July–October 1461." In *Secret Memoirs of a Renaissance Pope*, 189–209. London: The Folio Society, 1988.

Pizan, Christine de. "The Tale of Joan of Arc." In *The Selected Writings of Christine de Pizan*. Translated by Renate Blumenfeld-Kosinski and Kevin Brownlee, 252–62. New York: W. W. Norton & Company, 1997.

Military Treatises

Milner, N. P., trans. *Vegetius: Epitome of Military Science*. Second edition. Liverpool: Liverpool University Press, 2011.

Pizan, Christine de. *The Book of Deeds of Arms and of Chivalry*. Translated by Sumner Willard. University Park: Pennsylvania State University Press, 1999.

BIBLIOGRAPHIES AND SOURCE ANALYSES

Arden, Heather M. "Christine de Pizan's *Ditié de Jehanne d'Arc*: History, Feminism, and God's Grace." In *Joan of Arc and Spirituality*. Edited by Ann W. Astell and Bonnie Wheeler, 195–208. New York: Palgrave Macmillan, 2003.

Bouzy, Olivier. "Transcription Errors in Texts of Joan of Arc's History." *Fresh Verdicts on Joan of Arc*. Edited by Bonnie Wheeler and Charles T. Wood, 73–83. New York: Garland, 1996.

Clermont-Ferrand, Meredith. "Joan of Arc and the English Chroniclers: Monstrous Presence and Problematic Absence in *The Chronicle of London*, *The Chronicle of William of Worcester*, and *An English Chronicle 1377–1461*." *The Medieval Chronicle VII* (2011): 151–65.

Courroux, Pierre. "What Types of Sources Did Medieval Chroniclers Use to Narrate Battles? (England and France, Twelfth to Fifteenth Centuries)." *Journal of Medieval Military History* 18 (2020): 117–41.

Elliott, Dyan. "John Gerson and Joan of Arc." In *Proving Women: Female Spirituality and Inquisitional Culture in the Later Middle Ages*, 264–96. Princeton: Princeton University Press, 2004.

———. "Seeing Double: John Gerson, the Discernment of Spirits, and Joan of Arc." *American Historical Review* 107, no. 1 (2002): 26–54.

Fraioli, Deborah A. *Joan of Arc: The Early Debate*. Woodbridge: The Boydell Press, 2000.

———. "The Literary Image of Joan of Arc: Prior Influences." *Speculum* 56, no. 4 (1981): 811–30.

Giraudet, Luke. "Political Communication and the Public Opinion in the *Journal d'un bourgeois de Paris*, 1405–1449." PhD dissertation, University of York, 2019.

Hamblin, Vicki L. "*En l'honneur de la Pucelle*: Ritualizing Joan the Maid in Fifteenth-Century Orléans." In *Joan of Arc and Spirituality*. Edited by Ann W. Astell and Bonnie Wheeler, 209–26. New York: Palgrave Macmillan, 2003.

———. "The Fifteenth-Century French *Mistere du Siege d'Orleans*: An Annotated Edition." PhD dissertation, University of Arizona, 1984.

Hanawalt, Barbara A., and Susan Noakes. "Trial Transcript, Romance, Propaganda: Joan of Arc and the French Body Politic."

Modern Language Quarterly 57, no. 4 (1996): 605–31.

Hobbins, Daniel. "Jean Gerson's Authentic Tract on Joan of Arc: *Super facto puellae et credulitate sibi praestanda* (14 May 1429)." *Mediaeval Studies* 67 (2005): 99–155.

Le Brusque, Georges. "Chronicling the Hundred Years War in Burgundy and France in the Fifteenth Century." In *Writing War: Medieval Literary Responses to Warfare*. Edited by Corinne Saunders, Françoise Le Saux, and Neil Thomas, 77–92. Cambridge: D. S. Brewer, 2004.

Lightbody, Charles Wayland. *The Judgements of Joan*. Cambridge: Harvard University Press, 1961.

Margolis, Nadia. "Joan of Arc." In *The Cambridge Companion to Medieval Women's Writing*. Edited by Carolyn Dinshaw and David Wallace, 256–66. Cambridge: Cambridge University Press, 2003.

———. *Joan of Arc in History, Literature, and Film*. New York: Garland Publishing, 1990.

McWebb, Christine. "Joan of Arc and Christine de Pizan: The Symbiosis of Two Warriors in *Ditié de Jehanne d'Arc*." In *Fresh Verdicts on Joan of Arc*. Edited by Bonnie Wheeler and Charles T. Wood, 133–44. New York: Garland, 1996.

Rogers, Clifford. *The Hundred Years' War: Oxford Bibliographies Online Research Guide*. Oxford: Oxford University Press, 2010.

Ross, L. B. "The Good, the Bad, and the Ugly: Visions of Burgundy, France, and England in the *Oeuvres* of Georges Chastellain." In *The Hundred Years War (Part II): Different Vistas*. Edited by L. J. Andrew Villalon and Donald J. Kagay, 367–85. Leiden: Brill, 2008.

Spencer, Mark. *Thomas Basin, 1412–1490: The History of Charles VII and Louis XI*. Nieuwkoop: De Graaf Publishers, 1997.

Taylor, Larissa. "Joan of Arc." *Oxford Bibliographies*. https://www.oxfordbibliographies.com/view/document/obo-9780195399301/obo-9780195399301-0124.xml, 2012.

Visser-Fuchs, Livia. *History as Pastime: Jean de Wavrin and His Collection of Chronicles of England*. Donington: Shaun Tyas, 2018.

Waugh, W. T. "Joan of Arc in English Sources of the Fifteenth Century." In *Historical Essays in Honour of James Tait*. Edited by J. G. Edwards, et al., 387–98. Manchester, 1933.

Wijsman, Hanno. "History in Transition. Enguerrand de Monstrelet's *Chronique* in Manuscript and Print (c.1450–c.1600). In *The Book Triumphant. Print in Transition in the Sixteenth and Seventeenth Centuries*. Edited by Malcolm Walsby and Graeme Kemp, 199–52. Leiden: Brill, 2011.

JOAN OF ARC

Biographies

Brolis, Maria Teresa. "Joan the Rebel." In *Stories of Women in the Middle Ages*. Third edition. Translated by Joyce Myerson, 80–88. Montreal: McGill-Queen's University Press, 2018.

Castor, Helen. *Joan of Arc: A History*. New York: HarperCollins, 2015.

DeVries, Kelly. *Joan of Arc: A Military Leader*. Phoenix Mill: Sutton Publishing, 1999.

Fraioli, Deborah A. *Joan of Arc and the Hundred Years War*. Westport: 2005.

Gies, Frances. *Joan of Arc: The Legend and the Reality*. New York: Harper & Row, 1981.

Harrison, Kathryn. *Joan of Arc: A Life Transfigured*. New York: Doubleday, 2014.

Maddox, Joan Margaret. "Joan of Arc (ca. 1412–1431)." In *Icons of the Middle Ages: Rulers, Writers, Rebels, and Saints*. Edited by Lister M. Matheson, 2:417–49. Santa Barbara: Greenwood, 2012.

Pernoud, Régine, and Marie-Véronique Clin. *Joan of Arc: Her Story*. Translated by Jeremy du Quesnay Adams. New York: St. Martin's Griffin, 1998.

Richey, Stephen W. *Joan of Arc: The Warrior Saint*. Westport: Praeger, 2003.

Scott, W. S. *Jeanne: Her Life, Her Death, and the Myth*. London: Harrap, 1974.

Spoto, Donald. *Joan: The Mysterious Life of the Heretic Who Became a Saint*. New York: HarperCollins, 2007.

Taylor, Larissa Juliet. *The Virgin Warrior: The Life and Death of Joan of Arc*. New Haven: Yale University Press, 2010.

Warner, Marina. *Joan of Arc: The Image of Female Heroism*. New York: Alfred A. Knopf, 1981.

Wilson-Smith, Timothy. *Joan of Arc: Maid, Myth and History*. Thrupp: Sutton Publishing, 2006.

Military Career, Battles, and Sieges

Ambühl, Rémy. "Joan of Arc as *prisonnière de guerre*." *English Historical Review* 132 (2017): 1045–76.

Collins, Hugh. "Sir John Fastolf, John Lord Talbot and the Dispute over Patay: Ambition and Chivalry in the Fifteenth Century." In *War and Society in Medieval and Early Modern Britain*. Edited by Diana Dunn, 114–40. Liverpool: Liverpool University Press, 2000.

DeVries, Kelly. "'Because It Was Paris': Joan of Arc's Attack on Paris Reconsidered." In *Magistra Doctissima: Essays in Honor of Bonnie Wheeler*. Edited by Dorsey Armstrong, Ann W. Astell, and Howell Chickering, 123–31. Kalamazoo: Medieval Institute Publications, 2013.

———. "Joan of Arc." *Military History* 24, no. 10 (2008): 26–35.

———. "Joan of Arc's Call to Crusade." In *Joan of Arc and Spirituality*. Edited by Ann W. Astell and Bonnie Wheeler, 111–26. New York: Palgrave Macmillan, 2003.

———. "Successful Defenses against Artillery Sieges in the Fifteenth Century: Orléans, 1428–1429." In *Artillerie et Fortification, 1200–1600*. Edited by Nicolas Prouteau, Emmanuel de Crouy-Chanel, and Nicolas Faucherre, 81–85. Rennes Cedex: Presses Universitaires de Rennes, 2011.

———. "The Use of Gunpowder Weaponry by and against Joan of Arc during the Hundred Years War." *War and Society* 14 (May 1996): 1–15.

———. "A Woman as Leader of Men: Joan of Arc's Military Career." In *Fresh Verdicts on Joan of Arc*. Edited by Bonnie Wheeler and Charles T. Wood, 3–18. New York: Garland, 1996.

Hindley, Geoffrey. "Women at War." *Medieval Sieges & Siegecraft*, 125–36. New York: Skyhorse Publishing, 2009.

Jones, Michael K. "'Gardez mon corps, sauvez ma terre' – Immunity from War and the Lands of a Captive Knight: The Siege of Orléans (1428–29) Revisited." In *Charles d'Orléans In England (1415–1440)*. Edited by Mary-Jo Arn, 9–26. Cambridge: D. S. Brewer, 2000.

Manning, Scott. "3000 Miles to Rouen: Joan of Arc on Horseback." In *Saints and Sinners on Horseback*, edited by Miriam Bibby. Trivent Publishing, forthcoming.

———. "'. . . Otherwise, You Will Be Massacred': The Battle of Jargeau," *Medieval Warfare* 9, no. 2 (2019): 6–11.

Nicolle, David. *Orléans 1429: France Turns the Tide*. Oxford: Osprey Publishing, 2001.

O'Reilly, Don. "The Maid of Orléans." *Military History* 15, no. 1 (1998): 22–30.

Orgelfinger, Gail. "'We Have Burned a Saint': Joan of Arc and the English in France." In *Joan of Arc in the English Imagination, 1429–1829*, 13–35. University Park: Pennsylvania State Press, 2019.

Pinzino, Jane Marie. "Just War, Joan of Arc, and the Politics of Salvation." In *The Hundred Years War: A Wider Focus*. Edited by L. J. Andrew Villalon and Donald J. Kagay, 365–96. Brill: Leiden, 2005.

Spencer, Dan. "The Expeditions of 1430–2 and 1497." In *Royal and Urban Gunpowder Weapons in Late Medieval England*, 47–67. Woodbridge: Boydell, 2019.

Verbruggen, J. F. "Women in Medieval Armies." Translated by Kelly DeVries. *Journal of Medieval Military History* 4 (2006): 119–36.

Williams, Gareth. "Manipulation and the Maid: Joan of Arc and the Siege of Orléans." *Medieval Warfare* 4, no. 2 (2014): 25–32.

Spirituality

Astell, Ann W., and Bonnie Wheeler, eds. *Joan of Arc and Spirituality*. New York: Palgrave MacMillan, 2003.

Kelly, Henry Ansgar. "Saint Joan and Confession: Internal and External Forum." In *Joan of Arc and Spirituality*. Edited by Ann W. Astell and Bonnie Wheeler, 61–84. Basingstoke: Palgrave Macmillan, 2003.

Tavard, George H. "The Spirituality of Saint Joan." In *Joan of Arc at the University*. Edited by Mary Elizabeth Tallon, 43–58. Milwaukee: Marquette University Press, 1997.

Vauchez, André. "Joan of Arc and Female Prophecy in the Fourteenth and Fifteenth Centuries." In *The Laity in the Middle Ages: Religious Beliefs and Devotional Practices*. Edited by Daniel E. Bornstein and translated by Margery J. Schneider, 255–64. Notre Dame: University of Notre Dame Press, 1993.

Examinations, Condemnation Trial, and Nullification Proceedings

Astell, Ann W. "The Judgement of the Eucharist in the Trial of Joan of Arc." In *Witness of the Body: The Past, Present, and Future of Christian Martyrdom*. Edited by Michael Budde and Karen Scott, 82–103. Grand Rapids: Eerdmans, 2011.

Barstow, Anne Llewellyn. "Joan of Arc and Female Mysticism." *Journal of Feminist Studies in Religion* 1, no. 2 (1985): 29–42.

Clin, Marie-Véronique. "Joan of Arc and Her Doctors." In *Fresh Verdicts on Joan of Arc*. Edited by Bonnie Wheeler and Charles T. Wood, 295–302. New York: Garland Publishing, 1996.

Edwards, Lilas G. "Joan of Arc: Gender and Authority in the Text of the Trial of Condemnation." In *Young Medieval Women*. Edited by Katherine J. Lewis, Noël Menuge, and Kim M. Phillips, 133–52. New York: St. Martin's Press, 1999.

Fraioli, Deborah A. "The *Poitiers Conclusions*." In *Joan of Arc: The Early Debate*, 45–54. Woodbridge: Boydell Press, 2000.

Kelly, H. Ansgar. "Questions of Due Process and Conviction in the Trial of Joan of Arc." In *Religion, Power, and Resistance from the Eleventh to the Sixteenth Centuries: Playing the Heresy Card*. Edited by Karen Bollermann, Thomas M. Izbicki, and Cary J. Nederman, 81–100. New York: Palgrave, 2014.

———. "The Right to Remain Silent: Before and after Joan of Arc." *Speculum* 68, no. 4 (1993): 992–1026.

Little, Roger G. "The *Parlement*, The Siege of Orléans and Joan of Arc (c. 1429–1431)." In *The Parlement of Poitiers: War, Government and Politics in France, 1418–1456*, 90–123. London: Royal Historical Society, 1984.

Newhall, Richard A. "Payment to Pierre Cauchon for Presiding at the Trial of Jeanne d'Arc." *Speculum* 9, no. 1 (1934): 88–91.

Pinzino, Jane Marie. "But Where to Draw the Line? Colette of Corbie, Joan of Arc and the Expanding Boundaries of Women's Leadership in the Fifteenth Century." In *A Companion to Colette of Corbie*. Edited by Joan Mueller and Nancy Bradley Warren, 56–75. Leiden: Brill, 2016.

———. "Heretic or Holy Woman? Cultural Representation and Gender in the Trial to Rehabilitate Joan of Arc." PhD dissertation, University of Pennsylvania, 1996.

———. "Joan of Arc and *Lex Privata*: A Spirit of Freedom in the Law." In *Joan of Arc and Spirituality*. Edited by Ann W. Astell and Bonnie Wheeler, 85–109. New York: Palgrave Macmillan, 2003.

———. "Speaking of Angels: A Fifteenth-Century Bishop in Defense of Joan of Arc's Mystical Voice." In *Fresh Verdicts on Joan of Arc*. Edited by Bonnie Wheeler and Charles T. Wood, 161–76. New York: Garland, 1996.

Robins, P. R. "Discerning Voices in the Trial of Joan of Arc and 'The Book of Margery Kempe.'" *Fifteenth-Century Studies* 38 (2013): 175–234.

Schibanoff, Susan. "True Lies: Transvestism and Idolatry in the Trial of Joan of Arc." In *Fresh Verdicts on Joan of Arc*. Edited by Bonnie Wheeler and Charles T. Wood, 31–60. New York: Garland, 1996.

Sullivan, Karen. "'I Do Not Name to You the Voice of St. Michael': The Identification of Joan of Arc's Voices." In *Fresh Verdicts on Joan of Arc*. Edited by Bonnie Wheeler and Charles T. Wood, 85–111. New York: Garland, 1996.

———. *The Interrogation of Joan of Arc*. Minneapolis: University of Minnesota Press, 1999.

Taylor, Larissa Juliet. "Joan of Arc, the Church, and the Papacy, 1429–1920." *Catholic Historical Review* 98, no. 2 (2012): 217–40.

Weiskopf, Steven. "Readers of the Lost Arc: Secrecy, Specularity and Speculation in the Trial of Joan of Arc." In *Fresh Verdicts on Joan of Arc*. Edited by Bonnie Wheeler and Charles T. Wood, 113–32. New York: Garland, 1996.

Wood, Charles T. "Joan of Arc's Mission and the Lost Record of Her Interrogation at Poitiers." In *Fresh Verdicts on Joan of Arc*. Edited by Bonnie Wheeler and Charles T. Wood, 19–29. New York: Garland, 1996.

Appearance, Clothing, Armor, and Weapons

Bullough, Vern L. "Cross Dressing and Gender Role Change in the Middle Ages." In *Handbook of Medieval Sexuality*. Edited by Vern L. Bullough and James Brundage, 223–42. New York: Routledge, 2000.

Bychowski, Gabrielle. "Were There Transgender People in the Middle Ages?" *The Public Medievalist*. https://www.publicmedievalist.com/transgender-middle-ages/, 1 November 2018.

Crane, Susan. "Clothing and Gender Definition: Joan of Arc." *Journal of Medieval and Early Modern Studies* 26, no. 2 (1996): 297–320.

———. "Joan of Arc and Women's Cross Dress." In *The Performance of Self: Ritual, Clothing and Identity during the Hundred Years War*, 73–106. Philadelphia: University of Pennsylvania Press, 2002.

Edwards, Lilas G. "Joan of Arc: Empowerment and Risk in Androgyny." *Medieval Life* 5 (1996): 3–6.

Heerwarden, Jan van. "The Appearance of Joan of Arc." In *Joan of Arc: Reality and Myth*. Edited by Jan van Herwaarden, 19–74. Hilversum: Verloren, 1994.

Hotchkiss, Valerie R. "Tranvestism on Trial: The Case of Jeanne d'Arc." In *Clothes Make the Man: Female Cross Dressing in Medieval Europe*, 49–68. London: Routledge, 1996.

Jones, Robert W. "The Sword of Joan of Arc." *Historian in Harness*. https://www.historianinharness.co.uk/blog/joan-of-arc-sword, 24 July 2020.

Warren, Nancy Bradley. "The Sword and the Cloister: Joan of Arc, Margaret of Anjou and Christine de Pizan in England, 1445–1540." *Women of God and Arms: Female Spirituality and Political Conflict, 1380–1600*, 58–86. Philadelphia, 2005.

Wheeler, B. "Joan of Arc's Sword in the Stone." In *Fresh Verdicts on Joan of Arc*. Edited by Bonnie Wheeler and C. T. Wood, xi–xvi. New York: Garland Publishing, 1996.

Williamson, Allen. "Primary Sources and Context Concerning Joan of Arc's Male Clothing." *Historical Association for Joan of Arc Studies*. http://primary-sources-series.joan-of-arc-studies.org/PSS021806.pdf, 9 May 2006.

In the Footsteps of Joan of Arc

Chandler, David. "Orléans." In *A Guide to the Battlefields of Europe*, 108–12. Hertfordshire: Wordsworth, 1998.

Forristal, L. J. "On the Trail of Joan of Arc." *AlmaTourism* 4, no. 8 (2013): 45–60.

Robinson, Kirk Ward. "Jeanne." In *Hiking through History: Hannibal, Highlanders & Joan of Arc*, 258–365. North Charleston: CreateSpace Independent Publishing, 2011.

Starks, Michael. "The 'Goddams.'" In *The Hundred Years War in France*, 135–66. London: Cassell, 2002.

Special Topics

Foote-Smith, Elizabeth, and Lydia Bayne. "Joan of Arc." *Epilepsia* 32 (1991): 810–15.

McInerney, Maud Burnett. "Epilogue: Joan of Arc." In *Eloquent Virgins from Thecla to Joan of Arc*, 211. New York: Palgrave Macmillan, 2003.

Tavard, George H. "Jeanne and the Clergy." In *Joan of Arc and Spirituality*. Edited by Ann W. Astell and Bonnie Wheeler, 129–46. New York: Palgrave Macmillan, 2003.

Warren, Nancy Bradley. "The Sword and the Cloister: Joan of Arc, Margaret of Anjou, and Christine de Pizan in England, 1445–1450." In *Women of God and Arms: Female Spirituality and Political Conflict,*

1380–1600, 58–86. Philadelphia: University of Pennsylvania Press, 2005.

Post-Medieval Depictions

Astell, Ann W. *Joan of Arc and Sacrificial Authorship*. Notre Dame: University of Notre Dame Press, 2003.

Blaetz, Robin. *Visions of the Maid: Joan of Arc in American Film and Culture*. Charlottesville: University of Virginia Press, 2001.

Flower, John. *Joan of Arc: Icon of Modern Culture*. Hastings: Helm Information, 2008.

Harty, Kevin J. "The Lady *Is* for Burning: The Cinematic Joan of Arc and Her Screen Avatars." In *Medieval Women on Film: Essays on Gender, Cinema, and History*. Edited by Kevin J. Harty, 182–91. Jefferson: McFarland, 2020.

Heimann, Nora M., and Laura Coyle. *Joan of Arc: Her Image in France and America*. Washington: Corcoran Gallery of Art, 2006.

Manning, Scott. "Fit for Print, Not for Spectacle: Ringling Bros. and the Careful Exploitation of Joan of Arc." *Studies in Medievalism* 30 (2021): 229–52.

Orgelfinger, Gail. *Joan of Arc in the English Imagination, 1429–1829*. University Park: Pennsylvania State Press, 2019.

Vale, Malcolm. "The Legend of Joan of Arc." In *The Ancient Enemy: England, France and Europe from the Angevins to the Tudors*, 89–99. London: Hambledon Continuum, 2007.

Winock, Michel. "Joan of Arc." In *Realms of Memory: The Construction of the French Past*. Volume 3. Edited by Lawrence D. Kritzman and translated by Arthur Goldhammer, 433–80. New York: Columbia University Press, 1998.

BIOGRAPHIES

Key Personalities

Adams, Tracy. *The Life and Afterlife of Isabeau of Bavaria*. Baltimore: Johns Hopkins University Press, 2010.

———. "Recovering Queen Isabeau of France (c. 1370–1435): A Re-Reading of Christine de Pizan's Letters to the Queen." *Fifteenth-Century Studies* 33 (2008): 35–54.

Allmand, Christopher. *Henry V*. Berkeley: University of California Press, 1992.

Arn, Mary-Jo, ed. *Charles d'Orléans in England*. Cambridge: D. S. Brewer, 2000.

Cooper, Stephen. *The Real Falstaff: Sir John Fastolf and the Hundred Years War*. Barnsley: Pen & Sword Military, 2010.

Cooper-Davis, Charlotte. *Christine de Pizan: Life, Work, Legacy*. London: Reaktion Books, 2022.

Crowder, Susannah. "'Call me Claude': Female Actors, Impersonation, and Cultural Transmission." In *Performing Women: Gender, Self, and Representation in Late Medieval Metz*, 190–220. Manchester: Manchester University Press, 2018.

DeVries, Kelly. "Routier Perrinet Gressart: Joan of Arc's Penultimate Enemy." In *Routiers et mercenaires pendant la guerre de Cent ans: Homage á Jonathan Sumption*. Edited by Guilhem Pépin, Françoise Lainé, and Frédéric Boutoulle, 227–37. Bordeaux: Ausonius, 2016.

Gibbons, Rachel. "Isabeau of Bavaria, Queen of France (1385–1422): The Creation of an Historical Villainess." *Transactions of the Royal Historical Society* 6 (1996): 51–73.

———. "The Piety of Isabeau of Bavaria, Queen of France, 1385–1422." In *Courts, Counties and the Capital in the Later Middle Ages*. Edited by Dian E. S. Dunn, 205–24. Stroud: Sutton Publishing, 1996.

Griffiths, Ralph A. *The Reign of King Henry VI: The Exercise of Royal Authority, 1422–1461*. Second edition. Los Angeles: University of California Press, 1998.

Grummitt, David. *Henry VI*. London: Routledge, 2015.

Harriss, G. L. *Cardinal Beaufort. A Study of Lancastrian Ascendancy and Decline*. Oxford: Clarendon Press, 1988.

Kekwich, Margaret L. *The Good King: René of Anjou and Fifteenth Century Europe*. New York: Palgrave Macmillan, 2008.

Margolis, Nadia. *An Introduction to Christine de Pizan*. Gainesville: University Press of Florida, 2011.

McGuire, Brian Patrick. "In Search of Jean Gerson." In *A Companion to Jean Gerson*. Edited by Brian Patrick McGuire, 1–39. Leiden: Brill, 2006.

Odio, Elena. "Gilles de Rais: Hero, Spendthrift, and Psychopathic Child Murderer of the Later Hundred Years War." In *The Hundred Years War (Part III): Further Considerations*. Edited by L. J. Andrew Villalon and Donald J. Kagay, 145–84. Leiden: Brill, 2013.

Parsons, Ben. "Sympathy for the Devil: Gilles de Rais and His Modern Apologists." *Fifteenth-Century Studies* 37 (2012): 113–37.

Pollard, A. J. *John Talbot and the War in France, 1427–1453*. Yorkshire: Pen & Sword Military, 2005.

Rohr, Zita Eva. "On the Road Again: The Semi-Nomadic Career of Yolande of Aragon (1400–1439)." In *Travel and Exploration from the Atlantic to the Black Sea*. Edited by Felicitas Schmieder and Marianne O'Doherty, 215–44. Turnhout: Brepols, 2015.

———. *Yolande of Aragon (1381–1442) Family and Power: The Reverse of the Tapestry*. New York: Palgrave Macmillan, 2016.

Talbot, Hugh. *The English Achilles: The Life and Campaigns of John Talbot 1st Earl of Shrewsbury (1383–1453)*. London: Chatto & Windus, 1981.

Taylor, Aline S. *Isabel of Burgundy: The Duchess Who Played Politics in the Age of Joan of Arc, 1397–1471*. London: Madison Books, 2001.

Vale, M. G. A. *Charles VII*. Berkeley: University of California Press, 1974.

Vaughan, Richard. *John the Fearless: The Growth of Burgundian Power*. London: Longmans, 1966.

———. *Philip the Good: The Apogee of the Burgundian State*. Harlow: Longmans, 1970.

Williams, Ethel C. *My Lord Bedford, 1389–1435*. Londres: Longmans, 1963.

Wolffe, Bertram. *Henry VI*. New edition. New Haven: Yale University Press, 2001.

Collections

Allmand, C. T., and C. A. J. Armstrong. "Biographical Details of English Litigants." In *English Suits before the Parlement of Paris, 1420–1436*, 290–309. London: Royal Historical Society, 1982.

Champion, Pierre. "Partisans of France" and "Partisans of England." In *The Trial of Jeanne d'Arc Translated into English from the Original Latin and French Documents*. Edited and translated by Coley Taylor and Ruth H. Kerr, 255–336. New York: Gotham House, Inc., 1932.

Fraioli, Deborah A. "Biographies." In *Joan of Arc and the Hundred Years War*, 75–111. Wesport, CT: Greenwood Press, 2005.

Oxford Dictionary of National Biography. Sixty volumes. Prepared under various editors. New York: Oxford University Press, 1885–2004.

Pernoud, Régine, and Marie-Véronique Clin. "The Cast of Principal Characters." In *Joan of Arc: Her Story*. Translated by Jeremy duQuesnay Adams, 165–217. New York: St. Martin's Griffin, 1998.

Sullivan, Thomas. *Benedictine Monks at the University of Paris, A.D. 1229–1500: A Biographical Register*. Leiden: E. J. Brill, 1995.

HUNDRED YEARS WAR

General Narratives and Overviews

Allmand, Christopher. *The Hundred Years War: England and France at War, c. 1300 – c. 1450*. Revised ed. Cambridge: Cambridge University, 2001.

———, ed. *Society at War: The Experience of England and France during the Hundred Years War*. Edinburgh: Oliver & Boyd, 1973.

Barker, Juliet. *Conquest: The English Kingdom of France, 1417–1450*. Cambridge: Harvard University Press, 2012.

Curry, Anne. *The Hundred Years' War, 1337–1453*. Oxford: Osprey, 2002.

———, ed. *The Hundred Years War Revisited*. London: Red Globe Press, 2019.

DeVries, Kelly. "The Hundred Year Wars: Not One but Many." In *The Hundred Years War (Part II): Different Vistas*. Edited by L. J. Andrew Villalon and Donald J. Kagay, 3–34. Leiden: Brill, 2008.

Gilbert, James E. "A Medieval 'Rosie the Riveter'? Women in France and Southern England during the Hundred Years War." In *The Hundred Years War: A Wider Focus*. Edited by L. J. Andrew Villalon and Donald J. Kagay, 333–63. Leiden: Brill, 2005.

Green, David. *The Hundred Years War: A People's History*. New Haven: Yale University, 2014.

Keen, Maurice. "Henry VI and France: 1422–1453." In *England in the Later Middle Ages: A Political History*, 297–319. Second edition. London: Routledge, 2003.

King, Andy, and Claire Etty. "The Hundred Years War: War on Two Fronts, 1337–71." In *England and Scotland, 1286–1603*, 47–72. London: Palgrave, 2016.

Neillands, Robin. *The Hundred Years War*. Revised edition. London: Routledge, 2001.

Rogers, Clifford J. "The Age of the Hundred Years War" In *Medieval Warfare: A History*. Edited by Maurice Keen, 136–60. Oxford: Oxford University Press, 1999.

Seward, Desmond. *The Hundred Years War: The English in France, 1337–1453*. New York: Penguin, 1999.

The War from 1400 to 1428

Ambühl, Rémy. "Henry V and the Administration of Justice: The Surrender of Meaux (May 1422)." *Journal of Medieval History* 43, no. 1 (2017): 74–88.

Curry, Anne. "After Agincourt, What Next? Henry V and the Campaign of 1416." *Fifteenth Century England* 7 (2007): 23–51.

———. "Henry V's Conquest of Normandy 1417–1419: The Siege of Rouen in Context." In *Guerra y Diplomacia en la Europa Occidental. XXXI Semana de Estudios Medievales. Estellas 19–13 de julio 2004*, 237–54. Pamplona: Gobernio de Navarra, 2005.

———. "Representing War and Conquest, 1415–1429: The Evidence of College of Arms Manuscript M9." In *Representing War and Violence, 1250–1600*. Edited by Joanna Bellis and Laura Slater, 139–58. Cambridge: Cambridge University Press, 2016.

DeVries, Kelly. "John the Fearless' Way of War." In *Reputation and Representation in Fifteenth-Century Europe*. Edited by Douglas L Biggs, Sharon D. Michalove, and A. Compton Reeves, 39–55. Leiden: Brill, 2004.

Jones, Michael K. "The Battle of Verneuil (17 August 1424): Towards a History of Courage." *War in History* 9, no. 4 (2002): 375–411.

Lambert, Craig. "Henry V and the Crossing to France: Reconstructing Naval Operations for the Agincourt Campaign, 1415." *Journal of Medieval History* 43, no. 1 (2017): 23–39.

Milner, John D. "The Battle of Baugé, March 1421: Impact and Memory." *History* 91 (2006): 484–507.

———. "The English Commitment to the 1412 Expedition to France." *The Fifteenth Century* 11 (2012): 9–23.

Pépin, Guilhem. "The French Offensives of 1404–1407 against Anglo-Gascon Aquitaine." *Journal of Medieval Military History* 9 (2011): 1–40.

Spencer, Dan. "The Provision of Artillery for the 1428 Expedition to France." *Journal of Medieval Military History* 13 (2015): 179–92.

Sumption, Johnathan. *The Hundred Years War*. Volume 4, *Cursed Kings*. London: Faber & Faber, 2015.

Wadge, Richard. *Verneuil 1424: A Second Agincourt*. Stroud: Spellmount, 2015.

Warner, Mark. "Chivalry in Action: Thomas Montagu and the War in France, 1417–1428." *Nottingham Medieval Studies* 42 (1998): 146–73.

France

Bisson, Thomas N. *The Medieval Crown of Aragon: A Short History*. Oxford: Clarendon, 1986.

Chevalier, B. "The *bonnes villes* and the King's Council in the Fifteenth-Century France." In *The Crown and Local Communities: In England and France in the Fifteenth Century*. Edited J. R. L. Highfield and Robin Jeffs, 110–28. Gloucester: Alan Sutton, 1981.

Curry, Anne. "France and the Hundred Years War, 1337–1453." In *France in the Later Middle Ages*. Edited by David Potter, 90–116. Oxford: Oxford University Press, 2003.

Cuttler, S. H. "Treason and the Crown 1380–1422" and "Treason and the Crown 1422–1461." In *The Law of Treason and Treason Trials in Later Medieval France*, 181–212. Cambridge: Cambridge University Press, 1981.

Gibbons, Rachel. "'The Limbs Fail When the Head Is Removed': Reactions of the Body Politic of France to the Madness of Charles VI (1380–1422)." In *The Image and Perception of Monarchy in Medieval and Early Modern Europe*. Edited by Sean McGlynn and Elena Woodacre, 48–67. Cambridge Scholars Publishing, 2014.

Goldsmith, James L. "The Crisis of the Late Middle Ages: The Case of France." *French History* 9, no. 4 (1995): 417–50.

Le Goff, Jacques. "Reims, City of Coronation." In *Realms of Memory: The Construction of the French Past*. Volume 3. Edited by Lawrence D. Kritzman and translated by Arthur Goldhammer, 193–251. New York: Columbia University Press, 1998.

Lewis, P. S. "The Centre, the Periphery, and Power Distribution of Fifteenth-Century France." In *The Crown and Local Communities: In England and France in the Fifteenth Century*. Edited J. R. L. Highfield and Robin Jeffs, 33–50. Gloucester: Alan Sutton, 1981.

———. "France in the Fifteenth Century: Society and Sovereignty." In *Europe in the Late Middle Ages*. Edited by J. R. Hale, J. R. L. Highfield, and B. Smalley, 276–300. Evanston: Northwestern University Press, 1965.

———. *Later Medieval France: The Polity*. London: Macmillan, 1968.

Potter, David. "The King and His Government under the Valois, 1328–1498." In *France in the Later Middle Ages*. Edited by David Potter, 155–81. Oxford: Oxford University Press, 2003.

Solon, Paul D. "Popular Response to Standing Military Forces in Fifteenth-Century France." *Studies in the Renaissance* 19 (1972): 78–111.

Vale, Malcolm. "France at the End of the Hundred Years War (c. 1420–1461)." In *The New Cambridge Medieval History, Volume VII: c. 1415–c. 1500*. Edited by Christopher Allmand, 392–407. Cambridge: Cambridge University Press, 1998.

Burgundy

Armstrong, C. A. J. "The Golden Age of Burgundy: Dukes That Outdid Kings." In *The Courts of Europe: Politics, Patronage and Royalty, 1400–1800*. Edited by A. G. Dickens, 54–75. London: Thames & Hudson, 1977.

Bachrach, David S. "A Military Revolution Reconsidered: The Case of the Burgundian State under the Valois Dukes." *Essays in Medieval Studies* 15 (1999): 9–17.

Blockmans, Wim, and Prevenier, Walter. *The Promised Lands: The Low Countries under Burgundian Rules, 1369–1530*. Translated by Elizabeth Fackelman. Philadelphia: University of Pennsylvania Press, 1999.

Boulton, D'Arcy Jonathan Dacre. "The Order of the Golden Fleece and the Creation of Burgundian National Identity." In *The Ideology of Burgundy: The Promotion of National Consciousness, 1364–1565*. Edited by D'Arcy Jonathan Dacre Boulton and Jan R. Veenstra, 21–97. Leiden: Brill, 2006.

DeVries, Kelly. "Calculating Profits and Losses during the Hundred Years War: What Really Forced Philip the Good from the War?" In *Money, Markets and Trade in Late Medieval Europe: Essays in Honour of John H. A. Munro*. Edited by Lawrin Armstrong, Ivana Elbl, and Martin M. Elbl, 187–209. Leiden: Brill, 2007.

Harari, Yuval Noah. "Princes in the Cross-Hairs: The Rise and Fall of Valois Burgundy, 1407–83." In *Special Operations in the Age of Chivalry, 1100–1550*, 125–62. Woodbridge: Boydell, 2007.

Leguai, André. "The Relations between the Towns of Burgundy and the French Crown in the Fifteenth Century." In *The Crown and Local Communities: In England and France In the Fifteenth Century*. Edited J.

R. L. Highfield and Robin Jeffs, 129–45. Gloucester: Alan Sutton, 1981.

Small, Graeme. "For a Long Century of Burgundy: The Court, Female Power and Ideology." *BMGN–Low Countries Historical Review* 126, no. 1 (2011): 54–69.

———. "Of Burgundian Dukes, Counts, Saints and Kings (14 C.E. – c. 1500)." In *The Ideology of Burgundy: The Promotion of National Consciousness, 1364–1565*. Edited by D'Arcy Jonathan Dacre Boulton and Jan R. Veenstra, 151–87. Leiden: Brill, 2006.

———. "Some Aspects of Burgundian Attitudes towards the English during the Reign of Philip the Good: Georges Chastelain and His Circle." In *Publications du Centre Européen d'Etudes Bourguignonnes* 35 (1995): 15–26.

Smith, Robert Douglas, and Kelly DeVries. *The Artillery of the Dukes of Burgundy, 1363–1477*. Woodbridge: Boydell Press, 2005.

Vale, Malcolm G. A. "England and the Burgundian Dominions: Some Cultural Influences and Comparisons." In *Publications du Centre Européen d'Etudes Bourguignonnes* 35 (1995): 7–13.

Van Loo, Bart. *The Burgundians: The Vanished Empire, A History of 1111 Years and One Day*. Translated by Nancy Forest-Flier. London: Head of Zeus, 2021.

Vanderjagt, Arjo. "The Princely Culture of the Valois Dukes of Burgundy." In *Princes and Princely Culture, 1450–1650*. Volume 1. Edited by Martin Gosman, Alasdair MacDonald, and Arjo Vanderjagt, 51–79. Leiden: Brill, 2003.

Vaughan, Richard. *Valois Burgundy*. London: Allen Lane, 1975.

England and the English in France

Allmand, Christopher. *Lancastrian Normandy, 1415–1450: The History of a Medieval Occupation*. Oxford: Oxford University Press, 1983.

———. "Local Reaction to the French Reconquest of Normandy: The Case of Rouen." In *The Crown and Local Communities: In England and France in the Fifteenth Century*. Edited J. R. L. Highfield and Robin Jeffs, 146–61. Gloucester: Alan Sutton, 1981.

Butler, Raymond Reagan. *Is Paris Lost? The English Occupation, 1422–1436*. Staplehurst: Spellmount, 2003.

Castor, Helen. *The King, the Crown, and the Duchy of Lancaster: Public, Authority and Private Power, 1399–1461*. Oxford: Oxford University Press, 2000.

Curry, Anne. "Towns at War: Relations between the Towns of Normandy and Their English Rulers, 1417–1450." In *Towns and Townspeople in the Fifteenth Century*. Edited by John Thomson, 148–72. Gloucester: Alan Sutton, 1988.

Harriss, Gerald. "The English in France, 1413–1453." In *Shaping the Nation. England, 1360–1461*, 540–87. Oxford: Clarendon Press, 2005.

Keen, Maurice. "The End of the Hundred Years War: Lancastrian France and Lancastrian England." In *England and Her Neighbours, 1066–1453: Essays in Honour of Pierre Chaplais*. Edited by Michael Jones and Malcolm Vale, 297–311.

King, Andy. "Gunners, Aides and Archers: The Personnel of the English Ordnance Companies in Normandy in the Fifteenth Century." *Journal of Medieval History* 9 (2011): 65–75.

Labarge, Margaret Wade. *Gascony: England's First Colony, 1204–1453*. London: Hamish Hamilton, 1980.

Massey, Robert. "Lancastrian Rouen: Military Service and Property Holding, 1419–1449." In *England and Normandy in the Middle Ages*. Edited by David Bates and Anne Curry, 269–86. London: The Hambledon Press, 1994.

Murphy, Neil. "Ceremony and Conflict in Fifteenth-Century France: Lancastrian Ceremonial Entries into French Towns, 1415–1431." *Explorations in Renaissance Culture* 39, no. 2 (2013): 113–33.

Spencer, Dan. *Royal and Urban Gunpowder Weapons in Late Medieval England*. Woodbridge: Boydell, 2019.

Thompson, Guy Llewelyn. *Paris and Its People under English Rule: The Anglo-Burgundian*

Regime, 1420–1436. Oxford: Clarendon Press, 1991.

Brittany

Galliou, Patrick, and Michael Jones. "Brittany under the Montfort Dukes, 1365–1491." In *The Bretons*, 230–52. Oxford: Blackwell, 1991.

Jones, Michael. "The Defence of Medieval Brittany: A Survey of the Establishment of Fortified Towns, Castles and Frontiers from the Gallo-Roman Period to the End of the Middle Ages." *Archaeological Journal* 138 (1981): 149–204.

———. "The Duchy of Brittany in the Middle Ages." In *The Creation of Brittany: A Late Medieval State*, 1–12. London: Hambledon Press, 1988.

Kerhervé, Jean. "Taxation and Ducal Power in Late Medieval Brittany." Translated by J. A. Bergin. *French History* 6, no. 1 (1992): 1–23.

Other

Murphy, Neil. "Between France, England and Burgundy: Amiens under the Lancastrian Dual Monarchy, 1422–35." *French History* 26, no. 2 (2012): 143–63.

Armies, Soldiers, Ransoms

Allmand, Christopher T. "Changing Views of the Soldier in Late Medieval France." In *Guerre et société en France, en Angleterre et en Bourgogne XIVe–XVe siècle*. Edited by Philip Contamine, Charles Giry-Deloison, and Maurice Keen, 171–88. Lille: Publications de l'Institut de recherches historiques du Septentrion, 1991.

Ambühl, Rémy. *Prisoners of War in the Hundred Years War: Ransom Culture in the Late Middle Ages*. Cambridge: Cambridge University Press, 2013.

Baker, Gary Paul. "Armies." In *The Hundred Years War Revisited*. Edited by Anne Curry, 203–30. London: Red Globe Press, 2019.

Bell, Adrian R., Anne Curry, Andy King, and David Simpkin. *The Soldier in Later Medieval England*. Oxford: Oxford University Press, 2013.

Bell, Adrian R., Anne Curry, Adam Chapman, Andy King. "The Soldier in Later Medieval England: An Online Database. In *The Hundred Years War (Part III): Further Considerations*. Edited by L. J. Andrew Villalon and Donald J. Kagay, 19–46. Leiden: Brill, 2013.

Bennett, Matthew. "The Development of Battle Tactics in the Hundred Years War." In *Arms, Armies and Fortifications in the Hundred Years War*. Edited by Anne Curry and Michael Hughes, 1–20. Woodbridge: Boydell Press, 1994.

Boulton, D'Arcy Jonathan Dacre. *The Knights of the Crown: The Monarchical Orders of Knighthood in Later Medieval Europe 1325–1520*. Woodbridge: Boydell Press, 2000.

Contamine, Philippe. "The Soldiery in Late Medieval Urban Society." *French History* 8, no. 1 (1994): 1–13.

Curry, Anne. "English Armies in the Fifteenth Century." In *Arms, Armies and Fortifications in the Hundred Years War*. Edited by Anne Curry and Michael Hughes, 39–68. Woodbridge: Boydell Press, 1994.

———. "Foreign Soldiers in English Pay: Identity and Unity in the Armies of the English Crown, 1415–1450." In *Routiers et mercenaires pendant la guerre de Cent ans: Homage á Jonathan Sumption*. Edited by Guilhem Pépin, Françoise Lainé, and Frédéric Boutoulle, 303–16. Bordeaux: Ausonius, 2016.

———. "Guns and Goddams: Was there a Military Revolution in Lancastrian Normandy 1415–50?" *Journal of Medieval Military History* 8 (2010): 171–88.

Gaite, Pierre. "Exercises in Arms: The Physical and Mental Combat Training of Men-at-Arms in the Fourteenth and Fifteenth Centuries." *Journal of Medieval Military History* 16 (2018): 99–121.

Gravett, Christopher. *English Medieval Knight, 1400–1500*. Oxford: Osprey, 2001.

Grummitt, David. "The Changing Perceptions of the Soldier in Late Medieval England." *The Fifteenth Century* 10 (2011): 189–202.

Henneman, John Bell. "The Military Class and the French Monarchy in the Late Middle Ages." *American Historical Review* 83, no. 4 (1978): 946–65.

King, Andy. "The English Gentry and Military Service, 1300–1450." *History Compass* 12, no. 10 (2014): 759–69.

Michael, Nicholas. *Armies of Medieval Burgundy, 1364–1477*. London: Osprey, 1983.

Nicolle, David. *French Armies of the Hundred Years War*. Men-at-Arms 337. Oxford: Osprey Publishing, 2000.

Payling, Simon. "War and Peace: Military and Administrative Service amongst the English Gentry in the Reign of Henry VI." In *Soldiers, Nobles and Gentlemen: Essays in Honour of Maurice Keen*. Edited by Peter Coss and Christopher Tyerman, 240–58. Woodbridge: Boydell, 2009.

Taylor, Craig. *Chivalry and the Ideals of Knighthood in France during the Hundred Years War*. Cambridge: Cambridge University Press, 2016.

Wright, Nicholas. *Knights and Peasants: The Hundred Years War in the French Countryside*. Woodbridge: Boydell Press, 1998.

———. "Ransoms of Non-Combatants during the Hundred Years War." *Journal of Medieval History* 17, no. 4 (1991): 323–32.

Fortifications and Artillery

Allmand, Christopher T. "New Weapons, New Tactics, 1300–1500." In *The Cambridge Illustrated History of Warfare: The Triumph of the West*. Edited by Geoffrey Parker, 92–105. Cambridge: Cambridge University Press, 1995.

DeVries, Kelly. "Facing the New Technology: Gunpowder Defenses in Military Architecture before the *Trace Italienne*, 1350–1500." In *The Heirs of Archimedes: Science and the Art of War through the Age of Enlightenment*. Edited by Brett D. Steele and Tamera Dorland, 37–71. Cambridge: MIT Press, 2005.

———. "French and English Acceptance of Medieval Gunpowder Weaponry." *Journal of Medieval Military History* 11 (2015): 193–211.

———. "The Impact of Gunpowder Weaponry on Siege Warfare in the Hundred Years War." In *The Medieval City under Siege*. Edited by Ivy A. Corfis and Michael Wolf, 227–44. Woodbridge: Boydell, 1995.

———. "The Technology of Gunpowder Weaponry in Western Europe during the Hundred Years' War." In *XXII. Kongress der Internationalen Kommission für Militärgeschichte* (1997): 285–99.

———. "'The Walls Come Tumbling Down': The Campaigns of Philip the Good and the Myth of Fortification Vulnerability to Early Gunpowder Weapons." In *The Hundred Years War: A Wider Focus*. Edited by L. J. Andrew Villalon and Donald J. Kagay, 429–46. Brill: Leiden, 2005.

Hall, Bert S. *Weapons and Warfare in Renaissance Europe: Gunpowder, Technology, and Tactics*. Baltimore: Johns Hopkins University Press, 1997.

Hoskins, Peter. *Siege Warfare during the Hundred Years War: Once More unto the Breach*. Yorkshire: Pen & Sword Military, 2018.

Kaufmann, J. E., and H. W. Kaufmann. "The End of the Age of Castles, Part II." In *Castle to Fortress: Medieval to Post-Modern Fortifications in the Lands of the Former Roman Empire*, 81–115. Yorkshire: Pen & Sword Military, 2019.

———. *The Medieval Fortress: Castles, Forts and Walled Cities of the Middle Ages*. Cambridge: Da Capo Press, 2001.

Kelly, Jack. "The Most Pernicious Arts." *Gunpowder: Alchemy, Bombards, & Pyrotechnics: The History of the Explosive That Changed the World*, 39–72. New York: Basic Books, 2005.

Lepage, Jean-Denis G. G. "Transitional Fortifications in the 15th and 16th Centuries." In *Castles and Fortified Cities of Medieval Europe: An Illustrated History*, 178–249. Jefferson: McFarland, 2002.

Purton, Peter. "The Early Fifteenth Century: Changing Times." In *A History of the Late Medieval Siege, 1200–1500*, 206–80. Woodbridge: The Boydell Press, 2010.

Rogers, Clifford J. "The Artillery and Artillery Fortress Revolutions Revisited." In *Artil-*

lerie et Fortification, 1200–1600. Edited by Nicolas Prouteau, Emmanuel de Crouy-Chanel, and Nicolas Faucherre, 75–80. Rennes Cedex: Presses Universitaires de Rennes, 2011.

———. "Gunpowder Artillery in Europe, 1326–1500: Innovation and Impact." In *Technology, Violence and War. Essays in Honor of John F. Guilmartin, Jr.* Edited by Robert S. Ehlers Jr., Sarah K. Douglas, and Daniel P. M. Curzo, 39–71. Leiden: Brill, 2019.

———. "The Military Revolutions of the Hundred Years' War." *The Journal of Military History* 57, no. 2 (1993): 241–78.

Smith, Robert Douglas. "Artillery and the Hundred Years War: Myth and Interpretation." In *Arms, Armies, and Fortifications in the Hundred Years War.* Edited by Anne Curry and Michael Hughes, 151–60. Woodbridge: Boydell Press, 1994.

Vale, M. G. A. "New Techniques and Old Ideals: The Impact of Artillery on War and Chivalry at the End of the Hundred Years War." In *War, Literature and Politics in the Late Middle Ages: Essays in Honour of G. W. Coopland.* Edited by C. T. Allmand, 57–72. Liverpool: Liverpool University Press, 1975.

Wolfe, Michael. "*Bonnes Villes* and the Hundred Years' War." In *Walled Towns and the Shaping of France: From the Medieval to the Early Modern Era,* 57–74. New York: Palgrave Macmillan, 2009.

———. "Siege Warfare and the *Bonnes Villes* of France during the Hundred Years War." In *The Medieval City under Siege.* Edited by Michael Wolfe and Ivy A. Corfis, 49–66. Rochester: The Boydel Press, 1999.

Alliances, Treaties, and Peace Conferences

Bonner, Elizabeth. "Scotland's 'Auld Alliance' with France, 1295–1560." *History* 84, no. 273 (1999): 5–30.

Brill, Reginald. "The English Preparations before the Treaty of Arras: A New Interpretation of Sir John Fastolf's 'Report,' September, 1435." *Studies in Medieval and Renaissance History* 7 (1970): 213–47.

Brown, Michael. "French Alliance or English Peace? Scotland and the Last Phase of the Hundred Years War, 1415–53." *The Fifteenth Century* 7 (2007): 81–99.

Curry, Anne. "Two Kingdoms, One King: The Treaty of Troyes (1420) and the Creation of a Double Monarch of England and France." In *"The Contending Kingdoms": France and England 1420–1700.* Edited by Glenn Richardson, 23–42. Aldershot: Ashgate, 2008.

Dickinson, Jocelyne Gledhill. *The Congress of Arras, 1435: A Study in Medieval Diplomacy.* Oxford: Clarendon Press, 1955.

———. "The Congress of Arras, 1435." *History* 40, no. 138–139 (1955): 31–41.

Fowler, Kenneth A. "Truces." In *The Hundred Years War.* Edited by Kenneth Fowler, 184–215. London: Macmillan, 1971.

Lesaffer, R. C. H. "The Concepts of War and Peace in the 15th Century Treaties of Arras." In *Arras et la diplomatie européenne (XVe–XVe siècles).* Edited by Denis Clauzel, Charles Giry-Deloison, and Christopher Leduc, 163–83. Arras: Artois Presses Universitaires, 1999.

Lobanov, Aleksandr. "Anglo-Burgundian Military Cooperation, 1425–1430." PhD dissertation, University of Southampton, 2015.

———. "The Indenture of Philip the Good, Duke of Burgundy, of 12 February 1430 and the Lancastrian Kingdom of France." *English Historical Review* 130, no. 543 (2015): 302–17.

———. "The Treaty of Amiens (1423): Towards a Reconsideration." *Proslogion* 2 (2016): 244–63.

Munro, John H. "An Economic Aspect of the Collapse of the Anglo-Burgundian Alliance, 1428–1442." *English Historical Review* 335 (1970): 225–44.

Rogers, Clifford J. "The Anglo-Burgundian Alliance and Grand Strategy in the Hundred Years War." In *Grand Strategy and Military Alliance.* Edited by Peter R. Mansoor and Williamson Murray, 216–53. Cambridge: Cambridge University Press, 2016.

Rose, Susan. "Triumph and Disaster: Henry V, the Collapse of the Anglo-Burgundian

Alliance and the Resurgence of France." In *Calais: An English Town in France, 1347–1558*, 54–72. Woodbridge: Boydell, 2008.

Vale, M. G. A. "Sir John Fastolf's 'Report' of 1435: A New Interpretation Reconsidered." *Nottingham Mediaeval Studies* 17 (1973): 78–84.

Warner, Mark. "The Anglo-French Dual Monarchy and the House of Burgundy, 1420–1435: The Survival of an Alliance." *French History* 11, no. 2 (1997): 103–30.

Propaganda

Danbury, Elizabeth. "English and French Artistic Propaganda during the Period of the Hundred Years War: Some Evidence from Royal Charters." In *Power, Culture, and Religion in France c.1350–c.1550*. Edited by C. T. Allmand, 75–97. Woodbridge: Boydell, 1989.

Hutchison, Emily J. "Defamation, a Murder *More* Foul?: The 'Second Murder' of Louis, Duke of Orleans (d. 1407) Reconsidered." In *Medieval and Early Modern Murder*. Edited by Larissa Tracy, 254–80. Woodbridge: Boydell, 2018.

———. "'Pour le bien du roy et de son royaume': Burgundian Propaganda under John the Fearless, Duke of Burgundy, 1405–1419." PhD dissertation, University of York, 2006.

———. "Winning Hearts and Minds in Early Fifteenth-Century France: Burgundian Propaganda in Perspective." *French Historical Studies* 35, no. 1 (2012): 3–30.

Lewis, Peter S. "War Propaganda and Historiography in Fifteenth-Century France and England." *Transactions of the Royal Historical Society* 15 (1965): 1–21.

Lutkus, Anne D., and Julia M. Walker. "PR PAS PC: Christine de Pizan's Pro-Joan Propaganda." In *Fresh Verdicts on Joan of Arc*. Edited by Bonnie Wheeler and Charles T. Wood, 145–60. New York: Garland, 1996.

McKenna, J. W. "Henry VI of England and the Dual Monarchy: Aspects of Royal Political Propaganda, 1422–1432." *Journal of the Warburg and Courtauld Institutes* 28 (1965): 145–62.

Pons, Nicole. "Intellectual Patterns and Affective Reactions in Defence of the Dauphin Charles, 1419–1422." In *War, Government and Power in Late Medieval France*. Edited by Christopher Allmand, 54–69. Cambridge: Cambridge University Press, 2000.

Taylor, Craig. "War, Propaganda and Diplomacy in Fifteenth-Century France and England." In *War, Government and Power in Late Medieval France*. Edited by Christopher Allmand, 70–91. Cambridge: Cambridge University Press, 2000.

French Civil War (1407–1435)

Adams, Tracy. "The Armagnac-Burgundian Feud and the Languages of Anger." In *Writing War in Britain and France, 1370–1854: A History of Emotions*. Edited by Stephanie Downes, Andrew Lynch, and Katrina O'Loughlin, 57–72. London: Routledge, 2019.

———. "Feuding, Factionalism and Fictions of National Identity: Reconsidering Charles VII's Armagnacs." *Digital Philology: A Journal of Medieval Cultures* 1, no. 1 (2012): 5–31.

———. "Louis of Orleans, Isabeau of Bavaria, and the Burgundian Propaganda Machine, 1392–1407." In *Character Assassination throughout the Ages*. Edited by Eric Shiraev and Martijn Icks, 121–34. New York: Palgrave Macmillan, 2014.

Hutchison, Emily J. "Knowing One's Place: Space, Violence and Legitimacy in Early Fifteenth-Century Paris." *The Medieval History Journal* 20, no. 1 (2017): 38–88.

———. "Partisan Identity in the French Civil War, 1405–1418: Reconsidering the Evidence on Livery Badges." *Journal of Medieval History* 33, no. 3 (2007): 250–74.

———. "The Politics of Grief in the Outbreak of the Civil War in France, 1407–1413." *Speculum* 91, no. 2 (2016): 422–52.

Knecht, Robert J. "Armagnacs versus Burgundians." In *The Valois: Kings of France, 1328–1589*, 51–64. London: Hambledon Continuum, 2004.

Pollack-Lagushenko, Timur R. "The Armagnac Faction: New Patterns of Political Violence in Late Medieval France." PhD dissertation, Johns Hopkins University, 2003.

Rollo-Koster, Joëlle. "The Great Western Schism, Legitimacy, and Tyrannicide: The Murder of Louis of Orléans (1407)." In *Inventing Modernity in Medieval European Thought, ca. 1100–ca. 1550*. Edited by Bettina Koch and Cary J. Nedermann, 193–211. Kalamazoo: Medieval Institute Publications, 2018.

Slanicka, Simona. "Male Markings: Uniforms in the Parisian Civil War as a Blurring of the Gender Order (A.D. 1410–1420)." *Medieval History Journal* 2, no. 2 (1999): 209–44.

MEDIEVAL

General

Allmand, Christopher, ed. *The New Cambridge Medieval History, Volume VII: c. 1415–c. 1500*. Cambridge: Cambridge University Press, 1998.

Arnold, John H. *What Is Medieval History?* Second edition. Cambridge: Polity Press, 2021.

Classen, Albrecht, ed. *Handbook of Medieval Culture: Fundamental Aspects and Conditions of the European Middle Ages*. Three volumes. Berlin: De Gruyter, 2015.

———, ed. *Handbook of Medieval Studies: Terms–Methods–Trends*. Three volumes. Berlin: De Gruyter, 2010.

Duby, Georges. *France in the Middle Ages, 987–1460: From Hugh Capet to Joan of Arc*. Translated by Juliet Vale. Oxford: Blackwell, 1991.

Jones, Michael, ed. *The New Cambridge Medieval History, Volume VI: c. 1300–c. 1415*. Cambridge: Cambridge University Press, 2000.

Small, Graeme. *Late Medieval France*. Hampshire: Palgrave Macmillan, 2009.

Dictionaries and Encyclopedias

Bjork, Robert E., ed. *The Oxford Dictionary of the Middle Ages*. Four volumes. Oxford: Oxford University Press, 2010.

Carson, Thomas, and Joann Cerrito, eds. *The New Catholic Encyclopedia*. Second edition. Fifteen volumes. Farmington Hills: Gale, 2003.

Corédon, Christopher, and Ann Williams. *A Dictionary of Medieval Terms and Phrases*. Woodbridge: D. S. Brewer, 2004.

Dunphy, Graeme, ed. *Encyclopedia of the Medieval Chronicle*. Two volumes. Leiden: Brill, 2010.

Fritze, Ronald H., and William B. Robison, eds. *Historical Dictionary of Late Medieval England, 1272–1485*. Westport: Greenwood Press, 2002.

Kibler, William W., Grover A. Zinn, and Lawrence Earp, eds. *Medieval France: An Encyclopedia*. New York: Garland, 1995.

Rogers, Clifford J., ed. *The Oxford Encyclopedia of Medieval Warfare and Military Technology*. Three volumes. Oxford: Oxford University Press, 2010.

Strayer, Joseph R., ed. *Dictionary of the Middle Ages*. Thirteen volumes. New York: Charles Scribner's Sons, 1983–2004.

Wagner, John A. *Encyclopedia of the Hundred Years War*. Westport: Greenwood Press, 2006.

Warfare and Technology

Bachrach, Bernard S., and David S. Bachrach. *Warfare in Medieval Europe, c. 400–c. 1453*. Second edition. New York: Routledge, 2021.

Black, Jeremy. "The Medieval Castle." In *Fortifications and Siegecraft: Defense and Attack through the Ages*, 33–63. Lanham: Rowman & Littlefield, 2018.

Bradbury, Jim. *The Medieval Siege*. Woodbridge: The Boydell Press, 1992.

Contamine, Philippe. *War in the Middle Ages*. Translated by Michael Jones. New York: Basil Blackwell, 1984.

Curry, Anne. "Western Europe, 1300–1500." In *War and the Medieval World*. The Cambridge History of War 2. Edited by Anne Curry and David A. Graff, 349–88. Cambridge: Cambridge University Press, 2000.

Davies, Jonathan. *The Medieval Cannon, 1326–1494*. Oxford: Osprey, 2019.

DeVries, Kelly. "The Good, the Bad, and the Intoxicated: Guns in Battle." *Medieval Warfare Special* (2019): 26–39.

———. "Gunpowder Weaponry and the Rise of the Early Modern State." *War in History* 5, no. 2 (1998): 127–45.

DeVries, Kelly, and Robert Douglas Smith. "The Late Middle Ages, 1300–1500." *Medieval Weapons: An Illustrated History of Their Impact*. Santa Barbara: ABC-CLIO, 2007.

———. *Medieval Military Technology*. Second edition. Toronto: University of Toronto Press, 2012.

Hardy, Robert. "From Joan of Arc to Roger Ascham." In *Longbow: A Social and Military History*, 120–35. Fourth edition. Sparkford: Haynes, 2010.

Hindley, Geoffrey. *Medieval Sieges & Siegecraft*. New York: Skyhorse Publishing, 2009.

Keen, Maurice. "The Changing Scene: Guns, Gunpowder, and Permanent Armies." In *Medieval Warfare: A History*. Edited by Maurice Keen, 273–91. Oxford: Oxford University Press, 1999.

Loades, Mike. *The Longbow*. Oxford: Osprey, 2013.

Nicolle, David. *European Medieval Tactics (2): New Infantry, New Weapons 1260–1500*. Oxford: Osprey, 2012.

Nossov, Konstantin. *Ancient and Medieval Siege Weapons: A Fully Illustrated Guide to Siege Weapons and Tactics*. Guilford: The Lyons Press, 2005.

Purton, Peter. "The Late Fifteenth Century I: Britain, France, Central Europe and the Balkans." In *A History of the Late Medieval Siege, 1200–1500*, 281–42. Woodbridge: Boydell Press, 2010.

Rogers, Clifford J. "Gunpowder Artillery in Europe, 1326–1500: Innovation and Impact." In *Technology, Violence, and War: Essays in Honor of Dr. John F. Guilmartin, Jr.* Edited by Robert S. Ehlers Jr., Sarah K. Douglas, and Daniel P. M. Curzon, 37–71. Leiden: Brill, 2019.

Military Writings and Theory

Allmand, Christopher. *The* De Re Militari *of Vegetius: The Reception, Transmission and Legacy of a Roman Text in the Middle Ages*. Cambridge: Cambridge University Press, 2011.

Hall, Bert S. "'So Notable Ordynaunce': Christine de Pizan, Firearms, and Siegecraft in a Time of Transition." In *Cultuurhistorische Caleidoscoop aangeboden aan Prof. Dr. Willy L. Braekman*. Edited by C. De Backer, 219–40. Gent: Stichting Mens en Kultur, 1992.

Le Saux, Françoise. "War and Knighthood in Christine de Pizan's *Livre des faits d'armes et de chevallerie*." In *Writing War: Medieval Literary Responses to Warfare*. Edited by Corinne Saunders, Françoise Le Saux, and Neil Thomas, 93–105. Cambridge: D. S. Brewer, 2004.

Nall, Catherine. "Reading Vegetius in Fifteenth-Century England." In *Reading and War in Fifteenth-Century England: From Lydgate to Malory*, 11–47. Cambridge: D. S. Brewer, 2012.

Nicholson, Helen. *Medieval Warfare: Theory and Practice of War in Europe, 300–1500*. Gordonsville: Palgrave, 2004.

Whetham, David. *Just Wars and Moral Victories: Surprise, Deception and the Normative Framework of European War in the Later Middle Ages*. Leiden: Brill, 2009.

Nationalism

Allmand, Christopher. "National Reconciliation in France at the End of the Hundred Years War." *Journal of Medieval Military History* 6 (2008): 149–70.

Green, David. "National Identities and the Hundred Years War." *Fourteenth Century England* 6 (2010): 115–29.

Universities

Brockliss, L. W. B. "Patterns of Attendance at the University of Paris, 1400–1800." *The Historical Journal* 21, no. 3 (1978): 503–44.

Cobban, A. B. "Paris: Magisterial Archetype." In *The Medieval Universities: Their Development and Organization*, 75–95. London: Methuen, 1975.

Gabriel, Astrik L. "Intellectual Relations between the University of Louvain and the University of Paris in the 15th Century." In *The Universities in the Late Middle Ages*. Edited by Jozef Ijsewijn and Jacques Paquet, 82–132. Louvain: Leuven University Press, 1978.

Kibre, Pearl. *Scholarly Privileges in the Middle Ages: The Rights, Privileges, and Immunities, of Scholars and Universities at Bologna, Padua, Paris, and Oxford*. Cambridge: Mediaeval Academy of America, 1962.

Ridder-Symoens, Hilde de, ed. *A History of the University in Europe*. Volume 1: *Universities in the Middle Ages*. Cambridge: Cambridge University Press, 1992.

Skoda, Hannah. "Student Violence in Fifteenth-Century Paris and Oxford." In *Aspects of Violence in Renaissance Europe*. Edited by Jonathan Davies, 17–40. London: Routledge, 2016.

Verger, Jacques. "The University of Paris at the End of the Hundred Years' War." In *Universities in Politics: Case Studies from the Late Middle Ages and Early Modern Period*. Edited by John W. Baldwin, 47–78. Baltimore: John Hopkins University Press, 1972.

Weisheipl, James A. "The Structure of the Arts Faculty in the Medieval University." *British Journal of Education Studies* 19, no. 3 (1971): 263–71.

Church History, Heresy, Inquisition

Arnold, John. "Inquisition, Texts and Discourse." In *Texts and the Repression of Medieval Heresy*. Edited by Peter Biller and Caterina Bruschi, 63–80. Woodbridge: York Medieval Press, 2002.

Biller, Peter. "Christians and Heretics." In *Christianity in Western Europe, c. 1100–c. 1500*. The Cambridge History of Christianity 4. Edited by Miri Rubin and Walter Simons, 170–86. Cambridge: Cambridge University Press, 2009.

———. "Through a Glass Darkly: Seeing Medieval Heresy." In *The Medieval World*. Second edition. Edited by Peter Linehan, Janet L. Nelson, and Marios Costambeys, 345–67. London: Routledge, 2018.

Christianson, Gerald, Thomas M. Izbicki, and Christopher M. Bellitto, eds. *The Church, the Councils, & Reform: The Legacy of the Fifteenth Century*. Washington: The Catholic University of America Press, 2008.

Coakley, John. "Friars as Confidants of Holy Women in Medieval Dominican Hagiography." In *Images of Sainthood in Medieval Europe*. Edited by Renate Blumenfeld-Kosinski and Timia Szell, 222–46. Ithaca: Cornell University Press, 1991.

Cox, Roy. "The Hundred Years War and the Church." In *The Hundred Years War Revisited*. Edited by Anne Curry, 85–110. London: Red Globe Press, 2019.

Kelly, Henry Ansgar. "Inquisition and the Prosecution of Heresy: Misconceptions and Abuses." *Church History* 58 (1989): 439–51.

Kieckhefer, Richard. "The Office of Inquisition and Medieval Heresy: The Transition from Personal to Institutional Jurisdiction." *Journal of Ecclesiastical History* 46, no. 1 (1995): 36–61.

Logan, F. Donald. *A History of the Church in the Middle Ages*. London: Routledge, 2002.

Lynch, Joseph H., and Phillip C. Adamo. *The Medieval Church: A Brief History*. Second edition. London: Routledge, 2014.

Meyer, Andreas. "Papal Monarchy." In *A Companion to the Medieval World*. Edited by Carol Lansing and Edward D. English, 372–96. Malden: Wiley-Blackwell, 2009.

Müller, Heribert. "France and the Council." In *A Companion to the Council of Basel*. Edited by Michiel Decaluwe, Thomas M. Izbicki, and Gerald Christianson, 377–409. Leiden: Brill, 2017.

Stump, Phillip H. "The Council of Constance (1414–18) and the End of the Schism." In *A Companion to the Great Western Schism (1378–1417)*. Edited by Joëlle Rollo-Koster and Thomas M. Izbicki, 395–442 Leiden: Brill, 2009.

Thomsett, Michael C. *Heresy in the Roman Catholic Church: A History*. Jefferson: McFarland, 2011.

Van Engen, John. "The Church in the Fifteenth Century." In *Handbook of European His-*

tory 1400–1600: Late Middle Ages, Renaissance and Reformation. Volume 1. Edited by Oberman Thomas A. Brady Jr., Heiko A. Oberman, and James D. Tracy, 303–30. Leiden: Brill, 1994.

———. "Multiple Options: The World of the Fifteenth-Century Church." *Church History* 77, no. 2 (2008): 257–84.

ONLINE RESOURCES

The International Joan of Arc Society by Bonnie Wheeler: http://www.joanofarcsociety.org/.

Joan of Arc Archive by Allen Williamson: https://archive.joan-of-arc.org/.

The Soldier in Later Medieval England by Adrian R Bell, Anne Curry, Andy King, David Simpkin, and Aleksandr Lobanov: https://www.medievalsoldier.org/.

NON-ENGLISH SOURCES

Printed Medieval Sources Focused Primarily on Joan of Arc

Doncoeur, Paul, and Yvonne Lanhers, eds. *Documents et recherches relatifs à Jeanne la Pucelle*. Five volumes. Paris: Desclee de Brouwer, 1961.

Duparc, Pierre, ed. *Procès en nullité de la condamnation de Jeanne d'Arc*. Five volumes. Paris: Librairie C. Klincksieck, 1977–1989.

Quicherat, Jules, ed. *Procès de condamnation et de réhabilitation de Jeanne d'Arc. dite la Pucelle. Publiés pour la première fois d'après les manuscrits de la Bibliothèque Nationale, suivis de tous les documents historiques qu'on a pu réunir et accompagnées de notes et d'éclaircissements*. Five volumes. Paris: Jules Renouard, 1841–1849.

Tisset, Pierre, and Yvonne Lanhers, eds. and trans. *Procès de condamnation de Jeanne d'Arc*. Three volumes. Paris: Librairie C. Klincksieck, 1960–1971.

Medieval Chronicles and Journals

Basin, Thomas. *Histoire de Charles VII*. Edited by Charles Samaran and Henry de Surirey de Saint-Remy. Two volumes. Paris: Société d'édition Les Belles Lettres, 1933–1945.

Chartier, Jean. *Chronique de Charles VII: roi de France*. Three volumes. Paris: P. Jannet, 1858.

Chronique de Jean le Fèvre Seigneur de Saint Rémy. Second volume. Edited by François Morand. Paris: Librairie Renouard, 1881.

Chroniques de Perceval de Cagny. Paris: Société de l'Histoire de France, 1902.

Gruel, Guillaume. *Chronique d'Arthur de Richemont connétable de France, duc de Bretagne (1393–1458)*. Edited by A. Le Vavasseur. Paris: H. Laurens, 1890.

Journal du siege d'Orleans, 1429–1431. Edited by Paul Charpentier and Charles Cuissard. Orléans: Herluison, 1896.

Biographies

Jarry, Louis. "Biographiques sur les capitaines anglais du siège d'Orléans." In *Le Compte de l'armée anglaise au siège d'Orléans*, 205–26. Orléans: Herluison, 1892.

Liocourt, Ferdinand de. *La Mission de Jeanne d'Arc*. Two volumes. Paris: Nouvelles Éditions Latines, 1981.

Dictionaries and Encyclopedias

Ambrogi, Pascal-Raphaël, and Dominique Le Tourneau. *Dictionnaire encyclopédique de Jeanne d'Arc*. Paris: Desclée de Brouwer, 2017.

Contamine, Philippe, Olivier Bouzy, and Xavier Hélary. *Jeanne d'Arc: Histoire et dictionnaire*. Paris: Robert Laffont, 2012.

Online Sources

Ste Jeanne d'Arc: http://www.stejeannedarc.net/.

Index

12 Articles. *See* twelve articles
70 Articles. *See* seventy articles
100 Years War. *See* Hundred Years War

abbot, 9, 38, 76, 83, 170
abjuration of Joan of Arc, 9–10, 12, 30–31, 32, 35, 43, 46, 51, 53, 57, 59, 60, 62, 66–67, 69, 75, 76, 81, 83, 87, 99, 102, 123, 126, 138, 139, 142, 144, 178, 183, 184, 189, 191, 192, 203, 217, 219, 222
Achilles, 202
admiral of France, 71, 124, 197
Agde, 56
age of Joan of Arc, 10, 19, 36
Agincourt, 1, 4n1, 11, 18, 27, 30, 40, 52, 56, 60, 75, 85, 91, 100, 105, 121, 135, 146, 151, 157, 167, 179, 181, 189, 193, 197, 215, 216, 222. *See also* Hundred Years War
Agnes of Burgundy, 60
Albret, Charles II d' (?-1471), 10–11, 21, 34, 38, 63, 68, 98, 117–118, 121, 127, 131–132, 148, 187–188, 200
Alençon, John II, Duke of (C. 1409–1476), 3, 11–12, 21, 35, 40, 43, 45, 53, 56, 60, 63, 68, 70, 75, 85, 94, 103, 108, 111–112, 113, 115, 119, 121, 122, 145–146, 148, 152, 158, 162, 169–170, 175, 181, 197, 199, 200, 201, 204, 215–216, 218, 225; and the Loire Campaign, 31, 134–135, 143–144, 163
Alespée, Jean, 12
Allemagne. *See* Holy Roman Empire
Alnwick, William, 12
American Revolutionary War, 118
Amiens, 13, 69, 70
Amiens, Treaty of, 13, 33, 39, 40, 164

Angela of Foligno, 219
Angers, 83, 147; and the University of, 162
Anglo-Armagnac Alliance. *See* Bourges, treaty of
Anglo-Burgundian Alliance, 13–15, 18, 19, 31, 32–34, 41, 47, 50, 52, 65, 71, 75, 88, 101, 130, 144, 147, 165, 166, 178, 181, 207, 215, 216, 222, 227
Anglo-Scottish Truce. *See* Durham, treaty of
Anjou, 29, 75, 86, 96, 137, 179–180, 227
Anjou, Marie of. *See* Marie of Anjou
Anjou, René of. *See* René of
Anne of Burgundy, Duchess of Bedford, 13–15, 33, 46, 61, 164–165, 192, 217
Anthon, battle of, 15
Appellate Trial. *See* Nullification Proceedings
apostate, 15, 18, 59, 66, 83, 101–102, 107, 109, 180–181, 191, 209–210
Aragonois, François l', 187
Arc, Catherine d', 15–17, 46, 63,
Arc, Isabelle d', Rommée, 16–17, 39, 113, 154, 157, 162
Arc, Jacquemin d' (C. 1392 - C. 1450), 16
Arc, Jacques d' (?-C. 1439), 16–17, 28, 45, 74, 103, 125, 214
Arc, Jean d', Du Lys (?-C. 1476), 17, 19
Arc, Pierre d', Du Lys (?-C. 1478), 17, 19, 157–158, 221
archbishop, 17, 26, 34, 49, 87, 94, 135, 139, 154, 177; and the Coronation of Charles VII, 67–68. *See also* Chartres, Regnault of; Estouteville, Guillaume d'; Juvénal des Ursins, Jean; Roussel, Raoul
Aristotle, 79
Armagnac, Bernard VII, count of, 18, 91, 119
Armagnac, Bonne d', 18, 91, 160

INDEX

Armagnac, Jean IV, the count of, 18, 69, 168, 191; and correspondence with Joan of Arc, 64, 128, 131, 146
Armagnac, Termes d'. *See* Termes, Thibaut de
Armagnacs, 38, 48–49, 60, 88–89, 91, 105, 110, 160, 181, 185, 189, 216; and the origin of the term along with its misuse in the fifteenth century through today, 18–19.
Armenia, 38
Armoises, Claude des, 17, 19, 157, 174
Arras, Franquet d', 124, 176
Arras, Congress of. *See* Arras, Treaty of
Arras, Treaty of, 12, 14, 19–20, 31, 34, 41, 49, 55, 56, 70, 81, 86, 92, 98, 106, 110, 118, 119, 122, 125, 138, 144, 158, 161, 165, 166, 169, 180, 181, 198, 209
Arras, Peace of, 20, 91, 165
artillery, 20–22. *See also* battle; siege
assessor, 183–184; and assessors at Joan of Arc's condemnation trial, 26–27, 31–32, 56–57, 69–70, 76, 98, 104–105, 120, 125–126, 135, 142–143, 145, 196
Astesan, Antoine, 22, 37
Attila, 157
Auld Alliance. *See* Franco-Scottish Alliance
Aulon, Jean d', 10, 22–23, 50, 109, 113, 117, 136, 147–148, 154–155, 188, 195, 217, 218, 221, 227
Auxerre, 38, 178
Auxerre, Treaty of., 91. *See also* Bourges, Treaty of
Avignon, Marie Robine d', 171

bailiff, 25, 124, 176, 188, 191; and people with the title, 29, 36, 49, 88, 113, 147, 176, 187, 203, 225
bailli. *See* bailiff
banner, 62, 68, 87, 170, 196–197
Bar, Jean de, 182
Baretta, Bartolomeo, 25
Baron, 25; and people with the title, 73, 119, 173–175, 190–191, 201
Basel, Council of, 32, 49, 59, 69, 115, 135, 144; and suggestions that Joan of Arc appeal to, 120, 126
Basin, Thomas, 25–26, 29, 35, 48, 68, 79, 159
Basset, Jean, 26–27

Bastard, 27. *See also* Orléans, bastard of; Wandomme, Guillaume; Wavrin, Jean de
Bastard of Orléans. *See* Orléans, bastard of
bastille. *See* Compiégne, siege of; siege; Orléans, siege of
battle, 27–28. *See also* siege
Baudricourt, Robert de, 16, 28–29, 51, 55, 61, 75, 89, 102, 103, 125, 127, 136, 138, 141, 143, 145, 146, 151, 169, 171, 179, 180, 191, 194, 195, 199, 209, 214, 227
Baugé, battle of, 29, 32, 52, 90, 91, 100, 106, 118, 119, 158, 189
Bayeux, 45, 54, 55, 82
Bayonne, 214
Beaucaire, 23, 118
Beauchamp, Richard. *See* Warwick, Richard Beauchamp, earl of
Beauchamp, Thomas, 221
Beaufort, Henry, 30–31, 100–101, 103, 148, 152, 166, 182,
Beaufort, Joan, 77
Beaufort, John, duke of Somerset, 29, 77
Beaugency, battle of, 31, 35, 38, 55, 111, 119, 134, 144, 160, 163, 181, 189, 190, 194, 201
Beaumont, 48, 87
Beaupère, Jean, 31–32, 142, 153–154, 183
Beaurevior, tower of, 46, 81–82, 108, 138
Beauvais, 26, 31, 35, 45, 48, 65, 82, 113, 119, 124, 126, 176, 205–206
Bede, 170
Bedford, John of Lancaster, duke of, 32–34
Belgium, 88
Benedicite. *See* Estivet, Jean d'
Benedict XIII, Pope, 47, 97
Benedictine Order. *See* friar
Benefice, 34
Bermont Chapel, 74
Bernard VII, count of Armagnac. *See* Armagnac, Bernard VII, count of
Bernardine of Siena, 112
Berri, Herald of. *See* Bouvier, Gilles le
Berry, 34, 37, 38, 62, 75, 97–98, 117, 121, 143, 225
Berwoit, John 46, 183
Béthune, Jeanne de, 138
Béziers, 83
Bicêtre, peace of, 91
birth year of Joan of Arc. *See* age

bishop, 17, 34–35, 65, 109, 177, 204; and people in the role, 12, 26, 30–31, 33, 47–49, 55–56, 76, 82, 83, 97, 100, 113, 115, 126, 135, 137, 138, 149, 152, 154, 168, 176, 183, 187, 205–206, 212
blasphemy, 35, 62, 163, 209
Blois, 31, 35, 119, 128, 158, 160, 174
Bohemia, 30, 38, 69, 103, 132,
Boisguillaume. *See* Colles, Guillaume
bombard. *See* artillery
Bosquier, Pierre, 35–36, 92, 127
Boucher, Pierre, 144
Bouillé, Guillaume, 36, 83, 153
Boulainvilliers, Perceval de, 10, 22, 36–37, 218
boulevard, 40, 64–65, 70, 160
Bourbon, 75, 188
Bourbon, Charles I, duke of. *See* Clermont, Charles I, count of
Bourbon, John, duke of. *See* Clermont, John, count of
Bourgeois de Paris, Journal d'un, 10, 15, 18, 19, 29, 37, 49, 87, 97, 108, 110, 180, 219
Bourges, 34, 36, 37–38, 40, 51, 54, 57, 98, 117, 143, 161, 167, 188
Bourges, Treaty of, 38
Boussac, Marshal de. *See* Brosse, Jean de
Bouvier, Gilles le, 10, 38, 62, 117, 121–122, 138, 181, 187
Bower, Walter, 38–39, 182
Bréhal, Jean, 39, 51, 83, 121, 149, 153–154, 171, 184, 198, 219
Bretons. *See* Brittany
Bridget of Sweden, 95, 198, 219
Brittany, 39–40, 75, 88, 89, 124, 133, 173, 181, 202, 213. *See also* Brittany, Jean V, duke of
Brittany, Jean V, duke of, 13, 18, 33, 40, 52, 91, 103, 121, 139, 164, 181, 227
Brosse, Jean de, 40–41, 68, 71, 141, 148
Bruges, 198, 216
Buckingham, 196
Bulgnéville, battle of, 29, 179
Burgundy, 41
Buzançais, Treaty of. *See* Bourges, Treaty of
Byzantine, 20, 60

Cabochian Revolt, 48, 91
Caen, 26, 123, 152; and the University of, 49, 81, 221

Caesar, 55, 86, 157
Cagny, Perceval de, 10, 11, 43, 64, 87, 94, 108, 111, 117, 122, 123, 148
Calais, 89, 91, 100, 101, 105, 158, 196, 198, 221
Calixtus III, Pope, 113, 168
Calot, Laurent, 43, 139
caltrop, 44, 104, 107
camp followers, 11, 44–45, 70, 99, 199
Canivet, Gilles, 165
canon, 45
canon law, 45–46, 79–81
cannon, 12, 20–22, 71, 159, 190
captivity of Joan of Arc, 46
capture. *See* Compiégne, Siege of
cardinal of England. *See* Beaufort, Henry
Castel, Étienne du, 166
Castillon, battle of, 27, 50, 106, 194, 201, 202, 225
Catherine, Saint, 35, 46–47, 57, 80, 82, 85, 107, 108–109, 140, 144, 189, 197–199, 209, 218–219
Catherine de La Rochelle, 47, 128, 180, 189
Catherine of Siena, 219
Catherine of Valois, 13, 17, 29, 32, 47, 52, 60, 91, 100–101, 106, 100, 124, 166, 201, 208, 213, 221
Cauchon, Pierre, 30, 47–49, 57, 61, 63, 65–67, 68, 69, 74, 76, 82, 83–84, 97, 98, 118, 126, 127, 135, 139, 141, 154, 166, 168, 176, 182, 183–184, 204, 205, 205–207; and the abjuration of Joan of Arc, 9, 30, 35; and contemporary commentary on him, 35, 39, 87, 104, 120, 123, 154, 222; and his jurisdiction for the trial of Joan of Arc, 26, 33, 35, 48–49, 80, 109, 152, 212; and the ransom of Joan of Arc, 35, 41, 48, 65, 138, 176, 221; and the rumor of his desecrated grave, 137; and the Treaty of Arras, 49; and the University of Paris, 31, 35, 47, 65, 97
Chabannes, Antoine de, 49–50
Chabannes, Jacques de, 50, 88
Châteaudun, 107
chamberlain, 50, 83; and people who served as, 36, 70, 107, 121, 137, 159, 222
Chambéry, truce of, 50, 52, 56, 97, 117, 164
Champion des dames, 198
Chapitault, Simon, 50–51, 154, 170
Charité. *See* La Charité, siege of

Charlemagne, 51, 103, 137, 189, 218
Charles, Simon, 29, 51, 93, 145, 208
Charles II, duke of Lorraine. *See* Lorraine, Charles II, duke of
Charles V, 41, 51, 73, 117, 161, 166, 176, 213,
Charles VI, 51–52
Charles VII, 52–54
Charles VIII, 213
Chartier, Alain, 38, 54–55
Chartier, Guillaume, 50, 55, 154
Chartier, Jean, 10, 38, 45, 55, 58, 68, 108, 121, 123–124, 148, 200
Chartres, 17, 203
Chartres, Peace of, 91
Chartres, Regnault of, 17, 53, 55–56, 68, 87–88, 89, 94, 122
Chastellain, Georges, 18, 56, 123–124, 165
Châtillon, Jean Hulot de, 56–57, 59, 66, 99, 102, 184
chausse-trape. *See* caltrop
China, 20
Chinon, 10, 11, 51, 53, 57–58, 75, 93, 94, 121, 136, 147, 158, 162, 168, 173, 179, 203, 215, 217; and Robert de Baudricourt sends Joan of Arc to, 28–29, 125, 136, 138, 146, 171, 227; and the journey to, 17, 29, 41, 55, 61, 99, 103, 127, 143, 169, 199
Chronique de Jean Chartier. See Chartier, Jean
Chronique de La Pucelle, 44, 51, 58, 104, 107, 108, 113, 128, 137, 148, 194, 207, 217
Chronique de l'établissement de la fête du 8 Mai, 58, 147, 157, 190
Chronique dite des Cordeliers, 58, 73, 82
Chronique ou Mémoire sur l'institution de la Toison d'Or, 188
Chroniques de Charles VII. See Bouvier, Giles le
Church Militant, 9, 27, 39, 57, 58–59, 60, 66, 69, 98, 118, 126, 142, 184, 210
Church Triumphant, 58–59
Ciboule, Robert, 59–60
civil law, 60, 79–81
Clarence, Thomas, duke of, 29, 32, 38, 85, 100, 124, 189
Classidas. *See* Glasdale, William
Clement V, Pope, 157

Clement VIII, Antipope, 18
clerk, 86–87, 100, 134, 166, 183
Clermont, 119, 132, 200
Clermont, Charles I, count of, 49, 60–61, 68, 102, 148, 169
Clermont, John, duke of Bourbon, count of, 18, 60, 91
Clermont-en-Beauvaisis, 119
clothing of Joan of Arc, 61–62
Clovis I, 67, 157, 161, 177
coat of arms, *62*–63, 196
Colin, 15, 63
Colles, Guillaume, 63, 104, 135, 139, 143, 145, 183, 202, 205, 217
companion in arms, 63; of Joan of Arc, 11, 15, 40, 50, 71, 93, 135, 143, 158, 169, 173, 181, 225
Compiégne, siege of, 2, 10, 14, 18, 55, 64–65, 82, 124, 138, 148, 163, 164–165, 193, 216; and contemporary histories on, 38, 39, 55, 86–87, 113, 147, 182, 188; and gunpowder artillery at, 20–21 and Joan of Arc captured outside of, 10, 30, 33, 40, 41, 46, 47, 48, 53, 61, 64–65, 69, 75, 87–88, 92, 95, 104, 106, 113, 119, 122, 123, 133, 137–138, 162, 167, 174, 176, 197, 200, 212, 221, 227; and the relief of, 40, 49–50, 65, 87–88, 106, 146, 214, 215, 225; and those captured alongside Joan of Arc, 17, 22, 195, 225; and those who were present at, 17, 23, 25, 50, 56, 189, 196, 214, 215
condemnation trial of Joan of Arc, 9–10, 46, 48–49, 65–67, 79–80, 83–84, 109, 126–127, 165–166, 183–184, 191–192, 204, 205–207, 209–210
Constance, council of, 30, 48, 69, 94, 95, 97, 132, 168, 191
coronation of Charles VII, 67–68. *See also* Reims, march to
coulovrine. *See* artillery
council, ecclesiastical, 45, 69, 101, 177, 101, 177. *See also* Basel, Constance, Pavia-Siena
count, 69
Coutances, 76, 135, 153, 154
Courcelles, Thomas de, 57, 66–67, 69–70, 135, 140, 144, 154, 184, 192, 204, 205–207, 209
Couserans, 83

270

Coutes, Jeanne de, 107
Coutes, Louis de, 45, 70, 80, 107, 119, 197, 199, 217
Craon, Jean de, 173–174
Cravant, battle of, 13–14, 27, 52, 70–71, 90, 91–92, 96, 97, 106, 148, 163, 164, 189, 190, 197, 222, 225
Crecy, battle of, 105, 193
Crépy-en-Valois, 64
Cruisy, Jean de, 153
Culant, Louis de, 40, 68, 71
culverine. *See* artillery

dauphin, 73
Dauphiné, 15, 73, 93, 118, 203–204
dauphinists, 2, 18, 29, 73–74
De mirabilia victoria, 198
De puella aurelianensi dissertatio, 95
De quadam puella, 74, 97
Deborah, 59–60, 95, 198, 202
Desjardins, Guillaume, 165–166
Digne, 83
Diocletian, 187
Dissertatio. See Gélu, Jacques
Ditié de Jehanne d'Arc, 167, 202
doctor. *See* Physicians
Dominican Order, 35, 39, 76, 77, 92, 109, 120, 123, 126, 191, 205
Domremy, 16, 28, 36, 39, 46, 51, 63, 70, 74–75, 81, 85, 125, 136, 140, 151–152, 182, 214, 217
Dreux, 197
dual monarchy,
Duchemin, Jean, 75, 149
Dunois, Jean, count of. *See* Orléans, Jean, bastard of
duke, 75–76
Dupuy, Jean, 76
Duremort, Gilles de, 76, 104
Durham, Treaty of, 76–77, 90, 216
Duval, Guillaume, 77, 118, 120, 153, 222
Dynter, Edmund de, 108

earl. *See* count
ecclesiastical law. *See* canon law
education of Joan of Arc's judges and assessors, 79–80
Edward III, 68, 77, 105, 177
Embrun, 56, 94,
English, 80

ennoblement of Joan of Arc, 17, 62–63, 80–81, 139, 143, 196
Epistola de puella, 54–55
Érard, Guillaume, 9, 66, 81, 142, 178, 204
Érault, Jean, 81, 128, 171, 203
escape attempt, Joan of Arc's, 10, 35, 46, 47, 80, 81–82, 108, 189, 204, 209, 219, 221; and *Chronique dite des Cordeliers'* account, 58, 82
esquire, 96, 143, 195–196
estates general, 57
Esther, 202
Estivet, Jean d', 45, 82, 118, 120, 141, 154, 166, 183, 192, 203, 222
Estouteville, Guillaume d', 36, 39, 82–83, 121, 135, 153, 169, 170, 184–185
Euclid, 79
Eugene IV, Pope, 83, 168
Évrard, Guillaume. *See* Érard, Guillaume
examiner, 118, 126, 183
executioner, 19, 84, 142, 183
execution of Joan of Arc, 83–84
executor of mandates, 126, 141, 183
executor of writs, 183

Fabri, Jean. *See* Le Fèvre, Jean
fairy tree in Domremy, 39, 74, 85, 169
Falaise, 152, 201, 202
False Joan of Arc. *See* Armoises, Claude des
Fastolf, John, 85–86, 179, 190, 215, 222; and the battle of the Herrings, 102; and the Loire Campaign, 36, 130, 134–135, 144, 163, 201, 223
Fauquembergue, Clément de, 29, 37, 61, 68, 86–87, 108, 179, 199
Ferrebouc, François, 153
Favé, Jean, 87, 112, 140
Flanders, 64, 89, 204, 207
Flavy, Guillaume de, 64, 87–88
Fontaines, Riguard de, 88
France, 88–89
Franciscan Order, 92, 109, 151, 180
Franco-Burgundian Truce, 14, 50, 53, 56, 58, 64, 89, 92, 94, 121–122, 131, 132, 138, 146, 148, 152, 178, 215, 218
Franco-Scottish Alliance, 29, 56, 90, 115, 137
French Civil War, 90–92
French Revolution, 73, 94, 128, 200
Fresnay, 96

friar, 92, 109; and people with the title, 35, 39, 76, 77, 97, 120, 123, 126, 162, 191, 205. *See also* Richard, Friar.
Frontinus, 167

Gabriel, Saint, 93, 144, 189, 197
Gascony, 105–106, 199, 159, 202, 225,
Garde Écossaise, 93
Garter, Order of the, 30, 86, 163, 189, 190, 197, 201
Gastinel, Denis, 46
Gaucourt, Raoul de, 15, 57, 93–94, 122, 169; and negotiations with Philip the Good, 56, 89
Gélu, Jacques, 62, 94–95
Geoffrey of Monmouth, 170
George III, 105, 209
Germany, 167. *See also* Holy Roman Empire
Gerson, Jean, 95–96, 219; and misattributed works, 74; and *Super facto puellae et credulitate sibi praestanda*, 76, 198–199, 219
Gideon, 194, 202
Gien, 178, 207, 130
Gien, League of, 18, 91, 160
Gilles de Rais. *See* Rais, Gilles de
Giresme, Nicolas de, 96
Giustiniani, Pancrazio, 46
Glasdale, William, 37, 96, 120, 130, 160, 195–196
Gloucester, Humphrey, duke of, 31, 124, 190
goddam, 96
Gorkum, Henry of, 74, 96–97, 199
grand chamberlain. *See* chamberlain
Graverent, Jean, 35–36, 47, 97, 109, 126, 154, 181, 219
Great Schism, 30, 47, 69, 95, 97, 168
Gregory XII, Pope, 47, 97
Gressart, Perrinet, 34, 37–38, 97–98, 117–118, 122, 187–188
Grey, John, 46, 183
Grouchet, Richard de, 76, 98, 143
guards of Joan of Arc at Rouen. *See* roles and responsibilities
Guise, 138, 179
guns. *See* artillery
Guyenne, 38, 91, 181
Guyenne, Dauphin Louis, duke of, 91, 181, 216

hair, Joan of Arc's, 99–100, 132; and criticism of, 15, 57, 107; and support of, 95–96, 198; and its shaving after her abjuration, 9, 126
Hannibal, 55
Harfleur, 32, 83, 93, 100, 105, 152, 192, 216, 221
Hector, 55, 202
Henry II, 162
Henry IV, 30, 32, 38, 90, 91, 100, 105, 124, 181, 189, 221
Henry V, 100
Henry VI, 100–101
Henry VII, 182
heretic, 12, 36, 48, 49, 66, 69, 70, 75, 81, 98, 101–102, 107, 109, 127, 140, 145, 149, 180, 184, 191, 192, 209, 219. *See also* relapse; Richard, Friar
Herrings, battle of the, 27, 28, 37, 53, 90, 102–103, 115, 147, 148, 160, 163, 194; and participants at, 29, 40, 50, 60, 71, 86, 118, 119, 158, 179, 189, 203, 225
Heudicourt, 183
History of the Kings of Britain, 170
Holy Roman Empire, 41, 54, 59, 73, 103, 105, 136, 165, 214
horses: and Joan of Arc's interactions with them, 44, 64, 103–104, 107, 221; and those who contributed horses to Joan of Arc, 11, 29, 70, 125, 127, 136, 214
Houppeville, Nicolas de, 76, 104–105, 118, 120, 126, 167, 222
Hundred Years War, 105–106
Huss, John, 48, 69, 132
Hussites, 30, 97, 103, 112, 128, 132–133, 146, 148, 163, 169

idolater, 10, 101, 109, 192, 209
Île-de-France, 119
The Iliad, 202
Illiers, Florent d', 50, 107
illiteracy of Joan of Arc. *See* literacy
injuries of Joan of Arc, 44, 107–109, 111, 122–123, 160, 162
inquisition, 109
Isabeau of Bavaria, 48, 52, 109–110, 139, 177, 194–195
Isabella of Bavaria. *See* Isabeau of Bavaria

Islam, 20, 93, 144
Italy, 25, 36–37, 47, 54, 207, 214
Ivry, 181, 215

James I of Scotland, 38–39, 76–77, 90, 137
Janville, 111, 135, 163, 190
Jargeau, battle of, 21, 80, 111–112, 123, 134, 175, 194; and contemporary accounts of, 43, 86, 147, 148, 188; and participants at, 11, 12, 49, 94, 115, 174–175, 189, 197–198
Jargeau, Manifesto of, 91
Jean de Saint-Michel. *See* Kirkmichael, John of
Jean Lèfevre de Saint-Remy. *See* Saint-Remy, Jean Lèfevre de
Jerusalem, 30, 96, 180, 189
"Jesus Mary", 2, 35, 87, 112, 134, 182, 197, 209
John of Bridlington, 170
John the Fearless, 13–14, 18, 20, 30, 38, 41, 48, 50, 52, 60, 75, 91, 93, 95, 100, 105, 110, 121, 136, 137, 139, 145, 160, 164, 208, 211
John of Lancaster. *See* Bedford, John, duke of
John XII, Pope, 103
Joshua, 202
Journal du siège d'Orléans, 112–113; and its accounts, 21, 44, 68, 71, 96, 102, 104, 107, 119, 128, 148, 158, 190, 194, 197, 198, 199; as a source for other contemporary writings, 58, 147
judge. *See* roles
Judith, 202
Julian of Norwich, 219
Juvénal des Ursins, Jacques, 56
Juvénal des Ursins, Jean, 17, 23, 51–52, 113, 209, 215

Katherine, Saint. *See* Catherine, Saint
Katherine of Valois. *See* Catherine of Valois
Kirkmichael, John of, 115
knight, 115, 196; and people with the title, 36, 51, 85, 88, 96, 135–136, 137–138, 139, 179, 189, 190, 192, 201. *See also* Garter, Order of the; squire

La Brossinière, battle of, 52, 92, 106
La Chambre, Guillaume de, 9–10, 144, 165–166, 178, 222
La Charité, 34, 37–38, 50, 97–98, 187
La Charité, siege of, 47, 98, 117–118, 132, 188; and participants at, 11–12, 40
La Crique, Petrus de, 170
La Fayette, Gilbert Motier de, 29, 118, 141
La Fayette, Marquis de, 118
La Fontaine, Jean de, 118, 126, 183, 222
La Gravelle, battle of, 124
La Hire, 57, 118–119, 174, *226*; and blasphemy, 35; and his service in warfare, 11, 29, 49, 88, 93, 102, 135, 138, 148, 215, 225; and the Loire Campaign, 111–112, 134, 143, 163, 203; and the siege of Orléans, 158
La Mare, Simon de, 165
La Pierre, Isambard de, 10, 30–31, 59, 62, 77, 81, 104, 112, 118, 120, 126, 153, 222
La Pole, Alexander de, 130
La Pole, John de, 130
La Pole, Michael II de, 197
La Pole, William de. *See* Suffolk, William de La Pole, earl of
la Pucelle, 61, 99, 120–121; and Joan of Arc's use of the name, 45, 151, 171, 194, 216–217, 227
La Réole, siege of, 119
La Rochelle, Catherine de. *See* Catherine de La Rochelle
La Rose, Philippe de, 83, 121, 153
La Trémoille, Georges de, 11, 97, 98, 117, 118, 121–122, 148, 169–170, 173, 187–188; as an antagonist to Joan of Arc, 43, 94; and the Franco-Burgundian Truce, 53, 56, 89, 94; and his disputes with Arthur de Richemont, 14, 68, 181–182, 227
ladies' tree. *See* fairy tree
ladder, 3, 104, 108, 111, 122–123, 188, 194,
Ladvenu, Martin, 10, 81, 83, 104, 120, 123, 138, 153, 192, 205, 222
Lagny, 136
Lagny, battle of, 28, 56, 104, 106, 123–124, 147, 200; and participants at, 25, 176
Lagny, siege of, 40, 174
Lancaster, house of, 124
Lancaster, Humphrey of. *See* Gloucester, Humphrey, duke of
Lancaster, John of. *See* Bedford, John, duke of
Lancaster, Thomas of. *See* Clarence, Thomas, duke of

Laon, 70, 113
Laval, André de, 40, 124–125, 141
Laval, Guy XVI de, 40, 124–125
Laval Letter, 61, 104, 121, 124–125, 137, 146, 182, 200
Lavenu, Martin. See Ladvenu, Martin
Laxart, Durand, 16, 28, 125, 171, 214
L'Écrivain, Roland, 165
Le Comte, Denis, 153
Le Fèvre, Jean, 10, 112, 125–126, 138, 140
Le Franc, Martin, 198
Le Maistre, Jean, 35, 59, 63, 97, 109, 126–127, 154, 183, 202, 204
Le Mans, 86, 96, 179
Le Royer, Catherine, 28, 127, 171, 199, 214
Le Royer, Henri, 127, 214
Le Royer, Thevenin, 214
League of the Public Weal, 11, 26, 50, 127, 137
Lenizeul, Jean de, 81
Leparmentier, Mauger, 127, 204
letters of Joan of Arc, 127–133; and the letter to the English (22 March 1429), 33, 35, 80, 81, 100, 101, 115, 120, 128–129, 145, 167, 171, 175, 190, 197, 201, 203, 204, 209; and the letter to the English (5 May 1429), 129; and the letter to the people of Tournai (25 June 1429), 127–128, 129–130, 204–205; and the letter to the people of Troyes (4 July 1429), 130, 178, 180, 207, 208; and the letter to the duke of Burgundy (17 July 1429), 130–131; and the letter to the people of Reims (5 August 1429), 89, 131; and the letter to Jean IV, the count of Armagnac (22 August 1429), 18, 64, 128, 131, 168; and the letter to the people of Riom (9 November 1429), 21, 38, 98, 100, 117, 128, 131–132, 188, 200; and the letter to the people of Reims (16 March 1430), 128, 132; and the letter to the Hussites (23 March 1430), 103, 112, 128, 132–133, 146, 163; and the letter to the people of Reims (28 March 1430), 133
Leuven, 108
Leuven University, 56
Libellus d'Estivet. See seventy articles.
licentiate. See education
Ligny, 138
Limousin, 225

L'isle-Adam, Jean de Villiers de. See Villiers, Jean De
Lincoln, bishop of, 12, 30
Lisieux, 26, 49, 135, 205–206
literacy / illiteracy of Joan of Arc, 128, 133–134, 203, 215
Livre des fais d'armes et de chevalerie, 167
Livre des fais et bonnes meurs du sage roy Charles V, 166
Lodève, 83
Lohéac, André de. See Laval, André de
Loire Campaign, 31, 111–112, 134–135, 143–144, 163
Loiseleur, Nicolas, 123, 135, 140, 204
Longueil, Richard Olivier de, 50, 135, 154
Longueville-Giffard, 145, 170
Loré, Ambroise de, 135–136
Lorraine, 74–75 136–137, 214
Lorraine, Charles II, duke of, 28, 75, 103, 125, 136–137, 141, 151, 179, 214, 227
Louis, Saint, 51, 137
Louis VI, 157
Louis XI, 11, 17, 26, 38, 50, 52, 54, 55, 73, 90, 94, 122, 127, 135, 137, 141, 144, 145, 159, 165, 169, 180, 189, 203, 213, 225
Louis XII, 158, 213
Louis I, the Pious, 132
Loungueville, count of. See Orléans, Jean, bastard of
Louviers, 119, 205
Louvre, 216
loyalists, 137
Loyseleur, Nicolas. See Loiseleur, Nicolas
Luxembourg, 41, 88, 94
Luxembourg, Demoiselle of, 138
Luxembourg, Jacquetta of, 14, 33, 165,
Luxembourg, Jeanne of. See Béthune, Jeanne de
Luxembourg, John of, 30, 35, 46, 48, 64–65, 69, 87, 101, 127, 137–138, 139, 147, 152, 166, 176, 192, 196, 212, 221
Luxembourg, Louis of, 127, 138
Lyons, 95, 198, 203
Lys, Charles du, 131–133

Mâcon, Robert le, 139, 208
Macy, Haimond de, 43, 46, 139, 192, 193, 196, 222
maid. See la Pucelle

INDEX

Maine, 86, 137, 173, 190, 227

Manchon, Guillaume, 139–140, 205–207; and the compilation of the trial transcripts, 67, 69–70, 184; and his statements during the nullification proceedings, 57, 76, 104, 118, 126, 135, 153, 183, 192, 196, 217, 222; and his role as a notary during Joan of Arc's condemnation trial, 63, 183, 202

Margaret of Anjou, 43, 54, 101, 180

Margaret of Burgundy, 13, 33, 164, 181

Margaret of Scotland, 137

Margaret, Saint, 35, 57, 80, 107, 108, 109, 140, 197, 209, 218–219

Marie of Anjou, 37, 52, 101, 137, 141, 179, 180, 227

marriage contract, 141

marshal of France, 141; and people who held the title, 29, 40, 68, 118, 124, 174, 201, 216, 225

Martin V, Pope, 18, 76, 112, 132–133, 168, 173; and his election, 30, 48, 69, 94, 95, 97

Massieu, Jean, 141–142; and the abjuration of Joan of Arc, 9; and the execution of Joan of Arc, 19, 47, 144; as the executor of writs for Joan of Arc's condemnation trial, 46, 183; and statements made during the nullification proceedings, 9, 57, 76, 81, 82, 104, 118, 126, 135, 153, 183

master of arts, 79–80; and people with the degree of, 25, 31, 47, 50, 51, 54, 69, 83, 98, 118, 135

Maurice, Pierre, 142–143; and his admonishment of Joan of Arc, 57, 66, 184; and his testimony after the condemnation trial of Joan of Arc, 123, 205

Maximus, Valerius, 167

Mehun, 57, 143

Melun, 96, 201

men-at-arms, 143

Merlin, 39, 170

Metz, 38

Metz, Jean de, 90, 143, 195; and the journey to Chinon, 23, 28–29, 103, 169, 214

Meung, 119; and Salisbury's death at, 160, 190

Meung, battle of, 143–144; and the Loire Campaign, 31, 111, 112, 134–135, 163

Meuse River, 28, 74, 136, 151, 214

Michael, Saint, 46, 93, 107, 144, 189, 218, 219

Midi (Midy), Nicolas, 32, 59, 83, 144–145; and his work on the twelve articles, 66, 82, 184, 192, 209–210

Miget, Pierre, 145, 170; and his statements during the nullification proceedings, 10, 112, 135, 138

Mirepoix, 83

mission of Joan of Arc, 145–146, 170, 214; and Charles VII, 52–53, 136, 168, 177, 185, 194; and contemporary interpretations of, 51, 95, 167; and the duke of Orléans, 75, 158; and obstacles to, 14, 32, 89, 165; and phases of, 36–37, 100, 124, 128, 134, 152, 159, 160, 162, 176, 178, 209; and support for, 54, 55, 95, 128, 198, 227

Mistere du siege d'Orleans, 128, 146–147, 174

moat, 108, 117, 159, 162, 188

Mongols, 20

Monstrelet, Enguerrand de, 147; and his accounts, 10, 15, 21, 29, 33, 64, 65, 89, 91, 102, 104, 108, 111, 123–124, 148, 163, 165, 179, 180, 181, 215, 221; as a source for other chronicles, 56, 58, 188, 222

Mont-Saint-Michel, 83, 152

Montargis, 93, 121, 221–222

Montagu, Thomas. See Salisbury

Montéclair, Jean de, 22, 147–148

Montépilloy, battle of, 27, 48, 82, 97, 106, 130, 148–149, 168, 178; and contemporary accounts of, 38, 188; and participants at, 11, 30, 33, 90, 103, 104, 119, 121, 136, 158–159, 179, 215, 216

Montigny, Jean de, 149

Montmorillon, 119

Morel, Aubert, 75, 149, 204

Mortemert, Jeanne de, 139

Moses, 202

Moulins, 131

Muslim. See Islam

name of Joan of Arc, 151

Narbonne, 94

Neufchâteau, 16, 17, 28, 103, 136, 151–152, 214

Nicopolis, 93

Nicholas V, Pope, 83, 153, 169
Nîmes, 83, 118
Normandy, 152–153
Northampton, 191, 196
Norwich, Bishop of. *See* Alnwick, William
Notary. *See* roles and responsibilities
Notre-Dame, 31, 55, 63, 154, 162
Novelompont, Jean de. *See* Metz, Jean de
nullification proceedings / trial, 153–155

Orléans, 157–160
Orléans, Charles, duke of, 11, 17, 22, 35, 37, 70, 88, 91, 115, 119, 157–158, 160, 180, 213; and his captivity, 20, 49, 52, 75, 93, 165, 175, 191, 198; and Joan of Arc's mission, 146, 176
Orléans, Jean, bastard of, 26, 27, 29, 57, 69, 102, 147, 157, 158–160, 169 175, 198, 225; and his accounts of and interactions with Joan of Arc, 21, 35, 51, 53, 70, 96, 107, 108, 111, 119, 123, 127, 129, 134, 137, 146, 148, 174, 177–178, 203, 208, 217, 218
Orléans, Louis I, duke of, 18, 19, 47–48, 70, 90–91, 94, 95, 105, 110, 160,
Orléans, siege of, 1, 4n1, 20, 128–129, 159–160, 167, 227; and contemporary accounts of, 22, 23, 37, 38, 39, 55, 58, 76, 94, 96, 112–113, 147, 188, 202, 204; and its relief as a sign of Joan of Arc, 167, 188, 191, 194–195, 218; as a part of Joan of Arc's mission, 51, 53, 145–146; and participants at, 11, 14, 17, 22, 25, 33, 40, 50, 60, 70, 71, 86, 88, 93, 96, 107, 115, 118, 135, 141, 147, 158–159, 164, 179, 189–191, 197–198, 201–202, 203, 214, 225
Orléanais/Orléanists, 160
Otto I, Emperor, 103

Paris, 161–162; and Parlement of, 47, 86, 161, 167, 173, 189. *See also* University of Paris
Paris, siege of, 89, 162, 187; and contemporary accounts of, 37, 58, 87, 112; and participants at, 11–12, 33, 40, 70, 71, 118–119, 124, 179, 180, 215
parlement. *See* Paris; Poitiers
Parliament, 189, 191, 198
Pasquerel, Jean, 162–163; and his accounts of Joan of Arc, 18, 80, 94, 96, 108, 129, 215, 217, 218; and the letter to the Hussites, 112, 132–133
Patay, battle of, 27–28, 163; and contemporary accounts of, 38, 55, 58, 86, 121, 130, 147, 203, 204, 223; and participants at, 11, 14, 40, 49, 50, 70, 86, 90, 94, 115, 118, 119, 158, 175, 179, 181, 188, 189, 190, 201, 214, 215, 222, 225
Paul, Apostle, 216
pennon, 104, 196–197
Pepin the Short, 67
Philip the Good, 164–165
Philip I, 157
Philip VI, 73, 105, 213
physicians in the condemnation trial, 165–166
Picardy, 87, 97
Pius II, Pope, 10, 62, 108, 169
Pizan, Christine de, 166–167, 217; and *The Tale of Joan of Arc*, 10, 144, 168, 170, 202, 203–204; and her writings on warfare, 22, 44, 86, 122, 202, 215
Poitiers, 167–168; and Parlement of, 167, 173; and the University of, 55, 168, 191
Pole, William de La. *See* Suffolk, William de La Pole, earl of
Pont-Audemer, 26
Pont-del'Arche, 201
Pontoise, Peace of, 91
Pontorson, 96
pope, 168–169; and Joan of Arc's appeals to, 60, 81, 118
Poulengy, Bertrand de, 23, 28, 169, 195, 199, 214; and the journey to Chinon, 28–29, 103, 143
Poulnoir, Hauves, 196
Pragmatic Sanction of Bourges, 38, 83, 135, 153, 169
The Praguerie, 169–170, 225; and participants in, 50, 60, 69, 122, 137, 159, 215
Preuilly, Jeanne de, 94
Prévosteau, Guillaume, 51, 170
prior, 170; and people in the position, 39, 96, 126, 145, 162
prison. *See* captivity
prisoner of war. *See* ransom
promoter. *See* Chapitault, Simon; Estivet, Jean D'; roles and responsibillties

Prophecies Foretelling Joan Of Arc, 170–171; and contemporary reactions and interpretations, 39, 110, 120–121, 125, 188, 202, 203–204, 217; and Robert de Baudricourt, 28, 127
prostitutes. *See* sex workers
Pucelle. *See* La Pucelle
Provins, 96, 131
Puy du Fou, 182

Rabateau, Jean, 173
Rais, Gilles de Laval, Baron of, 3–4, 40, 68, 118, 124, 147, 173–175, 204; and his presence on the campaigns of Joan of Arc, 134, 148, 141, 148; and his trial, 65, 204
Rampston, Thomas. *See* Rempston, Thomas
ransom, 175–176; of Joan of Arc, 30, 46, 48, 53–54, 77, 80, 82, 138, 176, 196; and those who were ransomed, 11, 17, 37, 38–39, 117, 124, 146, 158, 179–180, 190, 198, 201, 214
Recollectio, 39, 154, 198, 219
rape. *See* sexual assault and rape
Raymond, 70
Récit du Herault Berri. *See* Bouvier, Gilles le
regent, 176–177
Registre delphinal, 129, 203
Regnault, Guillaume, 53
rehabilitation. *See* nullification proceedings
Reims, 177
Reims, march to, 177–178, 207–208; and contemporary accounts of, 39, 43, 55, 71, 103, 112, 130, 147, 188; and the debate on whether to, 53, 56, 158, 163; and participants in, 11, 38, 40, 49, 50, 51, 60, 68, 71, 90, 94, 96, 119, 121, 125, 136, 139, 141, 158–159, 174, 181, 189, 203, 215, 225
relapse of Joan of Arc, 65, 67, 178; and arguments against, 51, 154–155; and those who voted to abandon her to secular authorities, 12, 57, 76, 81, 98, 120, 135, 149
Rempston, Thomas, 50, 115, 135, 137–138, 175–176, 179
René of Anjou, 28, 54, 101, 136–137, 148, 179–180, 227
rescue of Joan of Arc, 53–54, 119, 159, 174, 189, 212
retrial. *See* nullification proceedings

Richard, Friar (Brother), 47, 92, 130, 180–181, 208; and attempts to discredit Joan of Arc through association, 33–34, 97
Richard II, 30, 100, 124
Richemont, Arthur de, 40, 88, 161, 179, 181–182, 216; and his disputes with Georges de La Trémoille, 68, 121–122, 227; and the Loire Campaign, 31, 40, 75, 134; and the Treaty of Amiens, 13, 14, 33, 164
rings of Joan of Arc, 112, 134, 182
Riquier, Jean, 12, 19, 183
roles and responsibilities in Joan's of Arc's condemnation trial, 183–184
Roman law. *See* civil law
Rome, 10, 16, 30, 38, 39, 76, 83, 112, 131, 149, 168, 169, 185, 198, 206, 211–212, 221, 222
Rotseläer, Lord of, 108
Rouen, 184
Rouen trial. *See* condemnation trial
Roussel, Raoul, 83, 184–185, 204
Rouvray, battle of. *See* Herrings
royalists, 185
Royer, Catherine Le. *See* Le Royer, Catherine
Russia, 20

Saint-Denis, 55, 71, 144, 162, 187, 216; and a sword of Joan of Arc, 12, 45, 199–200
Saint-Lo, 170
Saint-Pierre-Le-Moutier, Siege of, 98, 117, 146, 187–188; and contemporary accounts of, 131; and participants in, 11, 22, 122
Saint-Remy, Jean Lèfevre de, 162, 188
Sainte-Catherine-de-Fierbois, 46, 128, 199
Sainte-Sévère, Marshal de. *See* Brosse, Jean de
saints, 46–47, 51, 93, 137, 140, 144, 187, 188–189, 218–219
Salazar, Jean de, 189
Salisbury, Thomas Montagu, earl of, 29, 71, 96, 189–190, 215; and contemporary sources on his death, 37, 58; and his wounding and death, 22, 30, 143, 159–160, 197, 201
Salisbury's 1428 Expedition, 31, 35, 53, 92, 106, 111, 135, 143, 147, 151, 159, 163, 179, 187, 190; and logistics, 122, 193
Scales, Thomas, baron of, 143, 160, 190–191; and his capture and ransom, 115,

130, 135, 163, 175–176; and Joan of Arc's letter to, 115, 128, 201
schismatic, 18, 97, 101–102, 109 191, 209
Seguin, Seguin de, 191, 199, 218; and the mission of Joan of Arc, 145–146
Seine River, 31, 32, 84, 161, 207
seneschal, 191; and people in the role, 23, 36, 118, 190, 214, 225
Senlis, 124, 148, 176
seventy articles of accusation, 183, 191–192, 206–207, 209; and commentary on them outside of the condemnation trial, 39, 149, 154; and specific articles, 18, 35, 47, 59, 61, 63, 80, 85, 99, 101, 103, 108–109, 112, 129, 131, 141, 151, 181, 182, 187, 189, 197, 199; and their presentation to Joan of Arc, 26, 66–67, 69, 82, 101, 184
sex worker, 45, 199
sexual assault and rape, 46, 62, 120, 123, 140, 183, 192–193, 205, 217, 222
Shepherd, battle of, 225
Shrewsbury, earl of. *See* Talbot, John
Sicily, Queen of. *See* Yolande of Aragon
siege, 193–194
signs of Joan of Arc, 57, 60, 167, 191, 194–195, 218
Sixtus IV, Pope, 26
Sorel, Agnès, 141
Spain, 20
squire, 195–196; and people with the title, 22, 25, 96, 115, 119, 169, 188, 198, 203
Stafford, Humphrey, 196; and his attempted assault of Joan of Arc, 96, 139, 222
standard of Joan of Arc, 196–197; and its design, 35, 63, 87, 93, 112, 134, 144, 162; and its use, 22, 60, 61, 68, 103, 108, 123, 148, 180, 199, 200
Stewart, John, of Buchan, 29, 70–71, 90
Stewart, John, of Darnley, 90, 102
Suffolk, William de La Pole, Earl of, 191, 197–198; and Joan of Arc's letter to, 115, 128–129; and the Loire Campaign, 111–112, 130, 134, 175, 201; and the siege of Orléans, 160, 190, 201
suicide, accusations of, 81–82
Sully-sur-Loire, 132, 133
Summarium, 39, 153
Super facto puellae et credulitate sibi praestanda, 74, 76, 95, 198–199

swords of Joan of Arc, *44*, 199–200; and the assault of a camp follower, 11–12, 45, 70; and Clermont, 132, 200; and Franquet d'Arras, 124; and Saint-Denis, 187; and Sainte-Catherine-de Fierbois, 46, 128; and Robert de Baudricourt and Vaucouleurs, 29, 169
Sybil, 170
Syria, 180

Talbot, John, 124, 201–202; and the battle of Castillon, 50; and his dispute with John Fastolf, 86; and the exchange of manuscripts, 43, 54; and his ransom, 36 176, 225; and Joan of Arc's letter to, 115, 128; and the Loire Campaign, 31, 130, 134–135, 160, 163, 175, 190; and the siege of Orléans, 160, 190
Talbot, William, 46, 183
The Tale of Joan of Arc, 144, 170–171, 202, 204
Taquel, Nicolas, 10, 63, 126, 135, 139, 183, 202–203, 205
Termes, Thibaut de, d'Armagnac, 203
Thérage, Geoffroy, 84, 183
Thérouanne, 70, 138
Thérouanne, bishop of. *See* Luxembourg, Louis of
Thibault, Gobert, 81, 128, 133, 203
Thierry, Reginald, 188
Thiboust, Henri, 165
Thomassin, Mathieu, 129, 203–204
Thouars, Catherine de, 173
Tiphaine, Jean, 166
Tours, Truce of, 180, 198, 202
torture, 109, 204; and the debate to use on Joan of Arc, 59, 66, 69, 70, 81, 120, 126, 135, 149, 184, 207; and Gilles de Rais, 175; and the threat of against Joan of Arc, 57, 66, 81, 127, 149
Touraine, 57, 75, 181
Touraine, Jean, duke of, 52, 110
Tournai, 68, 204–205; and Joan of Arc's letters to, 127–128, 129–130
Toutmouillé, Jean, 83, 123, 153, 192, 205
transcripts of Joan of Arc's condemnation trial, 66–67, 205–207
trebuchet, 22
tree of fairies / ladies. *See* fairy tree

Troyes, 207
Troyes, siege of, 56, 130, 139, 178, 207–208
Troyes, Treaty of, 208–209
Turkey, 38
twelve articles of accusation, 63, 66–67, 142–143, 144, 183–184, 191–192, 209–210; and commentary on them outside of the condemnation trial, 36, 39, 59–60, 140, 149, 154; and opinions from assessors in the condemnation trial, 12, 26–27, 75, 76, 98, 149; and their contents, 15, 59, 61–62, 82, 85, 99, 101, 141, 182, 189, 197, 199, 219; and the University of Paris, 31, 35, 69, 82, 101–102, 107, 165, 212

University of Paris, 211–212
University of Prague, 132
usher, 142, 183,
Utrecht, 26, 96

Valentina of Milan, 158
Valois, House of, 41, 165, 213
Valpergue, Théodore de, 213–214
Vandonne, bastard of. *See* Wandomme, Guillaume
Vaucouleurs, 28–29, 214
Vegetius, 54, 122, 167, 214–215
Vendôme, Guillaume, bastard of. *See* Wandomme, Guillaume.
Vendôme, Louis de Bourbon, count of, 68, 70–71, 148, 169, 215
Verneuil, battle of, 27, 29, 77, 215–216; and participants in, 11, 13, 33, 49, 50, 86, 90, 96, 118, 119, 164, 189, 190, 197, 213, 222, 225

Vexin, 57
Vignolles, Étienne de. *See* La Hire
Villiers, Jean de, 91, 161, 216
Villiers, Philippe de, 182
virginity, 45, 107, 209, 216–217; and tests used against Joan of Arc, 46, 94, 104, 139, 192, 227. *See also* La Pucelle
viscount, 218
voices, visions, and revelations, 65–67, 191–192, 209–210, 218–219

Wandomme, Guillaume, bastard of, 64, 195, 221
Warwick, Richard Beauchamp, earl of, 43, 215, 221–222, 225; and his involvement in Joan of Arc's captivity, 46, 77, 80, 82, 118, 135, 139, 140, 166, 183, 196
Wavrin, Jean de, 222–223; and his accounts, 21, 33, 73, 86, 108, 163, 181, 215, 216
Wayman, Dorothy, 74, 199
wedding. *See* marriage contract
Western Schism. *See* Great Schism
William de La Pole. *See* Suffolk, William de La Pole, earl of
Winchester, bishop of. *See* Beaufort, Henry
Windeck, Eberhard, 45
World War II, 49, 74, 127–128, 130, 205
wounds. *See* injuries
Wycliffe, Jon, 12, 69

Xantrailles, Poton de, 215, 218, 225, *226*; and negotiations with Philip the Good, 164

Yolande of Aragon, 54, 136, 141, 217, 227
Yonne River, 71

About the Author

Scott Manning is a historian and independent scholar published in *The Year's Work in Medievalism*, *Studies in Medievalism*, and *Film & History*, as well as chapters and papers in several edited volumes. With Kevin J. Harty, Manning is coediting *Cinema Medievalia: New Essays on The Reel Middle Ages*, slated for publication in 2024. Manning has served as the VP of Conference for the Mid-Atlantic Popular & American Culture Association, and he is the cochair of the association's Medieval & Renaissance Area. Since 2019, he has been the session organizer for the International Joan of Arc Society's panels at the International Congress on Medieval Studies, held annually in Kalamazoo, Michigan. Manning holds a master's in history and a bachelor's in military history from American Military University.

CPSIA information can be obtained
at www.ICGtesting.com
Printed in the USA
LVHW061231080323
741116LV00005B/541

MAR 2023